REDEEMED BY GOD - 2

Salvation Through Jesus, New World Order, and Time of the End

3rd Edition

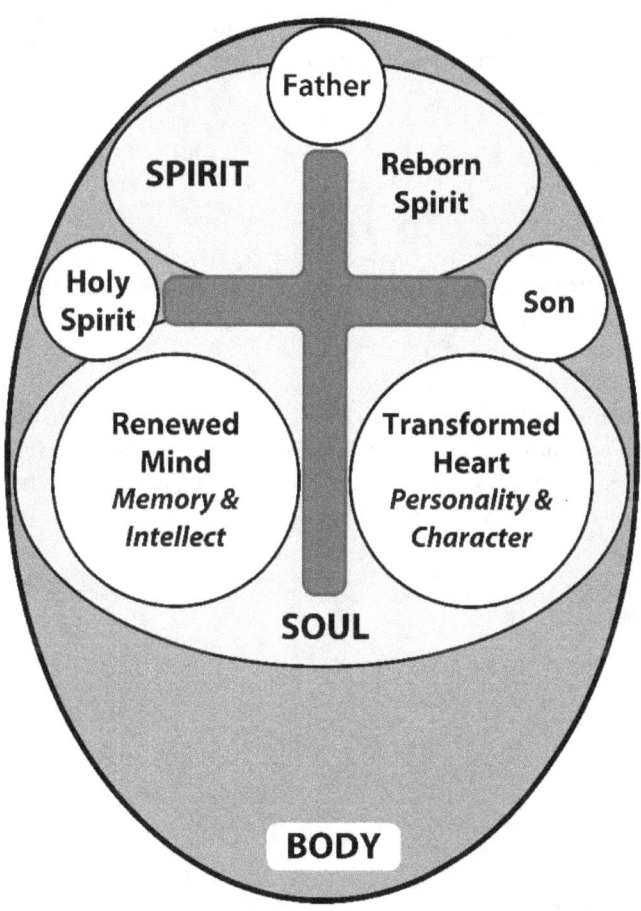

By
Douglas D. Reynolds, Ph.D.

ISBN: 978-1-960093-62-2   (Paperback)
ISBN: 978-1-960093-63-9   (eBook)

Scriptures taken from the NEW AMERICAN STANDARD BIBLE® Copyright © 1960, 1962, 1963, 1968, 1971, 1972, 1973, 1975, 1977, 1995, 2020 by the Lockman Foundation. Used with permission.

Because of the dynamic nature of the Internet, any web addresses or links contained in this book may have changed since publication and may no longer be valid. The views expressed in this work are solely those of the author and do not necessarily reflect the views of the publisher, and the publisher hereby disclaims any responsibility for them.

Book Ordering Information:
Atticus Publishing
548 Market St PMB 70756
San Francisco, CA 94104
(888) 208-9296
info@atticuspublishing.com
www.atticuspublishing.com

Printed in the United States of America

TITLE PAGE IMAGE

The apostle Paul stated in 1 Thessalonians 5:23 we are born with a spirit, soul and body. The outer ellipse in the title page image represents our physical body. Our body interacts with the physical world through our five physical senses of sight, hearing, touch, taste, and smell. The two inner ellipses in the outer ellipse of the body represent our spirit and soul. Our spirit gives life to our physical body and interacts with the spiritual realm where God exists. Our soul functions through our body and spirit as we interact with the physical world and the spiritual realm. Our spirit and soul are integrally linked. Our body dies and returns to dust when our spirit no longer can support physical life. Our spirit and soul continue in an eternal existence beyond physical death. They continue either in the kingdom of heaven in the presence of God, Jesus and the Holy Spirit or separated from Them in Hades (hell) before and in the lake of fire after the great white throne judgement.

Our soul is comprised of our mind and heart. Our mind is the seat of our memory and intellect. Our memory is the repository of information and experiences we have processed and assimilated throughout our life. Our intellect is the knowledge and wisdom we acquire from this information and these experiences. Our heart is the seat of our personality and character. Our personality is the organized pattern of behavioral characteristics that identify and define who we are. Our character defines the moral and ethical qualities of our personality.

Our soul possesses memory, acquires knowledge, experiences emotions, creates thoughts, forms habits, and initiates actions through our body and spirit. It develops as our mind and heart process and assimilate information it receives through our life experiences. It controls how we encounter, interpret and respond to new life experiences based on how it has processed and assimilated information it has received from prior life experiences.

The Bible teaches we relate to God as Father, Son and Holy Spirit. There are three eternal Persons within the Godhead even though there is one God. They each possess all the eternal attributes of God and interact with perfect agreement. However, they relate to and interact with us in distinct and unique ways. God, the Father, is our Creator and the One who is behind everything and to whom everyone in heaven and on earth is accountable. God's Son, Jesus, is our Lord and Savior. He is the One for and through whom all things have been created and are held together and through whom we approach God, the Father. The Holy Spirit, our Comforter and Helper, reveals the mind of God to us and makes our needs and requests known to God, the Father, through our prayers.

The Bible teaches we are born into this world with a sin nature that separates us from God. We are born spiritually dead because God's spirit is not present in us. However, the

Bible also teaches God loves us, desires to commune and fellowship with us, and is active in us through the Holy Spirit. The Holy Spirit makes us aware of sins in our life, leads us to repent of these sins, and creates a desire within us to enter a relationship with God. God has made this relationship possible through the sacrificial death and resurrection of Jesus. God extends His mercy and grace to us, and He makes known to us His desire to redeem and reconcile us to Himself through Jesus' death and resurrection. However, we must seek God's grace and forgiveness and acknowledge and repent of our sins to enter a reconciled relationship with Him through Jesus. God loves and forgives us, and He communes and fellowships with us when we approach Him through Jesus.

Jesus stated in John 14:6 we can only approach God, the Father, through Him. Therefore, being a good, moral and generous person independent of a relationship with God through Jesus does not gain us entrance into the kingdom of God while we are alive, nor does this gain us entrance into the kingdom of heaven after we die. God redeems and reconciles us to Himself through our faith and trust in and obedience to Jesus as a gift. This gift for us is free because we can do nothing to earn or obtain it independent of our relationship with God through Jesus. The Holy Spirit leads us to repent of our sins, profess with our mouth Jesus is Lord, and believe in our heart God raised Him from the dead to receive God's salvation through His gift of grace (Romans 10:9-10). This saves us from eternal separation from God, Jesus and the Holy Spirit after we die. We are spiritually reborn because God's Spirit along with Jesus and the Holy Spirit take up residence in us.

Paul instructed us in 1 Corinthians 3:10 - 15 to build our life on the foundation of Jesus. We begin building this foundation by reading and study God's word in the Bible. The Holy Spirit opens our mind to understand and internalize what we read and study in the Bible. Our mind is renewed as we internalize and assimilate the words Jesus spoke in the four Gospels, and the Holy Spirit enters our heart to transform our personality and character as our mind is renewed. We are transformed into the person God has created us to be as we continue to have faith in and trust Jesus and become obedient to the words He spoke in the four Gospels.

To the members of my family
my wife, Linda;
my son and daughter-in-law, John and Latricia, and son, Jeff (deceased);
my granddaughters, Janet, Jennifer and Ashlin;
my grandson, Jerry; and
my great grandchildren, Jered, Michael, Hailey,
Alex, Dustin, Ian, Mason and Jackson.

To the Rev. James "JD" Hilliard who reviewed the manuscript for this book and provided helpful guidance for its improvement.

TABLE OF CONTENTS

PREFACE

ACTIONS OF THE HOLY SPIRIT IN MY LIFE

God through the Holy Spirit indicated in 1982 He wanted me to write a book that addressed spiritual life principles associated with His word in the Bible. My initial response was why me? I am a Ph.D. mechanical engineer. I am not a pastor, Bible scholar or theologian. The Holy Spirit initiated a process when I committed to write this book that would enable and equip me to write and publish it. 2 Timothy 3:16-17 motivated me as I engaged in this process. Paul stated:

> "All Scripture is inspired by God and profitable for teaching, for reproof, for correction, for training in righteousness, so that the man of God may be adequate, equipped for every good work."

I again received God's call in 2000 for me to be one of His servants. He indicated He would reveal to me by my reading and studying the Bible and through the Holy Spirit an understanding of Scriptures related to the future. 2 Peter 1:20-21 provided significance to this understanding. Peter stated:

> "But know this first of all, that no prophecy of Scripture is a matter of one's own interpretation, for no prophecy was ever made by an act of human will, but men moved by the Holy Spirit spoke from God."

God indicated difficult days will arise in the future, and He wanted me to be a messenger who shares this understanding with others. He indicated He will be with and support those who trust and have faith in Jesus and obey His words. The future God referred to in 2000 is now here.

The Holy Spirit has revealed to me through the Bible and life experiences the love God extends to us through Jesus and Him. He has helped me to understand the:

- Significance of the infinite sacrifice God made for us through the sacrificial death and resurrection of His Son, Jesus:
- Significance of the infinite sacrifice Jesus made through His death and shed blood on a cross so God, His Father, can redeem us;

- Importance of our receiving the redemption and reconciliation God extends to us through His grace and our faith and trust in and obedience to Jesus; and

- Significance of God's holiness in the context of His relationship with His creation and with us through Jesus.

God will execute His justice that is an extension of His holiness when we stand before and are judged by Jesus on the last day.

I initially wrote and published three books in response to the leadership of the Holy Spirit. My first book, *REDEEMED BY GOD, Our Relationship with God through His Son, Jesus Christ*, was published in 2003. This book addressed the:

- The nature and character of God as Father, Son and Holy Spirit;

- The nature and character of Satan and sin;

- The nature of our creation as spirit, soul and body;

- Spiritual death we experience because of sin;

- Spiritual rebirth and life we receive from God by means of His grace extended to us through our faith and trust in and obedience to Jesus;

- Spiritual growth we experience through Bible study, prayer and a transformed heart;

- Spiritual gifts the Holy Spirit gives to us to enable and equip us to engage in ministry and service to others;

- Spiritual life principles that equip us to effectively address life challenges;

- The Christian Church through which we engage in ministry and service to others; and

- The seven-year tribulation through which God will execute His judgement on a fallen and rebellious world that has rejected Him, Jesus and the Holy Spirit.

The Holy Spirit led me in 2013 to revise and separate my original book into two books:

- *REDEEMED BY GOD - 1, Spiritual Growth and Life Principles Associated with the Gospel of Jesus*, and

- REDEEMED BY GOD - 2, A Christian Perspective of the End Time and a New World Order.

These books were in 2015. Discussion on the seven-year tribulation was placed in *REDEEMED BY GOD – 2, A Christian Perspective of the End Time and a New World Order* with discussions on the:

- Nature and character of God and Satan,
- Functions of our soul and spirit,
- Our relationship with God through our faith and trust in and obedience to Jesus, and
- Events associated with the establishment of a New World Order.

This book introduced cultural conflicts between secular humanism and Christianity, progressivism and conservatism, and socialism and capitalism. These conflicts and their consequences are evident today in the United States and other countries. They will lead to the formation of a New World Order. The topics covered in REDEEMED BY GOD, Our Relationship with God through His Son, Jesus Christ without material on the seven-year tribulation were revised and presented in REDEEMED BY GOD – 1, Spiritual Growth and Life Principles Associated with the Gospel of Jesus. Two subsequent revised editions of these two books were published.

REDEEMED BY GOD – 1 and REDEEMED BY GOD -2 were updated and re-released in 2020 as part of the three-book series with titles:

- REDEEMED BY GOD – 1, Spiritual Life Principles Associated with God's Word;
- REDEEMED BY GOD – 2, Time of the End, Return of Jesus and a New World Order; and
- REDEEMED BY GOD – 3, God's Redemption through Jesus and His Plan for Eternity.

The new releases of REDEEMED BY GOD – 1 and REDEEMED BY GOD – 2 contained revised materials presented in their prior releases. REDEEMED BY GOD – 3 was condensed from REDEEMED BY GOD – 2 and addressed the:

- Nature and character of God and Satan;
- Origin and nature of sin;
- Nature of our creation as spirit, soul and body;
- Functions of our soul and spirit;
- Our relationship with God through our faith and trust in and obedience to Jesus;
- God's future judgments of the unrighteous and righteous; and
- The destruction of the existing heaven and earth and the creation of a new heaven, earth and Jerusalem.

Revised 2nd editions of the above three REDEEMED BY GOD books were published in 2024.

My *REDEEMED BY GOD* books were written from an evangelical perspective of what I perceived the Bible was saying to and teaching me. My writing style as a Ph.D. mechanical engineer is that of a technical writer. Cultural influences on non-biblical topics in *REDEEMED BY GOD – 2* were addressed. This was not done in *REDEEMED BY GOD – 1* and *REDEEMED BY GOD - 3.*

My *REDEEMED BY GOD* books have been written for individuals who are struggling to cope with real life situations related to the cultural conflicts that are occurring in the world. Many are seeking a relationship with God through Jesus and the Holy Spirit to better equip themselves to address these conflicts and the life struggles they are creating. The revised 2nd edition releases of my *REDEEMED BY GOD* books are written for individuals who:

- Have entered a reconciled relationship with God through their faith and trust in and obedience to Jesus and want to grow and mature in this relationship through the presence of the Holy Spirit in their lives (*REDEEMED BY GOD – 1*);

- Have entered a reconciled relationship with God through their faith and trust in and obedience to Jesus and want to grow in their knowledge and understanding of events that will lead to the formation of a New World Order and the seven-year tribulation (*REDEEMED BY GOD – 2*); and

- Do not know God but who the Holy Spirit is nudging to seek and enter a redeemed relationship with Him through Jesus (*REDEEMED BY GOD -3*).

Bible scriptures are presented in these books to document that the spiritual life principle and precepts addressed in my books are from God. These Bible scriptures have been selected to aid in the spiritual growth of those who read my books.

SPIRITUAL ORIGIN OF TODAY'S CULTURAL CONFLICTS

The cultural conflicts addressed in *REDEEMED BY GOD - 2* are being discussed and framed today as a conflict between the progressive left and the conservative right. What is not being discussed is the spiritual origin of these conflicts. This origin is traced back to ancient secret societies that existed at the time of the Tower of Babel and after its fall described in Genesis 11:1-9. These secret societies opposed God and were led by illuminists who were the intellectual elite of their day. These illuminists were disciples of Lucifer and had as their objectives the:

- Absolute rule over the world,
- Elimination of private prosperity,

- Elimination of religions, and
- Elimination of nation-states.

These objectives after the death and resurrection of Jesus found their way into later anti-Christian secret societies that included the Luciferians, Rosicrucians and the Levellers. They eventually found their way into a secret society called the Illuminati.

The Illuminati controlled global movement was made popular by Adam Weishaupt during the latter part of the 18th century. The Illuminati wanted to establish a deistic, global and dictatorial government that will abolish:

- Governments of all nation-states;
- All private property;
- All inheritance rights;
- Patriotism to national causes;
- Social relationships within families,
- Sexual prohibition laws and moral codes; and
- Religious disciplines based on faith in a transcendent God, while promoting faith in nature, man and reason.

These objectives have been incorporated into the progressive left agenda that opposes the presence of God, Jesus and the Holy Spirit in our lives and culture.

SIGNIFICANCE OF GOD'S GRACE

I mention in my REDEEMED BY GOD books that we enter a redeemed relationship with God through our **faith** and **trust** in and **obedience** to Jesus. **Faith** is our strong belief in the **truth** of the Bible's discussions regarding our relationship with God and the roles Jesus and the Holy Spirit play in this relationship. **Trust** is our assured reliance on this **truth** and on God's and Jesus' ability to honor Their covenants and promises presented in the Bible. **Obedience** is our submission to the reality and requirements of this **truth** on our life and to God's laws and the words Jesus spoke in the four Gospels.

Paul stated in Ephesians 2:8 we are saved by God's **grace** through **faith**. God's **grace** is His conscious and deliberate extension of His love and good will to provide us with something we can neither earn nor provide for ourself. Paul stated God extends His **grace** to us as a gift, and he referred to this gift as being free in Romans 5:15-17. God extends His **grace** to us with no cost to us because we can do nothing to obtain it independent of His love for us, and so we cannot claim we are entitled to His grace because of actions we initiate. Paul continued in Ephesians 2:9 we cannot be redeemed by our own works independent of God's **grace**. He then stated in Ephesians 2:10 we become new creations by God in Christ Jesus to perform **good works** He has prepared beforehand for us to perform.

We are redeemed by God's **grace** when we profess with our mouth Jesus is Lord and believe in our heart God raised Him from the dead (Romans 10:8-10). The Holy Spirit then begins to reside in us, and we enter a bilateral relationship with God through Jesus and the presence of the Holy Spirit in our life. God, Jesus, the Holy Spirit and we have obligations in a relationship that results from our being redeemed by God's **grace**. God and Jesus will honor their covenants and promises regarding our relationship with Them that are presented in the Bible. We are to develop, grow and mature in our **faith** and **trust** in and **obedience** to Jesus with the assistance of the Holy Spirit in our relationship with God through Jesus.

Paul indicated in Romans 10:17 **faith** comes from hearing and proceeds from the words of Jesus. The Holy Spirit in our life facilitates the development and growth of our **faith** as we hear and are taught the words of Jesus in the four Gospels. These words, as we internalize them, facilitate the development and growth of our **faith** through a process that transforms our life by renewing our mind (Romans 12:2). Renewing our mind transforms our life choice from being defined and determined by our culture to being defined and determined by the words of Jesus.

Our **faith** and **trust** in and **obedience** to Jesus develop, grow and mature as we:

- Read, study and internalize God's word in the Bible (1 Peter 2:1–3);
- Incorporate the spiritual life principles associated with God's word in the Bible into our life (1 Timothy 4:13–16);
- Grow and mature in our relationship with God through Jesus and the presence of the Holy Spirit in our life (Philippians 2:12–13);
- **Obey** the words Jesus spoke in the four Gospels (John 14:15, 21, 23); and
- Do **good works** God has prepared for us to perform (Ephesians 2:10). The Holy Spirit, as we study and internalize the words of Jesus, equips us with unique supernatural spiritual gifts that enable us to perform **good works** God prepares for us to perform (Romans 12:4-8, 1 Corinthians 12:3-11, 28, and Ephesians 4:11-13).

We do **good works** because Jesus instructed us in Matthew 5:16:

> "Let your light shine before men in such a way that they may see your **good works**, and glorify your Father who is in heaven."

We do **good works** because Paul stated in Ephesians 2:10:

> "For we are [God's] workmanship, created in Christ Jesus for **good works**, which [He] prepared beforehand so that we would walk in them."

He affirmed in 2 Timothy 3:16-17 our understanding of the Bible enables and equips us to do the **good works** Jesus instructed and God has prepared for us to perform.

God through Jesus and the Holy Spirit draws us close to Himself to receive and grow in His love. The Holy Spirit motivates us to engage in the above activities to spiritually grow and mature in our relationship with God through Jesus. He enables us to love, minister to and serve others in Jesus' name. This equips us to perform **good works** out of love for God and others in **obedience** to Jesus with guidance from the Holy Spirit. God and Jesus bless and reward us when we engage in activities to spiritually grow and mature, and we perform **good works** Jesus instructs and God prepares for us to perform. However, we risk losing Their blessings and rewards when we fail to engage in activities to spiritually grow and mature, and we do none of the **good works** Jesus instructs and God prepares for us to perform after we have entered our relationship with Them (John 15:1-11).

GOOD WORKS

Our good works are fruit that proceeds from the vine of Jesus (John 15:1-6). They are activities God prepares for us to perform (Ephesian 2:10) to glorify Himself (Matthew 5:16). Good works are our response of love and obedience for receiving the gift of grace and redemption God extends to us through Jesus, and they are an integral part of our relationship with God through Jesus. They:

- Are our love-offerings to God that we extend to others (2 Timothy 2:15);
- Are performed to glorify God (Matthew 5:16);
- Are positions of leadership and service we perform in and through our local church (Ephesians 4:11-13);
- Are how we minister to and serve the needs of others (1 Peter 4:10).
- Are our witness to those who have not received Jesus as their Lord and Savior (Hebrews 13:2);
- Are our witness to fellow Christians (Colossians 3:16).
- Show we are God's workmanship, created in Christ Jesus to perform good works (Ephesians 2:10); and
- Reveal the presence of the Holy Spirit in our life (Matthew 5:14-16).

The Holy Spirits provides us with supernatural spiritual gifts that enable and equip us to perform our good works (Romans 12:4-8, 1 Corinthians 12:3-11, 28, and Ephesians 4:11-13). Paul instructed us in 1 Timothy 4:14-16:

> "Do not neglect the spiritual gift within you, which was bestowed on you through prophetic utterance with the laying on of hands by the presbytery. Take pains with these things; be absorbed in them that your progress will be evident to all. Pay close attention to yourself and to your teaching; persevere in these things, for as you do this you will ensure salvation both for yourself and for those who hear you."

Paul also instructed us in Titus 3:14:

> "Our people must also learn to engage in good deeds to meet pressing needs, so that they will not be unfruitful."

His reference to good deeds is the same as his reference to good works in previous Bible verses. We learn how to perform good works in and through our local church so we can bear fruit on Jesus' vine. We are taught how to perform our good works in our local church by individuals who know how to perform them.

KINGDOM OF GOD AND KINGDOM OF HEAVEN

The kingdom of God is a spiritual realm where God is everywhere present with His righteousness and holiness and where His rule is accepted and respected. The kingdom of heaven is included in the kingdom of God. Only individuals on earth who have been redeemed by and reconciled to God through their faith and trust in and obedience to Jesus are received into the kingdom of God on earth while they are alive. All others on earth are separated from God because of sin. Loving, ministering to and serving others while we are alive because we love and obey Jesus ensure our entrance into the kingdom of heaven after we die (2 Peter 1:5-11).

The kingdom of heaven is a spiritual realm where God is present with His righteousness and holiness and where His rule is accepted and respected. The kingdom of heaven is separated from the earth because the earth has been corrupted by sin. God's angles are present in the kingdom of heaven. The spirits and souls of individuals on earth who have been redeemed by and reconciled to God through Jesus before they die are also present there. These include all those throughout the ages who have obediently responded to God's call and been loyal to Him.

Jesus stated in Matthew 7:21-23:

> "Not everyone who says to Me, 'Lord, Lord,' will enter the kingdom of heaven, but he who does the will of My Father who is in heaven will enter. Many will say to Me on that day, 'Lord, did we not prophesy in Your name, and in Your name cast out demons, and in Your name perform many miracles?' And then I will declare to them, 'I never knew you; DEPART FROM ME, YOU WHO PRATICE LAWLESSNESS.'"

The Bible instructs us to spiritually grow and mature in our relationship with Jesus through the presence of the Holy Spirit in our life after we enter our relationship with Him through Jesus. Paul stated in Ephesians 2:10 that we become "[God's] workmanship, created in Christ Jesus" to perform good works He prepares for us to perform when we enter this relationship. We perform our good works when we share God's love and grace with others, and we serve and minister to them in Jesus' name. We are to perform our good works for God's glory, not for our benefit nor to satisfy our personal needs. Jesus may not allow us to enter the kingdom of heaven after we die when we did not perform our good works for God's glory while we were alive, or when we have not repented of intentional sin in our life and asked Him to forgive us while we were alive.

COMMENT ON MY DISCUSSION OF THE SEVEN-YEAR TRIBULATION

The genesis of my discussion on the seven-year tribulation is Figure 9 on page 100. I address numbers as a Professor of Mechanical Engineering. Therefore, the number of days and time periods associated with events that will occur during the seven-year tribulation prophesied to occur in Daniel and Revelation had to line up in a coherent time line for them to be credible. Daniel was written around 603 B.C., and Revelation was written in 95 A.D. A time span of 698 years separated these two sets of prophecies. A lunar calendar was used when Daniel was written, and a solar calendar was used when Revelation was written. I was unable to develop a coherent time line between events prophesied in Daniel and Revelation, using a lunar calendar.

Daniel was instructed by Gabriel in Daniel 12:4:

> "But as for you, Daniel, conceal these words and seal up the book until the end of time; many will go back and forth, and knowledge will increase."

This instruction implied the prophecies related to the seven-year tribulation in Daniel and Revelation would not be fully understood until the "end of time" when they will be fulfilled.

This indicates a calendar in existence near the "end of time" must be used to develop a coherent time line associated with time spans and related events that will occur during the seven-year tribulation.

The Julian calendar first presented in 65 B.C. and updated in 1582 by the Gregorian calendar are based on a solar cycle. I was able to develop a coherent time line for time spans and related events that will occur during the seven-year tribulation using the Gregorian calendar. This time line is presented in Figure 9 on page 106.

MEANING OF THE TERMS KINGDOM OF GOD AND KINGDOM OF HEAVEN IN THE FOUR GOSPELS

Parables of Jesus in the Gospel of Matthew refer to the kingdom of heaven. The same parables in the other Gospels refer to the kingdom of God. This may be because the Gospel of Matthew was written for a Jewish audience while the other Gospels were written for non-Jewish audiences. Saying and writing the word for God is a sin for Jews. The use and meaning of the kingdom of heaven and the kingdom of God are the same in the four Gospels.

OLD TESTAMENT SUPERSCRIPTS

Many of the New Testament scriptures presented throughout this book have Old Testament superscript references embedded in them. These references identify the Old Testament sources for the texts contained in the scriptures.

Douglas D. Reynolds, Ph.D.

CHAPTER 1
INTRODUCTION

THE BIBLE AND THE TIME OF THE END

The Old Testament prophet Daniel spoke of events that may lead to the establishment of a one-world government referred to as a New World Order. Daniel described in Daniel 10-12 the visions he received from the LORD that were interpreted for him by the angel Gabriel concerning:

- The formation of a future ten kingdom federation that will trample the earth;
- Activities related to the rise to power of a king who will rule this federation as a dictator;
- This king's invasion of Israel and his committing the abomination of desolation in the temple in Jerusalem;
- A future "time of distress such as has not happened from the beginning of nations" until that time; and
- The king's judgment by God at the end of this time of distress.

This future king is often referred to as the Antichrist, and these events will occur during a time the Bible refers to as the end time, the end time and the last days. This time will be associated with God's final conflict with Satan that will culminate in the return of Jesus. Regarding Daniel's visions, Gabriel told him in Daniel 11:36:

> "Then the king will do as he pleases, and he will exalt and magnify himself above every god and will speak monstrous things against the God of gods; and he will prosper until the indignation is finished, for that which is decreed will be done."

The establishment of a New World Order may precede the formation of the ten kingdom federation referred to in Daniel.

Jesus stated in Matthew 24:4-25, Mark 13:5-23 and Luke 21:8-36 the world will experience a time of distress, which will be followed by a time of "great distress, unequaled from the

1

beginning of the world ... and never to be equaled again." Jesus indicated these will be times of:

- Great global distress;
- Wars and rumors of wars and nations fighting against nations;
- Spiritual darkness and deception designed to draw men and women away from God;
- Persecution and the martyring of Christians; and Jesus indicated all humanity would be destroyed during the time of great distress if it would not be for God intervening to shorten its days.

He further stated during the time between the times of distress and great distress:

- Israel will be invaded by Gentile nations, presumably led by the Antichrist (the king in Daniel's vision);
- The Antichrist will commit the abomination of desolation in the temple in Jerusalem referred to in Daniel; and
- Christians will be removed from the earth during an event referred to by Christians as the rapture.

Jesus stated in Luke 21:22 regarding the time of great distress:

> "Because these are days of vengeance, so that all things which are written will be fulfilled."

The time of distress and great distress described by Jesus is referred to as the tribulation that will occur over a period of seven years. The judgments of God, other related events, and the return of Jesus described in Revelation will occur during this seven-year period. The tribulation will occur during the time referred to in the Bible as the end time. The time of distress described in Daniel and of great distress described by Jesus are referred to as the great tribulation. This will occur during the last 1,260 days of the tribulation.

THE BIBLE AND THE RETURN OF JESUS

Appendix A lists 61 Old Testament prophesies concerning the birth, life, death and resurrection of Jesus reported in the New Testament Gospels of Matthew, Mark, Luke and John that were fulfilled by Him. It is statistically impossible for anyone but Jesus to have fulfilled these prophesies. Appendix A also lists 22 Old and New Testament prophecies related to events associated with the tribulation and return of Jesus. Future events associated with the judgments of God and return of Jesus are presented in Revelation.

The Bible refers to two events associated with the return of Jesus during the end time. The first will be His return at what Christians call the rapture. This will be the time during the middle of the tribulation when Jesus will return to remove Christians from the earth to heaven before the beginning of the great tribulation. Jesus addressed this event in Matthew 24:26-41, Mark 13:24-29 and Luke 17:22-37. The second will be when Jesus returns at the end of the tribulation to confront and defeat the armies of the kings of the earth at the battle of Armageddon. This battle is described in Revelation 19:1-16.

Jesus will establish His 1,000-year kingdom after the battle of Armageddon. The prophet Ezekiel reported instructions he received from the Lord that are associated with the establishment of this kingdom. He received:

- Instructions regarding the rebuilding of the Temple in Jerusalem (Ezekiel 40-42);
- A vision of the Glory of God filling the rebuilt Temple (Ezekiel 43);
- Instructions on how the land in Israel is to be divided among the twelve tribes of Israel (Ezekiel 48); and
- Instructions regarding the land in Israel that is to be set apart for Jerusalem, the Levities, the Priests and the rebuilding of the Temple and for the requirements for the offerings and feast that will be celebrated in the Temple (Ezekiel 45 and 48).

The 61 Old Testament prophesies concerning the birth, life, death and resurrection of Jesus were fulfilled by Him during His life. Regarding the times of distress and great distress discussed above, Gabriel told Daniel, "for what has been determined must take place," and Jesus stated, "all things which are written will be fulfilled." It is, therefore, reasonable to expect the 22 unfulfilled prophesies concerning the return of Jesus, the related events foretold by Daniel, Jesus and Ezekiel, and the events discussed in Revelation concerning the tribulation and return of Jesus will be fulfilled in the future. The Bible does not present information regarding the specific times of Jesus' return even though it presents information concerning His return during the end time. Jesus stated concerning His return:

"But of that day and hour no one knows, not even the angels of heaven, nor the Son of Man, but the Father alone." (Matthew 24:36)

"It is not for you to know times or epochs which the Father has fixed by His own authority." (Acts 1:7)

We are not told when Jesus will return even though we are told He will return.

A CALL FOR A NEW WORLD ORDER

Change is occurring throughout the world. Radical Islamic terrorism is spreading throughout the world. Massive Islamic migration from war torn regions in the Middle East into Western European countries is transforming the cultural character and balance of these countries. Massive legal and illegal immigration from Mexico, Central America and other countries into the United States is transforming the cultural character and balance of the United States. Multiculturalism is challenging the rights of countries to secure their borders and control immigration into their countries. The LGBT movement and related court rulings and legislation in countries around the world are redefining the structure of the family. The traditional family structure defined by the Bible and Christianity are under relentless attack in efforts to neutralize their global influence.

World leaders have and are calling for the establishment of a one-world global government, a New World Order, to more effectively address the global challenges created by the above and other related global events. Former president George H. W. Bush in the United States announce the desirability for the establishment of a New World Order in his 1991 State of the Union address. Former Vice President Joe Biden stated in his address to the 2014 graduating class of the U.S. Air Force Academy, "The graduating cadets will lead and shape a New World Order for the 21st century." French President Emmanuel Macron stated in his speech to the U.S. Congress on April 25, 2018, "We can build the 21st Century world order, based on a new breed of multilateralism, based on a more effective, accountable and results-oriented multilateralism, a stronger multilateralism." Pope John Paul II in 1990, Pope Benedict XVI in 2005, and Pope Francis in 2017 in the Catholic church have called for a one-world government, a New World Order, to lead the world in addressing climate, financial and other global challenges.

Wikipedia defines the New World Order as referring to the emergence of a totalitarian world government that will incorporate and replace the individual governments of sovereign nation-states around the world. Much has been published in books, other media and on the Internet concerning conspiracy theories related to the establishment of a future New World Order. The key words *New World Order* generate over 7,790,000,000 hits with the

Google search engine. Some refer to the establishment of a New World Order and its related ideology as the culminating event in the evolution of human progress.

CHRISTIANITY AND A CALL FOR A NEW WORLD ORDER

There is a relation between:

- Bible prophesies;
- Presentations in the Bible about the end time;
- Presentations in Revelation concerning the judgments of God and the return of Jesus; and
- Events associated with the establishment of a New World Order.

Most Christians know little about or choose to ignore Bible prophesies, information related to the end time, and presentations in Revelation. They are also unaware of or know little about the establishment of a New World Order. Therefore, they know little or nothing about the possible relation between these four subject areas.

Jesus stated in John 4:24, "God is spirit, and those who worship Him must worship in spirit and truth." We interact with God through our spirit and with the world around us through our physical body. We must examine information and events leading to the establishment of a New World Order in the context of our spiritual relationship with God and our relation to the physical world around us.

Media information and presentations concerning events associated with the end time, return of Jesus, and establishment of a New World Order focus primarily on their relations to the physical world. They do not effectively address these subject areas in the context of our spiritual relationship with God through Jesus. These four subject areas must be examined in the context of our spiritual relationship with God through Jesus and the conflict between God and Satan in the spiritual and physical realms to better understand them.

Information presented in this book regarding our spiritual relationship with God through Jesus:

- Emphasizes the importance of our seeking and receiving the redemption God extends to us through Jesus;
- Addresses the relation between Bible prophesies and information in the Bible associated with the end time, the seven-year tribulation and the return of Jesus; and
- Identifies a time line that documents when major events will occur during the seven-year tribulation.

Information that specifies future times when specific events associated with the seven-year tribulation and return of Jesus are not presented because the Bible does not reveal this information.

Information is presented in this book that:

- Identifies secret societies, groups and organizations involved in efforts to establish a New World Order;
- Describes ongoing spiritual, social-political and economic cultural conflicts that will facilitate the establishment of a New World Order;
- Identifies obstacles to the establishment of a New World Order;
- Describes global spiritual, social-political and economic transformations that must occur before a New World Order can be established; and
- Explains possible relations between the establishment of a New World Order and events that will lead to the beginning of the seven-year tribulation.

Information is not presented that specifies future times when specific events will occur that will lead to the establishment of a New World Order because such information would be pure speculation.

Discussions that address our relationship with God through Jesus and related future global events associated with this relationship require a faith response. These discussions and events can be interpreted differently, depending on your knowledge and understanding of Bible scriptures and prophesies. This is true for many of the discussions presented in this book. Some of these discussions may be unsettling and frightful. They present mental images of future global distress, destruction, desolation and death. You will have to decide what you will choose to believe. I pray you will let the Holy Spirit guide you in the choices you will make.

SECRET SOCIETIES AND A CALL FOR A NEW WORLD ORDER

The involvement of secret societies in the establishment of a New World Order is little understood by most individuals. Conspiracy theorists suggest that a secret society known as the Illuminati has been and continues to be involved in efforts to establish a global dictatorial government known as a New World Order. They indicate other secret societies have also been and continue to be involved in these efforts. The Illuminati and these other secret societies are anti-God, involved in occult activities, and are loyal to and worship Lucifer.

An individual who used the pseudonym Svali was interviewed by HJ Springer during 2000 - 2001. She was an Illuminati head trainer/programmer before she became a Christian and left the Illuminati. She used psychological mind control programing as a head trainer/

programmer like she was subjected to as a young child to program young children of Illuminati parents to be loyal to and pursue Illuminati objectives when becoming adults. Svali's 18-part interview with HJ Springer presented insights into the organizational structure of the Illuminati and their global agenda to establish a New World Order. (*2nd Series - The Illuminati in America*; by Svali as interviewed by HJ Springer; 2000-2001; http://www. bibliotecapleyades.net/sociopolitica/esp_sociopol_illuminati_svali01b.htm/menu2).

This book addresses the roles Satan and secret societies have played and continue to play in movements to establish an anti-God, global, dictatorial government. Information is presented that identifies efforts by the Illuminati, Freemasonry and the Committee of 300 to establish a New World Order. Other secret societies and groups who support and participate in this pursuit are also identified.

ETERNAL NATURE OF GOD AND HIS JUDGMENTS

God is *eternal*. He has no beginning and no ending. His existence is from everlasting to everlasting. He exists forever, and His judgments have eternal consequences. Jesus' judgments at the end of His 1,000-year kingdom will fix our position with God, Him and the Holy Spirit forever; it will never change.

Eternity spans a period defined as *infinity*. We can neither imagine nor comprehend a time span this long. Our life normally spans a period of 80 - 90 years. The age of the Universe is 13,800,000,000 years. *Infinity* is massively larger than the age of the Universe. Mathematically, any number divided by *infinity* equals *zero*. Therefore, our life span of 80 - 90 years represents a time span of *zero* years (e.g. 90/13,800,000,000 = 0.0000000065 = 0) when compared to *infinity*.

Our life choices and actions during this *zero* time span determine where we will spend *eternity*. They determine whether we will forever be in the kingdom of heaven in the presence of God, Jesus and the Holy Spirit or whether we will forever be separated from Them in torment in the lake of fire.

CONCLUDING COMMENTS

I do not consider myself to be a Bible scholar or an expert on Bible prophesy and secret societies. There are many others who are far more qualified to present the information I present in this book. The Holy Spirit, for reasons that only He knows, has created a burden within my heart and presented me with the opportunity and means to write and publish this book. I believe He has given me a unique understanding of Bible scriptures and prophesies, has led me to relevant reference materials, and has given me the spiritual insight and vision necessary to write this book.

The Bible is the source and foundation of much of the information presented in this book. God though His prophets has presented us with information in the Bible describing how He will interact with His creation and with us in the future. However, He has not given us enough information to accurately predict specific times and conditions associated with future events related to this interaction. Therefore, we can only speculate on specifics related to future events based on our understanding of information presented in the Bible and obtained from non-biblical sources. I have attempted to present reasonable, defendable and understandable narratives in this book that describe the possible relations between Bible prophesy, the tribulation and return of Jesus, and conditions and events that will lead to the establishment of a New World Order. The narratives and related observations presented in this book are based on my understanding of precepts, principles and past and future events discussed in the Bible. They are also based on my perceptions of past, current and potential future regional and global conditions and events. You may choose to agree or disagree with my narratives and observations based on your understanding of information presented in the Bible and perception of world conditions and events. Whatever choice you make is okay.

Whether you agree or disagree with my narratives and observations regarding what may occur in the future is not important. However, your ability and willingness to perceive and understand God is present and actively working in His creation to bring you into a reconciled relationship with Him through His Son, Jesus, is important. Whatever good and bad may occur in the future, you must understand and believe God is in control of conditions and events in His creation that have, are and will occur in the future. God will walk with you to prepare your way as you encounter life's experiences and challenges when you invite Him into your life through faith in Jesus and give Him permission. The Bible teaches in the end God will triumph.

CHAPTER 2
NATURES OF GOD AND SATAN

GOD - GOD OF GODS AND LORD OF LORDS

The Eternal Nature of God

God is *eternal*. The nature and attributes of His character have no beginning and no end, and they will never change. The Old Testament declares the eternal nature of God. In one of the earliest books of the Bible, Elihu, one of Job's companions, stated in Job 36:26:

> "Behold, God is exalted, and we do not know Him; the number of His years is unsearchable."

The Psalms declare the eternal nature of God.

> "Before the mountains were born or You gave birth to the earth and the world, even from everlasting to everlasting, You are God." (Psalms 90:2)

> "But the lovingkindness of the LORD is from everlasting to everlasting on those who fear Him, and His righteousness to children's children, to those who keep His covenant and remember His precepts to do them." (Psalm 103:17-18)

> "Forever, O LORD, Your word is settled in heaven. Your faithfulness continues throughout all generations; You established the earth, and it stands." (Psalms 119:89-90)

Isaiah stated in Isaiah 41:4:

> "Who has performed and accomplished it, calling forth the generations from the beginning? 'I, the LORD, am the first, and with the last. I am He.'"

The New Testament declares the eternal nature of God. Paul stated in Romans 1:20:

"For since the creation of the world His invisible attributes, His eternal power and divine nature, have been clearly seen, being understood through what has been made, so that they are without excuse."

Peter stated in 1 Peter 1:24:

"For all flesh is like grass, and all its glory like the flower of grass. The grass withers, and the flower falls off, but the word of the LORD endures forever." [Isaiah 40:6-8] (Note: *Superscript Bible references denote the Old Testament source for the preceding Scripture.*)

In Hebrews 1:8-12, the writer stated:

"But of the Son He says, 'Your throne, O God, is forever and ever,
And the righteous scepter is the scepter of His kingdom.
You have loved righteousness and hated lawlessness,
Therefore God, Your God, has anointed You
With the oil of gladness above Your companion.' [Psalms 45:6-7]
And
'You, LORD, in the beginning laid the foundation of the earth,
And the heavens are the work of Your hands;
They will perish, but You remain;
And they all will become old like a garment,
And like a mantle You will roll them up,
Like a garment they will also be changed.
But You are the same,
And Your years will not come to an end.'" [Psalm 102:25-27]"

God, Jesus and the Holy Spirit have eternal natures. In Hebrews 13:8 the author also stated, "Jesus Christ is the same yesterday and today and forever."

The Old and New Testaments confirm the eternal natures of God and Jesus. The Bible indicates the words They spoke will stand forever. Psalms 119:89-90 above indicates God's word is settled in heaven forever. Isaiah stated in Isaiah 40:8:

"The grass withers, the flower fades, but the word of our God stands forever."

Peter reaffirmed God's word endures forever. Jesus stated in Matthew 5:17-19:

"Do not think that I came to abolish the Law or the Prophets; I did not come to abolish but to fulfill. For truly I say to you, until heaven and earth pass away, not the smallest letter or stroke shall pass from the Law until all is accomplished. Whoever then annuls one of the least of these commandments, and teaches others to do the same, shall be called least in the kingdom of heaven; but whoever keeps and teaches them, he shall be called great in the kingdom of heaven."

God's word is the eternal standard by which we must live our life and form our character. God's word and commandments stand forever and will never change. This contrasts with cultural and social customs and laws which continually change.

Solomon stated in Ecclesiastes 3:11:

"He has made everything appropriate in its time. He has also set eternity in their heart, yet so that man will not find out the work which God has done from the beginning even to the end."

God has placed eternity in our heart. This leads us to engage in life activities and make life choices that have eternal consequences. These actions often require us to look outside ourself to obtain information necessary to make correct choices. We as Christians approach God through Jesus and the Holy Spirit to obtain this information. We may not initially understand why and how God desires to work in and through us. However, God reveals Himself to us through the Holy Spirit to give us the information we seek as we grow in our knowledge of and internalize God's word in the Bible.

The Sovereignty and Power of God

Yahweh is the most important name for God in the Old Testament. It means *I am who I am*. The four-letter Hebrew word YHWH is the name by which God revealed Himself to Moses in the burning bush (Exodus 3:14). The name Yahweh expresses God is the infinite God, who is behind everything and to whom everyone in heaven and on earth is ultimately accountable. The *I am who I am* specifies nothing else defines who God is but God Himself.

The Bible teaches God has dominion over the Earth and the heavens. In 1 Chronicles 29:11-12, the writer stated:

"Yours, O LORD, is the greatness and the power and the glory and the victory and the majesty, indeed everything that is in the heavens and the earth; Yours is the dominion, O LORD, and You exalt Yourself as head over all. Both riches and honor come from You, and You rule over all, and Your hand is power and might; and it lies in Your hand to make great and to strengthen everyone."

There is only one God even though there may be many so-called gods. God stated in Deuteronomy 32:39:

"See now that I, I am He, and there is no god besides Me; it is I who put to death and give life. I have wounded, and it is I who heal; and there is no one who can deliver from My hand."

Moses stated in Deuteronomy:

"To you it was shown that you might know that the LORD, He is God; there is no other besides Him. ... Know therefore today, and take it to your heart, that the LORD, He is God in heaven above and on earth below; there is no other." (Deuteronomy 4:35, 39)

"For the LORD your God is the God of gods and the LORD of lords, the great, the mighty, and the awesome God who does not show partiality, nor take a bribe." (Deuteronomy 10:17)

God stated in Isaiah 46:9:

"Remember the former things long past. For I am God, and there is no other; I am God, and there is no one like Me."

God is the Father of creation (Genesis 1:1, Revelation 4:11), Israel (Exodus 4:22-23, Jeremiah 31:9), Jesus (Matthew 3:16-17), and all who believe in Jesus (John 1:12-13, Romans 8:14).

The Spiritual Nature of God

God is a spiritual being. Jesus stated in John 4:24, "God is Spirit, and those who worship Him must worship in spirit and truth." God as a spiritual being:

- Creates (Genesis 1:1)
- Destroys (Genesis 19:24-25)
- Provides (Psalm 104:27-30)
- Promotes (Psalm 75:6-7)
- Cares (1 Peter 5:6-7)
- Heals (Deuteronomy 32:39)
- Hears (Psalm 94:9-10)
- Hates (Proverbs 6:16)
- Grieves (Genesis 6:6)
- Loves (John 3:16)

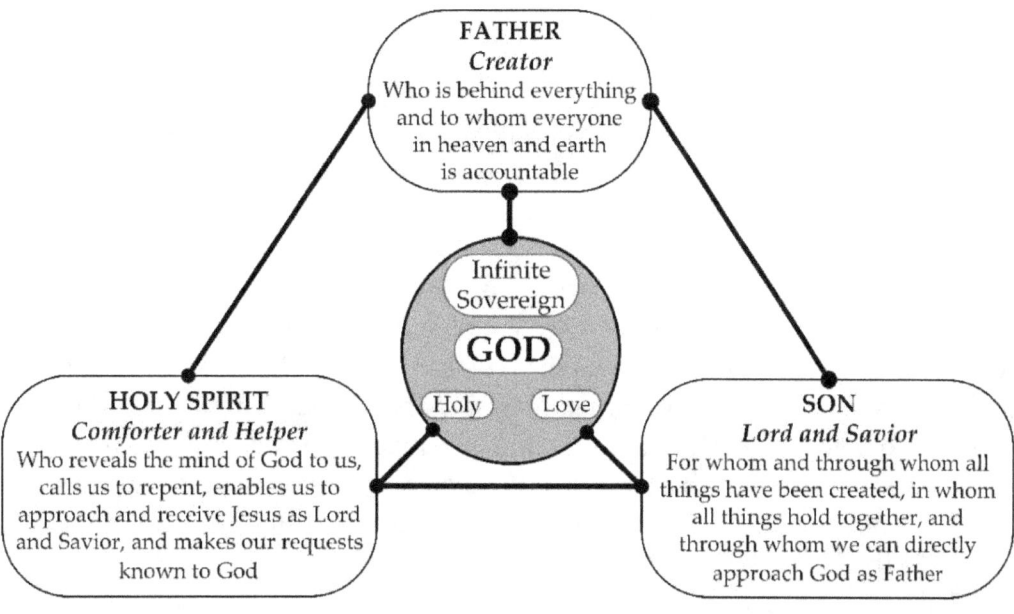

Figure 1

The Triune Nature of God

Even though there is one God, there are three eternal Persons within the Godhead who interact with each other and us. God is Father, Son and Holy Spirit (Figure 1). Each Person within the Godhead possesses all the eternal, infinite and sovereign attributes of Deity. They each interact with us in ways that are unique to their respective positions within the Godhead. However, they all interact with us in a unified manner that is perfectly consistent with God's sovereignty and His attributes of holiness and love. The Bible teaches:

- The Father is God (John 6:44-46, Romans 1:1-4, 1 Peter 1:2),
- Jesus, the Son of God, is God (John 1:1, Hebrews 1:1-3), and
- The Holy Spirit is God (Acts 2:16, Ezekiel 36:26-27).

Jesus stated in John 14:16-7:

> "And I will ask the Father, and He will give you another Helper, that He may be with you forever; that is the Spirit of Truth, whom the world cannot receive, because it does not behold Him or know Him, but you know Him because He abides with you, and will be in you."

He also stated in Matthew 28:19-20:

> "Go therefore and make disciples of all the nations, baptizing them in the name of the Father and the Son and the Holy Spirit, teaching them to observe all that I commanded you, and lo, I am with you always, even to the end of the age."

God, the Father, is the Creator of all things. He is the One who is behind everything and the one to whom everyone in all creation is accountable. Jesus, God's Son, is the One through and for whom all things have been created, in whom all things hold together, and through whom we can approach God, the Father. The Holy Spirit is our Comforter and Helper. He is our Advocate before the Father and the One who reveals the mind of God to us. He calls us to repentance, enables us to approach and receive Jesus as Lord and Savior, and makes our requests known to God. The Holy Spirit opens our minds to receive and understand God's word in the Bible.

The Bible teaches, even though the Father, Son and Holy Spirit are God, there is a hierarchy within the Godhead. Paul stated in 1 Corinthians 11:3 and 15:28:

> "But I want you to understand that Christ is the head of every man, and the man is the head of a woman, and God is the head of Christ. And when all things are subjected to Him, then the Son Himself also will be subjected to the One who subjected all things to Him, that God may be all in all."

Jesus is God, but He was and is obedient to God, the Father. He stated in John 5:30, 6:38, 14:28:

> "I can do nothing on My own initiative. As I hear, I judge; and My judgment is just, because I do not seek My own will, but the will of Him who sent me. ... For I have come down from heaven, not to do My own will, but the will of Him who sent Me. ... If you loved Me, you would have rejoiced, because I go to the Father; for the Father is greater than I."

Jesus stated the Holy Spirit proceeds from the Father (John 15:26) and was sent by the Father (John 14:6) and Him (John 15.26). The Holy Spirit was sent to glorify Jesus (John 16:14), bring to our remembrance all Jesus has taught us (John 14:26), and reveal the mind and thoughts of God as God wanted them revealed (1 Corinthians 2:11).

Relative to creation, Paul stated in 1 Corinthians 8:5-6:

"For even if there are so-called gods whether in heaven or on earth, as indeed there are many gods and many lords, yet for us there is but one God, the Father, from whom are all things, and we exist for Him; and one Lord, Jesus Christ, by whom are all things, and we exist through Him."

All things come from God, the Father, through Jesus as Lord. We exist and live for God through Jesus. Paul continued in 1 Corinthians 12:3:

"Therefore, I make known to you, that no one speaking by the Spirit of God says, 'Jesus is accursed'; and no one can say, 'Jesus is Lord,' except by the Holy Spirit."

In summary:

- We exist for the pleasure of God (the Father) through Jesus as our Lord;
- We can only come to God (the Father) through Jesus as our Savior; and
- The Holy Spirit enables us to receive Jesus as our Savior and Lord of our life.

The Laws of God

God has given us laws that direct how we are to relate to Him and interact with others. The Bible refers to these laws as the Law. The Ten Commandments Moses received from God on Mount Sinai form the core of His laws that cover our relationships with Him and our parents and our interactions with others. They are (Deuteronomy 5:7-21):

- "You shall have no other gods before Me."
- "You shall not make for yourself an idol, or any likeness of what is in heaven above or on the earth beneath or in the water under the earth. You shall not worship them or serve them; for I, the LORD your God, am a jealous God, visiting the iniquity of the fathers on the children, and on the third and the fourth generations of those who hate Me, but showing loving kindness to thousands, to those who love Me and keep My commandments.
- "You shall not take the name of the LORD your God in vain, for the LORD will not leave him unpunished who takes His name in vain."
- "Observe the Sabbath day to keep it holy, as the LORD your God commanded you. Six days you shall labor and do all your work, but the seventh day is a Sabbath of the

LORD your God; in it you shall not do any work, you or your son or your daughter or your male servant or your female servant or your ox or your donkey or any of your cattle or your sojourner who stays with you, so that your male servant and your female servant may rest as well as you."

- "Honor your father and your mother, as the LORD your God has commanded you, that your days may be prolonged, and that it may go well with you on the land which the LORD your God gives you.

- "You shall not murder."

- "You shall not commit adultery."

- "You shall not steal."

- "You shall not bear false witness against your neighbor."

- "You shall not covet your neighbor's wife, and you shall not desire your neighbor's house, his field or his male servant or his female servant, his ox or his donkey or anything that belongs to your neighbor."

Old Testament laws received by Moses in addition to the Ten Commandments are treated as extensions of the Ten Commandments. The Ten Commandments plus these laws form what is referred to as the Law. Jesus indicated in Matthew 5:18 that "not the smallest letter or stroke" shall be removed from the Law until heaven and earth pass away. Therefore, the Law defines and convicts us of sin.

Sexual sins associated with the commandment on adultery include:

- **Adultery** (Leviticus 20:10; Deuteronomy 22:13-22): Adultery is sexual contact between a man and woman, one or both who are married, but not to each other.

- **Fornication** (Exodus 22:16-17; Deuteronomy 22:20-30): Formication is sexual contact between a man and woman neither of whom is married nor engaged to be married. A man and woman engaged to be married are not to have sexual contact until after they are married.

- **Homosexuality** (Leviticus 18:22, 20:13): Homosexuality is sexual contact between men and women of the same gender.

- **Incest** (Leviticus 20:11-12, 14; Deuteronomy 27:20, 22-23): Incest is sexual contact between parents and children of opposite gender, between brothers and sisters, and between aunts, uncles, nieces, nephews and cousins of opposite gender.

- **Bestiality** (Exodus 22:20; Leviticus 18:23, 20:15-16): Bestiality is sexual contact between a man or woman and an animal.

- **Exposing of Nakedness** (Leviticus 18:8-17, 20:17): Exposing of nakedness in a family is looking at the nude body of a family member of different gender other than a spouse. This includes viewing modern-day pornography.

Sin in our life creates a barrier that separates us from God. The Bible teaches the Law cannot remove this barrier and redeem us from sin. It can only convict us of sin and condemn us to spiritual death and eternal separation from God, Jesus and the Holy Spirit.

SATAN - GOD OF THIS WORLD

There are many who doubt the existence of Satan. They may believe there is something or someone who is a personification of evil in the world, but they do not believe there is a real spiritual being named Satan. The Bible clearly teaches Satan's existence (Ron Rhodes, *Angels Among Us*, 1994). He is mentioned in seven Old Testament books: Genesis, 1 Chronicles, Job, Psalms, Isaiah, Ezekiel, and Zechariah. He is mentioned in nineteen of the twenty-seven books in the New Testament. He is mentioned by every New Testament writer:

- Matthew (Matthew 4:1)
- Mark (Mark 5:15)
- Luke (Luke 22:3)
- John (1 John 3:8)
- Paul (Romans 16:20)
- Peter (1 Peter 5:8)
- James (James 4:7)
- Jude (Jude 9)

He is mentioned by Jesus some twenty-five times in the Gospels. References are found in Matthew 4:10, Matthew 16:23, Matthew 25:41, Luke 10:18, John 8:44, and Luke 22:31. To deny the existence of Satan is to deny the validity of statements concerning his existence in the Bible and Jesus' own testimony.

God created three angels who had special positions. One was Michael, referred to as an archangel (Daniel 10:13, Jude 1:9). Another was Gabriel, identified as a special messenger angel from the very presence of God (Daniel 9:21, Luke 1:19). The third was Lucifer, who some believe was given the special task of watching over the throne of God. Ezekiel described Lucifer, the son of dawn, in Ezekiel 28:12-17:

> "Again the word of the LORD came to me saying, 'son of man, take up a lamentation over the king of Tyre, and say to him, 'Thus says the LORD God, you had the seal of perfection, full of wisdom and perfect in beauty. You were in Eden, the garden of God; every precious stone was your covering; the ruby, the topaz, and the diamond; the beryl, the onyx, and the jasper; the lapis lazuli, the turquoise, and the emerald; and the gold,

the workmanship of your settings and sockets, was in you. On the day that you were created they were prepared. You were the anointed cherub who covers, and I placed you there. You were on the holy mountain of God; you walked in the midst of the stones of fire. You were blameless in your ways from the day you were created, until unrighteousness was found in you. By the abundance of your trade you were internally filled with violence, and you sinned; therefore I have cast you as profane from the mountain of God. And I have destroyed you, O covering Cherub, from the midst of the stones of fire. Your heart was lifted up because of your beauty; you corrupted your wisdom by reason of your splendor. I cast you to the ground; I put you before kings, that they may see you.'"

Lucifer according to this description was perhaps the most beautiful creature in heaven. He was the anointed cherub. A cherub is a special angelic being who magnifies the holiness and power of God and serves as a visible reminder of the majesty and glory of God and His abiding presence with His people. Some Bible scholars speculate Lucifer led the worship in heaven and had the special task of watching over the throne of God. However, pride entered his heart because of his beauty and position. He no longer wanted to worship and serve God; he wanted to be served and worshiped. Isaiah implied this in Isaiah 14:12-15:

> "How you have fallen from heaven, O star of the morning, son of the dawn! You have been cut down to the earth, you who have weakened the nations! But you said in your heart, 'I will ascend to heaven; I will raise my throne above the stars of God, and I will sit on the mount of assembly in the recess of the north. I will ascend above the heights of the clouds; I will make myself like the Most High.' Nevertheless you will be thrust down to Sheol, to the recesses of the pit."

Lucifer wanted to become independent of and take the place of God. Consequently, he and many of the angels in heaven rebelled with him against God. Lucifer and those angels who followed him were defeated and cast out of heaven. Jesus implied this when He stated in Luke 10:18, "I was watching Satan fall from heaven like lightning."

Lucifer's name was changed to Satan when he was cast out of heaven. A name change in the Bible usually denotes a corresponding change in relationship with God. Abram became Abraham. Sarai became Sarah. Jacob became Israel. Simon became Peter, and Saul became Paul. These name changes implied moving into a more favored and closer relationship with God. Satan's name changes corresponded to his moving into a relationship more removed from God and his resulting judgment.

Satan is a fallen angel who was corrupted by sin. He is a created being (Ezekiel 28:12-17). He does not possess any of the sovereign and infinite attributes of God even though he possesses great power. His powers are limited by God like all other created beings.

The Bible teaches Satan is the god of this world (2 Corinthians 4:3-4) and the world is under his control (1 John 5:10). When Jesus was tempted by Satan after His forty days in the wilderness, the following account is given in Matthew 4:8-9:

> "Again the devil took Him to a very high mountain and showed Him all the kingdoms of the world, and their glory; and he said to Him, 'All these things will I give You, if You fall down and worship me.' Then Jesus said to him, 'Go, Satan! For it is written, 'You shall worship the LORD Your God, and serve Him only.'" (Deuteronomy 6:13)"

Jesus did not dispute Satan's claim to dominion over the kingdoms of the world, but He rebuked and commanded him to depart. Satan is a trespasser who has dominion because men and women whose hearts have been darkened and blighted by sin have given it to him. He rules over the world today because men and women choose to follow and serve him instead of God. Regarding this, Jesus stated in John 8:41-44:

> "They said to Him, 'We were not born of fornication; we have one Father, God.' Jesus said to them, 'If God were your Father, you would love Me, for I proceeded forth and have come from God, for I have not even come on My own initiative, but He sent Me. Why do you not understand what I am saying? It is because you cannot hear My word. You are of your father the devil, and you want to do the desires of your father. He was a murderer from the beginning, and does not stand in the truth, because there is no truth in him. Whenever he speaks a lie, he speaks from his own nature, for he is a liar, and the father of lies.'"

God did not initially want Satan to have dominion over the earth. However, He allowed Satan to seize dominion because of Adam's and Eve's disobedience. They were originally given dominion over the earth (Genesis 1:28). Therefore, only a perfect man without sin, Jesus, could pay the required ransom to regain dominion from Satan (Matthew 20:28, 1 Timothy 2:6, Hebrews 9:15).

Jesus stated Satan is a murderer and liar; he is a thief who comes to kill, steal and destroy (John 8:44, 10:10). Peter stated in 1 Peter 5:8:

> "Be of sober spirit, be on the alert. Your adversary, the devil, prowls about like a roaring lion, seeking someone to devour."

John indicated in 1 John 3:8:

> "The one who practices sin is the devil; for the devil has sinned from the beginning."

Satan is a liar and master of deception. Paul indicated he is an angel of light who disguises himself to lure people away from God (2 Corinthians 11:14-15), and he works to put a veil over "the minds of the unbelieving, that they might not see the light of the gospel of the glory of Christ" (2 Corinthians 4:3-4).

The Bible teaches Satan has been judged and defeated through the death and resurrection of Jesus (John 12:21, John 16:11, 1 John 3:8). He has a lake of fire waiting for him (Revelation 20:10). Dominion is returned to us when God and Jesus take up residence in us through the Holy Spirit (Acts 26:16-18, Colossians 1:13). We then have authority in the name of Jesus over Satan, and he must obey. John stated 1 John 4:4:

> "You are from God little children, and have overcome them; because greater is He who is in you than he who is in the world."

James indicated in James 4:2, "Submit therefore to God. Resist the devil and he will flee from you."

DOMINION VERSUS OWNERSHIP

God has ultimate dominion over and ownership of the heavens and earth. Ezra stated 1 Chronicles 29:11-12:

> "Thine, O LORD, is the greatness and the power and the glory and the victory and the majesty, indeed everything that is in the heavens and the earth; thine is the dominion, O LORD, and thou dost exalt thyself as head over all. Both riches and honor come from thee, and thou dost rule over all, and in thy hand is power and might; and it lies in thy hand to make great, and to strengthen everyone."

David stated in Psalm 24:1:

> "The earth is the LORD's, and all it contains, the world, and those who dwell in it." (Psalm 24:1)

The LORD stated in Deuteronomy 10:14:

> "Behold, to the LORD your God belongs heaven and the highest heavens, the earth and all that is in it."

Leviticus 25:23 teaches God owns all land. Haggai 2:8 states God owns all gold and silver. Psalm 50:10-12 indicates all livestock belongs to God. The Bible teaches God is the creator and owner of all things in heaven and on earth. He did not transfer ownership even though He originally transferred dominion of His creation on earth to Adam. Therefore, Adam did not have the authority to transfer ownership even though he transferred dominion over the earth to Satan because of sin. Only God has this authority, and He has not given it to either man or Satan.

Dualism is often taught when addressing the conflict between God and Satan. It presumes God and Satan are equal: God representing good and Satan representing evil. The conflict between good and evil in the world is then portrayed as a conflict between God and Satan who are equally powerful. The Bible does not support this. Satan is an angelic being who was originally created to watch over the throne of God. He was cast out of heaven because of sin. His powers are defined and limited by God. The book of Job in the Old Testament indicates the pain and suffering with which Satan was allowed to afflict Job were limited by God. God has placed boundaries on what Satan can and cannot do to us.

We are influenced by Satan when we reject God and ignore His lordship over our life. Sin reigns in our life as a result, and Satan can exercise dominion over us. Satan has become the god of this world and claimed dominion over it because mankind has rejected God's lordship over His creation. God has placed boundaries on the dominion he can exercise. The earth belongs to God even though Satan has been given dominion over it because of sin. Everything that happens in heaven and on earth occurs in a manner consistent with God's physical and spiritual laws.

CHAPTER 3
STRUCTURE OF OUR SOUL

OUR SPIRIT, SOUL AND BODY

Paul stated in 1 Thessalonians 5:23:

> "Now may the God of peace Himself sanctify you entirely; and may your spirit and soul and body be reserved complete, without blame at the coming of our Lord Jesus Christ."

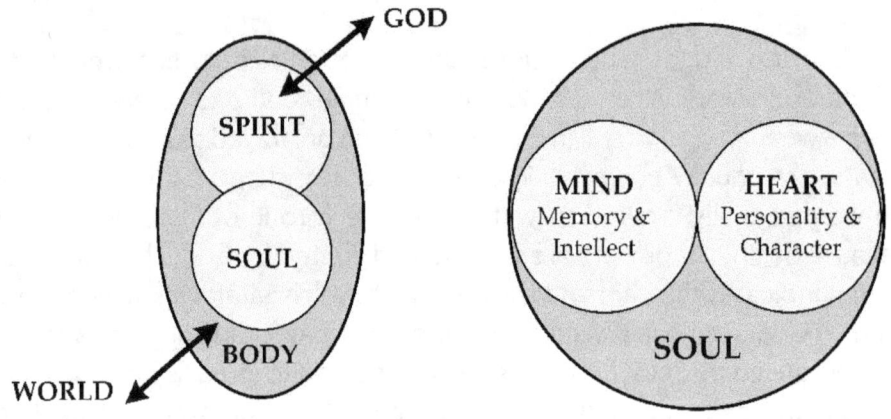

Figure 2

We are born with a spirit, soul and body (Figure 2). Our spirit interacts through our body with the spiritual realm where God exists. Our physical body interacts with the physical realm where we live through our five physical senses (sight, touch, hearing, smell and taste). Our spirit gives physical life to and functions in and through our body while we are alive. James stated in James 2:26 "the body without the spirit is dead." Our spirit and soul depart from our body when it is no longer able to support physical life and dies. Upon death our body decays and returns to dust while our spirit and soul leave our body. They continue in an eternal existence beyond physical death either in the presence of God in the kingdom of heaven or separated from Him in Hades and eventually in the lake of fire.

Our spirit and soul are linked but have separate functions. Our soul is comprised of our mind and heart (Figure 2) and functions through our spirit and body. Our mind is the seat of our memory and intellect. Our memory is the repository of information and experiences we have processed and assimilated throughout our life. Our intellect is the knowledge and wisdom we have acquired from this information and these experiences. Our heart is the seat of our personality and character. Our personality is the organized pattern of behavioral characteristics that identify and define who we are. Our character defines the moral and ethical qualities of our personality.

Our soul is an immaterial formless entity that:

- Possesses memory
- Creates thoughts
- Acquires knowledge
- Forms habits
- Experiences emotions
- Initiates actions

It develops as our mind and heart process and assimilate information they receive through our life experiences. Our soul controls how we encounter, interpret and respond to new life experiences based on how it has processed and assimilated information it has received from prior life experiences.

David stated in Psalm 139:13-16:

"For You formed my inward parts;
You wove me in my mother's womb.
I will give thanks to You, for I am fearfully and wonderfully made;
Wonderful are Your works,
And my soul knows it very well. My frame was not hidden from You,
When I was made in secret,
And skillfully wrought in the depths of the earth;
Your eyes have seen my unformed substance;
And in Your book were written
The days that were ordained for me,
When as yet there was not one of them."

David implied in this Psalm our soul instinctively moves us toward God and motivates us to be the person God has uniquely created us to be. Our soul is our moral compass that leads and enables us to live life with dignity, integrity and humility when it is nurtured by God through the Holy Spirit.

THE STRUCTURE OF AND PROCESSES WITHIN OUR SOUL

Our soul is the structure of our mind and heart - of memory, intellect, personality and character (Figure 2). Our soul governs how our spirit encounters, interprets and responds to life experiences through our physical body according to the way it assimilates and processes information it receives and experiences it encounters.

Chris Webb in his book, *The Fire of the Word: Meeting God on Holy Ground* (2011), presented the pictorial representation of our soul shown in Figure 3. The figure indicates our soul supports six actions and four processes. The six actions are senses, imagination, memory, reason, desires and drives. The four processes are perception, cognition, emotion and intention. Webb indicated the visual representation of the soul in Figure 3 was derived from ancient writings by Plato, Aristotle and the apostle Paul.

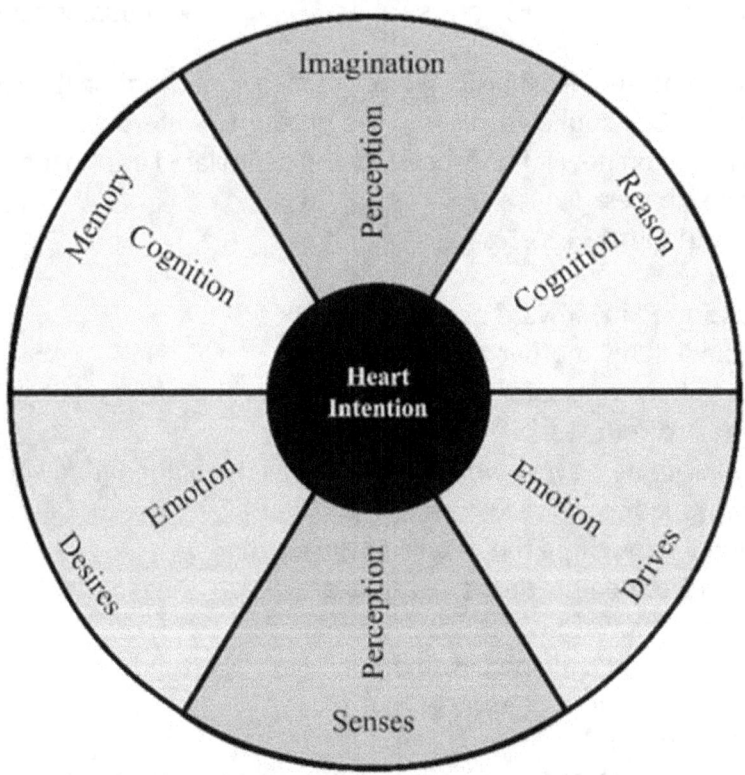

Figure 3

Inputs to our soul enter through the actions of *senses* and *imagination* in our mind. *Senses* receive information through our five physical senses (sight, hearing, touch, taste and smell) from the physical world and through our spirit from the spiritual realm. *Imagination* supplies supplemental information that further develops and embellishes information received into our mind. *Senses* and *imagination* allow us to receive information from God in the spiritual realm and from family, work and other environments where we are active in the physical world around us. *Senses* and *imagination* initiate the process of *perception*. *Perception* is the process through which we develop a coherent and unified awareness of the information we receive into our mind.

The actions of *memory* and *reason* interact in our mind to initiate the process of *cognition*. *Memory* is our repository of stored information received into our mind by *senses* and *imagination*. *Reason* is the action of our mind in which we assimilate and process this information in an orderly and systematic manner. *Cognition* is the process in our mind by which we acquire knowledge and gain insights and wisdom from this information. *Reason* and *cognition* combine to form *intellect*. The process of *cognition* facilitates the development of life skills. These skills enable us to engage in our life activities and challenges.

Desires and *drives* are actions within our heart. *Desires* are yearnings that predispose us to want to do certain activities and engage in specific tasks. *Drives* are strong urges that motivate and move us to do the activities and complete the tasks. *Desires* and *drives* initiate the process of *emotion* in our heart. *Emotion* is derived from the Latin words *emovere*, which means to disturb, and *movere*, which means to move. *Emotion* as it is used here is the process in our heart that motivates and moves us to act on information we process in our mind.

Our heart assimilates and processes outcomes from the processes of *perception*, *cognition* and *emotion* and initiates the process of *intention*. *Intention* is derived from the Latin word *intendere*, which means stretch, turn one's attention to. *Intention* as it is used here is the process that directs us to act in specific ways. It for example directs us to initiate a deliberate course of action, to form a new life habit, or to enter a new relationship. *Intention* is the process in our heart that directs us to stretch forth to engage in life's activities and challenges.

Figure 4 presents a more descriptive illustration of the actions and processes that occur within our soul. The development of this figure came to me in a dream. The emotional, psychological and functional interrelations between the actions and processes are complex. However, Figure 4 can be used with the preceding discussion to develop a more complete understanding of the interrelationships between the actions and processes shown in Figure 3.

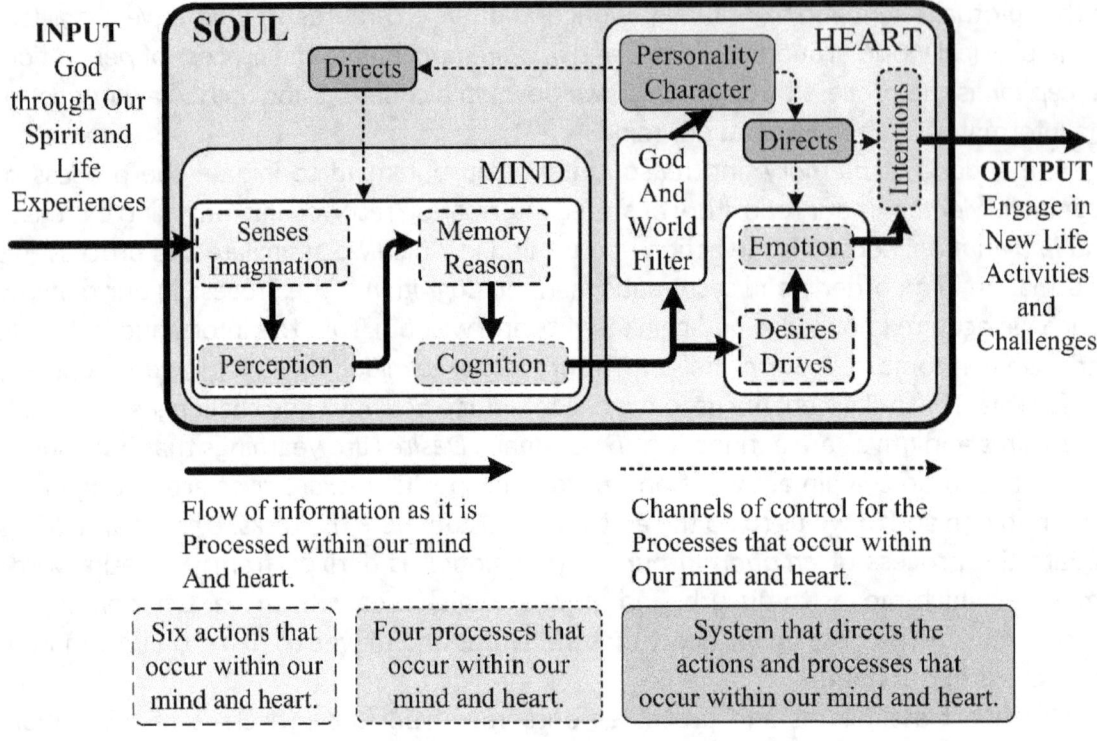

Figure 4

Figure 4 identifies additional processes that occur within and between our mind and heart. A *God and World Filter* is located between the symbol for the cognition process and the symbol for our personality and character. This filter can be referred to as the *God Site* in our soul. It performs an important function in the development of our personality and character. Its filter characteristics develop as we emotionally, psychologically and spiritually grow and mature. The development of the characteristics of this filter is influenced by two primary sources: God and the world. The filter characteristics most often are defined by God's laws and spiritual life principles when we live and grow up in an environment that affirms the existence of God and His presence in our life. The filter characteristics most often are defined by world and cultural norms and customs that may be hostile toward God when we live and grow up in an environment that denies His existence and may be hostile toward Him. The filter characteristics in many cases contain elements that are defined by both God and the world. This often results in struggles and conflicts within our soul that will be discussed later in this chapter.

Figure 4 indicates our personality and character direct:

- The senses, imagination, memory and reason actions and the perception and cognition processes within our mind, and
- The desires and drives actions and the emotion and intention processes within our heart.

Outputs from the cognition process in our mind with their associated knowledge, insights and wisdom continually influence the development of our personality and character as we assimilate and process life experiences. These outputs are filtered and often modified by the *God and World Filter* before they affect the development of or initiate changes in our personality and character. The effects of this filtering process depend on whether the filter characteristics are defined by God or by the world. This influences whether we grow into a life and life activities that honor and are obedient to God or into a life and life activities that reject and may be hostile toward God.

The redemption and reconciliation we receive from God through Jesus are gifts. God (Father, Son and Holy Spirit) takes up residence in us when we enter a relationship with Him through Jesus. How this occurs is a mystery, but it occurs. The place of this residence is the *God and World Filter* in our heart (Figure 4). It becomes the *God Site* in our soul when God is present. He reaches out from here through the Holy Spirit to begin the healing process of hurting and broken areas in our spirit and soul (mind and heart) and to initiate processes that will facilitate the transformation of our personality and character necessary for us to become obedient to Him and Jesus.

God requires us to read, study and internalize His word in the Bible to grow and mature in our relationship with Him through Jesus and the Holy Spirit. He reveals Himself to us through the Holy Spirit as we enter and continue this process, and He continues His healing process within our spirit and soul. God's, Jesus' and the Holy Spirit's imprint on our mind becomes clearer and more focused, and Their presence in our heart becomes stronger and more active as we grow and mature in our relationship with them.

The Holy Spirit adapts our personality and character to be sensitive, responsive and obedient to God's and Jesus' presence in our life as we grow in our understanding of and continue to internalize God's word in the Bible. This focuses Their presence on the perception and cognition processes that renew our mind and inserts Their presence into the emotion and intention processes that transform our heart. Paul stated relative to these processes in Philippians 4:6-7:

> "Be anxious for nothing, but in everything by prayer and supplication with thanksgiving let your request be made known to God. And the peace of God, which surpasses all comprehension, will guard your hearts and your minds in Christ Jesus."

Paul continued regarding our relationship with God in Philippians 4:8-9:

> "Finally, brethren, whatever is true, whatever is honorable, whatever is right, whatever is pure, whatever is lovely, whatever is of good repute, if there is any excellence and if anything worthy of praise, dwell on these things. The things you have learned and received and heard and seen in me, practice these things, and the God of peace will be with you."

God through the Holy Spirit transforms the characteristics of the *God and World Filter* in our heart. This filter becomes the *God Site* in our heart when we initially grow up or live in an environment that rejects and is hostile toward God, and we later enter a reconciled relationship with Him through Jesus. The renewing and transforming processes described above will begin when this occurs. These processes can begin at any age or stage in our life.

OUR SOUL WHEN NURTURED BY GOD

Our soul is the seat of our conscience, insight and sensitivity. God designed our mind to be the repository of His spiritual knowledge, insights and wisdom. A God consciousness develops in the God Site in our heart that facilitates the transformation of our personality and character as we fellowship and grow in our relationship with God through Jesus. This is essential for Him to renew our mind and transform our heart. The Holy Spirit then opens our mind and heart to receive, understand and assimilate God's spiritual laws and principles that govern our life. We grow in our understanding of the kind of person God has created us to be and how He wants us to interact with and relate to Him, others and the world around us as we read, study and internalize His word in the Bible and enter fellowship with other Christians. We learn our life is governed by these moral and spiritual laws and spiritual life principles, and the Holy Spirit creates within us the desire and gives us the ability to live according to them.

Our soul is also the seat of our creativity, inspiration and motivation. Our mind and heart process and assimilate information they receive from the spiritual realm of God and the physical world where we live, and they direct how we respond to this information. Life and meaning are given to ideas and beliefs that develop within our mind, and our heart inspires and motivates us to achieve tasks and to act on convictions that evolve from them.

Individuals whose minds and hearts are nurtured by the Holy Spirit:

- Experience the love, mercy, grace and forgiveness God gives to them through His Son, Jesus;
- Become sensitive to and reach out to and love others in the same way He reaches out to and loves them through Jesus.

- Are always able to approach life with a positive and balanced perspective;
- Have the energy, resiliency and motivation necessary to endure hardships and overcome obstacles they encounter;
- Develop insights into life and their relationship with God and others that are clearly inspired and motivated by the Holy Spirit;
- Radiate an enthusiasm for life that is contagious; and
- Have a zest for life that inspires and motivates others.

YEARNINGS WITHIN OUR SOUL

Our soul is created with built-in yearnings of the heart that drive us to move beyond ourself to seek meaning in life and our own distinct reality and destiny. Richard D. Grant and Andrea Wells Miller in their book, *Recovering Connections* (1993) and J. Keith Miller in his book, *The Secret Life of the Soul* (1997), indicate there are four basic yearnings within our soul. They are the yearning for:

- Perfect parenting,
- Perfect companionship,
- Perfect power and freedom, and
- Perfect meaning.

These yearnings begin at birth with our relationship with our parents. They progress to relationships with others, ultimately resulting in a relationship with God. They begin with our being dependent on our parents for meeting our physical, emotional and spiritual needs. We progress to where we want to be free and in control of our life, being dependent only on ourself for meeting these needs. We ultimately become dependent on God through the Holy Spirit for meeting these needs as we develop a relationship with Him through Jesus. Yearnings within our soul that occur in infancy are characterized by our being selfish and self-centered and caring only about satisfying our own physical, emotional and spiritual needs. We discover as we grow to adulthood true meaning in life is only achieved when we yield our life in obedience to God through Jesus and reach beyond ourself in selfless love to meet the legitimate needs of others.

Miller (The Secret Life of the Soul, 1997) indicated the above four yearnings can only be truly satisfied by God as Father, Son and Holy Spirit:

- Our yearning for a perfect parent is only satisfied when we enter an obedient and trusting relationship with God as Father.

- Our yearning for perfect companionship is only satisfied when we enter a surrendered relationship with Jesus within the fellowship and support of a local Christian community.

- Our yearning for perfect power and freedom is only satisfied when we invite the Holy Spirit into our life and allow Him to renew our mind and transform our heart.

- Our yearning for perfect meaning is only satisfied when our mind is renewed, our heart is transformed, and we seek and do God's will for our life.

Our personality develops the positive attributes God desires us to have and our moral and ethical values associated with our character become Christlike when our soul is nurtured by the Holy Spirit.

OUR SPIRIT WHEN NURTURED BY GOD

We will examine the functions of our spirit when we are spiritually alive, and our soul and spirit are nourished and nurtured by the Holy Spirit. Some functions are supported by the Bible while others are based on life experiences and observations (John and Paula Sandford, *Healing the Wounded Spirit*, 1985).

The first and most important function of our spirit is to worship God. Worship is our response to God's grace and His gift of redemption and reconciliation through our faith in Jesus. Paul stated in Romans 12:1:

> "I urge you therefore, brethren, by the mercies of God, to present your bodies a living and holy sacrifice, acceptable to God, which is your spiritual service and worship."

God has created us for His good pleasure to love and serve Him. Jesus stated in Mark 12:30 we are to love God with all our heart, mind, soul and strength. We are to focus our attention on, direct our affection toward, and use our talents for Him in everything we do. Jesus stated in John 4:23-24 we must worship God in spirit and truth. Real worship is a lifestyle through which we affirm the love we have for God. Everything we say and do in life must affirm His presence in our life and be done in a manner that brings Him glory and honor.

We approach God through corporate and private worship. Corporate worship is where we participate in singing and lifting praises, adoration and thanksgiving to God in fellowship with other Christians. Psalm 100:1-5 states:

> "Shout joyfully to the LORD, all the earth. Serve the LORD with gladness; come before Him with joyful singing. Know that the LORD Himself is God; it is He who has made us and not we ourselves; we are His people and the sheep of His pasture. Enter His gates with thanksgiving and His courts with praise. Give thanks to Him; bless His name. For the LORD is good; His loving kindness is everlasting and His faithfulness to all generations."

Corporate worship and fellowship are where we recognize God has created us and has facilitated our receiving all we possess. They are where we experience His love for us and receive strength to persevere.

Private worship and devotions are where we spend focused personal times with God. Our devotions are times when we approach Him through prayer and study His word in the Bible. We communicate with God through prayer, and He communicates with us through His word given to us in the Bible.

We receive knowledge of God's spiritual life principles that govern our life as we study His word in the Bible when we are spiritually alive. The Holy Spirit gives meaning and life to these principles and imprints them onto our mind and subconscious mind as we study and internalize them. We grow in our wisdom and insights related to these principles as we enter a deeper and more personal relationship with God through the guidance of the Holy Spirit. This enables us to incorporate them into our life more effectively.

God speaks to our mind and subconscious mind through the Holy Spirit, and we know He hears us when we speak to Him through prayer and lift our praises and adoration to Him in worship. Our soul is energized and receives strength from God through the Holy Spirit when we are spiritually alive. This enable us to engage life's challenges, endure its hardships, and live a life that glorifies God that is built on the foundation of His spiritual life principles and laws.

Our spirit plays an important role in our interaction and communication with other persons. Our spirit reaches out through time and space to interact with others. We sense their presence, emotions and sensitivity with our spirit. Sometimes without any verbal communication our spirit senses an individual's acceptance or rejection. Our spirit empathizes with and tunes into another person's feelings and emotions. We often desire to interact with and develop a relationship with a person when our spirit resonates with that person's spirit. We avoid a person when our spirit is repulsed. We have a sensitivity toward others that lowers barriers and establishes channels of communication with them necessary to develop and grow lasting relationships when we are spiritually alive.

Our spirit gives us stamina and buoyancy to confront life's challenges and hardships. We have the stamina and buoyancy to confront life's challenges and hardships and persevere when we are spiritually alive. Proverbs 18:14 states, "The spirit of a man can endure his sickness, but a broken spirit who can bear?" We can persevere through challenging and difficult times when our spirit is nourished and strengthened by the Holy Spirit. We can work through and look beyond these times with eyes of faith to see and experience God working in our life to bring us into a closer and more intimate relationship with Him.

Our spirit becomes united with the spirit of our spouse in marriage. We become one flesh with our spouse in marriage. God stated in Genesis 2:24:

> "For this cause a man shall leave his father and his mother and shall cleave to his wife; and they shall become one flesh."

Jesus reaffirmed this in Mark 10:6-8 where he stated:

> "But from the beginning of creation, God made them male and female. For this cause a man shall leave his father and mother and the two shall become one flesh; consequently they are no longer two, but one flesh."

The Bible implies marriage is consummated in the sexual union between a husband and wife. Paul implied this in 1 Corinthians 6:16-18:

> "Or do you not know that the one who joins himself to a harlot is one body with her? For [Jesus] says, 'The two will become one flesh.' But the one who joins himself to the Lord is one spirit with Him. Flee immorality. Every other sin that a man commits is outside the body, but the immoral man sins against his own body."

God has created marriage to be a holy and sacred covenant relationship between a husband and wife. It is the most intimate and sacred of all human covenants. Marriage is a relationship where all the functions of our spirit are active.

The spirits of a husband and wife resonant with each other when their spirits are alive and nourished by the Holy Spirit. Weaknesses and shortcomings of one are accepted and buoyed up by the strengths of the other. A husband and wife nurture and help each other, and they work to meet and satisfy each other's needs. They find their completeness in each other, and the most holy and sacred form of this completeness is manifested as they unselfishly give themselves to each other in sexual union. A husband and wife affirm each other's right to develop unique identities within the context of their marriage relationship as they experience life together. However, they develop these identities in the context of becoming one in spirit and developing a unified identity in their marriage that is formed through shared experiences.

STRUGGLES WITHIN OUR SOUL

God creates and brings each one of us into this world for specific purposes, and He has established behavioral boundaries. He gives us the freedom to choose if we will live according to the purposes for which He has created us and within the behavioral boundaries He has established. Our mind and heart will develop under the guidance of and be nurtured by the Holy Spirit when we choose to live according to God's will through Jesus. Our soul will be in communication with God through our spirit. However, this does not always occur in our life.

The Bible indicates our soul is a battleground in our life between good and evil, righteousness and unrighteousness, and obedience and disobedience. Our soul is where we decide we will live a life of dignity, integrity and humility in obedience to God through Jesus or a life of disobedience to God where we seek those things the world says we are entitled. How we resolve the struggles within our soul determines whether our life will be controlled by:

- The presence and guidance of God through the Holy Spirit, or
- Our desire to be in control and seek those things the world says are important.

The choices we make will affect our ability to find true meaning and purpose in life and to develop a healthy sense of self-esteem and self-worth.

The development and growth of our soul is influenced by our needs to:

- Be nurtured and supported (perfect parenting);
- Seek and enter relationships with others (perfect companionship);
- Achieve success and status in life (perfect power and freedom); and
- Find purpose in life and develop self-esteem and self-worth (perfect meaning).

The development and growth of our soul occurs in a fallen world that has been corrupted by sin and where we struggle with our sin nature. Our sin nature predisposes us to be hostile toward God and to seek what the world says is true and important.

We seek to satisfy the four yearnings of our soul in a hostile environment. In this environment:

- We sometimes do not have perfect parents as a child. Our parents may not give us the affection, support and nurturing we need. There are those who are emotionally, physically and sexually abused as children by their parents or other adults.

- We do not enter perfect relationships. We enter relationships where we are teased, tormented, rejected, used, manipulated, abused, molested, and assaulted. We enter personal, business and marriage relationships that fail.

- We do not make wise decisions in our quest for success and status in life. We make decisions that compromise our character and integrity. Just as we may become victims of others in their pursuit for success and status, we may make decisions and institute actions that victimize others. We experience disappointment and failure in our quest for success and status.

- Problems and failures we experience in our attempts to satisfy the first three yearnings of our soul can cause us to lose purpose and meaning in our life and leave us with a sense of a lack of self-esteem and self-worth. Our life can be devastated by negative experiences and appear to be out-of-control.

Consequences associated with not positively addressing our failures to satisfy the yearnings of our soul result in wounds within our soul and spirit. These wounds can derail God's purpose for our life and His desired development of our personality and character.

Serious wounds within our soul and spirit cause us to become angry at and shut God out of our life. This separates us from Him, and the continued development of our personality and character occurs in a manner that shields us from being wounded again. This intensifies battles, struggles and conflicts that occur within our soul.

Thoughts and what some describe as voices occur within our mind when our soul processes the battles, struggles and conflicts that occur within it. These thoughts/voices come from three sources:

- **The spiritual realm of God through angels and the Holy Spirit.** Thoughts/voices that originate from the spiritual realm of God direct us toward God who desires to heal our emotional and spiritual wounds. They affirm our value, dignity and worth in the eyes of God, and they encourage us to seek a life that is acceptable and pleasing to Him. They lead us to accept and receive the love, mercy, grace and forgiveness God extends to us through Jesus. They encourage us to give the Holy Spirit permission to enter our life to heal our emotional and spiritual wounds and to begin or continue the processes of renewing our mind and transforming our heart.

- **The spiritual realm of Satan through demonic sources.** Thoughts/voices that originate from the spiritual realm of Satan accuse and condemn us and work to draw us away from and make us hostile toward God. They attempt to shame us and take away our sense of value, dignity and worth. They create within us a sense that we are stupid, careless, worthless, etc. They imply we deserve the failures and bad and devastating experiences that have occurred in our life. They seek to drive us into a state of hopelessness and despair.

- **Our own mind.** Thoughts/voices that originate in our own mind and subconscious mind represent our perception of the state of our life. They reflect our concerns, fears, dreams, desires, plans, etc. They also reflect our emotional response to the thoughts/voices that come from the spiritual realms of God and Satan. How we process these thoughts/voices will either enhance our sense of self-worth and dignity or draw us into a deeper sense of hopelessness and despair.

The affirming thoughts/voices in our mind from the spiritual realm of God are ignored or repressed when our personality and character develop independent of God. The shaming and condemning thoughts/voices from the spiritual realm of Satan then become dominant, and the thoughts/voices originating within our own mind often condemn and shame us.

Thoughts/voices originating in our mind that condemn and shame us can occur whether we have entered a relationship with God through Jesus. This is certain to occur when we reject Jesus' claim on our life and are separated from God. However, it can occur when we invite Jesus into our life but do not give the Holy Spirit permission to perform His renewing and transforming processes. The Holy Spirit will not begin these processes in our soul until we give Him permission. The nurturing presence of God in our life is impaired when we fail to give the Holy Spirit permission to function within our soul.

Miller (*The Secret Life of the Soul*, 1997) indicated we enter activities directed at quieting and escaping the shaming and condemning thoughts/voices that exist in our mind when our personality and character develop independent of God. This leads us into compulsive and addictive behaviors. We may become overachievers and workaholics, hoping to find purpose and meaning in life and escape these thoughts/voices. We may become addicted to alcohol, drugs, pornography and sex because of their nagging presence. We ultimately discover these behaviors do not afford us any relief or escape. We experience a greater sense of hopelessness and despair as we enter further into these behaviors.

There are several potential negative consequences on our life when we allow our personality and character to develop independent of God.

- Spiritual communication with God is seriously impaired or cut off. As a result, our soul is unable to receive spiritual information from and to be nurtured by the Holy Spirit. Paul stated in 1 Corinthians 2:14:

  "But a nature man does not accept the things of the Spirit of God; for they are foolishness to him and he cannot understand them, because they are spiritually appraised."

- We become controlled by our interaction with the world when we take control of our life away from God, Jesus and the Holy Spirit. We become self-reliant and hostile toward God instead of developing a dependent, nurturing and loving relationship with Him.

- We are blind to God's absolute moral and spiritual laws that govern our life. The safeguards He has given us to keep our life in harmony with Him, others, ourself and the world are inoperable; they are dormant. Consequently, our life becomes controlled by our physical desires and appetites and by what the world says is important rather than by what God says is important. This increases our independence from and hostility toward God.

- We tend to become manipulative and controlling in nature and to relate to others in a way that can cause them to be apprehensive and defensive. We are unable to be compassionate and sensitive to others because we are unable to experience God's love and compassion. This results in the erection of barriers that impede the development of meaningful and trusting relationships.

- We are overcome and discouraged by hardships and crises in our life. We lack the stamina and buoyancy necessary to effectively confront them in a positive manner. They become devastating and destructive, particularly when we cannot see through or beyond them to the better times that will lie ahead. At a minimum, they become events that result in the development of a negative and defeated attitude. In more serious situations, they result in serious emotional and spiritual problems.

The beautiful story that runs throughout the Bible is God is loving, caring and patient. He continually reaches out to us with an invitation to come to Him through Jesus. God will remain in the background while we want to be in control of our life and allow our personality and character to develop independent of Him. He will permit us to sink deeper into hopelessness and despair until we ultimately give up and surrender to and seek Him. The voice of the Holy Spirit will quietly and gently break through the shaming and condemning thoughts/voices in our mind at this point to affirm God loves, forgives and desires to enter a loving, healing and nurturing relationship with us though His Son, Jesus.

We can begin to approach God on a more intimate bases through a process known as *Lectio Divina*. This process that is traditionally used in Catholicism to read and study the Bible can be used by anyone. It has four steps:

Read God's word in the Bible with reverence and the inspiration of the Holy Spirit;

Meditate by focusing our thoughts on what we have read;

Pray over the relevance of what we have read to our life; and

Contemplate on how we plan to apply what we have read to our life.

When we surrender and yield ourself to God through our faith in Jesus:

- The Holy Spirit will:

    1. Enter our life and initiate processes that result in the healing of our soul and spirit, renewal of our mind, and transformation of our heart, and

    2. Facilitate the growth of the positive personality attributes and Christlike character God has created within us.

- The dominant thoughts/voices in our mind will be those from the spiritual realm of God. They will:

    1. Affirm our value, dignity and worth in the eyes of God,

    2. Affirm our relationship with God through our faith in Jesus,

    3. Encourage us to live a life that is built on the foundation of God's spiritual life principle revealed to us in the Bible, and

    4. Transform the thoughts/voices that originate in our mind and subconscious mind to be compatible with the thoughts/voices we receive from the spiritual realm of God.

- We will develop and grow in our ability to live a life of faith and trust in and obedience to God through our faith and trust in and obedience to Jesus.

- Our soul will commune with and be nurtured and strengthen by God through actions of the Holy Spirit in our life.

- We will find true meaning and purpose in and for our life and experience true freedom and joy.

CHAPTER 4
JESUS - GOD'S SON AND OUR SAVIOR AND LORD OF OUR LIFE

JESUS AND THE BIBLE

God's love and plan for the redemption of His creation through Jesus after the fall of Adam and Eve in the Garden of Eden are the central themes throughout the Bible. Events prophesied about Jesus' life in the Old Testament were fulfilled by Him during His life in the New Testament. Table 2 lists some of the major events in Jesus' life that were prophesied in the Old Testament that were fulfilled by Him in the New Testament. According to Peter Stoner in his book, *Science Speaks: An Evaluation of Certain Christian Evidences* (1963), the probability the nine prophesies in the table that are preceded by an * were fulfilled by Jesus during His lifetime is 1 in 10^{17} (1 followed by 17 zeroes). 10^{17} silver dollars will cover the whole state of Texas to a depth of two feet. Imagine the probability of being able to pluck out one silver dollar that has been marked and randomly placed in that many silver dollars.

Table 2

Events in Life	Old Testament Prophesies	Fulfilled in the New Testament
Born of a virgin	Isaiah 7:14	Matthew 1:23,25
*Born in Bethlehem	Micah 5.2	Matthew 2:1 Luke 2:4-7
Herod to massacre infants	Jeremiah 31:15	Matthew 2:16
Would heal people	Isaiah 53:4	Matthew 8:16-17
*To be preceded by	Isaiah 40:3	Matthew 3:1-2
a messenger	Malachi 3:1	John 1:23, Mark 7:33-35
Would teach in parables	Isaiah 6:9-10	Matthew 13:10-15
Would be rejected	Psalm 69:8	John 1:11, 7:5
		Isaiah 53:3
*To enter Jerusalem on a donkey	Zechariah 9:9	Mathew 21:4-5

*To be betrayed by a friend	Psalm 41:9, 55:12-14	Matthew 10:4, 26:49-50
		John 13:21
*To be betrayed for 30 pieces of silver	Psalm 41:9, Zechariah 11:12-13	Matthew 26:14-16, 21- 25
*Silver to be used to buy Potter's field	Zechariah 11:13	Matthew 27:7
To be forsaken by His disciples	Zechariah 13:7	Matthew 26:31
		Mark 14:27,50
*To be dumb before accusers	Isaiah 53:7	Matthew 27:12-19
To be wounded and bruised	Isaiah 53:5 Zachariah 13:6	Matthew 27:26
*Hands and feet to be pierced	Psalm 22:16 Zechariah 12:10	Luke 23:33 John 20:25
*To be crucified between two thieves	Isaiah 53:12	Matthew 27:38 Mark15:27-28 Luke 22:37
Would rise from the dead	Psalm 16:10	Matthew 28:2-7
Would ascend into heaven	Psalm 24:7-10	Mark 16:19 Luke 24:51

JESUS - GOD'S AGENT FOR REDEMPTION AND RECONCILIATION

God set into motion how He planned to redeem fallen humanity following the fall of Adam and Eve in the Garden of Eden (Genesis 3). He accomplished this by impregnating a virgin named Mary through an act of the Holy Spirit so His Son, Jesus, could be born into the world. John stated in John 1:1-2:

> "In the beginning was the Word, and the Word was with God, and the Word was God. He was in the beginning with God."

Jesus is the Word who was with God in the beginning. Paul reaffirmed this in Colossians 1:15-17, 21-23 where he stated:

> "And He is the image of the invisible God, the firstborn of all creation. For in Him all things were created, both in the heavens and on earth, visible and invisible, whether thrones or dominions or rulers or authorities - all things have been created through Him and for Him. And He is before all things, and in Him all things hold together. ... And although you were formerly alienated

and hostile in mind, engaged in evil deeds, yet He has now reconciled you in His fleshly body through death, in order to present you before Him holy and blameless and beyond reproach - if indeed you continue in the faith firmly established and steadfast, and not moved away from the hope of the gospel that you have heard, which was proclaimed in all creation under heaven, and of which I, Paul, was made a minister."

Jesus is "the image of the invisible God," and all things in heaven and on earth have been created by and for Him. John stated in John 1:3 all things have come into being by Jesus. He is "the firstborn of all creation," and all things in creation are held together in and by Him. The Bible refers to Jesus in many ways. It refers to Him as:

- God (Hebrews 1:8-9),
- The Son of God (Matthew 16:16),
- The Word (John 1:1),
- The King of kings and Lord of lords (1 Timothy 6:15),
- Our Messiah (John 1:41), and
- Our Savior (1 John 4:14).

These refer to Jesus' deity. Jesus is also referred to as:

- The Son of Man (Luke 9:22),
- The Son of David (Matthew 9:27), and
- Man (John 10:5).

These refer to His humanity. Jesus referred to Himself as:

- The good shepherd (John 1:14, 27),
- The bread of life (John 6:35),
- The light of the world (John 8:12),
- The door (John 10:9),
- The resurrection and life (John 11:25-26),
- The way, the truth and the life (John 14:6), and
- The true vine (John 15:1-2).

These point to the facts Jesus:

- Reestablished the kingdom of God on earth and in the hearts of men and women;
- Is the king of God's Kingdom;
- Is the door through which we must pass to enter the kingdom of God; and
- Is the true vine through which the Spirit of God passes to breathe spiritual life into the hearts of men and women and to empower them to live according to the spiritual and life principles and laws of God.

Jesus stated in John 14:6, "No one comes to the Father but through Me."

JESUS - HE CAME TO ESTABLISH A NEW COVENANT IN HIS BLOOD AND SEND THE HOLY SPIRIT

Jesus came into this world from the presence of God. He stated in John 6:38:

> "For I have come down from heaven, not to do My own will, but the will of Him who sent Me."

He also stated in John 4:34, "My food is to do the will of Him who sent me, and to accomplish His work." Jesus came to reestablish the kingdom of God in the world. The disobedience of Adam introduced sin and death into God's creation and separated us from God. The perfect obedience of Jesus provides the way we can be reconciled to God and receive eternal life. Paul stated in Romans 5:18-21:

> "So then, as through one transgression there resulted condemnation to all men, even so through one act of righteousness there resulted justification of life to all men. For as through the one man's disobedience the many were made sinners, even so through the obedience of the One the many will be made righteous. The Law came in so that the transgressions would increase; but where sin increases, grace abounded all the more, so that, as sin reigned in death, even so grace would reign through righteousness to eternal life through Jesus Christ our Lord."

Jesus came to reveal the nature and character of God and His kingdom as God wanted them revealed in His own person. He came to bear witness to the truth of God that gives us freedom and life. He stated in John 8:31, 51:

"If you continue in My word, then you are truly disciples of Mine; and you will know the truth, and the truth will make you free. ... Truly, truly, I say to you, if anyone keeps My word he will never see death."

Jesus came to fulfill the Law. He stated in Matthew 5:17:

"Do not think that I came to abolish the Law or the Prophets; I did not come to abolish but to fulfill."

God gave us the Law to expose our sinful nature. The Law can only expose and convict us of sin; it cannot redeem or save us from the eternal consequences of sin. It is impossible to obey the 613 commandments of the Law. Therefore, it has become a curse to us that results in death. We cannot free ourself from this curse.

Jesus fulfilled the Law by establishing a new covenant that superseded the covenant of the Law. He sealed this new covenant with His blood shed on a cross. Jesus stated in Luke 22:20, "This cup which is poured out for you is the new covenant in My blood." In Hebrews 7:22, the author stated, "So much the more also Jesus has become the guarantee of a better covenant." The covenant Jesus established through His blood redeems and frees us from: the curse of the Law and reconciles us to God. Paul stated regarding this in Galatians 3:10-14:

"For as many as are of the works of the Law are under a curse, for it is written, 'Curst is everyone who does not abide by all things written in the book of the Law, to perform them.' (Deuteronomy 27:26) Now that no one is justified by the Law before God is evident; for 'The righteous man shall live by faith.' However, the Law is not of faith; on the contrary, 'He who practices them shall live by them.' (Leviticus 18:5) Christ redeemed us from the curse of the Law, having become a curse for us - for it is written, 'Cursed is everyone who hangs on a tree.' (Deuteronomy 21:22-23) - in order that in Christ Jesus the blessing of Abraham might come to the Gentiles, so that we would receive the promise of the Spirit through faith."

Jesus is the mediator of the new covenant He established and sealed with His blood. In Hebrews 9:15-16, the author wrote:

"And for this reason [Jesus] is the mediator of a new covenant, in order that since a death has taken place for the redemption of the transgressions that were committed under the first covenant, those who have been called may receive the promise of the eternal inheritance. For where a covenant is, there must of necessity be the death of the one who made it."

This new covenant is an eternal covenant, and it is the legal means through which our redemption and reconciliation to God can occur. This covenant allows us to approach God through Jesus to receive His grace, mercy and love. In Hebrews 10:15-18, the author stated the Holy Spirit said with respect to this covenant:

> "'This is the covenant that I will make with them after those days', says the LORD; 'I will put My Laws upon their hearts, and on their minds I will write them.' (Jeremiah 31:33) He then says, 'And their sins and their lawless deeds I will remember no more.' (Jeremiah 31:34) Now where there is forgiveness of these things, there is no longer any offering for sin."

This new covenant established through Jesus enables those who trust in and are obedient to Jesus to receive the eternal inheritance, and God will no longer remember "their sins and their lawless deeds."

Jesus came to be our savior. John stated in 1 John 4:14:

> "We have seen and testify that the Father has sent the Son to be the Savior of the world."

In Hebrews 2:9, the author stated:

> "But we do see Him who has been made for a little while lower than angels, namely, Jesus, because of the suffering of death crowned with glory and honor, that by the grace of God He might taste death for everyone."

God's holiness required the penalty of death for those guilty of sin. This meant all humanity. The justifiable wrath of God is directed against sin. It is directed against us when sin dwells in us. However, God in His mercy established a sacrificial means whereby His wrath could be diverted away from us toward a person who was willing to stand in our place. This person had to be without sin, acceptable to God, and willing to voluntarily die for our sins. This person was Jesus, who stated in John 10:17-18:

> "For this reason, the Father loves Me, because I lay down My life that I may take it up again. No one has taken it away from Me, but I lay it down on My own initiative. I have authority to lay it down, and I have authority to take it up again. This commandment I receive from My Father."

God's wrath was directed against Jesus when He shed His blood on a cross. Jesus was a propitiation for our sins; He stood in our place and accepted our death sentence for sin. John stated in 1 John 2:1-2:

> "My little children, I am writing these things to you so that you may not sin. And if anyone sins, we have an Advocate with the Father, Jesus Christ the righteous; and He Himself is the propitiation for our sins; and not for ours only, but also for those of the whole world."

Paul stated in Colossians 2:13-14:

> "And when you were dead in your transgressions and the uncircumcision of your flesh, He made you alive together with Him, having forgiven us all our transgressions, having canceled out the certificate of debt consisting of decrees against us and which was hostile to us; and He has taken it out of the way, having nailed it to the cross."

Jesus' holiness and obedience to God made it possible for His blood shed on a cross to be an acceptable sacrifice to cleanse us from our sins. John stated in 1 John 1:7:

> "If we walk in the light as He Himself is in the Light, we have fellowship with one another, and the blood of Jesus His Son cleanses us from all sin."

Jesus is our high priest in heaven. In Hebrews 4:15, 7:23-27, the author stated:

> "For we do not have a high priest who cannot sympathize with our weaknesses, but one who has been tempted in all things as we are, yet without sin. ... The former priests, on the one hand, existed in greater numbers because they were prevented by death from continuing, but He, on the other hand, because He abides forever, holds His priesthood permanently. Hence, also, He is able to save forever those who draw near to God through Him, since He always lives to make intercession for them. For it was fitting that we should have such a high priest, holy, innocent, undefiled, separated from sinners and exalted above the heavens; who does not need daily, like those high priest, to offer up sacrifices, first for his own sins, and then for the sins of the people, because this He did once for all when He offered up Himself."

Jesus understands our weaknesses because He has been tempted like us. He holds His priesthood forever and continually intercedes for us before His Father.

Genesis indicates God created men and women to have and exercise dominion over His creation. However, this dominion was transferred to Satan when Adam disobeyed God and sinned. Even though we may not intentionally serve Satan, we all experience the consequences of this transfer.

Jewish law in Leviticus 25:25 states:

> "If a fellow countryman of yours becomes so poor he has to sell part of his property, then his nearest kinsman is to come and buy back what his relative has sold."

Jew and his property could only be redeemed by a kinsman who was a blood relative and willing to pay his debt when he sold himself into bondage to pay his debt.

Adam's disobedience and sin in the Garden of Eden placed him and all humanity into bondage to Satan and transferred dominion of earth to him. Therefore, only a person who could act as our kinsman could pay the ransom to redeem us from this bondage and return to us the dominion God originally gave us. This person had to have the authority to carry out the required transaction to pay this ransom. He had to be perfectly obedient to God and without sin because Adam's disobedience and sin brought us into bondage to Satan. This person would have to be born into this world to have the authority to pay the ransom. This was accomplished by Jesus being born into this world through the seed of God being implanted in the womb of a virgin.

Jesus was our kinsman who had the authority to pay the ransom. Jesus' death, which satisfied the justifiable wrath of God against our sins, was the acceptable ransom to redeem us from bondage to Satan and return God's dominion to us when He died on a cross. Jesus stated in Mark 20:45:

> "For even the Son of Man did not come to be served, but to serve, and to give His life a ransom for many."

Paul stated in 1 Timothy 2:5-6

> "For there is one God, and one mediator also between God and men, the man Christ Jesus, who gave Himself as a ransom for all, the testimony borne at the proper time."

In Hebrews 2:14-15, the author stated:

"Since then the children share in flesh and blood, He Himself likewise also partook of the same, that through death He might render powerless him who had the power of death, that is the devil; and might deliver those who through fear were subject to slavery all their lives."

Jesus' sacrificial death rendered Satan's power over death powerless and ended his dominion over us. Jesus has removed the obstacles that stood between God and us. He replaced the Law that could only convict us of sin and bring death to us with a new covenant that reconciles us to God and gives us eternal life through Him. Jesus voluntarily accepted God's death penalty for our sins by dying on a cross in our place. He was the acceptable ransom to redeem us from our bondage to Satan and end his dominion over us. Jesus is our eternal high priest in heaven who is there to intercede to God for us. Therefore, when we approach God through Jesus, He no longer sees our sin natures; He sees us in the light of the righteousness of His Son, Jesus. Paul stated in Romans 8:9-10:

"However, you are not in the flesh but in the Spirit, if indeed the Spirit of God dwells in you. But if anyone does not have the Spirit of Christ, he does not belong to Him. And if Christ is in you, though the body is dead because of sin, yet the spirit is alive because of righteousness."

We are made spiritually alive when we come into the presence of God, the Father, through Jesus, His Son, and receive the Holy Spirit into our heart, so we can fellowship and commune with Them.

Jesus came to send the Holy Spirit into the world. He stated in John 14:16-18:

"I will ask the Father, and He will give you another Helper, that He may be with you forever, that is the Spirit of Truth, whom the world cannot receive, because it does not see Him or know Him, but you know Him because He abides with you and will be in you."

Jesus promised His disciples He would not leave them orphans or defenseless. He indicated the Holy Spirit would give them remembrance of all He had taught them. Jesus continued in John 16:7-11:

"But I tell you the truth, it is to your advantage that I go away; for if I do not go away, the Helper will not come to you; but if I go, I will send Him to you. And He, when He comes, will convict the world concerning sin and righteousness and judgment; concerning sin, because they do not believe in Me; and concerning righteousness, because I go to the Father and you no longer see Me; and concerning judgement, because the ruler of this world has been judged."

The Holy Spirit gave the disciples the ability to proclaim repentance for sin, preach the gospel of Jesus, witness to the presence of Jesus in their lives, and make disciples of others. When we accept Jesus as our Lord and Savior and invite the Holy Spirit, He dwells within us and gives us these same abilities.

OUR RELATIONSHIP WITH GOD THROUGH JESUS

Entering the Kingdom of God through Our Faith in Jesus

Jesus stated in Matthew 18:3:

"Truly I say to you, unless you are converted and become like children, you will not enter the kingdom of heaven."

We must turn from our love of the world to Jesus with a childlike faith to enter a relationship with God through Him. Jesus then stated in John 3:5-6:

"Truly, truly, I say to you, unless one is born of water and the Spirit he cannot enter into the kingdom of God. That which is born of the flesh is flesh, and that which is born of the Spirit is spirit."

We must be spiritually reborn to enter the kingdom of God.
Peter stated in Acts 3:19, 4:12:

"Therefore repent and return, so that your sins may be wiped away, in order that times of refreshing may come from the presence of the Lord. ... And there is salvation in no one else; for there is no other name under heaven that has been given among men by which we must be saved."

We receive God's redemption only through our faith in Jesus. We must approach God with a repentant heart. Repentance is an act of regret and remorse for living a life of sin apart from God. Jesus stated in Luke 13:3, "but unless you repent, you will all likewise perish." He then stated in Luke 15:7:

> "There will be more joy in heaven over one sinner who repents, than over ninety-nine righteous persons who need no repentance."

God forgives us and begins the process of regenerating and transforming us through the Holy Spirit in our life when we repent and approach Him through Jesus.

We must understand the relation between the Law of Moses and God's redemption that we receive through our faith in Jesus. Paul stated in Romans 3:19-26:

> "Now we know that whatever the Law says, it speaks to those who are under the Law, so that every mouth may be closed and all the world may become accountable to God; because by the works of the Law no flesh will be justified in His sight, for through the Law comes the knowledge of sin. But now apart from the Law the righteousness of God has been manifested, being witnessed by the Law and the Prophets, even the righteousness of God through faith in Jesus Christ for all those who believe; for there is no distinction; for all have sinned and fall short of the glory of God, being justified as a gift by His grace through the redemption which is in Christ Jesus; whom God displayed publicly as a propitiation in His blood through faith. This was to demonstrate His righteousness, because in the forbearance of God He passed over the sins previously committed; for the demonstration, I say, of His righteousness at the present time, so that He would be just and the justifier of the one who has faith in Jesus."

We are guilty of sins that separate us from God. The Law only gives us knowledge of our sins by defining them. It then convicts us of our sins and holds us accountable before God. As a result, the works of the Law cannot justify us before God. They cannot declare us to be innocent of our sins nor can they redeem and reconcile us to Him. Therefore, we need a Savior, Jesus, who can be a propitiation for our sins. He took our place on a cross and received God's death penalty for our sins. We are justified through Jesus' sacrificial death and declared to be innocent by the gift of God's grace. This grace is extended to us when we accept by faith the redemption and reconciliation, we receive through the blood of Jesus that God publicly displayed on a cross.

Jesus stated in John 14:6, "I am the way, and the truth, and the life; no one comes to the Father but through Me." We enter a reconciled relationship with God through Jesus by following Paul's instructions in Romans 10:8-10:

> "But what does it say? 'The word is near you, in your mouth and in your heart' (Deuteronomy 30:14) - that is, the word of faith which we are preaching,

that if you confess with your mouth Jesus as Lord, and believe in your heart that God raised Him from the dead, you will be saved; for with the heart a person believes, resulting in righteousness, and with the mouth he confesses, resulting in salvation."

The Holy Spirit creates the desire in our heart and gives us the ability through our mind to believe in and trust Jesus when He convicts us of sin. This enables us to publicly confess with our mouth Jesus is Lord. Righteousness is then accredited to us through Jesus as our heart is transformed by the Holy Spirit, and our salvation is assured when we confess Jesus is Lord.

Paul further stated in Ephesians 2:8-10:

"For by grace you have been saved through faith and that not of yourselves. It is the gift of God; not as a result of works, so that no one may boast. For we are His workmanship, created in Christ Jesus for good works, which God prepared beforehand so that we would walk in them."

Paul reaffirmed the salvation we receive through our faith in Jesus is a gift from God. We cannot boast that we have earned or deserve our salvation based on our own merit or efforts. We can only receive it as a gift extended to us by God. Paul indicated we have been created in Jesus to do good works even though we are not saved by good works.

Spiritual Growth and Maturity in Our Relationship with Jesus

Jesus becomes our Savior and the Lord of our life when we enter our relationship with God through Him. He restores our broken relationship with God caused by sin in our life as our Savior. We then need to allow Him to become ruler and master of all areas in our life, not just areas we select, as Lord of our life. Areas in our life where Jesus becomes Lord are determined by our life choices and actions after we receive Him as our Savior. Our relationship with Jesus as our Savior is impaired when areas remain in our life where we have not allowed Him to be Lord. However, Jesus restores impaired areas in our relationship with Him as our Savior when we repent, ask Him to forgive us, and allow Him to be the Lord of these areas in our life.

We need to internalize God's word in the Bible to grow in our relationship with Jesus as Lord of our life. The Holy Spirit then facilitates our spiritual growth and maturity through His presence in our life. Paul emphasized the importance of our internalizing God's word in the Bible when he stated in 2 Timothy 3:16-17:

"All Scripture is inspired by God and profitable for teaching, for reproof, for correction, for training in righteousness; that the man of God may be adequate, equipped for every good work."

Peter in 1 Peter 2:1-3 instructed us after we enter our relationship with Jesus:

"Therefore, putting aside all malice and all deceit and hypocrisy and envy and all slander, like newborn babes, long for the pure milk of the word, so that by it you may grow in respect to salvation if you have tasted the kindness of the Lord."

We are to "Therefore, putting aside all malice and all deceit and hypocrisy and grow in respect to [our] salvation" by reading, studying and internalizing God's word in the Bible when we receive the salvation He extends to us through Jesus.

Paul further instructed us in Philippians 2:12-13:

"So then, my beloved, just as you have always obeyed, not as in my presence only, but now much more in my absence, work out your salvation with fear and trembling, for it is God who is at work in you, both to will and to work for His good pleasure."

Paul indicated we are to work out our salvation even though the redemption and salvation we receive from God through Jesus is a gift. We do this by growing in our ability to live a life of faith and trust in and obedience to God and Jesus through the presence of the Holy Spirit in our life. This growth is accomplished through faithful and disciplined Bible study essential for us to:

- Learn and internalize God's spiritual life principles revealed in the Bible;
- Experience the resulting renewing of our mind and transforming of our heart through actions of the Holy Spirit in our life as we internalize these spiritual life principles; and
- Learn and take advantage of God's covenant promises available to us because of our relationship with Him through Jesus.

Paul indicated in 2 Timothy 3:16-17 our knowledge of the Scriptures equips us to live a life of obedience to God more effectively and makes it possible for Him "to will and to work for His good pleasure" through us.

Paul added in 1 Corinthians 3:9-15:

"For we are God's fellow workers; you are God's field, God's building. According to the grace of God which was given to me, like a wise master builder I laid a foundation, and another is building on it. But each man must be careful how he builds on it. For no man can lay a foundation other than the one which is laid, which is Jesus Christ. Now if any man builds on the foundation with gold, silver, precious stones, wood, hay, straw, each man's work will become evident; for the day will show it because it is to be revealed with fire, and the fire itself will test the quality of each man's work. If any man's work is burned up, he will suffer loss; but he himself will be saved, yet so as through fire."

Jesus must be the foundation of our life on which we continue to build as we grow in our faith, spiritually mature, and perform good works God prepares and places before us. Our motives for performing our good works and their quality will be revealed and tested by fire when Jesus examines them on the last day. Some will be accepted by Him and remain. Others may be rejected and burned up. We will suffer loss for those good works that are rejected, but we will not lose our salvation.

Jesus affirmed the importance of Him being the foundation of our life on which we continue to build when He stated in John 15:1-6:

"I am the true vine, and My Father is the vine dresser. Every branch in Me that does not bear fruit, He takes away; and every branch that bears fruit, He prunes it so that it may bear more fruit. You are already clean because of the word which I have spoken to you. Abide in Me, and I in you. As the branch cannot bear fruit of itself unless it abides in the vine, so neither can you unless you abide in Me. I am the vine, you are the branches; he who abides in Me and I in him, he bears much fruit, for apart from Me you can do nothing. If anyone does not abide in Me, he is thrown away as a branch and dries up; and they gather them, and cast them into the fire and they are burned."

Jesus indicated:

- We are to grow, mature and bear fruit in our relationship with Him;
- We will not be able to do these independent of Him; and
- God will remove us from our relationship with Him when we fail to grow, mature and bear fruit in this relationship.

Jesus' warning is often overlooked or ignored, but it is consistent with similar warnings He gave us in His parables of the talents in Mathew 25:14-30 and Luke 19:12-27. Jesus affirmed God will enable and equip us to bear more fruit as we grow and mature in our relationship with Him.

Peter stated in 2 Peter 1:5-11:

> "Now for this very reason also, applying all diligence, in your faith supply moral excellence, and in your moral excellence, knowledge; and in your knowledge, self-control, and in your self-control, perseverance, and in your perseverance, godliness; and in your godliness, brotherly kindness, and in your brotherly kindness, love. For if these qualities are yours and are increasing, they render you neither useless nor unfruitful in the true knowledge of our Lord Jesus Christ. For he who lacks these qualities is blind or shortsighted, having forgotten his purification from his former sins. Therefore, brethren, be all the more diligent to make certain about His calling and choosing you; for as long as you practice these things, you will never stumble; for in this way the entrance into the eternal kingdom of our Lord and Savior Jesus Christ will be abundantly supplied to you."

Peter's progression results from God's pruning transforms our faith into genuine love we can share with and extend to others without expecting something in return. Faith and trust in God, Jesus and the Holy Spirit precede and result in moral excellence. Moral excellence facilitates the acquisition of spiritual knowledge. Spiritual knowledge enables self-control. Self-control facilitates perseverance. Perseverance results in godliness. Godliness leads to brotherly kindness. Brotherly kindness results in genuine love. This progression enables and equips us to bear fruit as we spiritually grow, mature and engage in the good works God has prepared for us to perform. It assures our entrance into Jesus' eternal kingdom. Jesus instructed us in Matthew 5:16:

> "Let your light shine before men in such a way that they may see your good works, and glorify your Father who is in heaven."

Four Stages of Spiritual Growth

God requires us to spiritually grow and mature when we enter our relationship with Him through Jesus. We are to study, internalize and assimilate the solid food in the Bible. Spiritual growth, like physical and emotional growth, progresses through the four stages of infancy, childhood, adolescence and adulthood. The characteristics of each stage can be summarized with a two-word phrase: infancy - *feed me*, childhood - *teach me*, adolescence - *guide me*, and adulthood - *use me*.

Spiritual Infancy: We have no or little knowledge of God's word presented in the Bible during spiritual infancy. Therefore, God does not expect us to have this knowledge during spiritual infancy nor does He hold us accountable for our disobedience to Him and Jesus because we lack this knowledge. The development of our understanding of the Bible and our spiritual growth is influenced by the knowledge and integrity of Christians with whom we fellowship as spiritual infants. Therefore, we must be in an environment where we can be fed the pure milk of God's word and be protected from influences that will draw us away from God and Jesus as we begin our spiritual growth. This environment is present in a Christian church where we are taught God's unaltered word from the Bible and hear His word preached from the pulpit.

Spiritual Childhood: We enter spiritual childhood as we continue to feed on the pure milk of God's word in the Bible and begin to incorporate its precepts into our life. We are to grow in our knowledge and understanding of God's word in the Bible during spiritual childhood. We develop spiritual perspectives and life skills as we study the Bible and observe how spiritually mature Christians have incorporate biblical precepts into their lives. We often do not develop the spiritual maturity necessary to engage in the good works God has prepared for us during spiritual childhood even though we grow spiritually.

Spiritual Adolescence: We enter spiritual adolescence as our spiritual growth continues. This is often a difficult, troubled and rebellious time during our spiritual growth. We discover our desires and lifestyle conflict with our knowledge of God's word, and we must make changes in our life as we move closer to God through Jesus. These changes are often difficult to make and require we enter mentoring relationships with mature Christians we trust and with whom we can share sensitive and personal life issues. Our knowledge of God's word and related spiritual perspectives become convictions that form our character as we work through and make these life changes. We discover God's word is true and God is faithful to honor His word. We begin to develop spiritual maturity necessary to enable and equip us to perform the good works God has prepared for us as we progress through spiritual adolescence.

Spiritual Adulthood: We enter spiritual adulthood as we spiritually grow and develop spiritual maturity. These are lifelong processes that progress as we feed on and digest the solid food of God's word in the Bible. We become spiritual adults as we develop the ability to discern the differences between good and evil. We are then equipped to engage in the good works God has prepared for us.

The Relation between Faith, Grace and Good Works

Grace and faith are the foundation of our relationship with God through Jesus. He redeems and reconciles us through His grace. However, He requires us to enter the good works He calls us to enter. These good works are the ministries and service to others God calls us to enter in Jesus' name.

Many who understand the significance of grace and faith in our relationship with God through Jesus do not understand the significance of good works in this relationship. Two scripture verses help us understand the relation between grace, faith and good works. The first is Ephesians 2:8-10, where Paul stated:

> "For by grace you have been saved through faith and that not of yourselves. It is the gift of God; not as a result of works, so that no one may boast. For we are His workmanship, created in Christ Jesus for good works, which God prepared beforehand so that we would walk in them."

The second is James 2:14-26 where James stated:

> "What use is it my brethren, if a man says he has faith, but he has no works? Can that faith save him? If a brother or sister is without clothing and in need of daily food, and one of you says to them, 'Go in peace, be warmed and be filled,' and yet you do not give them what is necessary for their body, what use is that? Even so faith, if it has no works, is dead, being by itself. But someone may well say, 'You have faith, and I have works; show me your faith without works, and I will show you my faith by my works.' You believe that God is one. You do well; the demons also believe, and shudder. But are you willing to recognize, you foolish fellow, that faith without works is useless? Was not Abraham our father justified by works, when he offered up Isaac his son on the altar? You see that a man is justified by works, and not by faith alone. And in the same way was not Rahab the harlot also justified by works when she received the messengers and sent them out by another way? For just as the body without the spirit is dead, so also faith without works is dead."

There are two types of works referred to in these scripture verses. The first type of works are works referred to in Ephesians 2:8 that we use to justify ourself to God. Paul indicated these works will never justify us to God. The second type of works referred to in Ephesians 2:10 are "good works, which God prepared beforehand so that we would walk in them."

It is reasonable to belief the works referred to in James 2:17-26 are the same as the good works referred to in Ephesians 2:10.

Paul indicated in Ephesians 2:8 we are redeemed by God's grace through Jesus. James and Paul taught our faith in Jesus must result in our love for and obedience to Him. Our faith must motivate us to perform the good works God has prepared beforehand for us to perform. James stated our faith becomes useless and dies when we do not enter these good works. Our relationship with God is impaired when we do not live a life of faith and trust in and obedience to Jesus. Our faith dies when it does not motivate us to perform good works the Holy Spirit leads us to perform.

Four Responses to God's Word

Jesus stated in Matthew 7:13-14:

> "Enter through the narrow gate; for the gate is wide and the way is broad that leads to destruction, and there are many who enter through it. For the gate is small and the way is narrow that leads to life, and there are few who find it."

The Bible teaches we must:

- Study and internalize God's word in the Bible (1 Peter 2:1-3),
- Build our life on the foundation of Jesus (1 Corinthians 3:9-15), and
- Enter and perform the good works God has prepared for us to walk in (Ephesians 2:8-10).

These enable us to grow and mature in our relationship with God through Jesus. This requires commitment and perseverance to overcome the challenges, obstacles and hardships we will experience because of this relationship. Many who initially enter a relationship with God through Jesus lack this commitment and perseverance.

Jesus addressed this in His parable of the Sower in Matthew 13:3-9, 18-23. He indicated in Matthew 13:3-9 the spreading of God's word can be visualized as a sower spreading seeds. "Some seeds fell beside the road, and the birds came and ate them up." Other seeds fell on rocky places where they had insufficient soil in which to grow and immediately began to grow. Because they lacked depth of soil and roots, "when the sun had risen, they were scorched; and ... they withered away." Other seeds fell among thorns, and "the thorns came up and choked them out." Other seeds "fell on the good soil and yielded a crop, some a hundredfold, some sixty and some thirty."

Jesus explained His parable in Ma0tthew 13:18-23. He indicated:

- **Seeds that fall beside the road:** These seeds represent those who do not understand God's word when they hear it. Satan snatches it from their heart when this occurs.

- **Seeds that fall on rocky places:** These seeds represent those who initially receive God's word with joy when they hear it. However, they do not study and internalize God's word in the Bible. As a result, their faith is shallow, and they do not build their life on the foundation of Jesus. Therefore, they fall away when they experience affliction, persecution and hard times because of God's word.

- **Seeds that fall among thorns:** These seeds represent those who hear, study and internalize God's word in the Bible. They begin to build their life on the foundation of Jesus. However, the concerns of the world and the deceitfulness of wealth take root in their heart and grow. Eventually, these choke out God's word in their heart, and they fall away from God.

- **Seeds that fall on the good soil:** These seeds represent those who hear, study and internalize God's word in the Bible and who build their life on the foundation of Jesus. God's word bears much fruit in their life. Some bring forth a hundredfold, some sixty and some thirty.

In Hebrews 10:26-31, the author stated:

> "For if we go on sinning willfully after receiving the knowledge of the truth, there no longer remains a sacrifice for sins, but a terrifying expectation of judgement and the fury of a fire which will consume the adversary. [Isaiah 26:11] Anyone who has set aside the Law of Moses dies without mercy on the testimony of two or three witnesses. [Deuteronomy 17:6] How much severer punishment do you think he will deserve who has trampled underfoot the Son of God, and has regarded as unclean the blood of the covenant by which he was sanctified, and has insulted the Spirit of grace? For we know Him who said, 'Vengeance is mine, I will repay.' [Deuteronomy 32:35] And again, 'The LORD will judge His people.' [Deuteronomy 32:36] It is a terrifying thing to fall into the hands of the living God."

This Bible verse describes those who hear and receive God's word and continue in a life of willful sin. They are deceived by Satan into believing this is okay. The writer of Hebrews stated those who do this will have the "terrifying expectation of judgment." These individuals are represented by the Sower's seeds that fall beside the road.

Peter stated in 2 Peter 2:20-21:

> "For if, after they have escaped the defilement of the world by the knowledge of the Lord and Savior Jesus Christ, they are again entangled in them and are overcome, the last state has become worse for them than the firs. For it would be better for them not to have known the way of righteousness, than having known it, to turn away from the holy commandment handed on to them."

This Bible verse describes those who hear and receive God's word, but they do not study and internalize it and begin to build their life on the foundation of Jesus. As a result, they are drawn back into and entangled in the life of sin they left. Peter indicated the state of sin they reenter will be worse than the state of sin they left. These individuals are represented by the Sower's seeds that fall on rocky places.

In Hebrews 6:4-6, the author stated:

> "For in the case of those who have once been enlightened and have tasted of the heavenly gift and have been made partakers of the Holy Spirit, and have tasted the good word of God and the power of the ages to come, and then have fallen away, it is impossible to renew them again to repentance, since they again crucify to themselves the Son of God and put Him to open sham."

This Bible verse describes those who hear and receive God's word, study and internalize it, and begin to build their life on the foundation of Jesus. The concerns of the world and the deceitfulness of wealth then take root and grow in their heart. They eventually choke our God's word in the life of these individuals, and they abandon their relationship with God. The writer of Hebrews stated it will be "impossible to renew them again to repentance" when this occurs. These individuals are represented by the Sower's seeds that fall among thorns.

The fourth group of the Sower's seeds represents those who love and are obedient to Jesus. They have entered a relationship with God through Him. They study and internalize God's word in the Bible. They build their life on the foundation of Jesus. They enter and perform the good works God prepares for them. They demonstrate their love for, faith in and obedience to Jesus by keeping His commandments and His words. Jesus stated in John 14:15, 21 and 23:

> "If you love Me, you will keep My commandments. ... He who has My commandments and keeps them is the one who loves Me, and he who loves

Me will be loved by My Father, and I will love him and will disclose Myself to him. ... If anyone loves Me, he will keep My word; and My Father will love him, and We will come to him and make Our abode with him."

Reciprocal actions on the part of those who love and are obedient to Jesus and on the parts of God and Jesus are revealed in this scripture. Individuals who love and are obedient to Jesus demonstrate their love by keeping His commandments and words, and they demonstrate their love and obedience by their good works and their life choices and actions. Both God and Jesus reciprocate by loving them, disclosing Themselves to them, and taking up residence in them. The more of themselves these individuals yield in trust in and obedience to God and Jesus the more of Themselves will They disclose to them through the Holy Spirit. As a result, God's word bears much fruit in their lives, yielding a hundredfold in some and sixty and thirty fold in others.

Security of Our Relationship with God through Jesus

Our relationship with God through Jesus is secure. Paul stated in Romans 8:35-39:

> "Who will separate us from the love of Christ? Will tribulation, or distress, or persecution, or famine, or nakedness, or peril, or sword? Just as it is written, 'For your sake we are being put to death all day long, we were considered as sheep to be slaughtered.' (Psalms 44:22) But in all these things we overwhelmingly conquer through Him who loved us. For I am convinced that neither death, nor life, nor angels, nor principalities, nor things present, nor things to come, nor powers, nor height, nor depth, nor any other created thing, will be able to separate us from the love of God, which is in Christ Jesus."

Nothing in all creation will be able to separate us from the love of God extended to us through Jesus. Jesus confirmed the security of our relationship with God through Him when He stated in John 3:16-18.

> "For God so loved the world, that He gave His only begotten Son, that whoever believes in Him shall not perish, but have eternal life. For God did not send the Son into the world to judge the world, but that the world might be saved through Him. He who believes in Him is not judged; he who does not believe has been judged already, because he has not believed in the name of the only begotten Son of God."

He continued in John 6:35-40:

> "I am the bread of life; he who comes to Me will not hunger, and he who believes in Me will never thirst. But I said to you that you have seen Me, and yet do not believe. All that the Father gives Me will come to Me, and the one who comes to Me I will certainly not cast out. For I have come down from heaven, not to do My own will, but the will of Him who sent Me. This is the will of Him who sent Me, that of all that He has given Me I lose nothing, but raise it up on the last day. For this is the will of My Father, that everyone who beholds the Son and believes in Him will have eternal life, and I Myself will raise him up on the last day."

and in John 10:27-30:

> "My sheep hear My voice, and I know them, and they follow Me; and I give eternal life to them, and they will never perish; and no one will snatch them out of My hand. My Father, who has given them to Me, is greater than all; and no one is able to snatch them out of the Father's hand. I and the Father are one."

Closing Comments

In Hebrews 9:27-28, the author stated regarding our salvation through Jesus:

> "And inasmuch as it is appointed for men to die once and after this comes judgment, so Christ also, having been offered once to bear the sins of many, will appear a second time for salvation without reference to sin, to those who eagerly await Him."

We experience judgement immediately after we die because Jesus' death and resurrection did not do away with the Law even though they fulfilled it. The Law defines and convicts us of our sins. Therefore, it declares us guilty of our sins before the judgement seat of God when we have not sought nor received God's salvation through Jesus before we die. This declaration eternally separates us from God, Jesus and the Holy Spirit. The barrier of our sins that separates us from Them is only removed when we seek and have received God's salvation though Jesus before we die. It is not possible to seek God's salvation through Jesus after we die.

Paul stated in Romans 8:15-17:

"For you have not received a spirit of slavery leading to fear again, but you have received a spirit of adoption as sons by which we cry out, 'Abba! Father!' The Spirit Himself testifies with our spirit that we are children of God, and if children, heirs also, heirs of God and fellow heirs with Christ, if indeed we suffer with Him so that we may also be glorified with Him."

We become God's adopted children when we enter a reconciled relationship with Him through our faith and trust in and obedience to Jesus, and we grow and mature in this relationship through the indwelling presence of the Holy Spirit. We are fellow heirs with Jesus with the rights and privileges of being heirs of God.

CHAPTER 5
THE RETURN OF JESUS

TWO EVENTS

The Bible refers to two events associated with the return of Jesus to earth during the end time. The first is mentioned by Jesus in Matthew 24:29-31 where He stated:

> "But immediately after the tribulation of those days the sun will be darkened and the moon will not give its light, and the stars will fall from the sky, and the powers of the heavens will be shaken. And then the sign of the Son of Man will appear in the sky, and then all the tribes of the earth will mourn, and they will see the Son of Man is coming in the clouds of the sky with power and great glory. And He will send forth His angels with a great trumpet and they will gather together His elect from the four winds, from one end of the sky to the other."

He addressed the time when He will return to earth to remove Christians from the earth to heaven at an event referred to as the rapture. This event is discussed in more detail later in this chapter. The second return is mentioned in Revelation 19:11-16. John addressed the time following the end of the great tribulation (last 1,260 days of the tribulation) when Jesus will return to earth with the armies of heaven. He will destroy the armies of the Antichrist and kings of earth. He will then begin the process of establishing His 1,000-year kingdom. John stated in Revelation 19:11-17:

> "And I saw heaven open, and behold, a white horse, and He who sat on it is called Faithful and True, and in righteousness He Judges and wages war. His eyes are a flame of fire, and on His head are many diadems; and He has a name written on Him which no one knows except Himself. He is clothed with a robe dipped in blood, and His name is called The Word of God. And the armies which are in heaven, clothed in fine linen, white and clean, were following Him on white horses. From His mouth comes a sharp sword, so that with it He may strike down the nations, and He will rule them with a rod of iron, and He treads the wine press of the fierce wrath of God, the

Almighty. And on His robe and on His thigh He has a name written, 'KING OF KINGS, AND LORD OF LORDS.'"

Information on Jesus' return at the end of the great tribulation is presented in Chapter 10 and to establish His 1,000-year kingdom is presented in Chapter 11.

THE RETURN OF JESUS

As the disciples watched Jesus ascend into the clouds at their last meeting with Him, Luke stated in Acts 1:10-11:

> "And as they were gazing into the sky while He was going, behold, two men in white clothing stood beside them. They also said, 'Men of Galilee, why do you stand looking into the sky? This Jesus, who has been taken up from you into heaven, will come in just the same way as you have watched Him go into heaven.'"

This encounter with the men in white cloths has created the expectation Jesus will return. Jesus promised He will return to receive us unto Himself in John 14:2-3 and Matthew 24:29-31. Christians throughout the ages since His ascension into heaven have looked forward to His return to establish His kingdom on earth. Luke stated regarding the time of Jesus' return in Acts 1:6-8:

> "So, when they had come together, they were asking Him, saying, 'Lord, is it at this time You are restoring the kingdom to Israel?' He said to them, 'It is not for you to know time or epochs which the Father has fixed by His own authority.'"

The time when Jesus will return is unknown. Only God knows. However, we should live our life expecting Him to return at any time, and we need to be ready when He returns.

The time when Jesus will return to earth is referred to in the Bible as the last days, the end time, and the time of the end. This time is referred to in Daniel 12:12 as the time of distress, by Jesus in Matthew 24:4-31 as the times of distress and great distress, and in Revelation as the tribulation. The tribulation will end in the establishment of Jesus' 1,000-year kingdom (Revelation 20:1-6). The 1,000-year reign of Jesus will end in the great white throne judgment (Revelation 20:11-15). God will then destroy the existing heaven and earth, which have been corrupted by sin. He will create a new heaven and earth in which there will be no sin nor the effects of sin (Revelation 21-22). Peter discussed the destruction of the existing heaven and earth and creation of a new heaven and earth in 2 Peter 3:10-18, and John described the new heaven and earth in Revelation 21-22.

Paul stated regarding the end time or the time of the end in 2 Timothy 3:1-7:

> "But realize this, that in the last days difficult times will come. For men will be lovers of self, lovers of money, boastful, arrogant, revilers, disobedient to parents, ungrateful, unholy, unloving, irreconcilable, malicious gossips, without self-control, brutal, haters of good, treacherous, reckless, conceited, lovers of pleasure rather than lovers of God, holding to a form of godliness, although they have denied its power; avoid such men as these. For among them are those who enter into households and captivate weak women weighed down with sins, led on by various impulses, always learning and never able to come to the knowledge of the truth."

Peter stated in 2 Peter 3:3-9:

> "Know this first of all, that in the last days mockers will come with their mocking, following after their own lusts, and saying, 'Where is the promise of His coming? For ever since the fathers fell asleep, all continues just as it was from the beginning of creation.' For when they maintain this, it escapes their notice that by the word of God the heavens existed long ago and the earth was formed out of water and by water, through which the world at that time was destroyed, being flooded with water. But by His word the present heavens and earth are being reserved for fire, kept for the day of judgment and destruction of ungodly men. But do not let this one fact escape your notice, beloved, that with the Lord one day is like a thousand years, and a thousand years like one day. The Lord is not slow about his promise, as some count slowness, but is patient toward you, not wishing for any to perish but for all to come to repentance."

The last days or end time will be characterized by a substantial moral decline in men and women and their turning away from God and denying His lordship over His creation. There have been other times in history where these have occurred, and they characterize the attitudes of many today. There has been a significant moral free-fall and turning away from God in post-Christian western cultures, and Christians are being persecuted and martyred in many Third-World countries. These are significant considering Israel becoming a nation in 1948. Bible teachers indicate this must occur before the end time can begin.

The LORD instructed the prophet Joel to say the following concerning the last days:

"I will display wonders in the sky and on the earth,
Blood, fire and columns of smoke.
The sun will be turned into darkness
And the moon into blood
Before the great and awesome day of the LORD comes.
And it will come about that whoever calls on the name of the LORD
Will be delivered;
For on Mount Zion and in Jerusalem
There will be those who escape,
As the LORD has said,
Even among the survivors whom the LORD calls." (Joel 2:30-32)

"For behold, in those days and at that time,
When I restore the fortunes of Judah and Jerusalem,
I will gather all the nations
And bring them down to the valley of Jehoshaphat.
Then I will enter into judgment with them there
On behalf of My people and My inheritance, Israel,
Whom they have scattered among the nations;
And they have divided up My land.
They have also cast lots for My people,
Traded a boy for a harlot
And sold a girl for wine that they may drink." (Joel 3:1-3)

"Proclaim this among the nations:
Prepare a war; rouse the mighty men
Let all the soldiers draw near, let them come up
Beat your plowshares into swords
And your pruning hooks into spears;
Let the weak say, 'I am a mighty man.'
Hasten and come, all you surrounding nations,
And gather yourselves there.
Bring down, O LORD, Your mighty ones.
Let the nations be aroused
And come up to the valley of Jehoshaphat,
For there I will sit to judge
All the surrounding nations.
Put in the sickle, for the harvest is ripe.

Come, tread, for the wine press is full;
The vats overflow, for their wickedness is great.
Multitudes, multitudes in the valley of decision!
For the day of the LORD is near in the valley of decision.
The sun and moon grow dark
And the stars lose their brightness.
The LORD roars from Zion
And utters His voice from Jerusalem,
And the heavens and the earth tremble.
But the LORD is a refuge for His people
And a stronghold to the sons of Israel.
Then you will know that I am the LORD your God,
Dwelling in Zion, My holy mountain.
So Jerusalem will be holy,
And strangers will pass through it no more.
And in that day
The mountains will drip with sweet wine,
And the hills will flow with milk,
And all the brooks of Judah will flow with water;
And a spring will go out from the house of the LORD
To water the valley of Shittim.
Egypt will become a waste,
And Edom will become a desolate wilderness,
Because of the violence done to the sons of Judah,
In whose land they have shed innocent blood.
But Judah will be inhabited forever
And Jerusalem for all generations.
And I will avenge their blood which I have not avenged,
For the LORD dwells in Zion." (Joel 3:9-21)

The following observations can be drawn from Joel's statements. They are:

- God will restore the nation of Israel. He will honor the covenant promises He made to Israel during Old Testament times.

- The period of the end time that will precede the day of the Lord will be filled with worldwide suffering, destruction and desolation. This period will be characterized by wars and catastrophic natural disasters.

- God will support and sustain those who call upon His name and who will experience the suffering, destruction and desolation that will be associated with the day of the Lord.

- God will judge all who oppose Him. He will judge and destroy nations who have opposed Israel and brought suffering and desolation on and scattered His people.

- God will be a refuge and stronghold for His people.

The times when the end time and return of Jesus will occur are unknown. Jesus told his disciples in Acts 1:6-7 only the Father knows when events concerning the end time and restoration of Israel will occur. He stated in Matthew 24:36 that neither He nor angels in heaven know the exact day and hour when He will return. Anyone who claims to have precise information regarding the exact day and time of the return of Jesus must be treated with suspicion.

The Bible presents clues concerning world conditions that will exist before the beginning of the end time and the return of Jesus even though precise information associated with times of their occurrence is not available. Israel must become a nation, which occurred in 1948. There must be moral decline in men and women and a global turning away from God. These are occurring today, particularly in western cultures. The angel Gabriel told Daniel at the end of his discourse with him in Daniel 12:4:

> "But as for you, Daniel, conceal these words and seal up the book until the end of time; many will go back and forth, and knowledge will increase."

He characterized the end of time (or the end time) as a time when people will be able to travel and go wherever they desire with ease and by a rapid increase in knowledge. These characterize the world today. Recent history indicates events foretold in the Bible long ago that will precede the return of Jesus can begin at any time.

Interest has increased in what the Bible teaches about events associated with the return of Jesus. There is no unified consensus on what the Bible teaches about these events, and in many cases, there is much confusion. Hopefully, some of this confusion can be unraveled in this and the following chapters.

JESUS AND PROPHECY

The results of Peter Stoner's analysis of the probability of major Old Testament prophesies being fulfilled in the birth, life, death and resurrection of Jesus were presented in Chapter 4. His results imply it is virtually impossible for anyone but Jesus to have been the fulfillment of these prophesies. This gives an indication of the reliability of prophecies associated with His return. Daniel prophesied regarding the return of Jesus in Daniel 7:13-14:

> "I kept looking in the night visions,
> And behold, with the clouds of heaven
> One like a Son of Man was coming,
> And He came up to the Ancient of Days
> And was presented before Him.
> And to Him was given dominion,
> Glory and a kingdom,
> That all the peoples, nations and men of every language
> Might serve Him.
> His dominion is an everlasting dominion
> Which will not pass away;
> And His kingdom is one
> Which will not be destroyed."

Volumes have been written concerning prophesies associated with the end time and the return of Jesus. It is unreasonable to expect these prophesies can be discussed in detail in the short space of this and the following chapters. Information presented in these chapters will not represent a unified consensus because there are a wide range of beliefs concerning events associated with the return of Jesus. Prophesies associated with events related to the return of Jesus that will be discussed in this and the following chapters are found in:

- Isaiah, Jeremiah, Ezekiel, Daniel and Zechariah;
- The Gospels of Matthew, Mark and Luke; and
- Revelation.

What Jesus taught about the tribulation and rapture in Matthew, Mark and Luke will be examined. What He taught will be combined with related prophesies in Isaiah, Jeremiah, Ezekiel, Daniel, Zechariah and Revelation. This will help define a time line of events associated with the end time and Jesus' return to earth.

Events associated with the return of Jesus must be examined with the knowledge that God has redeemed us through our faith in Jesus. Prophesies associated with these events can be frightening and unsettling and cause us to become depressed and fearful of the future. God loves and has provided the means through Jesus for us to fellowship with Him.

He will be with, support and carry us through future difficult and troubled times as we go through them. He will always be our refuge and fortress.

Future events are examined when prophesies associated with the return of Jesus are studied. The Bible often does not present precise details concerning the events associated with these prophesies. Therefore, they often must be examined within a general framework. Hopefully, we will be able to recognize and understand them when they begin to be fulfilled in real life.

JESUS AND THE RAPTURE

The rapture will mark the removal of Christians and the Church from the earth (Matthew 24:30-31, Luke 17:24-31, 1 Corinthians 15:51-52, 1 Thessalonians 4:13-17, 2 Thessalonians 2:1-4). This will include all Christians who are alive at the time of the rapture and who have died down through the ages. The word *rapture* is not used in the Bible. It comes from the Latin word *rapio*, which means to be caught up. There are some who believe the rapture will occur: before the beginning of the tribulation (pre-tribulation rapture), at the end of the tribulation (post-tribulation rapture), and during the middle of the tribulation (mid-tribulation rapture).

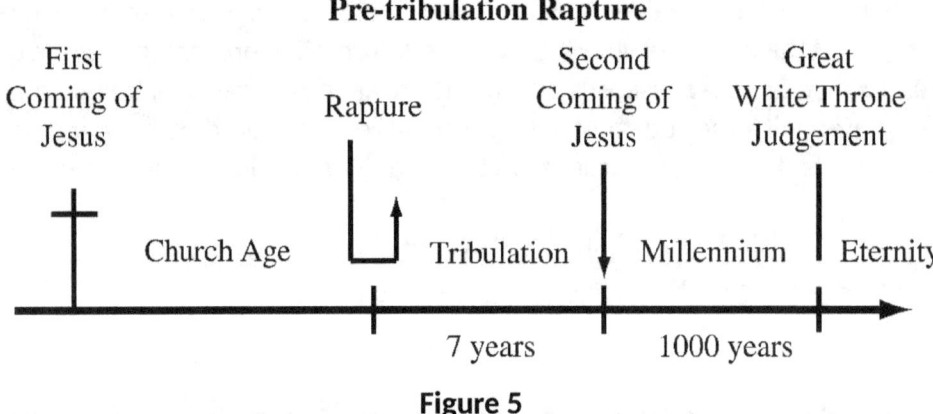

Figure 5

Pre-tribulation rapture (Figure 5): The pre-tribulation rapture implies the removal of Christians from the earth will occur before or at the beginning of the tribulation. Many believe the rapture will signal the beginning of the tribulation. Justification for the pre-tribulation rapture is found in Jesus' words in Revelation 3:10:

> "Because you have kept the word of my perseverance, I also will keep you from the hour of testing, that hour which is about to come upon the whole world, to test those who dwell on the earth."

and from Paul's words in 1 Thessalonians 1:10 and 5:9-10:

> "... and to wait for His Son from heaven, whom He raised from the dead, that is Jesus, who rescues us from the wrath to come. ... For God has not destined us for wrath, but for obtaining salvation through our Lord Jesus, who died for us, so that whether we are awake or asleep, we will live together with Him."

The Church is not mentioned after chapter 3 in Revelation even though it is mentioned several times in chapters 1-3. Many believe the reason for this is because the Church has been removed from earth by the rapture. This argument supports a pre-tribulation rapture. The removal of the Church will remove the restraining influence of the Holy Spirit on earth, so Satan will be free to do what he desires through the Antichrist (2 Thessalonians 2:6-9).

These are convincing arguments for a pre-tribulation rapture, but they are circumstantial. It is unclear as to what hour of testing Jesus is referring to in Revelation 3:10. It is reasonable to assume the hour of testing refers to an event or events in the tribulation. However, it is not clear whether the hour of testing refers to the whole tribulation or just to the great tribulation (the last 1,260 days of the tribulation). The same question applies to the wrath to come Paul referred to in 1 Thessalonians 1:10 and 5:9. This wrath may only occur during the great tribulation. The fact the Church is not mentioned after chapter 3 in Revelation is not clear proof it and Christians will not be present.

There are four potential problems with a pre-tribulation rapture that support the possibility the rapture may occur during the middle of the tribulation. The first and perhaps most significant problem is associated with Paul's statement in 2 Thessalonians 2:1-4 where he stated:

> "Now we request you, brethren, with regard to the coming of our Lord Jesus, and our gathering together with Him, that you may not be quickly shaken from your composure or be disturbed either by a spirit or a message or a letter as if from us to the effect that the day of the Lord has come. Let no one in any way deceive you, for it will not come unless the apostasy comes first, and the man of lawlessness is revealed, the son of destruction, who opposes and exalts himself above every so-called god or object of worship, so that he takes his seat in the temple of God, displaying himself as being God."

Both "the coming of our Lord Jesus, and our gathering together with Him" and "the day of the Lord" refer to the rapture. Paul stated the rapture will not occur until after "the man of lawlessness ... takes his seat in the temple of God, displaying himself to be God." This refers to the abomination of desolation by the Antichrist. Paul implied the rapture will not occur until after the abomination of desolation has occurred. The earliest the rapture can occur is during the middle of the tribulation if this is correct.

The second problem is associated with Gabriel's statements in Daniel. He presented information on activities of the Antichrist throughout the seven-year tribulation in Daniel 11-12. However, he discussed the "time of distress such as has not happened from the beginning of nations until then" in Daniel 12. This is a reference to the wrath of God that will be poured out on the earth during the great tribulation. Jesus also referred to this as a time of "great distress, such as has not occurred since the beginning of the world until now" in Matthew 24:21-22. Gabriel stated in Daniel 12:1 "everyone who is found written in the book, will be rescued" from this time of wrath. Two observations can be made with respect to this statement. First, the book referred to in Daniel 12:1 is the same as the book of life in Revelation 20:12, 15. Everyone whose name is written in the book of life will be delivered from the wrath of God during the great tribulation if this is correct. Second, Gabriel did not indicate everyone whose name is written in the book of life will be delivered from the wrath of God during the whole tribulation even though he indicated they will be delivered during the great tribulation. This implies Christians may not be delivered from the wrath of God during whole tribulation even though they will be delivered during the great tribulation. Therefore, Christians may be present on earth during the first 1,267 days of the tribulation. This supports a mid-tribulation rapture.

The last two potential problems with a pre-tribulation rapture are associated with two events that are described in Revelation. The first is associated with the 144,000 Jewish witnesses who will be sealed on their foreheads with the seal of the living God. This will occur during the first 1,267 days of the tribulation just before the seventh seal is opened (Revelation 7:1-8). These witnesses will be on earth during the first 1,267 days of the tribulation after they receive the seal of the living God. However, Revelation 14:1-5 indicates they will be in heaven with Jesus after the abomination of desolation occurs and before the beginning of the great tribulation. This will require a special resurrection for the 144,000 witnesses if the rapture occurs at the beginning of the tribulation. There is no mention in Revelation of such a resurrection or how the witnesses will get to heaven from earth. It is much easier to explain how they will get to heaven if the rapture occurs during the middle of the tribulation after the abomination of desolation.

The second event is the first resurrection discussed in Revelation 20:4-5. This resurrection will occur after the tribulation, but before Jesus sets up His 1,000-year kingdom. John described:

> "Then I saw thrones, and they sat on them, and judgment was given to them. And I saw the souls of those who had been beheaded because of the testimony of Jesus and because of the word of God, and those who had not worshiped the beast or his image, and had not received the mark on their

forehead and on their hand; and they came to life and reigned with Christ for a thousand years. The rest of the dead did not come to life until the thousand years were completed. This is the first resurrection."

One can argue that the "souls of those who had been beheaded" can refer to all saints who will be martyred during the tribulation. However, as will be discussed in the next chapter, the reference to the saints who "had not worshiped the beast or his image and had not received his mark on their foreheads or their hands" is a reference only to the saints who will be martyred during the great tribulation. What will happen to the saints who will be killed and martyred during the first 1,267 days of the tribulation if the rapture occurs before the beginning of the tribulation and the first resurrection refers only to the resurrection of those saints who will be martyred during the great tribulation? How will they get to heaven? There are no clear answers to these questions in Revelation. It is much easier to explain how they will get to heaven when the rapture occurs during the middle of the tribulation after the abomination of desolation.

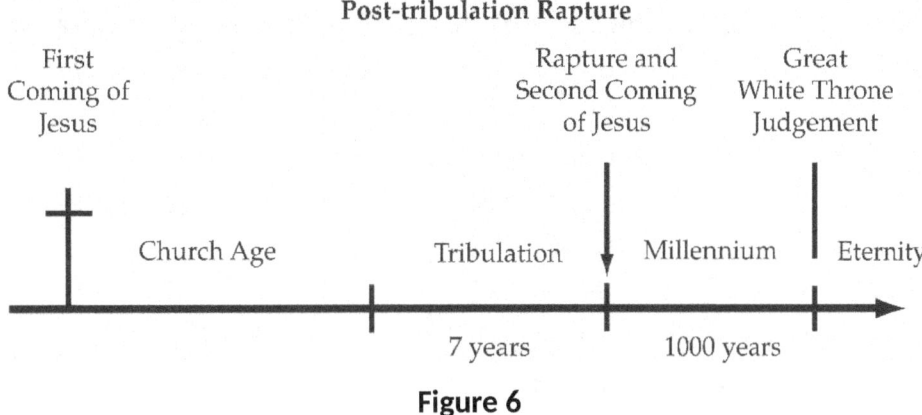

Figure 6

Post-tribulation rapture (Figure 6): A post-tribulation rapture implies the rapture will occur at or near the end of the seven-year tribulation. It will occur before the wedding of the Lamb. This will allow the raptured saints to return with Jesus when He returns to defeat the Antichrist and kings of the earth at the battle of Armageddon and to set up His 1,000-year kingdom. This position requires Christians, along with the Church, to be present on earth throughout the whole tribulation.

The primary justification for a post-tribulation rapture is the location of Jesus' statements concerning the rapture in His discourse on the last days in Matthew 24:4-44 and Mark 13:5-31. His statements concerning the rapture occur directly after His statements on the great tribulation. It is presumed this implies the rapture will occur after or near the end of the great tribulation. A second justification for a post-tribulation rapture is Paul's statement in 2 Thessalonians 2:1-4, where he stated the rapture will not occur until after the abomination of desolation.

There are two problems with a post-tribulation rapture. Gabriel stated in Daniel 12:1 that those whose name is written in the book of life will be delivered from the "time of distress such as never occurred since there was a nation until that time." This refers to the wrath of God that will occur during the great tribulation. Therefore, Christians cannot be present on earth during the great.

There is a conflict between the presumption of a post-tribulation rapture and the statements concerning the first resurrection in Revelation 20:4-6. The first resurrection will be the resurrection of Christians who will be martyred during the great tribulation because of their testimony to God's word and they will not worship the Antichrist nor receive the mark of the beast. This resurrection will occur after Jesus has returned to earth, defeated the Antichrist and kings of the earth at the battle of Armageddon, and set up His 1000-year kingdom. There will be no need for the first resurrection at the beginning of Jesus' 1,000-year kingdom if the rapture occurs at or near the end of the great tribulation before Jesus returns to earth. These problems imply the rapture will not occur at the end of the great tribulation.

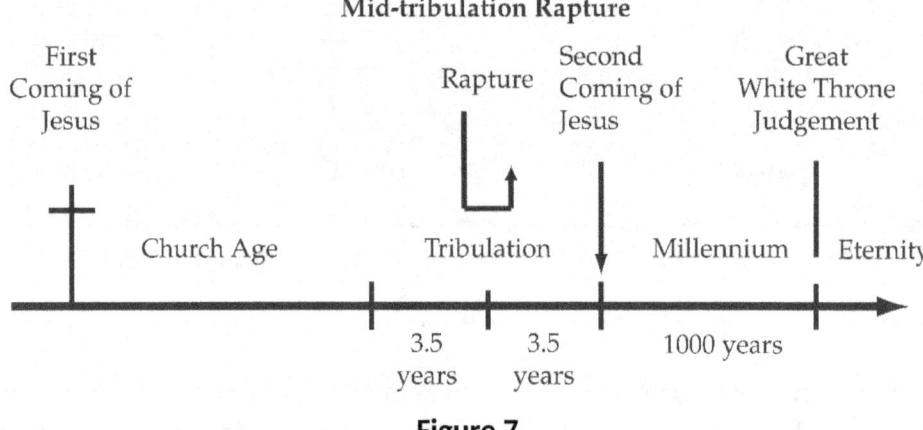

Figure 7

Mid-tribulation rapture (Figure 7): A mid-tribulation rapture implies the rapture will occur during the middle of the tribulation. The Bible persuasively supports a mid-tribulation rapture. Five major issues that support this have already been discussed. They are:

- Paul stated in 2 Thessalonians 2:1-4 the rapture will occur after the abomination of desolation, which will occur during the middle of the tribulation.

- Gabriel stated in Daniel 12 the persons whose names are written in the book of life will be delivered from the time of God's wrath during the great tribulation.

- The 144,000 Jewish witnesses appeared in heaven with Jesus after the abomination of desolation and before the beginning of the great tribulation (Revelation 7:1-8).

- Jesus' statement at the beginning of this chapter recorded in Matthew 24:29-31 indicates the rapture may occur during the middle of the tribulation. He stated in Matthew 24:31:

  "And He will send forth His angels with a great trumpet and they will gather together His elect from the four winds, from one end of the sky to the other."

- The saints who will be martyred during the great tribulation will be resurrected before Jesus establishing His 1,000-year kingdom (Revelation 20:4-6).

Paul stated regarding the gathering together of Jesus' elect at the rapture in 1 Corinthians 15:51-52:

  "Behold, I tell you a mystery; we will not all sleep, but we will all be changed, in a moment, in the twinkling of an eye, at the last trumpet; for the trumpet will sound, and the dead will be raised imperishable, and we will be changed."

and in 1 Thessalonians 4:13-17:

  "But we do not want you to be uninformed, brethren, about those who are asleep, so that you will not grieve as do the rest who have no hope. For if we believe that Jesus died and rose again, even so God will bring with Him those who have fallen asleep in Jesus. For this we say to you by the word of the Lord, that we who are alive and remain until the coming of the Lord, will not precede those who have fallen asleep. For the Lord Himself will descend from heaven with a shout, with the voice of the archangel and with the trumpet of God, and the dead in Christ will rise first. Then we who are alive and remain will be caught up together with them in the clouds to meet the Lord in the air, and so we shall always be with the Lord."

These Scriptures, when taken together, indicate the rapture will occur during the middle of the tribulation. It will be preceded by the voice of the archangel and the sound of a great trumpet (or trumpet of God). It will occur at the sound of the last trumpet.

An examination of the New Testament indicates the only divine trumpets that will be sounded during the time of the tribulation are those that are referred to in Revelation (Revelation 8:6-13, 9:1-20, 10:15-19). These are seven trumpets that will be associated with the seven trumpet judgments. The last trumpet that will be sounded will be the seventh trumpet. The first six trumpets will be associated with judgments God will pour out on earth and its inhabitants. The seventh trumpet will mark the moment when Jesus will begin to rule over His kingdom, judge the dead, and reward those who have been faithful to Him and feared His name. The seventh trumpet will precede the moment when "the kingdom of the world [will] become the kingdom of our Lord and of His Christ; and He will reign forever and ever (Revelation 11:15)." The twenty-four elders who are seated on the thrones before God will fall on their faces following this to worship God and say:

> "We give You thanks, O Lord God, the Almighty, who are and who were, because You have taken Your great power and have begun to reign. And the nations were enraged, and Your wrath came, and the time came for the dead to be judged, and the time to reward Your bond servants the prophets and the saints and those who fear Your name, the small and the great, and to destroy those who destroy the earth." (Revelation 11:17-18)

The sounding of the seventh trumpet, which may be the last trumpet referred to by Paul, will mark the beginning of the reign of Jesus over His kingdom on earth and the outpouring of the wrath of God on earth. The sounding of the seventh trumpet relative to its position in Revelation will mark the beginning of the transition from the tribulation to the great tribulation. The time following the sounding of the seventh trumpet will be the time of great distress referred to by Gabriel in Daniel 12 and the time of great tribulation referred to by Jesus in Matthew 24:20-22. This will be the time when the final conflict between God and Satan will begin. This conflict will occur over the forty-two months (1,260 days) the Antichrist will be given absolute dominion over the earth and allowed to wage war against the saints and overcome them. God will pour out the seven bowls of his wrath (referred to as the wrath of God) on the earth and those who receive the mark of the beast during this time. The sounding of the seventh trumpet could be the time when Jesus will come in the clouds to receive unto Himself the saints, both living and dead,.

Gabriel in Daniel 11:36 indicated the Antichrist "will prosper until the indignation is finished, for that which is decreed will be done." The period of the time of wrath referred to by the angel will begin after the Antichrist commits the abomination that causes desolation and will continue through the great tribulation. This may be the wrath Paul stated in 1 Thessalonians 5:9 for which God "has not destined us." The "hour of testing" Jesus indicated in Revelation 3:10 He will keep us from can refer to the choice the people of the earth will have to make during the great tribulation as to whether they will receive the mark of the beast and worship the Antichrist or be faithful to and worship Jesus.

All Bible verses used to support a pre-tribulation and post-tribulation rapture can be used to support a mid-tribulation rapture. They do not preclude the possibility of its occurrence. Therefore, the Bible strongly support the position the rapture will occur during the middle of the tribulation.

THE CHURCH AND THE RAPTURE

A wedding between the Lamb (Jesus) and His bride (the Church) will take place in heaven prior to the return of Jesus at the end of the great tribulation. The angel stated to John in Revelation 19:9:

> "Write, 'Blessed are those who are invited to the marriage supper of the Lamb.' ... These are true words of God."

The angel's statement implies the Church will be in heaven before the return of Jesus. We begin with Jesus' statement to Peter in Matthew 16:18 when He said:

> "I also say to you that you are Peter, and upon this rock I will build my church; and the gates of Hades will not overpower it."

This statement implied Satan, the Antichrist and false prophet will not be able to overcome and destroy His Church during the tribulation. The Church has and will prevail even though the Church has been and currently is being persecuted and oppressed and Christians have been and are currently being persecuted and martyred. This will also be true during the tribulation and great tribulation.

Gabriel told Daniel in Daniel 7:25 the saints will be handed over to the Antichrist for a period of 1,260 days. The messenger angel told John in Revelation 13:5-8 the Antichrist will be given power to make war against and conquer the saints during the 1,260 days of the great tribulation. The word saints, as used in these two instances, refer to Christians who will live on earth during the great tribulation.

God will never contradict Himself; He will not say one thing and then at some future time change His mind and say something different. Jesus stated in Matthew that Satan will never be able to overcome His Church. However, Gabriel in Daniel and the angel in Revelation both stated the Antichrist, who will be controlled by Satan, will be given power to make war against and conquer the saints (Christians) who will live on earth during the great tribulation. This can only occur if the Body of Christ, the Church, is not present on earth during the great tribulation.

John in Revelation was given two visions of martyred Christians

Revelation 6:9-11: These are martyred saints who were revealed to John at the opening of the fifth seal. They will be given white robes and be told "that they should rest for a little while longer, until the number of their fellow servants and their brethren who were to be killed even as they had been, would be completed also." These martyred saints will be those Christians who have already been and who will be murdered before the beginning of the great tribulation.

Revelation 7:9-17: John was told the "great multitude which no one could count" that he saw "from every nation and all tribes and peoples and tongues" were those who will be martyred during the great tribulation when the Antichrist will be given power to conquer the saints who will live on earth at that time.

John was told in Revelation 20:4-6 that saints who will be martyred during the great tribulation will be resurrected at the first resurrection before Jesus establishes His 1,000-year kingdom, and they will rule with Him in His kingdom. This accounts for martyred saints who will be murdered during the great tribulation. It does not address what will happen to the martyred saints who were revealed to John at the opening of the fifth seal. A mid-tribulation rapture presumes these martyred saints will be raptured with the rest of the saints, both living and dead, during the middle of the tribulation.

John was told in Revelation 7:1-8 the 144,000 witnesses from the twelve tribes of Israel who will receive the seal of the living God on their foreheads will be servants of God. Revelation 14:1-4 indicates these witnesses will be in heaven with Jesus during the great tribulation. They will be involved as servants of God in the evangelization of earth from the time of their being sealed until the beginning of the great tribulation. These witnesses will spread the message of salvation through Jesus throughout the earth during the first 1,267 days of the tribulation. It is reasonable to assume they along with other Christians will be the Church during the first 1,267 days of the tribulation. Gabriel in Daniel and the angel in Revelation do not indicate the Antichrist and Satan will be given authority to afflict these saints during the first 1,267 days of the tribulation that they will be given during the great tribulation.

Revelation 14 implies the Church that will exist before the great tribulation will not be present during the great tribulation. Evangelism by the 144,000 witnesses, the two witnesses and other Christians will cease. The two witnesses will be killed and resurrected (Revelation 11:1-12). The 144,000 witnesses will be in heaven with Jesus (Revelation 14:1-5). John was told in Revelation 14:14-16 that one "like the son of man" will be told, "Put in your sickle and reap, because the hour to reap has come, because the harvest of the earth is ripe." The term "son of man" may refer to Jesus. This reference to the son of man is also made in Daniel 7:13. This first harvesting may refer to a mid-tribulation rapture by Jesus of saints who are living and who have died. A second harvesting is referred to in Revelation 14:17-20. This may refer to the harvesting of the wicked for judgment. John stated in Revelation 14:12-13, regarding saints who will be martyred during the great tribulation:

> "Here is the perseverance of the saints who keep the commandments of God and their faith in Jesus. And I heard a voice from heaven, saying, 'Write, blessed are the dead who die in the Lord from now on!' 'Yes,' says the Spirit, 'that they may rest from their labors, for their deeds follow with them.'"

These saints will be resurrected by Jesus at the first resurrection before He establishes His 1,000-year kingdom (Revelation 20:4-6).

In summary, Jesus stated in Matthew Satan will never be able to overcome His Church. John stated in Revelation the Antichrist will be given authority only during the great tribulation to make war against and conquer the saints. These statements imply the Church may be present on earth during the first 1,267 days of the tribulation but not during the great tribulation. The Church will be raptured with the saints during the middle of the tribulation. These observations are further supported by:

- Saints who will be martyred during the great tribulation will experience a resurrection separate from saints who will live on earth and who will have been martyred before the great tribulation (Revelation 20:4-6).
- John indicated in Revelation 14:7 the salvation message of Jesus will be presented to people on earth by angels during the great tribulation.

WHAT JESUS SAID ABOUT THE TRIBULATION, GREAT TRIBULATION AND RAPTURE

Discussions associated with events during the seven-year tribulation and the rapture must be consistent with what Jesus presented about them in the Gospels of Matthew, Mark and Luke. Table 2 lists locations in these Gospels where Jesus addressed these events. His Mount of Olive discourse presented in:

- Matthew 24 addressed the sequence of events associated with the tribulation, abomination of desolation, great tribulation, and the rapture; and
- Matthew 25 addressed His criteria for judgement.

Jesus' presentation of the sequence of events in Matthew 24 will follow. His criteria for judgement are presented in Chapter 12 – JUDGEMENT OF GOD.

Table 2

Event	Gospel and Verses
Tribulation (first three and one-half years)	Matthew 24:4-14, Mark 13:5-13, Luke 21:8-19
Abomination of desolation (mid-point of Tribulation)	Matthew 24:15-18, Mark 13:14-16
Great Tribulation (last three and one-half years of Tribulation)	Matthew 24:16-26, Mark 13:17-23, Luke 21:20-36
Rapture (Christians caught up In middle of Tribulation to meet Jesus in the clouds)	Matthew 24:27-41, Mark 13:24-29, Luke 17:22-37

The Tribulation and Great Tribulation

Jesus stated in Matthew 24:4-14 concerning the part of the tribulation that will precede the abomination of desolation by the Antichrist:

> "See to it that no one misleads you. For many will come in My name, saying, 'I am the Christ,' and will mislead many. You will be hearing of wars and rumors of wars. See that you are not frightened, for those things must take place, but that is not yet the end. For nation will rise against nation, and kingdom against kingdom, and in various places there will be famines and earthquakes. But all these things are merely the beginning of birth pains."
>
> "Then they will deliver you to tribulation, and will kill you, and you will be hated by all nations because of My name. At that time many will fall away and will betray one another and hate one another. Many false prophets will arise and mislead many. Because lawlessness is increased, most people's love will grow cold. But the one who endures to the end, he will be saved. This

gospel of the kingdom shall be preached in the whole world as a testimony
to all the nations, and then the end will come."

Jesus did not give times in Matthew 24 when specific events He described will occur during the tribulation. He referred to the beginning of these events as the beginning of birth pains a woman experiences during the birth process. He presented this information so people will not be misled when they occur. Jesus divided His discussion into events that will occur before and after the abomination of desolation by the Antichrist that Daniel presented in Daniel 9:27.

Jesus addressed events that will occur after the beginning of the tribulation and before the abomination of desolation in Matthew 24:4-14. He indicated:

- False Christ will come who will mislead many.
- There will be rumors of wars and wars and nations and kingdoms will wage war against each other (revealed in the second seal judgement during that part of the tribulation that will precede the abomination of desolation).
- There will be famines and earthquakes (revealed in the third seal judgment during that part of the tribulation that will precede the abomination of desolation).
- Christians will experience tribulation and will be martyred.
- Christians will be hated because of their relationship with Jesus.
- Many will fall away from and turn against Jesus, and they will turn against and hate each other.
- Lawlessness will increase and people will cease to love one another.
- The Gospel of Jesus will be preached in the whole earth to all nations.

Jesus presented two promises relative to this part of the tribulation. He promised:

- Those who endure and survive the period of the tribulation that will precede the abomination of desolation will be saved.
- The Gospel of Jesus will be presented in the whole earth before the end of this period of the tribulation.

These promises imply Christians along with the Christian church will be present during the period of the tribulation preceding the abomination of desolation.

The abomination of desolation by the Antichrist will follow the events describe in Matthew 24:4-14. This event will occur during the middle of the seven-year tribulation

(See Figure 9 in Chapter 7). It will mark the transition between the period referred to as the tribulation and the period referred to as the great tribulation. The severity of events associated with the great tribulation will increase after the abomination of desolation. Jesus addressed this period in Matthew 24:15-26. He stated:

> "Therefore when you see the ABOMILATION OF DESOLATION which was spoken of through Daniel the prophet, standing in the holy place (let the reader understand), then those who are in Judea must flee to the mountains. Whoever is on the housetop must not go down to get the things out that are in his house. Whoever is in the field must not turn back to get his clock. But woe to those who are pregnant and to those who are nursing babies in those days! But pray that your flight will not be in the winter, or on a Sabbath. For then there will be a great tribulation, such as has not occurred since the beginning of the world until now, nor ever will. Unless those days had been cut short, no life would have been saved; but for the sake of the elect those days will be cut short. Then if anyone says to you, 'Behold, here is the Christ,' or 'There He is,' do not believe him. For false Christs and false prophets will arise and will show great signs and wonders, so as to mislead, if possible, even the elect. Behold, I have told you in advance. So if they say to you, 'Behold, He is in the wilderness,' do not go out, or, 'Behold, He is in the inner room,' do not believe them."

Jesus also addressed this in Luke 21:20-24. He stated:

> "But when you see Jerusalem surrounded by armies, then recognize that her desolation is near. Then those who are in Judea must flee to the mountains, and those who are in the midst of the city must leave, and those who are in the country must not enter the city, because these are days of vengeance, so that things which are written will be fulfilled. Woe to those who are pregnant and to those who are nursing babies in those days; for there will be great distress upon the land and wrath to this people; and they will fall by the edge of the sword, and will be led captive into all the nations; and Jerusalem will be trampled underfoot by the Gentiles until the times of the Gentiles are fulfilled."

Jesus indicated in the days that will follow the abomination of desolation:

- Jerusalem will be invaded and occupied by Gentiles until the time of the Gentiles is fulfilled.
- This will be a time of great tribulation and distress and of wrath.
- Those who believe in Jesus will be martyred and led as captives into all nations.
- False Christs and false prophets will arise who will show great signs and wonders to deceive even the elect, if possible.

The Rapture

Jesus addressed His return at the rapture in Matthew 24:29-31 that is presented at the beginning of this chapter. Many believe Jesus' statement refers to His second coming at the end of the great tribulation described in Revelation 19:11-16. However, His statement may refer to His coming at the rapture to remove His elect from the earth after the abomination of desolation. The following support this:

- Matthew 24:31 indicates Jesus will send fourth His angels with a great trumpet to gather His elect from the four winds from one end of the sky to the to the other.
- The armies of heaven who will return to the earth with Jesus as described in Revelation 19:11-16 will already be with Him in heaven when He returns to earth with them. Therefore, it will not be necessary for Jesus to gather them at this time from the four winds from one end of the sky to the other.
- There is no mention of the sound of a trumpet at Jesus' return to earth with His armies of heaven in Revelation 19:11-16.
- Paul stated regarding the rapture in 1 Corinthians 15:51-52 that we will be changed and rise to meet Jesus at the sound of the last trumpet.
- Paul stated in 1 Thessalonians 4:16-17 the Lord will descend from heaven with a shout, the voice of the archangel, and the trumpet of God, and the dead in Christ will be caught up with those who are alive in the clouds to meet Jesus in the air.

These statements indicate the rapture will occur after the abomination of desolation and before Jesus' return to earth with His armies of heaven at the end of the seven-year tribulation.

Jesus stated in Matthew 24:32-41 regarding the rapture:

"Now learn the parable from the fig tree: when its branch has already become tender and puts forth its leaves, you know that summer is near; so, you too, when you see all these things, recognize that He is near, right at the door. Truly I say to you, this generation will not pass away until all these things take place. Heaven and earth will pass away, but My words will not pass away."

"But of that day and hour no one knows, not even the angels of heaven, nor the Son of Man, but the Father alone. For the coming of the Son of Man will be just like the days of Noah. For as in those days before the flood they were eating and drinking, marrying and giving in marriage until the day that Noah entered the ark, and they did not understand until the flood came and took them all away; so will the coming of the Son of Man be. Then there will be two men in the field, one will be taken and one will be left. Two women will be grinding at the mill; one will be taken and one will be left."

The following observations regarding the rapture can be made with the Bible verses presented in this chapter section.

- Matthew 24:29-31 indicates Jesus will send forth His angels with the sound of a great trumpet to gather His elect from one end of the sky to the other.
- Matthew 24:32-35 indicates we will know the time of Jesus' return at the rapture may be near when we observe events recorded in Mathew 24:4-27.
- Matthew 24:36 indicates only God knows the exact day and time when the rapture will occur.
- Mathew 24:37-39 indicate global conditions will indicate when the rapture may be near.
- Matthew 24:40-41 describes the rapture.

Jesus gives us this warning in Matthew 24:42-51:

"Therefore be on the alert, for you do not know which day your Lord is coming. But be sure of this, that if the head of the house had known at what time of the night the thief was coming, he would have been on the alert and would not have allowed his house to be broken into. For this reason you also must be ready; for the Son of Man is coming at an hour when you do not think He will."

"Who then is the faithful and sensible slave whom his master put in charge of his household to give them their food at the proper time? Blessed is that slave whom his master finds so doing when he comes. Truly I say to you that he will put him in charge of all his possessions. But if that evil slave says in his heart, 'My master is not coming for a long time,' and begins to beat his fellow slaves and eat and drink with drunkards. The master of that slave will come on a day when he does not expect him and at an hour which he does not know, and will cut him in pieces and assign him a place with hypocrites; in that place there will be weeping and gnashing of teeth."

We are to live a life of faith and trust in and obedience to Jesus to be prepared to meet and be received by Him in the sky when He returns at the rapture. We may not be received by Jesus when He returns at the rapture when we have not lived a life of faith and trust in and obedience to Him. Paul indicated in 2 Corinthians 5:10 we will receive our reward after the rapture when we stand in judgement before Jesus.

CHAPTER 6
UNDERSTANDING THE LANGUAGE

RELATION BETWEEN DANIEL'S TEN KINGDOM FEDERATION, THE TRIBULATION, AND THE NEW WORLD ORDER

This book addresses the relation between the return of Jesus, the end time, and the establishment of a New World Order. The end time that includes events associated with the tribulation, great tribulation, and return of Jesus is initially discussed in Daniel and more fully discussed in Revelation. Jesus presented the framework for these events in Matthew 24. He indicated the end time will include a time of distress that will be followed by a time of "great distress, unequaled from the beginning of the world ... and never to be equaled again." The term tribulation refers to the seven-year period of the times of distress and great distress presented by Jesus and discussed in Revelation. The term great tribulation refers to the time of great distress that will occur during the last 1,260 days of the tribulation. Jesus indicated the invasion of Israel by Gentile nations, the abomination of desolation, and the removal of Christians from the earth (referred to as the rapture) will occur in between the times of distress and great distress.

The New World Order refers to the establishment of a dictatorial one-world government that will replace the governments of sovereign nation-states on earth. Daniel received a vision from the Lord concerning the formation of a future ten kingdom federation that will trample the earth and be ruled by a king as dictator. Revelation indicates the Antichrist will be the main political figure during the seven-year tribulation and will be given authority by God to rule the people and nations of earth as dictator during the great tribulation.

A major effort will be required by the Antichrist to establish the global economic and government framework and infrastructure necessary to rule the people and nations of the earth. It is unlikely this process could be accomplished starting with nothing during the first 1,267 days of the tribulation. It is also unlikely the Antichrist could facilitate the global political, economic and spiritual transformations necessary for the people of eartg to accept his dictatorial government during the first 1,267 days of the tribulation. These transformations could take decades and even centuries to be fully accomplished. Information in the open literature and on the Interned document activities have been ongoing for centuries to condition people on earth to accept the emergence of a one-world, dictatorial government. The future establishment of a New World Order can transition into the ten kingdom federation described in Daniel that will facilitate the development of the Antichrist's global dictatorship.

DESCRIPTION OF BASIC TERMS

The language used to describe the meaning and significance of future events associated with the tribulation, the return of Jesus, and God bringing an end to history as we recognize it must be understood to fully comprehend the significance of these events. Some terms associated with this language are defined and briefly discussed in this section. This discussion is divided into items, time periods, persons, places and events associated with prophesies concerning the end time, tribulation and return of Jesus.

Items

Abomination of desolation: An idol of a pagan or Gentile god placed in the Holy of Holies in the Temple in Jerusalem.

Book of life: The names of all who have and will accept Jesus as Lord and Savior will be contained in the book of life, which is referred to in Daniel 12:1 and Revelation 20:12, 15 and 21:27. Those whose names are written in the book of life will be spared from the wrath of God the world will experience during the great tribulation (the last three and one-half years of the tribulation) and the great white throne judgment at the end of the 1,000-year millennial rule of Jesus.

Mark of the beast: The false prophet will require "the small and the great, and the rich and the poor, and the free men and the slaves" to receive this mark on either their right hand or forehead to carry out acts of commerce during the great tribulation (Revelation 13:16-18). It will be associated with either the name or number (666) of the Antichrist. The wrath of God will be directed against those who receive this mark (Revelation 14:9-11). They will be judged and cast into the lake of fire at the great white throne judgment (Revelation 20:15).

Seal of the living God: This seal will be placed on the foreheads of the 144,000 Jews who will be selected by God to spread the gospel of Jesus throughout the world during the first three and one-half years of the tribulation (Revelation 7:2-8). Those who receive the seal of God will be supernaturally protected from the judgments of God during the first 1,267 days of the tribulation.

Places

Abyss: The abyss is the place, possibly deep within the earth, from where locust-like demonic creatures associated with the fifth trumpet judgment will come (Revelation 9:1-11). The abyss is also where Satan will be bound in chains during the 1,000-year millennial rule of Jesus (Revelation 20:1-2).

Babylon the Great: Babylon will be the world political and economic center during the tribulation (Revelation 18). It will be the place from where the Antichrist will rule the world. Bible scholars believe the Babylon of Revelation may be the restored ancient Babylon located in modern day Iraq.

Beth-tagarmah: Beth-tagarmah is a region in modern day Turkey (Ezekiel 38:6). Beth-tagarmah will be an ally of Russia in its invasion of Israel.

Cush (ancient Ethiopia): Cush is modern day northern Sudan (Ezekiel 38:5). Cush will be an ally of Russia in its invasion of Israel.

Gomer: Gomer is a region in modern day Turkey (Ezekiel 38:6). Gomer will be an ally of Russia in its invasion of Israel.

Heaven: Heaven is the dwelling place and paradise of God.

Lake of fire: The lake of fire will be the dwelling place of those who do not accept Jesus as Lord and Savior and oppose God during and after the seven-year tribulation. The Antichrist and false prophet will be placed there after the battle of Armageddon (Revelation 19:20). Death and Hades and all whose names are not written in the book of life will be placed there at the great white throne judgment (Revelation 20:14-15). Satan will be placed there when he and his armies are defeated in his final battle with God after the 1,000-year millennial reign of Jesus (Revelation 20:10). The lake of fire will be a place of judgment and punishment. Those who are placed there will be eternally separated from God.

Magog: Magog is modern day Kazakhstan, Kirghizia, Uzbekistan, Turkmenistan, and Tajikistan (Ezekiel 38:2). Magog will be an ally of Russia in its invasion of Israel..

Meshach: Meshach is a region in modern day Turkey (Ezekiel 38:3). Meshek will be ally of Russia in its invasion of Israel.

Magog: Magog is modern day Kazakhstan, Kirghizia, Uzbekistan, Turkmenistan, and Tajikistan (Ezekiel 38:2). These countries will be allies of Russia in its invasion of Israel.

Persia: Persia is modern day Iran (Ezekiel 38:5). Persia will be an ally of Russia in its invasion of Israel.

Petra: Petra is a place in southern Jordon where the remnant of Israel a secure place to hid during the great tribulation.

Put: Put is modern day Libya (Ezekiel 38:5). Put will be an ally of Russia in its invasion of Israel.

Rush: Rush is a region in modern day northern Russia, who will invade Israel.

Temple of the Lord: The temple will be rebuilt in Jerusalem possibly at the beginning of the tribulation. This is confirmed by John being asked to measure the temple in Revelation 11:1-2 and Daniel prophesying in Daniel 9:27 and 11:31 that the Antichrist will commit the abomination of desolation in the temple and suspend temple sacrifices during the middle of the tribulation. Jesus referred to the abomination of desolation described by Daniel in Matthew 24:15. The temple that will be built during the tribulation will possibly be destroyed by the Antichrist when he invades Israel during the middle of the tribulation. Ezekiel indicated in Ezekiel 40-48 the temple will be rebuilt again at the beginning of the 1,000-year rule of Jesus. The rebuilt temple will be the place where the glory cloud of God will dwell (Ezekiel 43) and a center for the King of glory (Ezekiel 43:7) during the 1,000-year rule of Jesus.

Tubal: Tubal is a region in modern day Turkey (Ezekiel 38:3). Tobal will be an ally of Russian in its invasion of Israel.

Time Periods

End time: This term (also referred to as the time of the end) used in Daniel refers to the time of the seven-year tribulation (Daniel 8:17-19, 11:35, 11:40, and 12:9).

Last day: Day of the great white throne judgement (John 6:35-40, John 12:47-50, Revelation 20:11).

Last days: The last days refer to the time preceding and during the seven-year tribulation (Ezekiel 38:16, 2 Timothy 3:1-7, and 2 Peter 3:3-7).

Time of great distress: The time of great distress was used by the angel Gabriel in Daniel 12:1 to refer to the great tribulation (the last three and one-half years of the tribulation).

Tribulation and Great Tribulation: The tribulation will be the seven-year period that will precede the return of Jesus. It will be marked by wars, catastrophic natural disasters, and an outpouring of God's judgments on the earth. The great tribulation will be the last three and one-half years of the seven-year tribulation (Daniel 12:1, Matthew 24:21, Revelation 7:14). The great tribulation will follow the abomination of desolation when the Antichrist declares himself to be God in the middle of the tribulation (Matthew 24:15-28, Daniel 12:1). It will be the time when the surviving people of the world will be required to receive the mark of the beast, the Antichrist will wage war against the saints of God, and the world will experience the wrath of God.

Persons

Apollyon: Apollyon (also Abaddon in Hebrew) is the angel (or demon) who is king over the abyss (Revelation 9:11). Apollyon's rank in Satan's kingdom may be equivalent to the archangel Michael's rank in the kingdom of God.

Antichrist: The term *antichrist* is introduced in 1 John 2: 18, 22 and in 2 John 1:7 and 4:3. John referred to an *antichrist* as a deceiver who denied Jesus is the Christ and One will return in the flesh. The king who will form and lead the ten kingdom confederation that will be formed at the beginning of the tribulation (Daniel 7:8, 24-25) is commonly referred to as the Antichrist. The "beast" referred to in Revelation 11:7 and several other places in Revelation is commonly called the Antichrist. The Antichrist will be the main world political leader during the seven-year tribulation (2 Thessalonians 2:1-10). He will initially be a popular leader, who will rise to power by using deception and guile. He will sign a covenant (or treaty) with Israel at the beginning of the tribulation, initially guaranteeing Israel's safety during the tribulation (Daniel 9:27). He will break this covenant and turn against Israel in the middle of the tribulation, set himself up as the world dictator, and declare himself to be God. The Bible indicates the Antichrist will be an intellectual genius (Daniel 8:23), an oratorical genius (Daniel 11:36), a political genius (Revelation 17:11-12), a commercial genius (Daniel 11:43, Revelation 13:16-17), and a religious genius (2 Thessalonians 2:4, Revelation 13:2). He will receive a fatal head wound from a sword, probably sometime before the abomination of desolation that will be supernaturally healed (Revelation 13:3, 14).

Death and Hades: They are possibly demonic princes who control the place where those who have died without receiving the salvation God gives to us through Jesus dwell. The names of the dead who dwell there will not be written in the book of life. Both will be thrown into the lake of fire after they give up their dead at the great white throne judgment (Revelation 6:8, 20:13-14).

False prophet: He will be the cohort and right-hand man of the Antichrist (Revelation 13:11-17). He will be able to perform miracles through satanic power and exercise the authority of the Antichrist on his behalf. The false prophet will force the inhabitants of the earth to worship the Antichrist, set up an image to honor the Antichrist, and force everyone to receive the mark of the beast to carry out acts of commerce during the great tribulation.

Four women in Revelation: The woman in Revelation 12 who is clothed with the sun, with the moon under her feet, and a crown of twelve stars on her head represents Israel. The woman in Revelation 17 who was sitting on a scarlet beast that was covered with blasphemous names and had seven heads and ten horns represents the world's religious system. This woman is referred to as the great prostitute in Revelation 17:1-2 and Revelation 19:2. The woman in Revelation 18 who has become a home for demons and a haunt for every evil spirit, a haunt for every unclean and detestable bird, represents the world's economic system. The pure bride in Revelation 19 represents the Church of Jesus.

Gog: He was the ruler of Magog and the prince of Rosh, Meshach and Tubal (Ezekiel 38:2-3). God will place a hook in his jaw and pull him and his allies to invade Israel (Ezekiel 38:4 and 8).

Male child: The male child who was born to the woman clothed with the sun, the moon under her feet, and a crown of twelve stars on her head refers to Jesus (Revelation 12:4-6). This child "was caught up to God and to his throne."

Red dragon: The enormous red dragon in Revelation 12 with seven heads and ten horns and seven crowns on his heads represents Satan.

The 144,000 witnesses: 144,000 witnesses from the twelve tribes of Israel will be sealed as servants of God during the first 1,267 days of the tribulation (Revelation 7:1-8). The seal of God will be placed on their foreheads. Jesus indicated in Matthew 24:14 that the end will not come until after His gospel of salvation has been proclaimed in all the world. The end Jesus refers to is the wrath of God that will be poured out on the world during the great tribulation. It is presumed God will use the 144,000 witnesses to spread this gospel to the whole world during the first 1,267 days of the tribulation. John indicated in Revelation 14:1-5 the 144,000 witnesses will be in heaven with Jesus at the beginning of the great tribulation. John stated they will be "purchased from among men and offered as first fruits to God and the Lamb."

Two witnesses: The two witnesses will be prophets sent directly from God to witness the gospel of Jesus to the earth during the first three and one-half years of the tribulation (Revelation 11:2-13). They will be given power to prevent it from raining when they prophesy, and they will have power to turn water into blood and strike the earth with every kind of plague as often as they want. No one will be able to harm them during the 1,260 days the Lord has given them to prophesy. The false prophet will be given power to overcome and kill them at the end of 1,260 days (Revelation 11:7). They will be refused burial when they are killed. Their bodies will lay on the ground for three and one-half days after which they will be resurrected from the dead. The two witnesses may be either Elijah and Enoch or Elijah and Moses. Elijah and Enoch are presumed because neither experienced physical death (2 King 2:11-12, Hebrew 11:5). They were directly translated into heaven without dying. Elijah and Moses are presumed because Elijah and Moses appeared to Jesus on the Mount of Transfiguration (Matthew 17:3), and Moses turned water into blood as one of the plagues God placed on the land of Egypt, which ultimately led Pharaoh to release the Israelites to travel to the land He had promised them (Exodus 7:17-21).

Events

Abomination of desolation: The abomination of desolation is the act that will be performed by the Antichrist during the middle of the tribulation when he will put an end to temple sacrifices and declare himself to be God (Daniel 9:27, 11:31, Matthew 24:15, 2 Thessalonians 2:4-10, Revelation 13:5). He will utter proud words and blasphemies against God. From the time the Antichrist declares himself to be God, he will be given forty-two months (three and one-half years) to exercise his authority. This forty-two-month period is referred to as the great tribulation when the Antichrist will wage war against the saints (Christians) and overcome them, and "authority over every tribe and people and tongue and nation will be given to him (Revelation 13:7)." His authority will end at the Battle of Armageddon at the end of the tribulation.

Battle of Armageddon: The battle of Armageddon will be the final battle that will take place between the armies of the Antichrist and kings of the earth and Jesus and the armies of heaven at the end of the tribulation (Revelation 16:16, 19:11-21). Some Bible scholars speculate the battlefield will stretch from the Plain of Jezreel north of Megiddo in the north to Edom in the south (120 - 180 miles) and from the Mediterranean Sea in the west to the hills of Moab in the east (60 - 100 miles) (Figure 8). Jerusalem will be in the middle of the battle field. The Valley of Jehosaphat (a valley east of Jerusalem between Jerusalem and the Mount of Olives) referred to in Joel 3:9-21 as the valley of decision will be in the battlefield.

Day of the Lord: The day of the Lord is a term used in both the Old and New Testaments to denote a day or time of great judgment by God. With respect to the tribulation, the expression the day of the Lord is used in reference to three separate events that are associated with a major judgment by God: the removal of Christians along with the Church from the face of the earth at the rapture (Joel 2:28-32, 1 Corinthians 5:5, 1 Thessalonians 5:1-3 and 2 Thessalonians 2:1-4), the defeat of the Antichrist and kings of the earth at the battle of Armageddon (Joel 3:1-21), and the consuming of the existing heaven and earth with intense heat and fire by God before he creates the new heaven and earth at the end of 1,000-year rule of Jesus (2 Peter 3:10-13, Revelation 20:11, Revelation 21-22).

First resurrection: The first resurrection will occur at the beginning of the 1,000-year rule of Jesus. It will be the resurrection of persons who have not received the mark of the beast and worshiped the Antichrist and have been martyred because of their testimony to God's word during the Great tribulation (Revelation 20:4-6).

Figure 8

Great white throne judgment: The great white throne judgment will be experienced by all who have rejected the salvation God extends to them through Jesus at the end of the 1,000-year rule of Jesus (Revelation 21:11-15). They will be judged and thrown into the lake of fire.

Jacob's distress: The judgement of Israel during the seven-year tribulation (Jeremiah 30 and 31.

Return of Jesus: The return of Jesus will occur at the end of the tribulation when He returns with the armies of heaven to defeat the armies of the Antichrist and kings of the earth at the battle of Armageddon and set up his 1,000-year kingdom on earth (Revelation 19:11-21, 20:1-7).

Second death: The second death will be experienced by all who will be cast into the lake of fire at the great white throne judgment. The second death will be associated with eternal separation from God (Revelation 20:14, 21:8).

Second resurrection: The second resurrection is not specifically mentioned in the Bible. It will be the resurrection at the great white throne judgment of all who have died since the beginning of time whose names are not written in the book of life and who have lived and died during the 1,000-year kingdom of Jesus (Revelation 20:11-15). All those resurrected at the second resurrection whose names are not written in the book of life will be cast into the lake of fire.

Wedding of the Lamb: The wedding of the Lamb is the marriage that will occur in heaven between the Lamb, Jesus, and his bride, the Church, before He returns to earth with the armies of heaven to defeat the armies of the Antichrist and kings of the earth at the battle of Armageddon (Revelation 19:1-9).

Wrath of God: The wrath of God refers to the seven bowls of God's wrath that will be poured out on earth during the great tribulation (Revelation 15:7, 16:1-21). These plagues will be associated with unimaginable catastrophic natural disasters. Gabriel in Daniel 12:1 referred to this as "a time of distress such as never occurred since there was a nation until that time." Jesus stated in Matthew 24:21-22:

> "... there will be a great tribulation, such as has not occurred since the beginning of the world until now, nor ever will. Unless those days had been cut short, no life would have been saved; but for the sake of the elect those days will be cut short."

Gabriel indicated in Daniel 12:2 persons whose names are written in the book of life will be delivered from this time of God's wrath. Paul stated in Romans 5:9 that Christians will be save from the wrath of God. battle of Armageddon will be the largest, boldest and bloodiest battle of all time.

CHAPTER 7
TIME LINE OF THE TRIBULATION IN DANIEL AND REVELATION

GOD'S PLAN FOR THE REDEMPTION OF HIS CREATION

Note: This and following chapters present events related to Bible prophecy associated with the end time. Bible prophecy can be separated into three categories:

- The first refers to future events at the time they were recorded in the Bible that, relative to the present, refer to past events. These refer to some events recorded in Daniel.

- The second refer to future events at the time they were recorded in the Bible that, relative to the present, refer to future events. This is true of events recorded in Revelation, as well as, to some events recorded in Daniel.

- The third refer to future events at the time they were recorded in the Bible that, relative to the present, refer to past events. However, some of these events also refer to the same events with different characters and conditions that, relative to the present, will occur in the future. These refer to some events recorded in Daniel.

These and similar events associated with the end time are presented in this and following chapters.

God's plan for the redemption of His creation is divided into three phases.

Phase 1: God has redeemed individual men and women through their faith and trust in and obedience to Jesus, has reconciled them to Himself, and has received them into his presence.

Phase 2: God will redeem the nation of Israel. He explains in Ezekiel 39:21-29 why He allowed them to be sent into exile and why He will redeem them in the future:

"And I will set My glory among the nations; and all the nations will see My judgment which I have executed and My hand which I have laid on them. And the house of Israel will know that I am the LORD their God from that day onward. The nations will know that the house of Israel went into exile for their iniquity because they acted treacherously against Me, and I hid My face from them, so I gave them into the hand of their adversaries, and all of them fell by the sword, according to their uncleanness and according to their transgressions I dealt with them, and I hid My face from them."

"Therefore thus says the LORD God 'Now I will restore the fortune of Jacob and have mercy on the whole house of Israel; and I will be jealous for My holy name. They will forget their disgrace and all their treachery which they perpetrated against Me, when they live securely on their own land with no one to make them afraid. When I bring them from the peoples and gather them from the lands of their enemies, then I shall be sanctified through them in the sight of the many nations. Then they will know that I am the LORD their God because I made them go into exile among the nations, and then gathered them again to their own land, and I will leave none of them there any longer. I will not hide My face from them any longer, for I will have poured out My Spirit on the house of Israel,' declares the LORD God."

Many believe the restoration of the nation of Israel in 1948 was a partial fulfillment of this promise by God. The rest of this promise may be fulfilled when Jesus sets up His 1,000-year kingdom after the seven-year tribulation.

Phase 3: God will redeem His creation at the end of Jesus' 1,000-year kingdom after He destroys the existing heaven and earth and create a new heaven and earth where there will be no sin.

TIME FRAME OF THE TRIBULATION

The Bible does not indicate a specific time when the tribulation will begin, but it does indicate when specific events will occur during the tribulation. Daniel in Daniel 9 entered intense prayer concerning his own sins and the sins of the people of Israel. He reminded God in his prayer of His covenant relationship with Israel and His mercy toward those who love Him. He asked God to bring Israel out of their Babylonian captivity, forgive their sins, and allow the temple to be rebuilt in Jerusalem. God sent Gabriel to Daniel to relay His response to Daniel's prayer and explain His plan for Israel's redemption. Gabriel stated regarding God's response in Daniel 9:24-27:

"Seventy weeks have been decreed for your people and your holy city, to finish the transgression, to make an end of sin, to make atonement for iniquities, to bring in everlasting righteousness, to seal up vision and prophecy and to anoint the most holy place. So you are to know and discern that from the issuing of a decree to restore and rebuild Jerusalem until Messiah the Prince there will be seven weeks and sixty-two weeks; it will be built again, with plaza and moat, even in times of distress. Then after the sixty-two weeks the Messiah will be cut off and have nothing, and the people of the prince who is to come will destroy the city and the sanctuary. And its end will come with a flood; even to the end there will be war; desolations are determined. And he will make a firm covenant with the many for one week, but in the middle of the week he will put a stop to sacrifices and grain offering; and on the wing of abominations will come one who makes desolate, even until a complete destruction, one that is decreed, is poured out on the one who makes desolate."

Gabriel's response indicated:

- The seventy sevens refers to a time period of 490 years (70 times 7 years). This is the time God indicated it will take to put an end to sin, atone for wickedness, bring in everlasting righteousness, fulfill all prophecy, and anoint the most holy place.

- The Anointed One refers to Jesus.

- The period of seven sevens or 49 years (7 times 7 years) refers to the time from 445 to 396 B.C. This period began with King Artaxerxes of Babylon allowing the people of Israel to return to Israel to begin building the walls of Jerusalem and ended with the completion of the project (Nehemiah 1-2).

- The period of sixty-two sevens or 434 years refers to the time from 396 B.C. to 32 A.D. when Jesus was crucified. The Messiah will be cut off refers to Jesus' crucifixions.

- The destruction of the city and sanctuary can refer to the destruction of Jerusalem and the Temple by the Roman general Titus in 70 A.D. It can also refer to the destruction of Jerusalem and the Temple that will be built during the first 1,267 days of the tribulation in the middle of the tribulation by the Gentiles who occupy Jerusalem and the Antichrist.

- The ruler in the phrase "people of the ruler" refers to the Antichrist.

- The one seven refers to the seven year period of the tribulation during the end time. There is an indefinite time span between the end of the first sixty-nine sevens and the beginning of the last seven. The time at which the seven-year tribulation period will begin is unknown.

- The covenant refers to the covenant the Antichrist will enter with Israel at the beginning of the tribulation. This covenant will guarantee security and peace for Israel for seven years. The Antichrist will break this covenant and commit the abomination that causes desolation during the middle of the seven-year tribulation.

Daniel and John in Revelation used four measures of time when describing events that will occur during the tribulation.

Years

- Duration of the tribulation - seven years (Daniel 9:24-27)

Months

- Time that gentiles will occupy and control the city of Jerusalem - 42 months (Revelation 11:2).

- Time during the great tribulation when the Antichrist will make war against and overcome the saints and rule over every tribe and people and tongue and nation on the earth - 42 months (Revelation 13:7).

Days

- Time between the abomination of desolation and end of the tribulation - 1,290 days (Daniel 12:11).

- Time between the abomination of desolation and beginning of the 1,000-year kingdom of Jesus - 1,335 days (Daniel 12:12).

- Time allotted for the two witnesses to prophesy during the first 1,267 days of the tribulation - 1,260 days (Revelation 11:1-13).

- Time allotted for the protection by God of the remnant of Israel during the great tribulation - 1,260 days (Revelation 12:6).

Time, times and a half time

- Time period Christians will be given into the hands of the Antichrist during the great tribulation - time, times and a half time (Daniel 7:25).

- Duration of the great tribulation - time, times and a half time (Daniel 12:7).

- Time allotted for the protection by God of the remnant of Israel during the great tribulation - time, times and a half time (Revelation 12:14). The protection of the remnant of Israel by God in the wilderness referred to in Revelation 12:6 and 12:14 refer to the same event. One event refers to a period of time of 1,260 days, and the other to a period of time of a time, times and a half time. Therefore, the period of a time, times and a half time is 1,260 days.

CALENDAR USED TO SPECIFY THE NUMBER OF DAYS IN THE TRIBULATION

Which calendar - Hebrew or Gregorian - should be used to determine the number of days in seven years and forty-two months? The Hebrew calendar is based on a lunar cycle of 29-1/2 days for each lunar month, while the Gregorian calendar is based on a solar cycle of 365-1/4 days in a year (*Pictorial Bible Dictionary*, 1971). The Gregorian calendar is adjusted every fourth year (designated a leap year) by adding an extra day to the month of February.

The Hebrew calendar and its relation to the Gregorian calendar are shown in Table 3. The Hebrew months are alternately 30 and 29 days to account for the half day in each lunar cycle. A year based on the Hebrew calendar is 354 days. Therefore, the Hebrew year is eleven days shorter than the solar year used in the Gregorian calendar. Approximately every three years an extra 29-day-month, designated Adar 2, was added between Adar and Nisan to adjust for this difference.

Table 3

Name of Months	Corresponds with	Number Days	Months of Civil Year	Months of Sacred Year
Tishri	Sep-Oct	30	1st	7th
Heshvan	Oct-Nov	29 or 30	2nd	8ths
Chistlev	Nov-Dec	29 or 30	3rd	9ths
Tebeth	Dec-Jan	29	4th	10th
Shebat	Jan-Feb	30	5th	11th

Adar	Feb-Mar	29 Or 30	6th	12th
Nisan	Mar-Apr	30	7th	1st
Iyar	Apr-May	29	8th	2nd
Sivan	May-Jun	30	9th	3rd
Tammuz	Jun-Jul	29	10th	4th
Ab	Jul-Aug	30	11th	5th
Elul	Aug-Sep	29	12th	6th

The Hebrew and solar year are aligned over a nineteen-year cycle by adding an extra 29-day-month (Adar 2) to the Hebrew year in the 3rd, 6th, 8th, 11th, 14th, 17th and 19th year of the nineteen-year cycle. The years in which these extra months are added are called leap years. The number of days in nineteen solar years (with four leap years) is 6,935 days. The number of days in nineteen Hebrew years plus seven extra months is 6,929 days. The additional six days are added by increasing the number of days in the original month of Adar to 30 during each leap year. Minor adjustments during each of the seven leap years are made by adjusting the number of days in the months of Heshvan and Chislev between 29 and 30 days. The Israelites used two cycles for their calendar. One was the civil year, which began with the month of Tishri. The other was the sacred year, which began with the month of Nisan.

Gabriel instructed Daniel in Daniel 12:4 to close his scroll that contained the vision he received from the LORD until the time of the end. This instruction implies the Gregorian calendar, which is based on the actual number of days in a solar year, should be used to specify the number of days in the seven-year period of the tribulation and in forty-two months. The Gregorian calendar specifies there are 2,557 days in seven solar years with two intervening leap years and 1,278 1/2 days in forty-two months with one intervening leap year.

The number of days in the tribulation will either be 2,538 or 2,568 when the Hebrew calendar is used to specify the number of days in seven years, depending on whether two or three leap years are assumed to occur during seven Hebrew years. The 1,260 days the two witnesses will witness the gospel of Jesus in Jerusalem during the first 1,267 days of the tribulation before they will be killed (Revelation 1:3, 7) when added to the 1,290 days between the abomination of desolation by the Antichrist and the end of the tribulation (Daniel 12:11) indicate the possible minimum number of days in the tribulation. If the two witnesses are killed before the abomination of desolation, the minimum number of days will be 2,550. This is greater than the 2,538 days based on seven Hebrew years plus two intervening leap years. The 2,568 days associated with seven Hebrew years plus three intervening leap years is greater than the 2,557 days in seven solar years plus two intervening leap years. These imply the Hebrew calendar should not be used to specify the number of days in the seven-year period of the tribulation or in forty-two months.

Figure 9 presents tabulated results based on the Gregorian calendar that show the time line of events prophesied to occur during the tribulation. This time line incorporates all the time intervals specified in Daniel and Revelation. While Figure 9 indicates when events will occur during the tribulation, it does not show when the tribulation will begin. Jesus stated in Matthew 24:34 only the Father knows when He will return and in Acts 1:7 it is not for us to know times the Father sets by His authority.

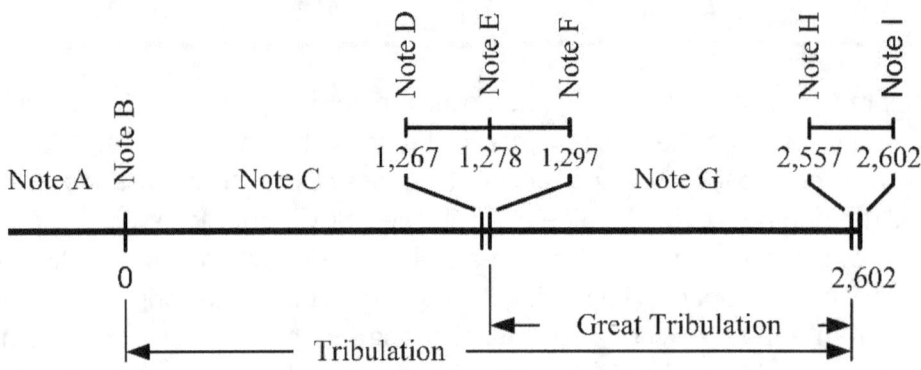

Number of Days Associated with the Tribulation

Figure 9

Notes for Figure 9:

Note A: Ten kingdom federation is formed before start of the tribulation. Antichrist becomes king of the ten kingdom federation (Daniel 7:19-27).

Note B: Antichrist signs covenant with Israel (Daniel 9:27). Tribulation period begins.

Note C: Two witnesses from God will prophesy for 1,260 days. They will start at the end of the first week or the beginning of the second week of the tribulation. They are killed by the false prophet (Revelation 11:3, 7) at end of 1,260 days and are resurrected three and one-half days later (Revelation 11:11-12). 144,000 witnesses from the twelve tribes of Israel will be sealed with the seal of the living God before the beginning of the 7th seal judgment (Revelation 6:1-8). They will witness the gospel of Jesus on earth during the remainder of the first 1,267 days of the tribulation. Seven seal and six trumpet judgments will occur during the first 1,267 days of the tribulation (Revelation 6-11).

Note D: The Antichrist ends temple sacrifices and sets up the abomination of desolation (Daniel 11:31, 12:11; Matthew 24:15-16).

Note E: Antichrist breaks covenant with Israel (Daniel 9:27).

Note F: Antichrist is given power to make war against and overcome the saints and authority to rule over every people, tongue and nation of the earth (Revelation 11:2, 13:5-7). The remnant of Israel go into hiding in a place prepared by God and saints given into the hands of the Antichrist for a period of 1,260 days (Revelation 12:6, Daniel 7:25).

Note G: The great harlot is killed by the Antichrist and ten kings (time of death unknown, but probably near the beginning of the great tribulation) (Revelation 17:8-18). World economic system is judged and destroyed by God (time of destruction unknown, but probably near the end of the great tribulation) (Revelation 18:4-19). The seven bowl judgments occur during the great tribulation (Revelation 16). The marriage of Jesus occurs at the end of the great tribulation (Revelation 19:7-8).

Note H: Jesus returns with the army of heaven to defeat the armies of the Antichrist and kings of the earth at the battle of Armageddon. Tribulation period ends (Daniel 12:7, 11, Revelation 13:7, 19:11-21).

Note I: Jesus establishes His 1,000-year kingdom (Daniel 12:11-12, Revelation 20).

Period between Days 1,267 and 1,297: The abomination of desolation occurs (Revelation 13:5, Matthew 24:15-16). 7th trumpet judgment occurs and Jesus begins to reign over His kingdom and raptures His saints from the earth to heaven (includes 144,000 witnesses) (Matthew 24:29-31; Luke 17:30-36, 40-41, 1 Corinthians 15:51-52, 2 Thessalonians 2:1-4, Revelation 11:15-17, 14:1-5). Satan and his angels are cast out of heaven and thrown down to earth (Relation 12:7-12).

Period between Days 2,557 and 2,602: Jesus resurrects saints martyred during the great tribulation and sets up His 1,000-year kingdom (Daniel 12:11-12; Revelation 20)

INFORMATION ASSOCIATED WITH THE TRIBULATION

Description of the Tribulation

The tribulation refers to a future seven year (2,557 day) period during which God will execute His judgements of the unrighteous on earth (Figure 9). He will also complete His judgement of the people of Israel associated with their disobedience during the tribulation. The great tribulation refers to the last forty-two months (1,260 days) of the tribulation (Figure 9). Jesus indicated in Matthew 24:21 the great tribulation will be a time "such as has not occurred since the beginning of the world until now, nor ever will." It will be a time on earth of hardships, desolations, destruction and death. The tribulation and great tribulation will occur during a time the Bible refers to as the time of the end or the end time.

Those who have faith and trust in and are obedient to Jesus are referred to as saints in this and the following three chapters. They will be hated, persecuted, and martyred in unimaginable numbers during the great tribulation. Jesus stated in Luke 21:16-19:

> "But you will be betrayed even by parents and brothers and relatives and friends, and they will put some of you to death, and you will be hated by all because of My name. Yet not a hair of your head will perish. By your endurance you will gain your lives."

God will execute His judgments of the unrighteous during the tribulation and great tribulation. However, He will receive into His presence during this time those who seek Him through their faith and trust in and obedience to Jesus. They may experience sever hardships and many may be martyred, but God's grace and love for them through Jesus will prevail. Satan, the Antichrist, the false prophet, and the unrighteous will be judged and cast into the lake of fire after the great white throne judgement described in Revelation 20:11-13. The righteous who had faith and trust in and were obedient to Jesus and persevered will live forever in the presence of God, Jesus and the Holy Spirit on the new earth God will create after the great white throne judgement (Revelation 21:.1-6).

Events Associated with the Tribulation and Great Tribulation

Three overlapping layers of events will occur during the tribulation and great tribulation. There will be events that will:

- Occur in heaven;
- Be associated with judgments of God (seal, trumpet and bowl judgments) on earth; and
- Be associated with individuals and groups of individuals on earth. These will include the Antichrist, the false prophet, the two witnesses, the 144,000 Jewish witnesses from the twelve tribes of Israel, the unrighteous, the saints, and the remnant of Israel who will go into hiding in the wilderness.

Daniel described in Daniel 7:1-8 a dream and visions he had in which he saw four great beasts come up from the sea. Gabriel told him these beasts represented four kings who will rise from the earth. The bests were:

- A **lion** with the wings of an eagle (Daniel 7:4). The king represented by the first beast is Nebuchadnezzar who was the king of Babylon;

- A **bear** raised up on one side (Daniel 7:5). The king represented by the second beast is Cyrus who was the king of the Medo-Persian Empire where Persia was the dominant partner;

- A **leopard** with four wings on its back and four heads (Daniel 7:6). The king represented by the third beast is Alexander the great who was the king of the Grecian Empire. This empire was divided into four parts after his death.

- A **terrifying, frightening and extremely strong beast with large iron teeth who devoured, crushed and trampled its prey and who had ten horns, among which a little horn emerged** (Daniel 7:7-8). The fourth beast represented the Roman Empire that was controlled by Rome and its kings. The ten horns on the fourth beast, among which emerged a little horn, represented ten kings and the Antichrist who will appear during the end time. They are presumed to come from a revived Roman Empire because the fourth beast represented the Roman Empire. The Bible, however, does not address a future revived Roman Empire.

Note: The Holy Roman Empire that existed from 800 to 1806 was formed from countries that are now in Central and Eastern Europe. The region occupied by these countries was the western region of the former Roman Empire. Therefore, the forty-seven kings of the Holy Roman Empire considered their empire to be a successor of the former Roman Empire. Countries that formed the Holy Roman Empire are now in the European Union. Therefore, the European Union may be the revived Roman Empire from which ten kings and the Antichrist will come during the end time.

- The fourth beast in Daniel's dream and vision was describe as (Daniel 7:7-8):

  "... dreadful and terrifying and extremely strong; and it had large iron teeth. It devoured and crushed, and trampled down the remainder with its feet; and it was different from all the beasts that were before it, and it had ten horns. While [Daniel] was contemplating the horns, behold, another horn, a little one, came up among them, and three of the first horns were pulled out by the roots before it; and behold, this horn possessed eyes like the eyes of a man, and a mouth uttering great boasts."

Daniel's vision continued to include the setting up of a court with thrones, among which the Ancient of Days (God) took His seat (Daniel 7:9-10), and where the Son of Man (Jesus) was presented before the Ancient of Days (Daniel 7:13-14). Two actions occurred in Daniels vision of this court:

- The beast represented by the little horn, who represents the Antichrist, was slain and its body was destroyed (Daniel 7:11).
- The Son of Man (Jesus) was given "dominion, Glory and a kingdom" in which all the people and nations of the earth will serve Him. His dominion will be an everlasting dominion that will not pass away, and His kingdom will never be destroyed (Daniel 7:14).

Daniel in his vision requested Gabriel to explain the meaning of the (Daniel 7:19):

- Fourth beast with ten horns; and
- The little horn that came up among the ten horns and that had eyes like a man and a mouth that uttered great boasts, and which was larger in appearance than its associates who:

> "... was waging war against the saints and overpowering them until the Ancient of Days came, and judgment was passed in favor of the saints of the Highest One, and the time arrived when the saints took possession of the kingdom (Daniel 7:21-22)."

Gabriel and other angels revealed the following to Daniel:

- The fourth beast in Daniel 7:7-8 represented a fourth kingdom that will be different from other kingdoms (Daniel 7:23-27). The beast had ten horns that represented ten kings who will come from this fourth kingdom. The little horn represented an eleventh king who will come among the ten kings and who will subdue three of the ten kings.
- The following was revealed to Daniel regarding the little horn (Daniel 8:23-25):

> "And in the latter period of their rule, when the transgressors have run their course, a king will arise insolent and skilled in intrigue. And his power will be mighty, but not by his own power, and he will destroy to an extraordinary degree and prosper and perform his will; he will destroy mighty men and the holy people. And through his shrewdness he will cause deceit to succeed by his influence; and he will magnify himself in his heart and he will destroy many while they are at ease. He will even oppose the Prince of princes, but he will be broken without human agency."

The king represented by the little horn is the Antichrist who will receive his power from Satan. His kingdom is referred to as Babylon the great in Revelation 17 and 18. He will oppose the Prince of princes (Jesus) and wear down the saints of the Most High who will be given into his hands for a time span of a time, times and half a time (1,260 days) during the great tribulation (Daniel 7:25, Revelation 13:5-7). The court will sit for judgement and the Antichrist's dominion will be taken from him, annihilated and destroyed forever (Daniel 7:26). The angel then stated in Daniel 7:27:

> "Then the sovereignty, the dominion and the greatness of all the kingdoms under the whole heaven will be given to the people of the saints of the Highest One; His kingdom will be an everlasting kingdom, and all the dominions will serve and obey Him."

This kingdom will be Jesus' 1,000 year kingdom that will be established after the great tribulation and continue to the new earth God will create after the great white throne judgement (Revelation 20:11-15 and 21:1-9)

- The time of distress such as never occurred since there was a nation until that time will be the great tribulation that will occur over a time span of a time, times and half a time (1,260 days) (Daniel 12:1-4) (Figure 9).
- The time span between the suspension of temple sacrifices and abomination of desolation and the end of the great tribulation will be 1,290 days (Daniel 12:11) (Figure 9).
- Daniel stated in Daniel 12:12, "How blessed is he who keeps waiting and attains to the 1,335 days!" This is the time span between the abomination of desolation and the time Jesus will establish His 1,000 year kingdom (Figure 9).

Other events not mentioned above that will occur during the tribulation and great tribulation include:

- Two witnesses will prophesy for 1,260 days, starting during the first week of the tribulation (Revelation 11:3-12) (Figure 9).
- Saints will be raptured when the seventh trumpet is sounded during the middle of the tribulation (1 Corinthians 15:51-52, 2 Thessalonians 2:1-4) (Figure 9).
- Gentiles will occupy and control Jerusalem during the great tribulation for 42 months (1,260 days) (Revelation 11:2) (Figure 9).
- The remnant from Israel will go into hiding in a place prepared for them in the wilderness for a time span of a time, times and half a time (1,260 days) (Revelation 12:6, 14) (Figure 9).
- The Antichrist will make war with the saints and overcome them during the great tribulation for a time span of a time, tines and half a time or 42 months (1,260 days) (Revelation 13:5-7, Daniel 7:21) (Figure 9).

INVASION OF ISRAEL BY RUSSIA AND ITS ALLIES

Ezekiel in Ezekiel 38 and 39 described a future invasion of Israel by Rosh (modern day northern Russia) and its allies. Ezekiel 38:5-6 identifies Rosh's allies. They will include:

Magog – modern day Kazakhstan, Kirghizia, Uzbekistan, Turkmenistan, and Tajikistan
Meshek, Tubal, Gomer and Beth Togarmah – modern day regions in Turkey
Persia – modern day Iran
Cush (ancient Ethiopia) – modern day Sudan
Put – modern day Libya

These countries, except for Russia, surround Israel in the Middle East, and they all are Muslim countries.

Ezekiel did not indicate when Israel will be invaded in the future. However, Bible commentators indicate this invasion may occur before the start of the tribulation. A justification for this is found in Ezekiel 39:9-10 where he indicated the weapons of the defeated armies of the invaders of Israel will provide fuel for fires in the cities of Israel for seven years (the length of the tribulation).

Ezekiel indicated in Ezekiel 38:1-4 God will draw Russia and its allies out to invade Israel. Their motivation for the invasion will be to plunder the wealth of Israel. It will be impossible for Israel to defend itself against this invasion. Therefore, Ezekiel indicated God will intervene to defend Israel, and He will defeat the armies of Russia and its allies. The LORD stated in Ezekiel 38:21-23:

> "'I will call for a sword against him on all My mountains,' declares the LORD God. 'Every man's sword will be against his brother. With pestilence and with blood I will enter into judgment with him; and I will rain on him and on his troops, and on the many peoples who are with him, a torrential rain, with hailstone, fire and brimstone. I will magnify Myself, sanctify Myself, and make Myself known in the sight of many nations and they will know that I am the LORD.'"."

God will magnify and sanctify Himself through His actions and make Himself known in the sight of many nations through these actions.

CHAPTER 8
THE TRIBULATION
DAYS 1 - 1,267

THE TRIBULATION – THE SEVENTYTH WEEK

Daniel indicated in Daniel 9:24 that seventy weeks have been decreed for Israel to finish:

> "... the transgressions, to make an end of sin, to make attornment for iniquities, to bring in everlasting righteousness, to seal up vision and prophecy and to anoint the most holy place."

A discussion associated with this decree in Daniel 9:24-27 is presented in the beginning of Chapter 7. Sixty-nine weeks, which represent 483 years, associated with this decree have been completed. The seventieth week remains to be completed. This week that represents seven years will be the tribulation and great tribulation.

It is unknown when the tribulation will occur in the future. However, Bible commentators indicate the tribulation will begin after Israel has been invaded by Russia and its allies. This invasion that is described in Ezekiel 38 and 39 is discussed at the end of Chapter 7. A seven year covenant that guarantees Israel's security and right to exist will be approved by the Antichrist and Israel after the armies that invaded Israel have been destroyed by God (Ezekiel 38:21-23). This covenant that is described in Daniel 9:27 stated:

> "And he will make a firm covenant with the many for one week, but in the middle of the week he will put a stop to sacrifice and grain offering; and on the wing of abominations will come one who makes desolate, even until a complete destruction, one that is decreed, is poured out on the one who makes desolate."

The "he" and "one who makes desolate" in this verse refer to the Antichrist, and "the many" refers to Israel. The tribulation will begin after this covenant is adopted.

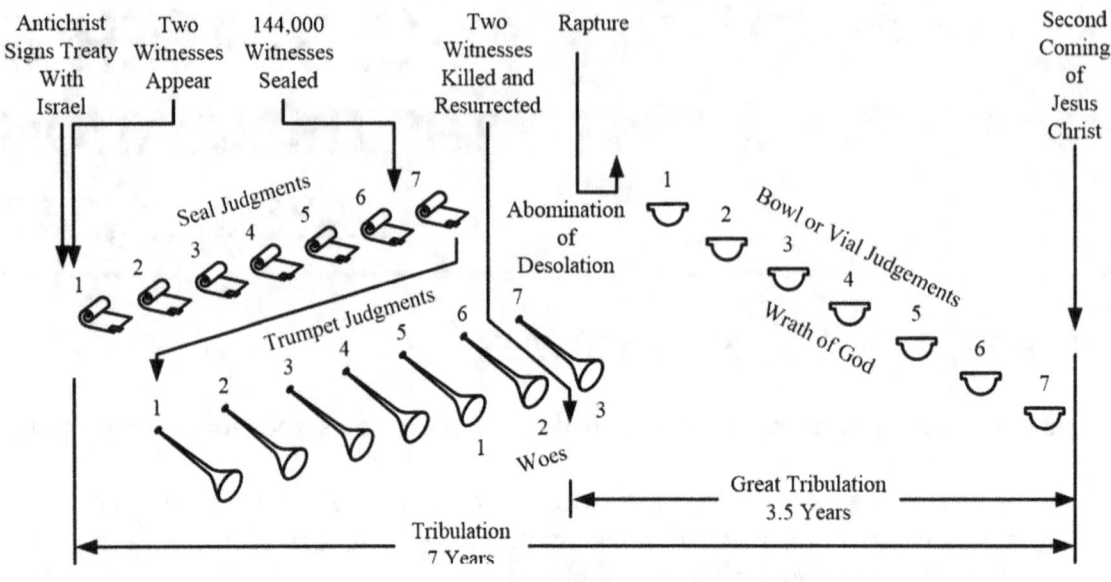

Figure 10

EVENTS THAT WILL OCCUR DURING DAYS 1 - 1,267

Several events will occur during the first 1,267 days of the tribulation (Figures 9 and 10). These events will include:

- Two witnesses from God who will appear at the beginning of the tribulation and prophesy for 1,260 days, after which they will be murdered by the false prophet, as indicated in Revelation 11:3, 7 (Figure 10):

   "And I will grant authority to my two witnesses, and they will prophesy for twelve hundred and sixty days, clothed in sackcloth. ... When they have finished their testimony, the beast that comes up out of the abyss will make war with them, and overcome them and kill them."

- 144,000 witnesses from the 12 tribes of Israel will be sealed with the seal of the living God (Revelation 7:4-8). This will occur before the seventh seal judgment (Figure 10). They will spread the gospel of Jesus throughout the earth for the remainder of the first 1,267 days of the tribulation (Figures 10).

- Seven seal and six trumpet judgments (Figure 10) will occur during the first 1,267 days of the tribulation (Revelation 6-11) (Figure 10).

THE SEAL JUDGMENTS

The seal judgments will be the first seven judgments that will start near the beginning of the tribulation (Figure 10). Only the Lamb (Jesus) who is in heaven will be worthy and able to take the scroll and open the seven seals (Revelation 5:1-14). The first four seals are associated with four different riders on four different horses. John saw the following when the Lamb opened the seven seals of the scroll:

1st Seal: When the Lamb opened the first seal, a rider on a white horse who held a bow and was given a crown appeared and "he went out conquering, and to conquer." (Revelation 6: 2)

2nd Seal: When the Lamb opened the second seal, a rider on a red horse went out, and:

> "... to him who set on it, it was granted to take peace from the earth, and that men should slay one another; and a great sword was given to him." (Revelation 6:4)

3rd Seal: When the Lamb opened the third seal, a rider on a black horse appeared, "and he who sat on it had a pair of scales in his hand." When John saw this rider, he heard the four living creatures around the throne of God say:

> "A quart of wheat for a denarius, and three quarts of barley for a denarius; and do not harm the oil and the wine." (Revelation 6: 5-6)

4th Seal: When the Lamb opened the fourth seal, a rider on a pale horse went forth. This rider had the name of Death, and Hades was following him.

> "And authority was given to them over a fourth of the earth, to kill with the sword and with famine and with pestilence and by the wild beasts of the earth." (Revelation 6:8)

5th Seal: When the Lamb opened the fifth seal, John:

> "... saw underneath the altar the souls of those who had been slain because of the word of God, and because of the testimony which they had maintained."

These saints:

> "Were told they should rest for a little while longer, until the number of their fellow servants and their brethren who were to be killed even as they had been, should be completed."

John was given a vision of the saints who had been martyred and who will be martyred during the first 1,267 days of the tribulation because of their public testimony to their trust and faith in Jesus as their Lord and Savior with the opening of the fifth seal. (Revelation 6:9-11)

6th Seal: When the Lamb opened the sixth seal, John saw a great earthquake where:

> "... the sun became black as sackcloth made of hair, and the whole moon became like blood; and the stars of the sky fell to the earth, as a fig tree casts its unripe figs when shaken by a great wind. And the sky was split apart like a scroll when it is rolled up; and every mountain and island were moved out of their places."

This earthquake will be like none that will have preceded it. According to its description, it will cause horrendous devastation throughout the world. (Revelation 6:12-17).

7th Seal: When the seventh seal was opened by the Lamb, there was silence in heaven for about one-half hour. The opening of the seventh seal will mark the beginning of the seven trumpet judgments (Revelation 8:1-5). The silence in heaven possibly was in response to a change in the nature of the seven trumpet judgments that will follow, as compared to the nature of the previous six seal judgments.

The seal judgements will be associated with actions of people on earth and from acts of nature. The first four seal judgments will be associated with actions of the Antichrist to set up and consolidate his control of earth. This will result in wars, famines and deaths of people on earth. The fifth seal judgement will be associated with an event viewed in heaven. The major earthquake associated with the sixth seal judgement will be an act of nature. Therefore, people on earth may fail to recognize the judgements of God in these actions and events.

Ten kings will form a ten kingdom federation that will be controlled by the Antichrist before the start of the tribulation. Chapters 7 and 19 present information regarding the formation of this federation. The rider on the white horse in the first seal judgement represents the Antichrist who sets out to conquer the earth, as described in Daniel 7, 8 and 11.

Daniel was told in Daniel 11:38 the Antichrist will "honor a god of fortresses," indicating he may use military force to accomplish his objectives. Three kings in the ten kingdom federation may be subdued by the Antichrist (Daniel 7:20) during a war with them. The rider on the red horse in the second seal judgement symbolizes war.

Famines have followed devastating region and global wars in the past. A possible Third World War before the start of the tribulation and regional wars associated with the Antichrist's effort to consolidate his control over the earth will result in famines. Chapter 19 addresses the possibility of a Third World War before the start of the tribulation. The rider on the black horse in the third seal judgement symbolizes famine.

Death is a consequence of wars and famines. Therefore, the rider on the pale horse in the fourth seal judgement symbolizes death. This rider is given the name of Death, and Hades will follow him. Hades is the location of the dead whose names are not written in the book of life.

The devastation from regional wars associated with the Antichrist's rise to power and the aftermath of a possible Third World War before the start of the tribulation may result in a global famine associated with the third seal judgement. These wars and resulting famine will result in the deaths of one-fourth of the earth's population (Revelation 6:8).

The four horses and riders in the first four seal judgements are associated with the Antichrist's rise to power. He will be the king of the ten kingdom federation at the start of the tribulation, and he will become a global dictator at the beginning of the great tribulation. Chapters 7 and 19 present information on the Antichrist's rise to power.

The Bible does not indicate the time over which the first four seal judgements will occur. It is reasonable to presume the first four seal judgements may occur within the first year of the tribulation, given the desire of the Antichrist to consolidate his control over the earth and his use of war to accomplish this.

John was given a vision of saints who had been martyred from the birth of Christianity to the beginning of the tribulation and who will be martyred during the first 1,267 days of the tribulation when the Lamb opened the fifth seal (Figure 9). The Antichrist will not be given authority to make war against and overcome saints during the first 1,267 days of the tribulation that he will be given during the 1,260 days of the great tribulation. Nevertheless, he will still hate saints and persecute and cause many of them to be murdered. Also, those who have not and will not accept Jesus as their Savior during the tribulation will hate, persecute, and murder saints.

The earth will suffer a major catastrophic earthquake after the wars and famine that will occur during the first four seal judgments, and there will be terrifying disturbances in the heavens. Jesus stated concerning these events in Luke 21:9-11:

> "When you hear of wars and disturbances, do not be terrified; for these things must take place first, but the end does not follow immediately. ... Nation will rise against nation, and kingdom against kingdom, and there will be great earthquakes, and in various places plagues and famines; and there will be terrors and great signs from heaven."

The large magnitude of the earthquake associated with the sixth seal judgment is implied by the statement in Revelation 6:14:

> "And the sky was split apart like a scroll when it is rolled up; and every mountain and island were moved out of their places."

The splitting apart and rolling up of the sky is a phenomenon that occurs during a nuclear explosion. This implies there may possibly be huge volcanic eruptions and explosions during this earthquake that will cause the sky to split and roll up. The magnitude of this earthquake is also implied in what John observed after his vision of the earthquake in Revelation 6:15-17:

> "And the kings of the earth and the great men and the commanders and the rich and the strong and every slave and free man, hid themselves in the caves and among the rocks of the mountains; and they said to the mountains and to the rocks, 'Fall on us and hide us from the presence of Him who sits on the throne, and from the wrath of the Lamb; for the great day of their wrath has come; and who is able to stand?'"

This earthquake will get the attention of the people of earth. They may begin to recognize the judgments of God are being directed against them if they did not recognize this before this event.

John saw a "angel ascending from the rising of the sun" who had the seal of the living God before the Lamb opened the seventh seal (Revelation 7:1-3). This angel cried out to four other angels who were standing at the four corners of the earth, holding back the four winds of the earth, and to whom it was granted the power to harm the earth and the sea. He commanded them:

> "Do not harm the earth or the sea or the trees, until we have sealed the bondservants of our God on their foreheads."

The bondservants to whom the angel referred will be the 144,000 Jewish witnesses who will receive the seal of the living God on their foreheads between the sixth and seventh seal judgments.

THE TRUMPET JUDGMENTS

John saw seven angels standing before God who were given seven trumpets when the Lamb opened the seventh seal (Revelation 8:2-6) (Figure 10). Then he saw another angel who stood at the altar before the throne of God with a golden censer filled with much incense that represented the prayers of the saints, which continually went up before God. The angel then filled the censer with fire from the altar and threw it to the earth, and "there followed pearls of thunder and sounds and flashes of lightning and an earthquake." The seven angels then prepared to sound their trumpets. The seven trumpet judgment that follow will begin to give a clear indication God is responsible for the judgments.

1st Trumpet: When the first trumpet sounded:

> "... there came hail and fire, mixed with blood, and they were thrown to the earth; and a third of the earth was burned up, and a third of the trees were burned up, and all the green grass was burned up (Revelation 8:7)."

Trees and green vegetation supply oxygen that is needed to support breathing. The destruction of one-third of the green vegetation and all the green grass will result in a major ecological disaster. Plant life was the first type of life to be created on earth during the third day of creation (Genesis 1:11-13), and it will be the first type of life to be destroyed during the trumpet judgments.

2nd Trumpet: When the second trumpet sounded:

> "... something like a great mountain burning with fire was thrown into the sea; and a third of the sea became blood; and a third of the creatures, which were in the sea and had life, died; and a third of the ships were destroyed (Revelation 8:8-9)."

This possibly refers to a flaming meteor that will fall into one of the earth's oceans. The resulting tsunami waves from this meteor will destroy one-third of the earth's ships, along with many of the coastal regions around the earth. One-third of the saltwater oceans and seas will become red like blood (possibly from a toxic red algae), and one-third of the saltwater ocean and sea animals will die. Birds of the air and sea animals were the second types of life to be created on the fifth day of creation (Genesis 1:20-23), and the sea animals will be the second type of life to die during the trumpet judgments.

3rd Trumpet: When the third trumpet sounded:

> "... a great star fell from heaven, burning like a torch, and it fell on a third of the rivers and on the springs of waters; and the name of the star is called Wormwood; and a third of the waters became wormwood, and many men died from the waters, because they were made bitter (Revelation 8:10-11)."

This possibly refers to another flaming meteor that will experience a massive air burst over the earth. The debris from this meteor will be dispersed throughout the earth and pollute and poison many fresh water lakes, streams and rivers around the earth. Wormwood usually refers to calamity and injustice when used in the Bible. Even though the first two trumpet judgments will result in ecological disasters, the third trumpet judgment will result in an even greater ecological disaster. Wormwood is a bitter plant. The reference to a third of the waters becoming wormwood indicates one-third of the fresh water lakes, streams and rivers of the earth will become bitter or poisoned. This trumpet judgment is the first trumpet judgment that specifically states men and women will die because of it.

4th Trumpet: When the fourth trumpet sounded:

> "... a third of the sun and a third of the moon and a third of the stars were smitten, so that a third of them might be darkened and the day might not shine for a third of it, and the night in the same way (Revelation 8:12)."

The debris associated with the meteor impacts of the previous two trumpet judgments will be thrown into the upper atmosphere and spread around the earth. It will block the light from the sun, moon and stars and prevent a third of the light from reaching the surface of the earth. God made the sun, moon and stars "to give light to the earth and to govern the day and the night and to separate the light from the darkness on the fourth day of creation (Genesis 16:19)." Many of the ecological and life cycles on earth depend on a proper balance between sunlight during the day and moonlight during the night. This is particularly true for growing cycles of plants, vegetation and food. Reducing light from the sun, moon and stars by one-third will have a catastrophic effect on these cycles.

5th Trumpet: This trumpet judgement will be the first of three woes the earth will experience. A prince of Satan named Apollyon had the key to the abyss when the fifth trumpet sounded (Revelation 9:1-12). Smoke like that from a great furnace came forth that darkened the sun and air when he opened the opening to the abyss. Hordes of locust-like creatures came forth from this smoke who had the power to sting like scorpions. John described these locusts like creatures in Revelation 9:7-10:

"The appearance of the locusts was like horses prepared for battle; and on their heads, as it were, crowns like gold, and their faces were like the faces of men. And they had hair like the hair of women, and their teeth were like the teeth of lions. And they had breastplates like breastplates of iron; and the sound of their wings was like the sound of chariots, of many horses rushing to battle. And they have tails like scorpions, and stings; and in their tails is their power to hurt men for five months. These locusts will possibly be small demonic creatures who will be under the control of Satan. They will be prohibited from destroying or eating any green vegetation. They will only be allowed to attack men and women who do not have the seal of God on their foreheads. They will not be allowed to kill these men and women, but their sting, which will be like the sting of a scorpion, will cause torment in their victims that will last for five months. This torment will be so severe men and women who are stung will want to die, but they will not be allowed to die. This judgment is the first one that will be specifically directed at men and women who have rejected the lordship of Jesus. It will result in immerse suffering even though it will not result in their death."

6th Trumpet: This trumpet judgment will be the second of three woes the earth will experience. When the sixth trumpet sounded, the angel who sounded the trumpet was instructed to (Revelation 9:14-15):

"Release the four angels who are bound at the great river Euphrates. And the four angels, who had been prepared for the hour and day and month and year, were released, so that they might kill a third of mankind. And the number of the armies of the horsemen was two hundred million."

John saw regarding the horsemen (Revelation 9:17-19):

"The riders had breastplates the color of fire and of hyacinth and of brimstone; and the heads of the horses are like the heads of lions; and out of their mouths proceed fire and smoke and brimstone. A third of mankind was killed by these three plagues, by the fire and the smoke and the brimstone, which proceeded out of their mouths. For the power of the horses is in their mouths and in their tails; for their tails are like serpents and have heads; and with them they do harm."

These horsemen may also be demonic and under Satan's control. The demonic creatures in the fifth trumpet judgment will only be allowed to inflict suffering on men and women who have rejected the lordship of Jesus. The demonic creatures in this trumpet judgment will be allowed to kill men and women who have rejected the lordship of Jesus, up to one third of the earth's population.

7th Trumpet: This trumpet judgment will be the third of three woes the earth will experience. This trumpet judgment will be discussed later.

"There was silence in heaven for about half an hour" when the seventh seal was opened by the Lamb, ushering in the seven trumpet judgments (Revelation 8:1). This may be a time of mourning in heaven for what will occur on earth when the seven trumpet judgments are executed. The trumpet judgments will be directed at specific parts of the earth and its people. The first four trumpet judgments will be directed at:

- Plants, trees and vegetation (1st trumpet);
- The oceans and seas and ocean and sea animals (2nd trumpet);
- Freshwater lakes, streams and rivers (3rd trumpet); and
- The sun, moon and stars (4th trumpet).

These four trumpet judgments will result in catastrophic ecological crises that will result in the deaths of many people on earth. The next two trumpet judgments will be directed at men and women who have rejected the lordship of Jesus. The seventh trumpet judgment, which will be presented in the next chapter, will be associated with the beginning of the reign of Jesus over the "kingdom of the world (Revelation 11:15)."

Between the sounding of the fourth and fifth trumpets, John saw and heard (Revelation 8:13):

> "... an eagle flying in mid heaven, saying with a loud voice, 'Woe, woe, woe, to those who dwell on the earth, because of the remaining blasts of the trumpet of the three angels who are about to sound!'"

Therefore, the fifth through seventh trumpet judgments are referred to as the three woes. The warning from the eagle between the fourth and fifth trumpet judgments will signify a major shift in the nature of the judgments God will execute on the inhabitants of the earth. The judgments associated with the sounding of the first four trumpets will be directed against nonhuman elements of God's creation on the earth. However, the judgments associated with the sounding of the last three trumpets will be directed against men and women who have rejected the lordship of Jesus.

One would expect individuals to turn to Jesus as their Savior after experiencing the events associated with the seal and trumpet judgments because of the catastrophic nature of these judgments. Over one-half of the earth's population will be killed by the seven seal and six trumpet judgments, but John observed after the completion of his vision of the sixth trumpet judgement (Revelation 9:20-21):

> "And the rest of mankind, who were not killed by these plagues, did not repent of the works of their hands, so as not to worship demons, and the idols of gold and of silver and of brass and of stone and of wood, which can neither see nor hear nor walk; and they did not repent of their murders nor of their sorceries nor of their immorality nor of their thefts."

EVANGELISM DURING THE FIRST 1,267 DAYS OF THE TRIBULATION

Jesus stated concerning the beginning of the great tribulation in Matthew 24:14:

> "And this gospel of the kingdom shall be preached in the whole world for a witness to all the nations, and then the end shall come."

The context in which Jesus made this statement implied the gospel of the kingdom of God will be proclaimed to all nations and peoples of earth before the abomination of desolation occurs during the middle of the tribulation. This implies the first 1,267 days of the tribulation may be a time of intense worldwide evangelism.

Gabriel stated to Daniel in Daniel 12:10 regarding the tribulation. He stated:

> "Many will be purged, purified and refined; but the wicked will act wickedly, and none of the wicked will understand; but those who have insight will understand."

This statement implies the wicked will continue to act wickedly during the tribulation, and they will not understand what is at stake regarding the judgments of God. However, saints will understand what is occurring, and they will share the gospel of Jesus with others, so those who have not accepted Jesus as Lord and Savior will have an opportunity to do so before it is too late. The Bible implies saints will be present during the first 1,267 days of the tribulation and will be involved in spreading the gospel of Jesus along with the 144,000 Jewish witnesses.

John was given two visions of others who will be servants of God and involved in witnessing the gospel of Jesus during the first 1,267 days of the tribulation.

1st Vision: The first vision was the sealing of 144,000 Jewish witnesses from the twelve tribes of Israel with the seal of the living God (Revelation 7:8). 12,000 from each of the twelve tribes will be sealed with the seal of God on their foreheads before the opening of the seventh seal by the Lamb (Figure 10). When this will occur during the first 1,267 days of the tribulation is unknown even though we know it will occur before the opening of the seventh seal.

2nd Vision: The second vision was associated with the two witnesses who Bible commentators believe may be either Elijah and Enoch or Elijah and Moses (Revelation 11:4-5). They will be given power to prophesy for 1,260 days before they will be murdered by the false prophet. They will:

> "... have the power to shut up the sky, in order that rain may not fall during the days of their prophesying; and they [will] have power over the waters to turn them into blood; and to smite the earth with every plague, as often as they desire (Revelation 11:6.)."

The exact time these two witnesses will first appear is not known. However, referring to Figures 9 and 10 and assuming the witnesses will be killed before the abomination of desolation, they may first appear during the first week of the tribulation.

John indicated the 144,000 witnesses and the two witnesses will receive special protection during the first 1,267 days of the tribulation. He stated the 144,000 witnesses will not be harmed during the fifth trumpet judgement. The demonic creatures in this judgment will not be allowed to sting anyone who has the seal of God on his/her forehead (Revelation 9:4). It can be presumed the 144,000 witnesses will not be harmed during the sixth trumpet judgment since this judgment is also associated with demonic creatures. John does not indicate the 144,000 witnesses will be protected during the other judgments of God during the first 1,267 days of the tribulation. However, they may receive special protection during these judgments.

No one will be able to harm the two witnesses during the 1,260 days they will be given power to prophesy. John stated in Revelation 11:4-6:

> "And if anyone desires to harm them, fire proceeds out of their mouth and devours their enemies; and if anyone would desire to harm them, in this manner he must be killed."

The false prophet at the end of 1,260 days will be given power to kill the two witnesses (Revelation 11:7-14). This will occur near the end of the first 1,267 days of the tribulation. Their bodies will lie on the ground for three and one-half days, after which they will be resurrected. A major earthquake will occur in Jerusalem during the hour they are resurrected, destroying a tenth of the city and killing 7,000 people. This earthquake will mark the end of the second woe (Revelation 11:14).

John does not indicate in Revelation whether saints (separate from the 144,000 sealed Jews) will be given special protection during the first 1,267 days of the tribulation. His vision of martyred Christians in the opening of the fifth seal (Revelation 6:9-11) indicates saints will be persecuted and martyred during the first 1,267 days of the tribulation. Jesus stated concerning this in Luke 21:12-17:

> "But before all these things they will lay their hands on you and will persecute you, delivering you to the synagogues and prisons, bringing you before kings and governors for My name's sake. It will lead to an opportunity for your testimony. So make up your minds not to prepare beforehand to defend yourselves; for I will give you utterance and wisdom which none of your opponents will be able to resist or refute. But you will be delivered up even by parents and brothers and relatives and friends, and they will put some of you to death, and you will be hated by all on account of My name."

Those who do and do not follow Jesus will be killed during seal and trumpet Judgements that will occur during the first 1,267 days of the tribulation. Possible exceptions may be during the fifth and sixth trumpet judgments.

The Bible indicates we are given authority in the name of Jesus over Satan and demons who follow him. James stated in James 4:2, "Submit therefore to God. Resist the devil and he will flee from you." John stated in 1 John 4:4:

> "You are from God little children and have overcome them; because greater
> is He who is in you than he who is in the world."

The second "he" in John's statement refers to Satan. God will allow him to use demonic creatures in the fifth and sixth trumpet judgments to inflict suffering and death on the wicked. However, God has given saints authority in the name of Jesus over Satan and his demons. Therefore, it is reasonable to presume:

- The authority given to saints over Satan and demons in the New Testament will also be given to them during the tribulation;

- Saints may be spared from suffering and death associated with the fifth and sixth trumpet judgments; and
- Saints may spread the gospel of Jesus along with the 144,,000 Jewish witnesses during the first 1,267 days of the tribulation.

FALSE CHRISTS AND FALSE PROPHETS

Jesus indicated many false Christs and prophets who will mislead many will arise during the first 1,267 days of the tribulation. Jesus stated in his discourse on the end of the age (Matthew 24:5, 11):

> "For many will come in My name, saying, 'I am the Christ,' and will mislead many. ... And many false prophets will arise, and will mislead many."

REBUILDING OF THE TEMPLE IN JERUSALEM

The Temple will be rebuilt, and temple sacrifices will be initiated during the first 1,267 days of the tribulation. When these will occur is not known. John in his vision was told in Revelation 11:1-2 "to measure the temple of God, and the altar, and those who worship in it." Gabriel told Daniel in Daniel 9:27 the Antichrist will put a stop to sacrifice and grain offering during the middle of the tribulation.

TIME FRAME OF THE SEAL AND TRUMPET JUDGMENTS

The sequence of the seal and trumpet judgments during the first 1,267 days of the tribulation is presented in Revelation and in this chapter. However, the times when these judgments will occur is unknown. The first four seal judgments may occur during the first year of the tribulation. The following can be stated with some certainty:

- There will be around a five-month gap between the fifth and sixth trumpet judgments (Revelation 9:10). This gap may be longer, depending on the time the demonic creatures associated with the fifth trumpet judgment will be given to afflict men and women who do not have the seal of God on their foreheads.
- The seventh trumpet will not be sounded until after the two witnesses have been killed and resurrected (Revelation 11:14-15). The seventh trumpet judgement may not occur until just before or at the beginning of the middle of the tribulation (Figure 9). The killing and resurrection of the two witnesses will mark a major turning point in the tribulation.

THE FINISHING OF THE MYSTERY OF GOD

After the sounding of the sixth trumpet but before the end of the second woe, John saw in his vision and heard (Revelation 10:5-7):

> "And the angel whom I saw standing on the sea and on the land lifted up his right hand to heaven, and swore by Him who lives forever and ever, who created heaven and the things in it, and the earth and the things in it, and the sea and the things in it, that there shall be delay no longer, but in the days of the voice of the seventh angel, when he is about to sound, then the mystery of God is finished, as he preached to His servants the prophets."

What mystery of God will be finished "in the days of the voice of the seventh angel" is not known. However, we can speculate. There are four mysteries in the New Testament that have not been finished or fully revealed. The main mystery of these four is stated by Paul in Ephesians 1:9-10:

> "[God] made known to us the mystery of His will, according to His kind intentions which He purposed in [Christ] with a view to an administration suitable to the fullness of the times, that is, the summing up of all things in Christ, things in the heavens and things upon the earth. In Him also we have obtained an inheritance, having been predestined according to His purpose who works all things after the counsel of His will, to the end that we who were the first to hope in Christ should be to the praise of His glory. In Him, you also, after listening to the message of truth, the gospel of your salvation - having also believed, you were sealed in Him with the Holy Spirit of promise, who is given as a pledge of our inheritance, with a view to the redemption of God's own possession, to the praise of His glory."

Paul made the following observations concerning this mystery:

- All things in heaven and on earth will find their final completion in Jesus.
- We have as saints received an inheritance according to God's purpose, which is salvation through our faith in Jesus. This inheritance is sealed with the Holy Spirit, who is given to us as a pledge of our inheritance.
- God will redeem His possessions. These include us and the nation of Israel.
- God will administer His will as He purposes in the fullness of time to the praise of His own glory. These will find their final completion during the tribulation.

Three other mysteries that have not been finished will be associated with the completion of the mystery of God's will during the middle of the tribulation.

1st Mystery: The first mystery will be the rapture of the saints along with the Church from earth to heaven. Paul stated regarding this in 1 Corinthians 15: 51-52:

> "Behold, I tell you a mystery; we shall not all sleep, but we shall be changed, in a moment, in the twinkling of an eye, at the last trumpet; for the trumpet will sound, and the dead will be raised imperishable, and we shall be changed."

The trumpet referred to by Paul may be the seventh trumpet that will be sounded by the seventh angel during the middle of the tribulation.

2nd Mystery: The second mystery will be removing the restraints on the Antichrist, so he will be able to make war on and overcome the saints and rule over every tribe and people and tongue and nation (Revelation 13:7). Paul stated regarding this in 2 Thessalonians 2:6-9:

> "And you know what restrains [the man of lawlessness] now, so that in his time he may be revealed. For the mystery of lawlessness is already at work; only he who now restrains will do so until he is taken out of the way. And then that lawless one will be revealed whom the Lord will slay with the breath of his mouth and bring to an end by the appearance of his coming; that is, the one whose coming is in accord with the activity of Satan, with all power and signs and false wonders."

This will occur during the middle of the tribulation when the Antichrist will be given authority over all nations and people of the earth and allowed to overcome the saints.

3rd Mystery: The third mystery will be the redemption of the remnant from the nation of Israel. Paul stated regarding this in Romans 11:25-29:

> "For I do not want you, brethren, to be uninformed of this mystery, lest you be wise in your own estimation, that a partial hardening has happened to Israel until the fullness of the Gentiles has come in; and thus all Israel will be saved; just as it is written, 'The Deliverer will come from Zion, He will remove ungodliness from Jacob. And this is My covenant with them, when I take away their sins.' From the standpoint of the gospel they are enemies for your sake, but from the standpoint of God's choice they are beloved for the sake of the fathers; for the gifts and the calling of God are irrevocable."

Satan will make war against the people of Israel through the Antichrist when he is cast out of heaven with his angels. God has prepared a place in the wilderness where they will be able to escape and hide (Revelation 12:6, 14). The beginning of "the fullness of the Gentiles" will mark the beginning of the forty-two months the Antichrist will be given authority to control the nations of the earth (Revelation 13:5) and of when Gentiles will occupy Jerusalem (Revelation 11:2).

JUDGEMENT OF ISRAEL DURING THE TRIBULATION AND JACOB'S DISTRESS

God will judge Israel during the tribulation. Jeremiah 30 and 31 describes this judgement. God indicated, concerning Israel and Judah in Jeremiah 30:5-9, 11:

> "For thus says the LORD, 'I have heard a sound of terror,
> Of dread, and there is no peace.
> Ask now, and see if a male can give birth.
> Why do I see every man
> With his hands on his loins, as a woman in childbirth?
> And why have all faces turned pale?
> Alas! for that day is great,
> There is none like it;
> And it is the time of **Jacob's distress**,
> But he will be saved from it.'
> 'It shall come about on that day,' declares the LORD of hosts, 'that I will break
> his yoke from off their neck and will tear off their bonds; and strangers will
> no longer make them their slaves. But they shall serve the LORD their God
> and David their king whom I will raise up to them.'
> ...
>
> 'For I am with you,' declares the LORD, 'to save you;
> For I will destroy completely all the nations where I have scattered you,
> Only I will not destroy you completely.
> But I will chastise you justly
> And will by no means leave you unpunished.'"

God's judgement of Israel during the tribulation described in Jeremiah 30 and 31 is referred to as Jacob's distress or Jacob's troubles. God will destroy those nations where He will scatter the people of Israel during this judgment, but He will save and not completely destroy Israel. God will chastise and not let Israel go unpunished for their sins. However,

He will redeem Israel after the tribulation and establish a new covenant with them. He stated in Jeremiah 31:31-34:

> "'Behold, days are coming,' declares the LORD, 'when I will make a new covenant with the house of Israel and with the house of Judah, not like the covenant which I made with their fathers in the day I took them by the hand to bring them out of the land of Egypt, my covenant which they broke, although I was a husband to them,' declares the LORD. 'But this is the covenant which I will make with the house of Israel after those days,' declares the LORD, 'I will put my law within them, and on their heart I will write it; and I will be their God, and they shall be my people. And they shall not teach again, each man his neighbor and each man his brother, saying 'Know the LORD,' for they shall all know Me, from the least of them to the greatest of them,' declares the LORD, 'for I will forgive their iniquity, and their sin I will remember no more.'"

God will accomplish this by showing Israel He is their God and Jesus is their Savior.

CHAPTER 9
MIDDLE OF THE TRIBULATION
DAYS 1,267 - 1,297

EVENTS DURING THE MIDDLE OF THE TRIBULATION – DAYS 1,267 – 1,297

The middle of the tribulation will be between days 1,267 and 1,297 (Figure 9). This period is bracketed by the abomination of desolation by the Antichrist (Revelation 13:5-6) and the time the remnant of Israel will go into hiding in the wilderness and the saints will be given into the hands of the Antichrist, both for 1,260 days (Daniel 7:25, Revelation 12:5-6). Several events will occur during this 30 days. They include:

- Gentiles will have invaded and occupy Israel (Zechariah 13:8-9, Revelation 11:2).
- The Antichrist will be revealed (Revelation 13:1-4).
- The abomination of desolation by the Antichrist will occur, and he will put an end to sacrifices and offerings in the Temple (Daniel 9:27, 11:31, Matthew 24:15, 2 Thessalonians 2:4-10, Revelation 13:5-6).
- The false prophet will be revealed (Revelation 13:11-18).
- The seventh trumpet judgement and the rapture will occur.
  - "The kingdom of the earth will become the kingdom of our Lord, and of his Christ," and Jesus will take his great power and begin to reign (Revelation 11:15-17).
  - The rapture of the saints from earth to heaven by Jesus will occur after the abomination of desolation (Matthew 24,29-31, Luke 17:22-36, 1 Corinthians 15:51-52, 1 Thessalonians 4:13-17, 2 Thessalonians 2:1-4).
- War in heaven will occur, resulting in Satan and his angels being cast out of heaven and thrown down to earth (Revelation 12:7-12).
- War on earth will occur and one-third of the remnant of Israel will go into hiding for a period of 1,260 days in a place in the wilderness prepared for them by God (Daniel 11:41, Zechariah 13:8-9, Revelation 12:6, 14).

The times and sequence when these events will occur is unclear. However, the Bible presents clues to the times and sequence.

INVASION OF ISRAEL BY GENTILES

Jesus indicated in Matthew and Luke that Israel will be invaded by Gentiles before or during the tribulation. Daniel in Daniel 11:30-35 indicated this invasion will occur before the abomination of desolation. Jesus stated in Luke 21:20-24:

> "But when you see Jerusalem surrounded by armies, then recognize that her desolation is at hand. Then let those who are in Judea flee to the mountains, and let those who are in the midst of the city depart, and let not those who are in the country enter the city; because these are days of vengeance, in order that all things which are written may be fulfilled. Woe to those who are with child and to those who nurse babes in those days; for there will be great distress upon the land, and wrath to this people, and they will fall by the edge of the sword, and will be led captive into all the nations; and Jerusalem will be trampled underfoot by the Gentiles until the times of the Gentiles be fulfilled."

The desolation of Jerusalem when it "will be trampled underfoot by Gentiles until the times of the Gentiles be fulfilled" is the 42 months (1,260 days) in Revelation 11:2 when the holy city will be controlled by Gentiles. This control will occur during the great tribulation Jesus stated regarding the abomination of desolation in Matthew 24:15-18:

> "Therefore when you see the abomination of desolation which was spoken of through Daniel the prophet, standing in the holy place (let the reader understand), then let those who are in Judea flee to the mountains; let him who is on the housetop not go down to get the things out that are in his house; and let him who is in the field not turn back to get his cloak. But woe to those who are with child and to those who nurse babes in those days."

REVELING OF THE ANTICHRIST

John stated in Revelation 13:1-4:

> "Then I saw a beast coming up out of the sea, having ten horns and seven heads, and on his horns were ten diadems, and on his heads were blasphemous names. And the beast which I saw was like a leopard, and his feet were like those of a bear, and his mouth like the mouth of a lion. And the dragon gave him his power and his throne and great authority. I saw one of his heads as if it had been slain, and his fatal wound was healed. And

the whole earth was amazed and followed the beast, they worshiped the dragon because he gave his authority to the beast, and they worshiped the beast, saying, 'Who is like the beast, and who is able to wage war with him?'"

The dragon refers to Satan, and the beast coming out of the sea refers to the Antichrist. The Antichrist will possess some of the characteristics of the first three kings Gabriel revealed to Daniel in Daniel 7:4-6. The ten horns refer to ten kings who will rule with the Antichrist during the tribulation.

ABOMINATION OF DESOLATION

Gabriel indicated in Daniel 12:11 there will be 1,290 days between the abomination of desolation and the end of the tribulation (Daniel 12:11). Therefore, the abomination of desolation will occur on day 1,267 of the tribulation (Figure 9). The angel told John in Revelation 13:5-6:

> "There was given to him a mouth speaking arrogant words and blasphemies, and authority to act for forty-two months was given to him. And he opened his mouth in blasphemies against God, to blaspheme His name and His tabernacle, that is, those who dwell in heaven."

The Antichrist will be given authority to act for forty-two months (1,260 days), which is the length of the great tribulation. Gabriel stated regarding this event in Daniel 11:36-37:

> "Then the king will do as he pleases, and he will exalt and magnify himself above every god and will speak monstrous things against the God of gods, and he will prosper until the indignation is finished, for that which is decreed will be done. He will show no regard for the gods of his fathers or for the desire of women, nor will he show regard for any other god, for he will magnify himself above them all."

The king refers to the Antichrist who will magnify himself above all gods.

REVELING OF THE FALSE PROPHET

John was told in Revelation 13:11-18 that a second beast will arise from the earth. This beast will be the false prophet. He will possess all the powers of the Antichrist in his presence, and he will force people and nations of earth to worship the Antichrist and to receive his mark of the beast.

SEVENTH TRUMPET JUDGEMENT

The seventh angel will sound the seventh trumpet after the completion of the second woe, and the third woe will begin. A transition will occur on earth with the sounding of the seventh trumpet. John heard voices in heaven in his vision with the sounding of the seventh trumpet that said (Revelation 11:15):

> "The kingdom of the world has become the kingdom of our Lord, and of His Christ, and He will reign forever and ever."

John heard after this the twenty-four elders, who sit on their thrones before God, say (Revelation 11:17-18):

> "We give You thanks, O Lord God, the Almighty, who are and who were, because You have taken Your great power and have begun to reign. And the nations were enraged, and Your wrath came, and the time came for the dead to be judged, and the time to reward Your bondservants the prophets and saints and those who fear Your name, the small and the great, and to destroy those who destroy the earth."

Revelation 11:15 and 11:17-18 refer to the fulfillment of Daniel's prophesy in Daniel 7:14 in which he indicated Jesus will be given an everlasting dominion and a kingdom that will never be destroyed. The unsaved dead will be judged and the prophets and saints will receive their rewards during this transition. This may occur at or near the rapture of the saints if the seventh trumpet is the last trumpet Paul referred to in 1 Corinthians 15:51-54.

RAPTURE OF THE SAINTS

Paul stated in 2 Thessalonians 2:1-7 the rapture will occur after the abomination of desolation. The actual day and time when the rapture will occur are unknown. However, it may occur before the start of the great tribulation (day 1,297 in Figure 9). Saints who will receive Jesus as their Savior and Lord after the rapture will live on earth during the great tribulation. The Antichrist will martyr these saints in exceedingly large numbers during the great tribulation.

The rapture occurring before the great tribulation is consistent with what Jesus stated in the parable of the fig tree (Matthew 24:32-41). He indicated people will know summer is near when the branches of a fig tree become tender and put forth their leaves. People on earth during the tribulation who have received Jesus as their Savior and Lord will know the rapture is near by observing the nature of the days and events that will precede it. Jesus indicated the days that will precede the rapture will be like those in the time of Noah when God destroyed the earth with a flood (Exodus 6-9). These were days of lawlessness, rebellion against God, and moral decay. These will characterize the days during the tribulation that will precede the rapture.

There will be great signs and wonders in the heavens and on earth during the time preceding the rapture. Jesus stated in Luke 21:25-27:

> "And there will be signs in sun and moon and stars, and upon the earth dismay among nations, in perplexity at the roaring of the sea and the waves, men fainting from fear and the expectation of the things which are coming upon the world; for the powers of the heavens will be shaken. And then they will see the Son of Man coming in a cloud with power and great glory."

This statement by Jesus follows His statement in Luke 21:20-24 that addressed the invasion of Israel by Gentiles. This implies the rapture will occur after Israel is invaded by Gentiles. Jesus stated regarding the rapture in Luke 17:30-31, 34-36:

> "It will be just the same on the day that the Son of Man is revealed. On that day, let not the one who is on the housetop and whose goods are in the house go down to take them away; and likewise let not the one who is in the field turn back. ... I tell you, on that night there will be two men in one bed; one will be taken, and the other will be left. There will be two women grinding at the same place; one will be taken, and the other will be left. Two men will be in the field; one will be taken and the other will be left."

The beginning of Jesus' statement at the beginning of this verse is similar to His statement in Matthew 24:15-18. However, His statement in Matthew begins with:

> "Therefore when you see the ABOMINATION OF DESOLATION which was spoken of through Daniel the prophet."

Daniel indicated in Daniel 11:30-35 the invasion of Israel will precede the abomination of desolation. Therefore, the rapture describe in Jesus' statement will occur after the invasion of Israel by Gentiles and the abomination of desolation.

Many will understand the nature of events that will occur during the first 1,267 days of the tribulation and that will precede the rapture. This will be facilitated by efforts to evangelize the earth during these days. However, many will have rejected Jesus and God at the time of the rapture. Therefore, they will be left behind after the rapture. This will account for the perplexity and dismay among the people and fear in the hearts of people that are left behind, concerning events that will occur on earth after the rapture during the great tribulation. These individuals will understand the significance of the rapture they have missed and the horror that awaits them during the great tribulation. ***The mystery of the rapture will be fully revealed and finished*** (1 Corinthians 15:51-52).

SUMMARY OF INVASION OF ISRAEL, ABOMINATION OF DESOLATION, AND RAPTURE

The invasion of Israel by Gentiles, the abomination of desolation, and the rapture will occur before and during the middle of the tribulation in the order listed (days 1,267 to 1,297 in Figure 9). Figure 9 indicates the abomination of desolation will occur at the start of the middle of the tribulation on day 1,267. Daniel in Daniel 11:30-35 indicated Israel will be invaded by Gentiles before the abomination of desolation. Therefore, this invasion may occur before the start of the middle of the tribulation (Figure 9). Revelation 11:2 indicates Gentiles will occupy Jerusalem for 42 months (1,260 days). This occupation may first be consolidated during and then begin after the middle of the tribulation (figure 9). Revelation 13:7 indicates saints will be given into the hands of the Antichrist for forty-two months (1,260 days). Therefore, the two previous events will occur during the great tribulation and will be 1,260 days in length (Figure 9). It is reasonable to presume saints who have died before and who are alive during the middle of the tribulation will be raptured before the start of the great tribulation. Therefore, the rapture of these saints will occur sometime during the middle of the tribulation (Figure 9).

WAR IN HEAVEN

Characters associated with events in heaven recorder in Revelation 12:1-9 are:

- "A woman clothed with the sun, and the moon under her feet, and on her head a crown of twelve stars" who was pregnant with a male child (Revelation 12:1-2). The woman refers to the remnant of Israel, and the male child refers to Jesus.
- A great red dragon with seven heads and ten horns and on his heads were seven diadems. (Revelation 12:3). The great red dragon refers to Satan.
- The angel Michael (Revelation 12:7).

The woman gave birth to the male child (Jesus) who is to rule all nations of the earth with a rod of iron. The male child was caught up to God and His thrown after being born, so Satan could not devour him. The woman (the remnant of Israel) then fled into the wilderness where a place was prepared for her by God where she will be supported for 1,260 days (the length of the great tribulation) (Revelation 12:6).

Revelation 12:7-9 indicates Satan and his angels will enter a war in heaven with Michael and his angels where Michael and his angels will prevail in this war. There will then be no place in heaven for Satan and his angels. Therefore, they will be cast out of heaven and thrown down to earth.

John heard after Satan and his angels were cast out of heaven and thrown down to earth a loud voice in heaven saying (Revelation 12:10-12):

> "Now the salvation, and the power, and the kingdom of our God and the authority of His Christ have come, for the accuser of our brethren has been thrown down, who accuses them before our God day and night. And they overcame him because of the blood of the Lamb and because of the word of their testimony, and they did not love their life even to death. For this reason, rejoice, O heavens and you who dwell in them. Woe to the earth and the sea, because the devil has come down to you, having great wrath, knowing that he has only a short time."

The coming of the salvation, power and kingdom of God and authority of Christ refer to Jesus taking His authority and beginning to rule at the sound of the seventh trumpet (Revelation 12:17-18). This will be a fulfillment of the prophesy in Daniel 7:14. The time when Satan and his angels will be cast out of heaven and thrown down to earth may be at or near the sounding of the seventh trumpet.

WAR ON EARTH AND A REMNENT FROM ISRAEL HIDES IN THE WILDERNESS

Satan will act through the Antichrist to persecute the people of Israel when he is thrown down to earth from heaven (Revelation 12:13). However, God will provide a means for a remnant of Israel to flee to the place prepared for them in the wilderness for a time span of a time, times, and half a time (1,260 days - the length of the great tribulation) (Revelation 12:14). These events may occur near the end of the middle of the tribulation and beginning of the great tribulation.

Gabriel indicated in Daniel 11:41 the Antichrist will not be able to gain control of "Edom, Moab and the foremost of the sons of Ammon." Petra, which is a city hidden in the mountains in the eastern part of Jordan, is in this area. Some Bible commentators indicate

Petra may be the place prepared by God in the wilderness where his remnant from Israel will flee to for protection during the great tribulation (Revelation 12:6 and 13-14) (Refer to the maps in Figure 8 and Figure 14 for the location of Petra.).

Gabriel in Daniel 12:1 indicated the angel Michael will protect the remnant of Israel. The LORD stated concerning the remnant of Israel that will be saved in Zechariah 13:8-9:

> "'And it will come about in all the land,' declares the LORD, 'That two parts in it will be cut off and perish; but the third will be left in it. And I will bring the third part through the fire, refine them as silver is refined, and test them as gold is tested. They will call on My name, and I will answer them; I will say, 'They are My people,' and they will say, 'The LORD is My God.'"

Two parts of Israel will be cut off and perish by the sword as indicated by Jesus in Luke 21:20-26. The third part is the "all Israel" Paul indicated in Romans 11:25-29 who will be saved and redeemed by God. *The mystery of the redemption of Israel* will be fully revealed and finished (Romans 11:25-29).

Satan through the Antichrist will turn his rage on the "[woman's] children, who keep the commandments of God and hold to the testimony of Jesus (Revelation 12:17)" when he is prevented from attacking the remnant of Israel. Satan through the Antichrist will wage war against saints during the great tribulation. Gabriel stated in Daniel 7:25 saints will be given into the hands of the Antichrist for a time span of a times, time, and half time (1,260 days) during the great tribulation.

John indicated in Revelation 13 people will worship and follow Satan because he will give "his power and his throne and great authority" to the Antichrist. All restraints will be removed from Satan and the Antichrist at the beginning of the great tribulation. The Antichrist will be given authority for a period of forty-two months (1,260 days) when he will rule "over every tribe and people and tongue and nation," during which time he will make war on and overcome the saints (Revelation 13:5-7). The people of earth, as a result, "whose name has not been written from the foundation of the world in the book of life of the Lamb" will worship the Antichrist. They will say, "Who is like the beast, and who is able to wage war with him." *The mystery of lawlessness* (removing the restraints from Satan and the Antichrist) will be fully revealed and finished (2 Thessalonians 2:1-12). The great tribulation will begin.

CHAPTER 10
THE GREAT TRIBULATION
DAYS 1,297 - 2,557

EVENTS THAT WILL OCCUR DURING THE GREAT TRIBULATION - DAYS 1,297 - 2,557

The following events will occur between days 1,297 - 2,557 of the tribulation (Figure 9):

- The seven bowl judgments occur.
- The judgement and fall of Babylon the great.
- The marriage of the Lamb (Jesus) and saints take place in heaven.
- Jesus returns to earth with the armies of heaven and defeats the armies of the Antichrist and kings of earth at the battle of Armageddon.

THE GREAT TRIBULATION

The great tribulation will start after the remnant of Israel has gone into hiding in the place prepared for them by God in the wilderness and the saints who will live on earth during the great tribulation have been given into the hands of the Antichrist. Gabriel indicated in Daniel 12:1-7 the length of the great tribulation will be a time, times and half a time, which will be 1,260 days. He further indicated this "will be a time of distress such as never occurred since there was a nation until that time." Jesus stated concerning the great tribulation in Matthew 24:21-22:

> "For then there will be a great tribulation, such as has not occurred since the beginning of the world until now, nor ever shall. And unless those days had been cut short, no life would have been saved; but for the sake of the elect those days shall be cut short."

As bad as the first 1,267 days of the tribulation will be, the great tribulation will be much worse. It will be a time of unimaginable worldwide destruction, desolation and suffering. The restraints restricting activities of Satan and the Antichrist on earth will be removed

(2 Thessalonians 2:6-9). Therefore, the great tribulation will be a time of unimaginable lawlessness, moral decay and evil. It will be a time when Satan through the Antichrist without restriction and with great vengeance will persecute and murder saints who seek to follow God and Jesus. It will also be a time when the undiluted wrath of God will be directed against the people of earth in the form of the final seven bowl judgments.

SAINTS DURING THE GREAT TRIBULATION

Many will turn to Jesus during the great tribulation. Two factors will facilitate this. Many who will be left on earth after the rapture will understand the significance of the rapture and the events that will follow. God in His mercy will reach out to those who will be left behind even though the Church will not be present after the rapture to present the Gospel of Jesus to others and explain how one receives salvation through Jesus.

John saw the following after his vision in Revelation 14:1-5 of the 144,000 witnesses following the Lamb in heaven (Revelation 14:6-13):

> "And I saw another angel flying in mid heaven, having an eternal gospel to preach to those who live on the earth, and to every nation and tribe and tongue and people; and he said with a loud voice, 'Fear God, and give Him glory, because the hour of his judgment has come; worship Him who made the heaven and the earth and sea and springs of waters.' And another angel, a second one, followed, saying, 'Fallen, fallen is Babylon the great, she who has made all the nations drink of the wine of the passion of her immorality.' Then another angel, a third one, followed them, saying with a loud voice, 'If anyone worships the beast and his image, and receives a mark on his forehead or on his hand, he also will drink of the wine of the wrath of God, which is mixed in full strength in the cup of his anger; and he will be tormented with fire and brimstone in the presence of the holy angels and in the presence of the Lamb. And the smoke of their torment goes up forever and ever; they have no rest day and night, those who worship the beast and his image, and whoever receives the mark of his name.' Here is the perseverance of the saints who keep the commandments of God and their faith in Jesus. And I heard a voice from heaven, saying, 'Write, blessed are the dead who die in the Lord from now on!' 'Yes,' says the Spirit, 'so that they may rest from their labors, for their deeds follow with them.'"

God will reach out to those who are left behind on earth through His angels because the Church will no longer be present on earth. The time of John's vision in Revelation implies

God's message will be delivered by three angles to people on earth after the rapture but before the false prophet requires them to receive the mark of the beast. There will be four parts to the message presented by the angels to "those who [will] live on the earth, and to every nation and tribe and tongue."

- First, they will be asked to continue to fear God and to have faith in and worship Him.

- Second, they will be told Babylon the great has fallen. Bible commentators indicate Babylon the great may refer to the kingdom of ten kings the Antichrist will rule during the great tribulation. He will rule his kingdom with the assistance of the false prophet.

- Third, the people of earth will be warned not to worship the Antichrist and receive his mark of the beast. They will be told those who worship the Antichrist and receive his mark of the beast will experience the same judgment and eternal punishment the Antichrist will experience, and they and the Antichrist will experience the eternal undiluted divine wrath of God.

- Fourth, the saints who die from this point forward will be blessed, and they will be able to rest from their labors. This refers to saints who will be martyred by the Antichrist during the great tribulation.

People who live on earth during the great tribulation will be given a promise with this message. They will be promised "those who keep the commandments of God and their faith in Jesus" will be counted as blessed.

Gabriel indicated in Daniel 7:25 those who live on earth and follow Jesus during the great tribulation will be given into the hands of the Antichrist. John was told in Revelation 13:5-6 the Antichrist will be given power "to make war with the saints and to overcome them" during the great tribulation.

Satan is and will be restricted before the rapture in how he can afflict saints, and Jesus indicated in Matthew 16:18 Satan will not be able to overcome His Church. This will change during the great tribulation after the rapture during the middle of the tribulation. The Church along with saints will have been removed from earth to heaven before the start of the great tribulation. All restraints after this on how Satan through the Antichrist can afflict, persecute and martyr saints during the great tribulation will be removed. The Antichrist will then pursue saints with a vengeance during the great tribulation.

John was given a vision in Revelation 7:9-17 of the "great multitude, which no one could count, from every nation and all tribes and peoples and tongues" who follow Jesus who will be martyred by the Antichrist. One of the elders before the throne of God told John regarding these martyred saints (Revelation 7:14-17):

"These are the ones who come out of the great tribulation, and they have washed their robes and made them white in the blood of the Lamb. For this reason, they are before the throne of God; and they serve Him day and night in His temple; and He who sits on the throne will spread His tabernacle over them. They will hunger no longer, nor thirst anymore; nor will the sun beat down on them, nor any heat; for the Lamb in the center of the throne will be their shepherd, and will guide them to springs of the water of life; and God will wipe every tear from their eyes."

The saints who will be martyred during the great tribulation will experience a separate resurrection before the start of Jesus' 1,000-year kingdom (Revelation 20:4-6). They will be resurrected at the first resurrection and "they will be priest of God and of Christ and will reign with Him" in His 1,000-year kingdom (Revelation 20:6).

SATAN, THE ANTICHRIST AND FALSE PROPHET DURING THE GREAT TRIBULATION

Satan, the Antichrist and false prophet will form an unholy counterfeit trinity during the great tribulation. John saw in his vision in Revelation 13:1-8 that men will worship Satan because he will give his power, throne and great authority to the Antichrist. John further saw that the people of earth whose names are not written in the book of life will worship the Antichrist. The false prophet will be given power to do miraculous signs on behalf of the Antichrist (Revelation 13:11-17). He will require the inhabitants of earth to worship the Antichrist and receive the mark of the beast to carry out acts of commerce during the great tribulation.

John saw in Revelation 12:9-12 that Satan and his angels will be cast out of heaven and thrown down to earth. He then heard a loud voice in heaven say;

"Woe to the earth and the sea, because the devil has come down to you, having great wrath, knowing that he has only a short time (Revelation 13:12)."

Jesus indicated in Matthew 24:24 false Christs and false prophets will appear during the great tribulation, and they will perform great signs and miracles. These false Christs and prophets will appear because of demonic activity associated with the presence of Satan.

The Antichrist with Satan and the false prophet will be given authority to rule over the earth during the great tribulation (Revelation 13:5). Daniel implied in Daniel 11:36-45 the Antichrist will exercise his authority through great military might. The Antichrist will attempt to destroy the people of Israel, but he will be prevented by God from doing this (Revelation 12:13-17). He will then turn his attention to saints living on earth during the great tribulation who will refuse to receive his mark of the beast and worship him. Revelation 7:9-17 indicates the Antichrist will murder multitudes of saints that are so great that no one will be able to count them from every nation, tribe, people and tongue.

THE BOWL JUDGMENTS

The bowl judgments will be the final seven judgments God will execute against the people of earth (Figure 10). John heard from the temple of God in heaven a command to the seven angels who were given the seven bowls of God's wrath (Revelation 16:1) to "Go, pour out the seven bowls of God's wrath on the earth."

1st Bowl.   When the first angel poured out his bowl over the face of the earth:

> "... it became a loathsome and malignant sore on the people who had the mark of the beast and who worshiped his image." (Revelation 16:2)

2nd Bowl.   When the second angel poured out his bowl into the sea waters:

> "... it became blood like that of a dead man; and every living thing in the sea died." (Revelation 16:3)

3rd Bowl.   When the third angel poured his bowl into the rivers and the springs of, "they became blood." (Revelation 16:4) After this had been done, John heard the angels of the waters say:

> "Righteous are You, who are and who were, O Holy One, because You judged these things; for they poured out the blood of saints and prophets, and You have given them blood to drink. They deserve it." (Revelation 16:5-6)

4th Bowl.   When the fourth angel poured out his bowl unto the sun:

> "... it was given to it to scorch men with fire. Men were scorched with fierce heat, and they blasphemed the name of God who has the power over these plagues, and they did not repent so as to give Him glory." (Revelation 16:8-9)

5th Bowl.   When the fifth angel poured out his bowl on the throne of the beast:

"... his kingdom became darkened; and they gnawed their tongues because of pain, and they blasphemed the God of heaven because of their pains and their sores; and they did not repent of their deeds." (Revelation 16:10-11)

6th Bowl.   When the sixth angel poured out his bowl on the great river, the Euphrates:

"... its water was dried up, so that the way would be prepared for the kings from the east (Revelation 16:12)."

After the Euphrates river was dried up, John saw:

"coming out of the mouth of the dragon and out of the mouth of the beast and out of the mouth of the false prophet, three unclean spirits like frogs; for they are spirits of demons, performing signs, which go out to the kings of the whole world, to gather them together for the war of the great day of God, the Almighty. ... And they gathered them together to the place which in Hebrew is called Har-Magedon [Armageddon]." (Rev 16:13-14, 16)

7th Bowl.   When the seventh angel poured out his bowl upon the air:

"a loud voice came out of the temple from the throne, saying, 'It is done.' And there were flashes of lightning and sounds and peals of thunder; and there was a great earthquake, such as there had not been since man came to be upon the earth, so great an earthquake was it, and so mighty. The great city was split into three parts, and the cities of the nations fell. Babylon the great was remembered before God, to give her the cup of the wine of his fierce wrath. And every island fled away, and the mountains were not found. And huge hailstones, about one hundred pounds each, came down from heaven upon men; and men blasphemed God because of the plague of the hail, because its plague was extremely severe." (Revelation 16:17-21)

The destruction, desolation and suffering that will be associated with the bowl judgments will be beyond comprehension. The first four bowl judgments will be directed at people on earth who will worship the Antichrist and receive his mark of the beast. The second and third bowl judgments will be replications of the second and third trumpet judgments. However, the bowl judgments will be much worse. The angel's statement following the third bowl judgment implies saints who will live on earth during the great tribulation will not experience the consequences of these judgments. This will certainly be true of the first bowl judgment.

The description of the fourth bowl judgment implies the ozone layer around the earth will be seriously damaged, exposing people on earth to direct ultraviolet radiation from the sun. Scientists indicate a massive solar flare on the surface of the sun much larger than previous solar flares can create a solar storm with enough intensity to seriously damage or destroy the ozone layer when it reaches the earth.

The last three bowl judgments will be directed at the Antichrist and his kingdom. The fifth bowl judgment will be directed at the Antichrist and his throne. The sixth bowl judgment will be directed at clearing the way to draw the kings of earth and their armies to Armageddon for the Antichrist's and their final battle with Jesus and the armies of heaven. The location of Armageddon is thought to be the hill country surrounding the plain of Megiddo. This is around sixty miles north of Jerusalem. The seventh bowl judgment will be a global mega earthquake that will split Jerusalem into three parts and destroy the major cities on earth. Destruction from this earthquake will destroy the economies of the nations of earth. In addition, one hundred-pound hailstones will rain down on the people on earth.

The bowl judgments will not start until after the beginning of the great tribulation. The times when the bowl judgements will occur during the great tribulation are unknown.

One would presume, with the major catastrophic effects of each bowl judgment, people on earth during the great tribulation would turn to and trust God. Many will, and they will be martyred in unimaginable large numbers by the Antichrist and those who follow him. However, the wicked will continue to curse and blaspheme God.

FALL AND JUDGMENT OF BABYLON THE GREAT

Babylon in the Old Testament was a place of luxury, wealth and opulence. It was also a place of wickedness that opposed God. Babylon the great referred to in Revelation 17 and 18 is a future kingdom that, like Babylon in the Old Testament, will be a place of luxury, wealth and opulence. It will also be a place of wickedness that will oppose God. Babylon the great, as used here, is a metaphor that refers to the end time kingdom of the Antichrist.

An angel told John in Revelation 17:1-7:

"Come here, I will show you the judgement of the great harlot who sits on many waters, with whom the kings of the earth committed acts of immorality, and those who dwell on the earth were made drunk with the wine of her immorality. And he carried me away in the Spirit into a wilderness; and I saw a woman sitting on a scarlet beast, full of blasphemous names, having seven heads and ten horns. The woman was clothed in purple and scarlet, and adorned with gold and precious stones and pearls, having in her hand a gold cup full of abominations and of the unclean things of her immorality, and on her forehead a name was written, a mystery, 'BABYLON THE GREAT, THE MOTHER OF HARLOTS AND OF THE ABOMINATIONS OF THE EARTH.' And I saw the woman drunk with the blood of the saints, and with the blood of the witnesses of Jesus. When I saw her I wondered greatly. And the angel said to me, 'Why do you wonder? I will tell you the mystery of the woman and of the beast that carries her, which has the seven heads and the ten horns'"

The following observations can be made with respect to the angel's statement:

- The scarlet beast refers to the Antichrist and his end time kingdom.
- The seven heads refer to five kingdoms that have existed and fallen in the past and to two kingdoms that will emerge in the future.
- The ten horns refer to ten kings the Antichrist will rule with during the great tribulation.
- Babylon the great refers to the evil end time kingdom of the Antichrist.
- The "great harlot who sits on many waters" refers to the evil political, economic and religious system that will rule the nations and people of the earth during the Antichrist's end time kingdom during the great tribulation.

Observations with respect to the great harlot are:

- She is the "mother of harlots and abominations" refers to religious heresies that will originate and spread throughout the earth during the Antichrist's end time kingdom. Proverbs 6:16–19 list abominations to God that can occur in the Antichrist end time kingdom. They are: haughty eyes, a lying tongue, hands that shed innocent blood, a heart that devises wicked schemes, feet that are swift in running to mischief, a false witness who utters lies, and one who spreads strife among brothers.
- She will be "drunk with the blood of the saints, and with the blood of the witnesses of Jesus." This refers to the large number of saints who will be martyred during the Antichrist's end time kingdom.

An angel indicated in Revelations 17:16-18 the Antichrist and ten kings of his kingdom will grow to hate and turn against the great harlot and murder her. This may occur during the middle of the tribulation after the abomination of desolation by the Antichrist when he declares himself to be god and the false prophet requires the people on earth to worship the Antichrist and receive his mark of the beast. The angle stated God will lead them in these actions to accomplish His purpose. They will have a common objective with God regarding these actions. The ten kings at this time will give their kingdoms (swear allegiance) to the Antichrist to fulfill the words of God. This will result in the fall of Babylon the great referred to in Revelation 18.

John was told by an angel in Revelation 18:2-3:

> "Fallen, fallen is Babylon the great. She has become a dwelling place of demons and a prison of every unclean spirit, and prison of every unclean and hateful bird. For all the nations have drunk of the wine of the passion of her immorality. And the kings of the earth have committed acts of immorality with her, and the merchants of the earth have become rich by the wealth of her sensuality."

The angel indicate the end time kingdom of the Antichrist during the great tribulation will be a kingdom populated with demons, unclean spirits and hateful birds. It will also be a kingdom of extravagant luxury and great wealth.

John was then told by a voice from heaven in Revelation 18:4-8:

> "Come out of her, my people, so that you will not participate in her sins and receive of her plagues; for her sins have piled up as high as heaven, and God has remembered her iniquities. Pay her back even as she has paid, and give back to her double according to her deeds; in the cup which she has mixed, mix twice as much for her. To the degree that she glorified herself and lived sensuously, to the same degree give her torment and mourning; for she says in her heart, 'I sit as A QUEEN AND I AM NOT A WIDOW, and will never see mourning.' For this reason in one day her plagues will come, pestilence and mourning and famine, and she will be burned up with fire; for the Lord God who judges her is strong."

God will encourage the people on earth not to participate in the sins of the Antichrist's end time kingdom, so they will escape His coming judgment of the Antichrist and his kingdom. God will judge the Antichrist and bring his kingdom to an end. The previously presented seven bowl judgements that God will pour out on earth during the great tribulation will be judgements He will execute against the Antichrist and his kingdom to bring his kingdom to an end.

IT IS DONE

The use of the phrase "It is done" in Revelation 16:17 is the second of three times this phrase is used in the New Testament. The first time was when Jesus stated, "It is finished," and yielded His spirit to God and died (John 19:30). Jesus had completed his atonement for sin. The third time the phrase "It is done" will be used is in Revelation 21:6. Its use here will refer to the destruction of the existing heaven and earth, the judgment of all whose names are not written in the book of life at the great white throne judgment, the final judgment of Satan, and the creation of a new heaven and earth.

The use of the expression "It is done" in Revelation 16:17 refers to the judgment and destruction of the end time kingdom of the Antichrist by God. He will judge and destroy the Antichrist's evil global religious, political and economic system. Therefore, the source of Satan's power over and control of earth by false religions and corrupt political and economic systems will be judged and destroyed. Jesus will be ready to return to earth to establish His 1,000-year kingdom.

MARRIAGE OF THE LAMB

John heard after the angel showed him the vision of the judgments and destruction of Babylon the great in Revelation 17 and 18 (Revelation 19:6-10):

> "... something like the voice of a great multitude and like the sound of many waters and like the sound of mighty peals of thunder, saying, 'Hallelujah! For the LORD our God, the Almighty, reigns. Let us rejoice and be glad and give the glory to Him, for the marriage of the Lamb has come and His bride has made herself ready.' It was given to her to clothe herself in fine linen, bright and clean; for the fine linen is the righteous acts of the saints. Then [the angel] said to [John], 'Write, 'Blessed are those who are invited to the marriage supper of the Lamb." And he said to [John], 'These are true words of God.'"

The event referred to in this verse is the marriage of Jesus in heaven at the end of the tribulation before He returns to earth. He is referred to as the Lamb in this verse. Jesus referred to Himself as the bridegroom in Matthew 9:15, Mark 2:19, and Luke 5:34-35. John the Baptist referred to Jesus as the bridegroom in John 3:29. "Those who are invited to the marriage supper of the Lamb" will be the saints who will be in heaven because of the rapture during the middle of the tribulation and the first resurrection at the end of the tribulation.

Jesus' bride is not identified in Revelation 19:6-9. Paul compared in Ephesians 5:22-32 the marriage of a husband and wife to Jesus' relationship with the church. He indicated, "For the husband is the head of the wife, as Christ is the head of the church." Paul indicated in Colossians 1:18 Jesus "is head of the body, the church." Therefore, Christians believe Jesus' bride in Revelation 19:6-9 will be the body of Christ, the church.

Jesus after His marriage to His bride in heaven will return to earth. He will engage the armies of the Antichrist and kings of the earth at the battle of Armageddon and set up His 1,000-year kingdom.

RETURN OF JESUS AND BATTLE OF ARMAGEDDON

The battle of Armageddon will mark the end of the great tribulation. It will be the final battle between the armies of the Antichrist and kings of the earth and Jesus and the army of heaven. The sixth bowl judgment will set into motion the events that will draw the armies of the Antichrists and kings of the earth to Israel "to gather them for the battle on the great day of God Almighty." (Revelation 16:14) The prophet Joel stated regarding this battle in Joel 3:9-17:

> "Proclaim this among the nations: Prepare a war; rouse the mighty men. Let all the soldiers draw near, let them come up. Beat your plowshares into swords and your pruning hooks into spears; let the weak say, 'I am a mighty man.' Hasten and come, all you surrounding nations, and gather yourselves there. Bring down, O LORD, Your mighty ones. Let the nations be aroused and come up to the valley of Jehoshaphat, for there I will sit to judge all the surrounding nations. Put in the sickle, for the harvest is ripe. Come, tread, for the wine press is full; the vats overflow, for their wickedness is great. Multitudes, multitudes in the valley of decision! For the day of the LORD is near in the valley of decision. The sun and moon grow dark and the stars lose their brightness. The LORD roars from Zion and utters His voice from Jerusalem, and the heavens and the earth tremble. But the LORD is a refuge for his people and a stronghold to the sons of Israel. Then you will know that I am the LORD your God, dwelling in Zion, My holy mountain. So Jerusalem will be holy, and strangers will pass through it no more."

Joel implied the battle of Armageddon will be a time of judgment for nations who have opposed Israel. This will be the second major judgment that will occur during the tribulation. The earth will know the LORD is God after this battle, and Jerusalem will be restored to its place of holiness as the center of worship for the earth.

John stated in Revelation 19:1-16 and 19-21 regarding the battle of Armageddon:

"And I saw heaven opened and behold, a white horse, and He who sat upon it is called Faithful and True; and in righteousness He judges and wages war. And His eyes are a flame of fire, and upon His head are many diadems; and He has a name written upon Him which no one knows except Himself. And He is clothed with a robe dipped in blood; and His name is called the Word of God. And the armies which are in heaven, clothed in fine linen, white and clean, were following Him on white horses. And from His mouth comes a sharp sword, so that with it He may smite the nations; and He will rule them with a rod of iron; and He treads the wine press of the fierce wrath of God, the Almighty. And on His robe and on His thigh He has a name written, 'KING OF KINGS, and LORD OF LORDS.' ... And I saw the beast and the kings of the earth and their armies, assembled to make war against Him who sat upon the horse, and against His army. And the beast was seized, and with him the false prophet who performed the signs in his presence, by which he deceived those who had received the mark of the beast and those who worshiped his image; these two were thrown alive into the lake of fire which burns with brimstone. And the rest were killed with the sword which came from the mouth of Him who sat upon the horse, and all the birds were filled with their flesh."

The LORD stated in Zechariah 14:1-8 with respect to the battle of Armageddon:

"Behold, a day is coming for the LORD when the spoil taken from you will be divided among you. For I will gather all the nations against Jerusalem to battle, and the city will be captured, the houses plundered, the women ravished and half of the city exiled, but the rest of the people will not be cut off from the city. Then the LORD will go forth and fight against those nations, as when He fights on a day of battle. In that day His feet will stand on the Mount of Olives, which is in front of Jerusalem on the east; and the Mount of Olives will be split in its middle from east to west by a very large valley, so that half of the mountain will move toward the north and the other half toward the south. You will flee by the valley of My mountains, for the valley of the mountains will reach to Azel; yes, you will flee just as you fled before the earthquake in the days of Uzziah king of Judah. Then the LORD, My God, will come, and all the holy ones with Him! In that day there will be no light; the luminaries will dwindle. For it will be a unique day which is known to the LORD, neither day nor night, but it will come about that at evening time there will be light. And in that day living waters will flow out of Jerusalem, half of them toward the eastern sea and the other half toward the western sea; it will be in summer as well as in winter."

The statement by John in Revelation 19:1-16, 19-21 and by the LORD in Zechariah 14:1-8 indicate:

- Only God knows the day Jesus will return to earth. This is consistent with Jesus' statements in Matthew 24:36 and Acts 1:7 concerning the times of the rapture and the restoration of the kingdom of Israel.

- God will initially draw the nations of the earth to Jerusalem to do battle. The reference in Zechariah 14:2 to Jerusalem being captured and plundered is a reference to when Jerusalem will come under the control of the Antichrist and Gentiles during the great tribulation. The reference to the LORD going forth to do battle in Zechariah 14:3 refers to the return of Jesus to fight against the armies of the Antichrist and kings of the earth. The vision of John concerning the sixth bowl judgment implies God will draw the nations to Israel for the battle of Armageddon by means of demonic spirits who will proceed from Satan, the Antichrist and the false prophet (Revelation 16:13-14).

- Jesus will return with His army from heaven by way of the Mount of Olives, which overlooks Jerusalem from the east. Luke stated in Luke 24:50-51 Jesus ascended into heaven from a place near Bethany, which is on the Mount of Olives. The angel told the disciples in Acts 1:10-11 Jesus will return to earth in the same manner He was taken into heaven. Jesus departed from earth on the Mount of Olives and will return by way of the Mount of Olives.

- The Mount of Olives will split in two with half of the mountain moving to the north and half moving to the south when Jesus arrives there (Zechariah 14:4). The valley between the two halves will provide an escape route for those whom the LORD will allow to flee from Jerusalem.

- Living waters will flow from Jerusalem toward the Mediterranean Sea to the west and toward the Dead Sea to the east in the day Jesus returns to earth and after the Mount of Olives will have split in two (Zechariah 14:8). This water will flow during both summer and winter. This water will flow from the new temple that will be built in Jerusalem at the beginning of the 1,000-year rule of Jesus.

- Joel indicated in Joel 3:15 the sun and moon will grow dark, and the stars will lose their brightness on the day of the LORD at the battle of Armageddon. Zechariah implied the same in Zechariah 14:6-7.

- Jesus will destroy the army of the Antichrist and kings of the earth assembled for the battle of Armageddon (Revelation 19:11-19). John saw in his vision that these armies will be destroyed by a sword that will proceed from the mouth of Jesus. The LORD told Zechariah in Zechariah 14:12-13:

"Now this will be the plague with which the LORD will strike all the peoples who have gone to war against Jerusalem; their flesh will rot while they stand on their feet, and their eyes will rot in their sockets, and their tongues will rot in their mouth. And it will come about in that day that a great panic from the LORD will fall on them; and they will seize one another's hand, and the hand of one will be lifted against the hand of another."

The description of rotting flesh is similar to what occurs in a nuclear explosion. How Jesus will destroy the armies of the Antichrist and kings of the earth is unknown. However, the power at His disposal will be beyond comprehension. Those who will not be killed directly by Jesus will kill each other in the ensuing panic.

- The Antichrist and false prophet will be seized after the battle of Armageddon and placed alive in the lake of fire (Revelation 19:20). They will be the first to be judged and placed in the lake of fire.

CHAPTER 11
JESUS SETS UP HIS 1,000-YEAR KINGDOM - DAYS 2,557 - 2,602

STATE OF THE WORLD AT THE END OF THE TRIBULATION

It is difficult to visualize the world that will exist after Jesus returns to earth, defeats the armies of the Antichrist and kings of the earth at the battle of Armageddon, and begins to set up His 1,000- year kingdom. Revelation indicates:

- The world population at the midpoint of the tribulation will be reduced by more than one-half (Revelation 6:8, 9:15). John was shown in Revelation 7:9-17 the "great multitude, which no one could count, from every nation and all tribes and peoples and tongues" who will be killed during the great tribulation because they will not worship the Antichrist or receive his mark. Even though no specific information is given in the Bible, it is reasonable to assume multitudes of those who do worship the Antichrist and receive his mark will be killed during the seven bowl judgments God will pour out over the earth during the great tribulation. Therefore, the population of earth at the beginning of the 1,000-year kingdom of Jesus will be but a small fraction of what it will be at the beginning of the tribulation.

- All life in the oceans and seas will have been destroyed during the second bowl judgment (Revelation 16:3).

- All life in the fresh water rivers, streams and lakes will have been destroyed during the third bowl judgment (Revelation 16:4-7).

- The ozone layer around the earth will have been seriously diminished during the fourth bowl judgment (Revelation 16:8-9).

- The earthquake in the seventh bowl judgment will have destroyed the major cities of the world (Revelation 16:17-21).

- All world religions except the one that worships the Antichrist will have been destroyed by the Antichrist and kings of the earth (Revelation 17). Jesus will judge and destroy this religion when He throws the Antichrist and false prophet into the lake of fire and Satan is bound and sealed in the abyss (Revelation 19:19, 20:1-3).

- The world economic system will have been judged and destroyed by God (Revelation 18).

- All armies of the world who gathered to make war against Jesus and His heavenly army will have been destroyed by Jesus at the battle of Armageddon (Zechariah 14:12-15, Revelation 19:19-21).

- Satan will have been bound and imprisoned in the abyss so he will be unable to interfere with world affairs or deceive men and women for a period of 1,000-years (Revelation 20:1-3). It is reasonable to assume his fallen angels (or demons) will also have been bound up with him.

- Both those who will have received the mark of the beast and worshiped the Antichrist and those who will have remained faithful to God and worshiped Jesus during the great tribulation will populate the earth at the beginning of the 1,000-year reign of Jesus (Zechariah 14:16-21, Matthew 24:22, Mark 13:20). These people will have survived to the end of the tribulation.

- With Jesus will be the Christians who will have been taken to heaven at the rapture during the middle of the tribulation and the martyred saints who will have been killed during the great tribulation and resurrected by Jesus at the beginning of His 1,000-year kingdom (Revelation 20:4). These people will rule the earth with Jesus in His 1,000-year kingdom (Daniel 7:21-22, 27, 2 Timothy 2:11-13, Revelation 3:21, 5:9-10, 20:4).

- Jesus will rule the nations of earth with a rod of iron during His 1,000-year reign (Revelation 2:26- 27, 12:5, 19:15). Even though people will reject Jesus during His 1,000-year reign, they will not be allowed to rebel against Him until after Satan is released for a short period of time at the end of the 1,000 years (Revelation 20:7-9).

This will be the state of the world when Jesus establishes His 1,000-year kingdom.

Gabriel told Daniel in Daniel 12:11-12 there will be 45 days between the end of the tribulation (day 2557) and the beginning of Jesus' 1,000-year kingdom (day 2602). The Bible presents no information regarding what will occur during this period.

THE 1,000-YEAR KINGDOM OF JESUS

The term millennium refers to the 1,000-year kingdom Jesus will establish and govern between the end of the tribulation and the great white throne judgment and day of the Lord referred to in Revelation 20:1-6. There are three interpretations by Christians regarding the 1,000-year kingdom of Jesus. They are: Postmillennialism, amillennialism and premillennialism.

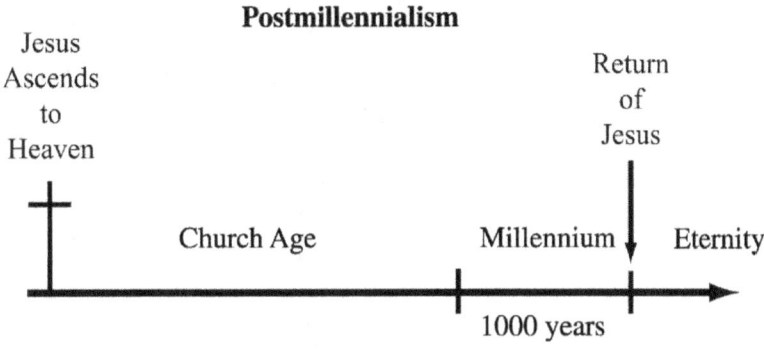

Figure 11

Postmillennialism (Figure 11): Postmillennialism presumes the world will eventually embrace Christianity through preaching the gospel of Jesus. It presumes Christian men and women have the collective ability to make societies and cultures better places to live. Postmillennialist believe Jesus will return after they have successfully achieved this objective. However, history has shown that as time moves forward things get progressively worse. Postmillennialism became popular in the seventeenth century and flourished until the middle of the twentieth century. As a result of the worldwide devastation associated with World Wars I and II, interest in Postmillennialism has died out. *Order of events*: Millennium occurs during latter part of church age; Christ returns near the end of the millennium, followed by the resurrection of the saved and unsaved; after this comes judgment and then eternity.

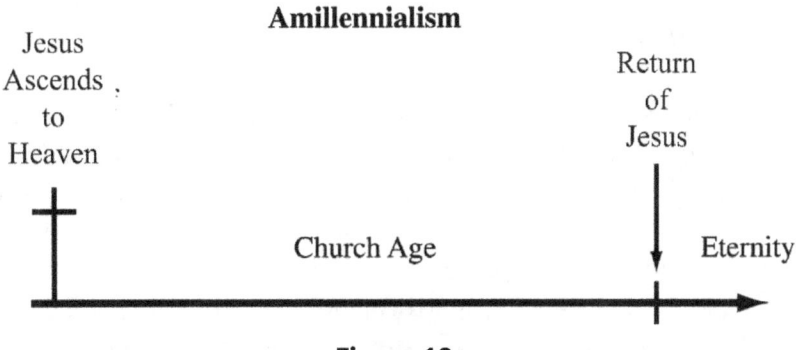

Figure 12

Amillennialism (Figure 12): Amillennialism believe there will be no literal 1,000-year reign of Jesus and the New Testament church will inherit the promises associated with Old Testament prophesies relating to the future of Israel. Amillennialism tend to spiritualize unfulfilled prophecies concerning the return of Jesus. They prefer a spiritualized and symbolic rather than a real-life literal interpretation of these prophesies. Amillennialist conclude we are currently living in a 1,000-year kingdom, which is a spiritual kingdom residing in the hearts of men and women rather than an actual kingdom that is or will be ruled by Jesus. *Order of events*: There is no 1,000-year kingdom of Jesus; church age ends in a time of trouble; Christ returns at the end of the church age, followed by the resurrection of the saved and unsaved; after this comes judgment and then eternity.

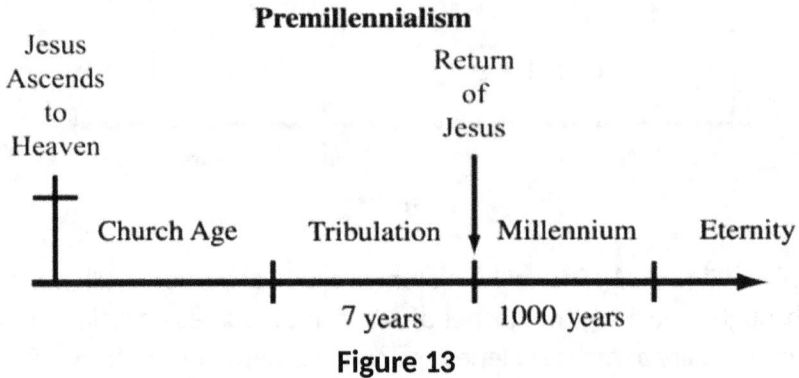

Figure 13

Premillennialism (Figure 13): Premillennialists believe Jesus will return after the seven-year tribulation just prior to establishing his 1,000-year kingdom. This position is taught in the Bible, was taught by the early church fathers, and is believed by most evangelical Christians today. *Order of events*: The church age ends in the seven-year tribulation; Jesus returns at the end of the tribulation and sets up his 1,000-year kingdom; His 1,000-year kingdom ends in the resurrection of the saved and unsaved and judgment, after which eternity comes.

THE NATION OF ISRAEL

God will honor the covenants He made with Abraham, Isaac and Jacob to establish the nation of Israel. Isaiah described the restoration of the nation of Israel during the 1,000-year rule of Jesus in Isaiah 60-62. The LORD specified the boundaries of the nation in Genesis 15:18-21:

> "On that day the LORD made a covenant with Abram [Abraham], saying, 'To your descendants I have given this land, from the river of Egypt as far as the great river, the river Euphrates: the Kenite and the Kenizite and

the Kadmonite and the Hittite and the Perizzite and the Rephaim and the Amorite and the Canaanite and the Girgashite and the Jebusite.'"

God further elaborated on the overall boundaries of Israel in Deuteronomy 1:7-8:

"Turn and set your journey, and go to the hill country of the Amorites, and to all their neighbors in the Arabah, in the hill country and in the lowland and in the Negev and by the seacoast, the land of the Canaanites, and Lebanon, as far as the great river, the river Euphrates. See, I have placed the land before you; go in and possess the land which the LORD swore to give to your fathers, to Abraham, to Isaac, and to Jacob, to them and their descendants after them."

and in Deuteronomy 11:24:

"Every place on which the sole of your foot shall tread shall be yours; your border shall be from the wilderness to Lebanon, and from the river, the river Euphrates, as far as the western sea."

These scriptures imply the boundaries of Israel will be the Brook of Egypt and the Mediterranean Sea to the West and the Euphrates River to the East. It will be the Sinai Peninsula, the Negev and southern Jordan to the South and the norther part of Lebanon and Syria to the North.

The LORD indicated in Numbers 34:1-12 the boundaries of the land in Canaan that was to be an inheritance for the sons of Israel (Figure 14):

"Then the LORD spoke to Moses, saying, 'Command the sons of Israel and say to them, 'When you enter the land of Canaan, this is the land that shall fall to you as an inheritance, even the land of Canaan according to its borders. Your southern sector shall extend from the wilderness of Zin along the side of Edom, and your southern border shall extend from the end of the Salt Sea eastward. Then your border shall turn directions from the south to the ascent of Akrabbim and continue to Zin, and its termination shall be to the south of Kadesh-barnea; and it shall reach Hazaraddar and continue to Azmon. The border shall turn direction from Azmon to the brook of Egypt, and its termination shall be the sea.'

'And this shall be your north border: you shall draw your border line from the Great Sea to Mount Hor. You shall draw a line from Mount Hor to the Lebo-hamath, and the termination of the border shall be at Zedad; and the border shall proceed to Ziphron, and its termination shall be at Hazar-enan. This shall be your nor border.'

'For your eastern border you shall also draw a line from Hazar-enan to Shepham, and the border shall go down from Shepham to Riblalh on the east side of Ain; and the border shall go down and reach to the slope of the east side of the Sea of Chinnereth. And the border shall go down to the Jordan and its termination shall be at the Salt Sea. This shall be your land according to its border all around.'"

The LORD also specified in Ezekiel 47:13-21 the boundaries of the land that will be divided as an inheritance among the twelve tribes of Israel during the 1,000-year kingdom of Jesus (Figure 14):

"Thus says the LORD God, 'This shall be the boundary by which you shall divide the land for an inheritance among the twelve tribes of Israel; Joseph shall have two portions. And you shall divide it for an inheritance, each one equally with the other; for I swore to give it to your forefathers, and this land shall fall to you as an inheritance. And this shall be the boundary of the land; on the North side, from the Great Sea by the way of Hethlon, to the entrance of Zedad; Hamath, Berothah, Sibraim, which is between the border of Damascus, and the border of Hamath; Hazer-hatticon, which is by the border of Hauran. And the boundary shall extend from the sea to Hazarenan at the border of Damascus, and on the North toward the North is the border of Hamath. This is the North side. And the East side, from between Hauran, Damascus, Gilead, and the Land of Israel, shall be the Jordan; from the North border to the eastern sea you shall measure. This is the East side. And the South side toward the South shall extend from Tamar as far as the waters of Meribath- kadesh, to the brook of Egypt, and to the Great Sea. This is the side toward the South. And the West side shall be the Great Sea, from the South border to a point opposite Lebo-hamath. This is the West side. So you shall divide this land among yourselves according to the tribes of Israel.'"

Figure 14 shows the land to be given to the twelve tribes of Israel as an inheritance per the instructions of the LORD. It includes present-day Israel (includes the Gaza Strip and the West Bank) plus Lebanon and a small portion of western Syria. There are no clear explanations as to why there are differences in the land area the LORD promised to give to Israel in Genesis 15:2, Deuteronomy 1:7-8, 11:24, Numbers 34:1-12 and Ezekiel 47:14-21. It is possible the eastern border of Israel in Jesus' 1,000-year kingdom may extend eastward to the Euphrates River. However, the only land that will specifically be given as an inheritance to the twelve tribes of Israel will be that which is described in Numbers and Ezekiel.

The LORD in Numbers 34 and Ezekiel 48 specified how the land in Israel will be divided among the twelve tribes. He also specified a portion of the land will be set aside for the temple, priests, Levites, the city of Jerusalem and the prince. The portion of the land that will be set apart for the temple and the priests is referred to by the LORD as the holy allotment (Ezekiel 45:1-4, 48:9-12). The land minus the area that will be set aside for the temple, the priests, the Levites, the city of Jerusalem and the prince will be divided equally among the twelve tribes. The North and South borders of the land occupied by each tribe will be parallel to each other and will run horizontally from the west boundary to the east boundary of Israel. The land north of the holy allotment will be divided among seven of the twelve tribes. From North to South, the following tribes will occupy the land: Dan, Asher, Naphtali, Manasseh, Ephraim, Reuben and Judah. South of the holy allotment the land will be divided among the remaining five tribes. From North to South, the following tribes will occupy the land: Benjamin, Simeon, Issachar, Zebulum and Gad.

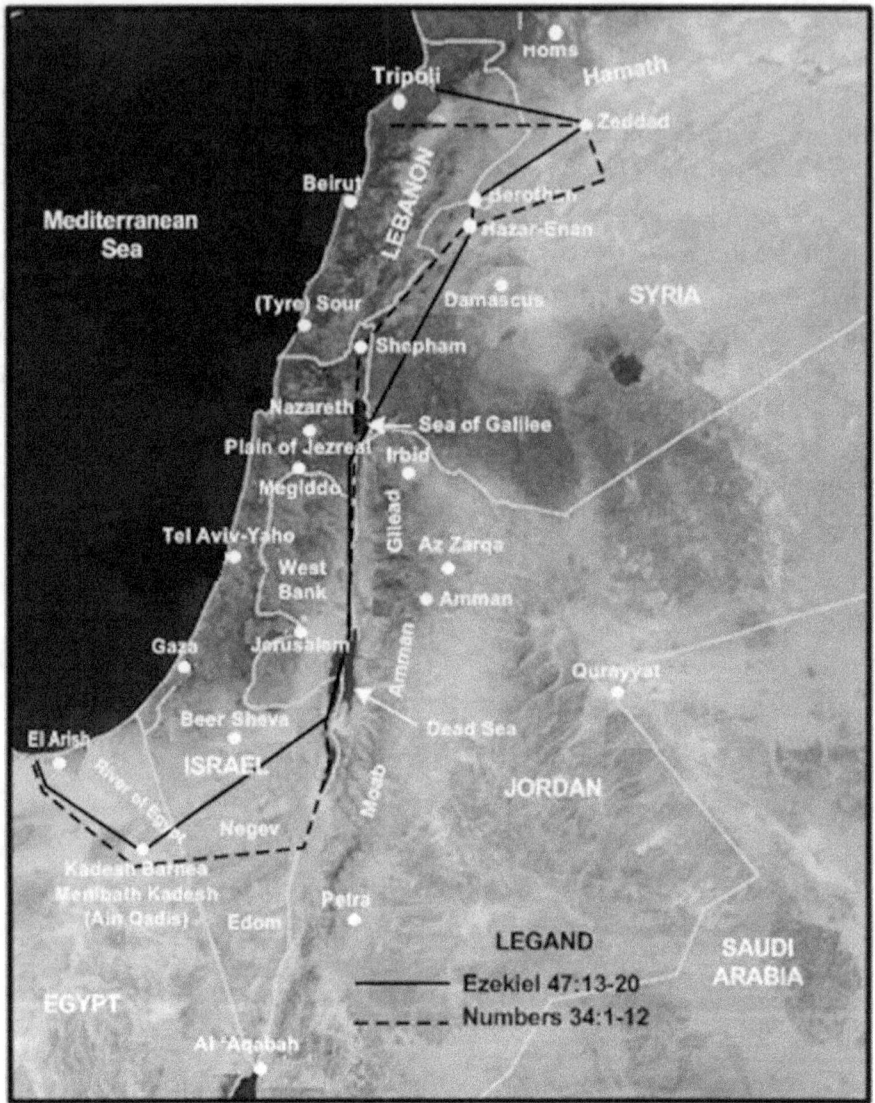

Figure 14

The land that will be set aside for the temple, the priests, the Levites and the city of Jerusalem will be near present-day Jerusalem. It will be a square section of land approximately 8.1 miles square (Ezekiel 48:8-20). Figure 15 shows how this area will be divided. The LORD stated in Ezekiel 48:8 the sanctuary or temple will be placed in the middle of this section of land. It can assume the location of the temple will be near to or at the same location of the temple during the time of Jesus. The LORD's statements in Ezekiel 48:8-20 indicate the Levites will occupy the northern 8.1 mile by 3.24 mile section, the priests and temple the central 8.1 mile by 3.24 mile section, and the city of Jerusalem the southern 8.1 mike by 1.64 mile section of this land. Extending from both sides of the land allotted for the temple, the priests, the Levites and Jerusalem will be land that will be allotted to the prince (Ezekiel 48:21-22). This land will extend to the Mediterranean Sea on the west and the Dead Sea on the East.

The section of land allotted for the city of Jerusalem will be 1.64 miles square. Sections of land 3.24 by 1.64 miles will be located to the East and West of the city and will be used to produce food for the workers of the city. The population of Jerusalem will probably be highly controlled during Jesus' 1,000-year kingdom because of the size of the city.

THE PRINCE

Ezekiel 45:9-17 specifies the laws governing the Prince. The Prince will be expected throughout Israel "to remove violence and plundering, execute justice and righteousness, and stop dispossessing [God's] people." He will be required to have honest scales and related honest units of measure. The people of Israel will make offerings required by the Law to the Prince. The Prince will then be required to:

- Give burnt offerings, grain offerings and drink offerings at the feasts, the new moons, the Sabbaths, and at all the appointed seasons of the house of Israel; and

- Prepare the sin offerings, the grain offerings, the burnt offerings and the peace offerings to make atonement for the house of Israel.

THE TEMPLE

The LORD indicated in Ezekiel 48:8 the sanctuary or temple will be in the middle of the 8.1 by 8.1-mile section of land that will be set aside for the Levites, priests and the city of Jerusalem (Figure 15). This will place the temple in the section of land that will be set aside for the holy allotment. The LORD stated in Ezekiel 45:1-4 the holy allotment will be holy within its boundaries. He stated in Ezekiel 45:4:

> "It shall be the holy portion of the land; it shall be for the priests, the ministers of the sanctuary, who come near to minister to the LORD, and it shall be a place for their houses and a holy place for the sanctuary."

The LORD specified how the temple area is to be laid out and the layout of the temple itself in Ezekiel 40-43.

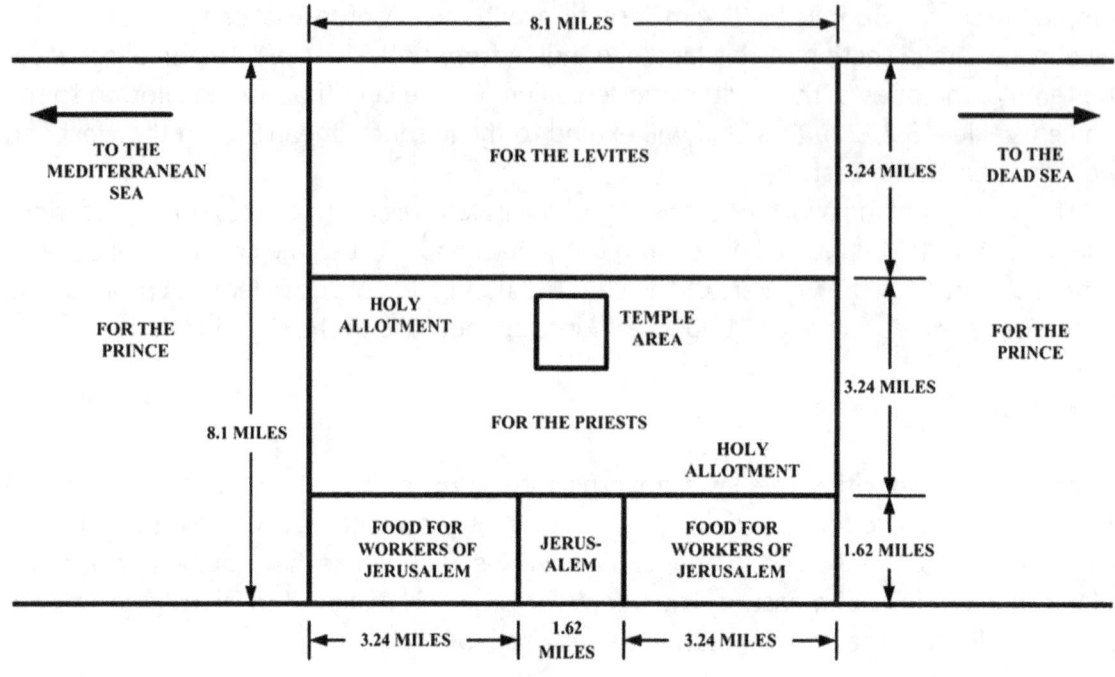

Figure 15

The LORD specified the duties of those who will minister to Him in Ezekiel 44. He stated the Levites will be responsible for keeping charge of the temple, all its services, and all that will be done in the temple. This will include preparing the sacrifices and offerings. The Levites will not be allowed to minister to or bring the sacrifices and offerings into the presence of the LORD because they "became a stumbling block of inequity to the house of Israel,". These tasks will be given to descendants of the sons of Zadok. The LORD stated in Ezekiel 44:15:

> "But the Levitical priests, the sons of Zadok, who kept charge of My sanctuary when the sons of Israel went astray from Me, shall come near to Me to minister to Me; and they shall stand before Me to offer Me the fat and the blood."

Ezekiel in Ezekiel 9-11 described the vision he had seen concerning God's judgment of Israel and Jerusalem and the departure of the glory of the God of Israel from Israel. Ezekiel cried out to the LORD near the end of his vision, "Alas, LORD God! Wilt Thou bring the remnant of Israel to a complete end (Ezekiel 11:13)?" The LORD replied to this (Ezekiel 11:15-20):

"Son of man, your brothers, your relatives, your fellow exiles and the whole house of Israel, all of them, are those to whom the inhabitants of Jerusalem have said, 'Go far from the LORD; this land has been given us as a possession.' Therefore say, 'Thus says the LORD God, 'Though I had removed them far away among the nations, and though I had scattered them among the countries, yet I was a sanctuary for them a little while in the countries where they had gone.'' Therefore say, 'Thus says the LORD God, 'I shall gather you from the peoples and assemble you out of the countries among which you have been scattered, and I shall give you the land of Israel.' When they come there, they will remove all its detestable things and all its abominations from it. And I shall give them one heart, and shall put a new spirit within them. And I shall take the heart of stone out of their flesh and give them a heart of flesh, that they may walk in My statutes and keep My ordinances, and do them. Then they will be My people and I shall be their God."

Regarding this promise, Ezekiel described his vision of the return of the glory of the God of Israel who will again dwell in His sanctuary during the 1,000-year kingdom of Jesus, in Ezekiel 43:1-2, 4:

"Then he led me to the gate, the gate facing toward the East; and behold, the glory of the God of Israel was coming from the way of the East. And His voice was like the sound of many waters; and the earth shone with His glory. And the glory of the LORD came into the house by the way of the gate facing toward the East."

Isaiah affirmed the return of the glory of the God of Israel in Isaiah 4:2-6:

"In that day the Branch of the LORD will be beautiful and glorious, and the fruit of the earth will be the pride and the adornment of the survivors of Israel. And it will come about that he who is left in Zion and remains in Jerusalem will be called holy - everyone who is recorded for life in Jerusalem. When the LORD has washed away the filth of the daughters of Zion, and purged the bloodshed of Jerusalem from her midst, by the spirit of judgment and the spirit of burning, then the LORD will create over the whole area of Mount Zion and over her assemblies a cloud by day, even smoke, and the brightness of a flaming fire by night; for over all the glory will be a canopy. And there will be a shelter to give shade from the heat by day, and refuge and protection from the storm and the rain."

The city of Jerusalem during the 1,000-year kingdom of Jesus will be called Jehovah-Shammah, which means the LORD is there, because God will again dwell in His temple (Ezekiel 48:35).

Several articles present in the Temple during Old Testament times will not be present in the temple that will be built at the beginning of Jesus' 1,000-year kingdom. Notably absent will be the ark of the covenant, which was placed in the Holy of Holies, and the veil that separated the Holy of Holies from the Holy Place in the Temple. The ark of the covenant represented our rebellion against God and His resulting judgment of our rebellion. Our rebellion and God's judgment separated us from Him. The veil between the Holy of Holies and the Holy Place represented another barrier or point of separation between God and us. Jesus through His death on the cross and resurrection and ascension into heaven to be our high priest before the Father has removed these barriers. Therefore, they will not be present in the temple in Jesus' 1,000-year kingdom.

Ezekiel in Ezekiel 47:1-12 described his vision of the river that will flow from the temple eastward toward and into the Dead Sea. This river will give life to the land and turn the Dead Sea into a fresh water sea that will contain many types of fish that will be used for food. Many types of trees for food will grow on both banks of the river. These trees "will bear every month because their water flows from the sanctuary, and their fruit will be for food and their leaves for healing."

OFFERINGS AND FEASTS

The LORD in Ezekiel 45-46 specified the offerings and feasts that will be observed in His temple during the 1,000-year kingdom of Jesus. The significance of these offerings and feasts in the Old Testament must be understood to understand their significance in Jesus' 1,000-year kingdom. God instituted the Old Testament offerings and feasts as part of the covenant relationship He established with Israel through Moses.

Moses recorded the instructions given to him by God as they related to the offerings He established in Leviticus 1-7. He specified five offerings that were to be made to Him by the Israelites. The first three were to maintain fellowship with God, and the last two were to restore fellowship. These offerings were:

Burnt offering (Leviticus 1:1-17, 6:8-13): A burnt offering was an animal without blemish that was to be totally consumed by fire as a sacrifice to God. This was possibly the most solemn of the five offerings. It symbolized worship of God in the fullest sense. It was made as a general atonement for sin and represented adoration, devotion, dedication and supplication with respect to one's relationship with God.

Grain offering (Leviticus 2:1-16, 6:14-23): A grain offering was confined to raw or roasted cereals that were ground to flour or baked and then mixed with oil and frankincense. The grain offering was given as a gift to God from the fruits of one's labors on the soil God had entrusted to his care. A portion of the offering was to be consumed by fire, and the remainder belonged to the priests. Grain offerings were often made in conjunction with other offerings.

Peace offering (Leviticus 3:1-17, 7:11-38): A peace offering was a sacrifice that was made to thank God and seek communion with Him. Only part of the animal, which was without blemish, was consumed by fire as a sacrifice to the LORD. The remainder belonged to the priests and was to be consumed during the day it was offered.

Sin offering (Leviticus 4:1-5:13, 6:24-30): A sin offering was a sacrifice made to atone for the general nature of sin and its effects on God's creation and unintentional sins that may have been committed by the one offering the sacrifice. The offering temporarily restored fellowship with God by removing the barrier of sin between God and the offeror. Only part of the animal, which was without blemish, was consumed by fire as a sacrifice to the LORD. The remainder could be eaten by the priest.

Guilt offering (Leviticus 5:14-6:7, 7:1-10): A guilt offering was a sacrifice that was made to atone for acts of unfaithfulness to the LORD resulting in unintentional sins and for specific sins that the offeror knew he had committed. The offering was made to temporarily restore fellowship with God by removing the barrier of sin between God and the offeror. Only part of the animal, which was without blemish, was consumed by fire as a sacrifice to the LORD. The remainder of the offering could be eaten by the priest.

These offerings pointed to acts Jesus was to undertake when He offered Himself as an offering to God for our sins. His death, resurrection and ascension removed the barrier of sin that stood between God and us and made it possible for us to enter fellowship with God. The LORD stated in Ezekiel 45:18-46:24 all these offerings will be observed during the 1,000-year kingdom of Jesus. They will serve as a reminder and memorial of what Jesus accomplished for us on the cross.

Moses recorded the instructions given to him by God for the feasts Israel was to observe in Leviticus 23. God commanded the Israelites to celebrate seven feasts over a seven-month period. Four feasts were to be observed during the spring, beginning with the month of Nisan (refer to Table 3 in Chapter 7). These were Passover, Unleavened Bread, First Fruits and Pentecost.

Passover (Leviticus 23:5, Deuteronomy 16:2-7): The Feast of Passover was celebrated on the 14th of Nisan. It commemorated the salvation the Israelites received when the angel of death passed over their homes, which were marked with blood from a lamb. Death of the firstborn sons in Egyptian households was the final plague the LORD visited on Egypt before Pharaoh released the Israelites to return to the land He had promised them. Passover served as a reminder there is no atonement for sin apart from the shedding of blood from an innocent lamb. It pointed to Jesus as our Passover lamb whose blood was shed on the cross for our sins.

Unleavened *Bread* (Leviticus 23:6-8, Deuteronomy 16:3-8, 16): The Feast of Unleavened Bread was celebrated from the 15th through 21st of Nisan. It immediately followed Passover and was a reminder to the Israelites of their swift departure from Egypt. Their departure was so swift they did not have time to put leaven into their bread after Pharaoh released them to return to the land the LORD had promised them. Leaven is a symbol of sin in the Bible. Therefore, the Feast of Unleavened Bread was a reminder of God's call for Israel to be a holy nation, set apart from the world as a witness to Him. It pointed to Jesus' sinless life, which made Him a perfect sacrifice for our sins. Jesus was in the grave during the first two days of this feast. He was like a kernel of wheat planted in the ground, waiting to spring forth as the bread of life.

First Fruits (Leviticus 23:10-14): The Feast of First Fruits was celebrated on the 16th of Nisan. It was a feast where the first fruits of the early spring harvest were presented as a sacrifice to God. The feast was a reminder to the Israelites to put God first in their lives. The Feast of First Fruits pointed to the resurrection of Jesus when He became the first fruits of those who are dead (1 Corinthians 15:20-25).

Pentecost - the Feast of Weeks (Leviticus 23:15-22): The feast was the last of the spring feasts. It was a celebration of the completion of the spring harvest season and reminded the Israelites God was the source of all blessings. The Feast of Weeks (Pentecost) pointed to Jesus and the Father sending the Holy Spirit at Pentecost, signaling the birth of the Church. It also pointed to the harvest of souls that was to occur during the Church Age.

These four feasts pointed to events in the life of Jesus and the Church that were literally fulfilled when He first came to earth as our Messiah and Savior.

There was an interval of three months when there were no feasts established by God. Some teach this was intended to represent the Church Age - the time between the first and second coming of Jesus to earth.

The final three feasts were to be observed during the fall. These were Trumpets, Day of Atonement and Tabernacles:

Trumpets (Leviticus 23:23-25): The Feast of Trumpets (called Rosh Hashanah today) was celebrated on the 1st of Tishri at the new moon. It was the first of the fall feasts and marked the beginning of the Jewish civil year (refer to Table 8). The feast begins the "ten days of awe" that precedes the Day of Atonement. The feast was a day of rest and a reminder of the ongoing need for repentance to the Israelites. The Feast of Trumpets points to the coming rapture of Christian men and women and the Church when, at the sound of a great trumpet, Jesus will appear in the clouds to receive His elect into heaven (Matthew 24:31, 1 Corinthians 15:51-52, 1 Thessalonians 4:14-18).

Day of Atonement (Leviticus 23:26-32): The Feast of the Day of Atonement (called Yom Kippur) was celebrated on the 10th of Tishri. This was the day when the high priest went into the Holy of Holies to spread the blood of a slain innocent lamb on the seat of the ark of the covenant to atone for the sins of the nation of Israel. The Day of Atonement was a solemn day of rest and introspection to the Israelites. It was a reminder of God's promise to send a Messiah who would fulfill the demands of the Law. The Feast of the Day of Atonement points to the day of the second coming of Jesus. It will be a day when the remnant of Israel will look upon Jesus whom they have pierced, repent of their sins, and receive Him as their Messiah (Zechariah 12:10, Romans 11:1-6, 25-32).

Tabernacles (Leviticus 23:33-44, Deuteronomy 16:13-16): The Feast of Tabernacles (called Sukkot today) was celebrated on the 15th through 22nd of Tishri. It was also referred to as the Feast of Booths. The Feast of Tabernacles was a reminder to the Israelites of God's dwelling with, providing for and protecting them as they wandered in the wilderness for forty years. It was a celebration of God's faithfulness, even when the Israelites were unfaithful. The Feast of Tabernacles points to the time when God will again dwell with, provide for and protect His people during the 1,000-year reign of Jesus.

The first four feasts pointed to events in the life of Jesus and the Church that have already occurred. The last three feasts point to events that are related to Jesus' second coming when He will return as Lord and King. They will occur during the tribulation and millennial reign of Jesus.

The LORD indicated in Ezekiel 45:18-24 and Zechariah 14:16-21 only two of the seven feasts will be observed during the 1,000-year kingdom of Jesus. They are Passover and the Feast of Tabernacles (Booths). Three of the seven feasts were pilgrimage feasts that required males of Israel to travel to Jerusalem to celebrate the feasts. These were the Feast of Unleavened Bread, the Feast of Pentecost (Weeks) and the Feast of Tabernacles (Booths) (Deuteronomy 16:16-17). The LORD indicated in Zechariah 14:16-19 during the 1,000-year kingdom of Jesus the Feast of Booths will be a pilgrimage feast. He stated in Zechariah 14:16:

"Then it will come about that any who are left of all the nations that went against Jerusalem will go up from year to year to worship the King, the LORD of Hosts, and to celebrate the Feast of Booths."

The King refers to Jesus. The LORD stated nations who do not annually go to Jerusalem to celebrate the Feast of Booths and worship the King will be punished. He stated in Zechariah 14:18:

"And if the family of Egypt does not go up or enter, then no rain will fall on them; it will be the plague with which the LORD smites the nations who do not go up to celebrate the Feast of Booths."

Nations who do not go to Jerusalem to celebrate the Feast of Booths will experience drought the following year.

WORLD GOVERNMENT

The world government during the 1,000-year kingdom of Jesus will be a theocracy. The government will be headed by Jesus as its King. The seat of government will be Jerusalem (Isaiah 2:1-5, Zechariah 14:16-20). God described the restoration of Israel and Jerusalem during the 1,000-year kingdom of Jesus in Isaiah 60-62. Jesus will rule the nations of the world with a "rod of iron" (Revelation 12:5). He will rule with absolute authority. The 1,000-year kingdom of Jesus will be a time of rest, peace and prosperity throughout the earth because Jesus will be king, and Satan and his fallen angels will be bound and imprisoned in the abyss. This will be a time when the world will heal and rebuild itself from the horrendous devastation that will occur during the tribulation. Even though there will be people who will not accept the lordship of Jesus during the time of His kingdom, they will not be allowed to act out their rebellion. The world will be governed in a manner that will be perfectly compatible with the Laws of God. However, it will be governed in a manner that will clearly show the love and mercy of God toward the people of His creation.

The Bible indicates saints who are caught up with Jesus at the rapture during the middle of the tribulation and resurrected at the first resurrection at the beginning of the 1,000-year rule of Jesus will rule with Jesus in His kingdom (Daniel 7:21-22, 27, 1 Timothy 2:11-13, Revelation 3:31, 5:9-10, 20:4). The Bible does not present information on how Jesus will set up His government and what responsibilities and authority saints will be given in His government. We will have to wait until He sets up His government to learn how He will address these issues. The Bible also indicates Israel will play a central role in Jesus' government, and He will rule from Jerusalem.

THE FINAL REBELLION

Individuals who will have received the mark of the beast and worshiped the Antichrist and who will have remained faithful to God and worshiped Jesus during the great tribulation will enter the 1000-year kingdom of Jesus. The world will be repopulated with people who will accept the lordship of Jesus and who will reject His lordship. Those who reject Jesus during His 1,000-year rule will not be allowed to act out their rebellion because He will rule the world with a rod of iron and Satan and his angels will be imprisoned in the abyss and not be free to deceive people.

Satan and his angels will be released from the abyss when the 1,000 years of Jesus' kingdom are completed (Revelation 20:7-10). He will then deceive people from the nations of the world who have rejected the lordship of Jesus. The number of these persons will be "like the sand of the seashore." Satan will gather them to make war against Jesus and His saints. Fire will come down from heaven and devour them when they surround the camp of the saints and Jerusalem. Satan and his angels will then be cast into the lake of fire with the Antichrist and the false prophet where they will be tormented day and night forever.

CHAPTER 12
JUDGMENTS OF GOD

GOD'S FIXED DAY FOR JUDGMENT

Paul stated in Acts 17:30-31:

> "Therefore having overlooked the times of ignorance, God is now declaring to men that all people everywhere should repent, because He has fixed a day in which He will judge the world in righteousness through a Man whom He has appointed, having furnished proof to all men by raising Him from the dead."

God has "fixed a day in which He will Judge the world" through His Son, Jesus. We normally think in terms of a life span of 80 - 90 years. This governs the life choices we make and the characters we develop. We must think in terms of eternity when we address the judgments of God through Jesus. The positions the unrighteous and righteous with God, Jesus and the Holy Spirit will be fixed forever after they have been judged by Jesus. They will never change. The unrighteous will be separated from God, Jesus and the Holy Spirit in the lake of fire forever. The positions of the righteous in the kingdom of heaven will be fixed forever.

JESUS' CRITERIA FOR JUDGMENT

Jesus stated at the beginning of His ministry in Matthew 5:17-19:

> "Do not think that I came to abolish the Law or the Prophets; I did not come to abolish but to fulfill. For truly I say to you, until heaven and earth pass away, not the smallest letter or stroke shall pass from the Law until all is accomplished. Whoever then annuls one of the least of these commandments, and teaches others to do the same, shall be called least in the kingdom of heaven; but whoever keeps and teaches them, he shall be called great in the kingdom of heaven."

Jesus addressed three major points in His statement. First, He came to fulfill the Law and Prophets, not do away with them. Second, nothing shall be removed from or changed in the Law until heaven and earth pass away. This will not occur until just before the great white throne judgment the unrighteous will experience after the completion of Jesus' 1,000-year kingdom (Revelation 20:11, 21:1-2). Third, Jesus indicated the righteous who enter the kingdom of heaven will be separated into two groups. The righteous who have changed one of the least of the commandments of the Law and have taught others to do the same shall be called least in the kingdom of heaven, while the righteous who have obeyed and taught them to others shall be called great in the kingdom of heaven. Jesus' statement indicated God's grace and redemption will apply to the righteous who have changed one of the least of the commandments of the Law and have taught others to do the same. However, their position in the kingdom of heaven will be different from the righteous who have obeyed the commandments of the Law and have taught them to others.

Jesus presented the criteria we will be judged by. He stated in John 12:48-49:

> "He who rejects Me and does not receive My sayings, has one who judges him; the word I spoke is what will judge him at the last day. For I did not speak on My own initiative, but the Father Himself who sent Me has given Me a commandment as to what to say and what to speak."

Jesus stated in John 14:23, "If anyone loves Me, he will keep My word." John stated in 2 John 1:8-9:

> "Watch yourselves, that you do not lose what we have accomplished, but that you may receive a full reward. Anyone who goes too far and does not abide in the teaching of Christ, does not have God; the one who abides in the teaching, he has both the Father and the Son."

The unrighteous who have not abided in the teaching of Jesus have rejected God. Therefore, their names will not be written in the book of life. They will be judged and thrown into the lake of fire when they stand before Jesus at the great white throne judgment. However, the righteous who have been faithful to and abided in the teaching of Jesus will have "both the Father and Son," and their names will be written in the book of life. They will "receive a full reward" for the good works they have done in Jesus' name when they stand before Him. More will be said about this later.

Jesus addressed the judgment of the righteous and unrighteous in Matthew 25:31-46. He stated:

"But when the Son of Man comes in His glory, and all the angels with Him, then He will sit on His glorious throne. All the nations will be gathered before Him; and He will separate them one from another, as the shepherd separates the sheep from the goats, and He will put the sheep on His right, and the goats on the left."

"Then the King will say to those on His right, 'Come, you who are blessed of My Father, inherit the kingdom prepared for you from the foundation of the world. For I was hungry, and you gave Me something to eat; I was thirsty, and you gave Me something to drink; I was a stranger, and you invited Me in; naked, and you clothed Me; I was sick, and you visited Me; I was in prison, and you came to Me.' Then the righteous will answer Him, 'Lord, when did we see You hungry, and feed You, or thirsty, and give You something to drink? And when did we see You a stranger, and invite You in, or naked, and clothe You? When did we see You sick, or in prison, and come to You?' The King will answer and say to them, 'Truly I say to you, to the extent that you did it to one of these brothers of Mine, even the least of them, You did it to Me.'"

"Then He will also say to those on His left, 'Depart from Me, accursed ones, into the eternal fire which has been prepared for the devil and his angels; for I was hungry, and you gave Me nothing to eat; I was thirst, and you gave Me nothing to drink; I was a stranger, and you did not invite Me in; naked, and you did not clothe Me; sick, and in prison, and you did not visit Me.' Then they themselves also will answer, 'Lord, when did we see You hungry, or thirsty, or a stranger, or naked, or sick, or in prison, and did not take care of You?' Then He will answer them, 'Truly I say to you, to the extent that you did not do it to one of the least of these, you did not do it to Me.' These will go away into eternal punishment, but the righteous into eternal life."

Jesus will separate those who have performed works in His name as a shepherd separates sheep from goats when He returns. Sheep conjugate in flocks with a shepherd who protects, cares for, leads, and keeps them from straying from the flock. Goats gather in herds with a herdsman who cares for them. Goats are more independent than sheep and are by nature curious and often stray into new and unfamiliar areas. Sheep represent individuals who seek Jesus to lead and guide them through the presence of the Holy Spirit in their lives as they study, lean and internalize His words in the Gospels. Goats represent individuals with independent attitudes who stray from Jesus' words in the Gospels to follow beliefs His words do not confirm or support.

Jesus is our good shepherd who protects, cares for and leads us (John 10:11). He is also the Light of life and the Light of the world who guides us (John 8:12). Those who love and follow

Jesus have the Light of life who enables them to walk in the Light of the world. He leads and guides them through the presence of the Holy Spirit in their lives as they grow and mature in their relationship with Him. This equips them to perform good works in His name that honor and glorify God, His Father. Jesus will receive them into His presence when He returns.

Those who stray from Jesus' words in the Gospels often walk in darkness, and they often perform works in His name that are motivated by beliefs His words in the Gospels do not confirm or support. These works may not honor and glorify God. Mainline liberal protestant churches and denominations who support the LGBT agenda stray from Jesus' words in the Gospels. The LGBT agenda supports same sex and bisexual sexual relations between men and women, same sex marriages, and the right for individuals to change the gender with which they were born. The moral Law defines all sexual relations between men and women outside of marriage as sin. God stated in Genesis 2:18, 21-24 and Jesus affirmed in Matthew 19:4-6 that marriage is to be a union between a man and a woman as husband and wife.

God's and Jesus' words in the Bible are immutable. They will never change or pass away. Jesus stated in Matthew 24:35, "Heaven and earth will pass away, but My words will not pass away." He stated in John 12:48-50 we will be judged by His words in the Gospels. Jesus' words will judge and condemn those who deliberately choose to stray from them. He will remove from His presence those who have not repented and been forgiven for straying from His words when He returns.

Jesus stated in Matthew 6:1-7:

> "Beware of practicing your righteousness before men to be noticed by them; otherwise you have no reward with your Father who is in heaven."
>
> "So when you give to the poor, do not sound a trumpet before you, as the hypocrites do in the synagogues and in the streets, so that they may be honored by men. Truly I say to you, they have their reward in full. But when you give to the poor, do not let your left hand know what your right hand is doing, so that your giving will be in secret; and your Father who sees what is done in secret will reward you."
>
> "When you pray, you are not to be like the hypocrites; for they love to stand and pray in the synagogues and on the street corners so that they may be seen by men. Truly I say to you, they have their reward in full. But you, when you pray, go into your inner room, close your door and pray to your Father who is in secret, and your Father who sees what is done in secret will reward you."
>
> "And when you are praying, do not use meaningless repetition as the Gentiles do, for they suppose that they will be heard for their many words. So do not be like them; for your Father knows what you need before you ask Him."

We will be noticed and appreciated by others when these activities are motivated by our desire to be noticed and appreciated. Our reward will be being noticed and appreciated by others. However, we will not receive a reward from Jesus.

God expects us to grow in our knowledge of and internalize His word in the Bible and to enter and perform the good works He prepares for us to perform when we enter a relationship with Him through Jesus (Ephesians 2:10). Jesus indicated we show our love for Him by obeying His commandments and keeping His word (John 14:15, 21, 23). Our love for and obedience to Jesus is the foundation on which we build our life and develop our character. These must motivate us to enter the ministries and service to others we do in Jesus' name. He stated in Matthew 7:21-23:

> "Not everyone who says to Me, 'Lord, Lord,' will enter the kingdom of heaven, but he who does the will of My Father who is in heaven will enter. Many will say to Me on that day, 'Lord, Lord, did we not prophesy in Your name, and in Your name cast out demons, and in Your name perform many miracles?' And then I will declare to them, 'I never knew you; depart from Me, you who practice lawlessness.' Psalms 6:8"

Jesus indicated not everyone who refer to Him as Lord and claim to perform works in His name will enter the kingdom of heaven. Only those who do the will of His Father will enter. We do the will of God when we receive and abide in the words of Jesus in the Gospels and obey His commandments. Jesus also indicated performing works in His name will not gain us entrance to the kingdom of heaven when we have intentional unrepentant sin in our life that we have not confessed and requested forgiven.

Jesus stated in a parable in Matthew 24:42-51, "the Son of Man is coming at an hour when you do not think He will." He then identified "the faithful and sensible slave whom his master put in charge of his household to give them their food at the proper time" as one "whom his master finds so doing when he comes." His master "will put him in charge of all his possessions" when he returns. Jesus identified the evil slave as one who believed "in his heart" his master will not return for a long time and who will begin "to beat his fellow slaves and eat and drink with drunkards." His master will "assign him to a place with the hypocrites" where "there will be weeping and gnashing of teeth" when he returns "on a day when he does not expect ... at an hour which he does not know." God expects us to perform good works He prepares for us to perform (Ephesians 2:10). We will receive our reward when our good works are examined by Jesus when we are properly motivated to perform them.

Jesus presented another parable in Matthew 25:1-13 in which He stated

"The kingdom of heaven will be comparable to ten virgins, who took their lamps and went out to meet the bridegroom. Five of them were foolish, and five were prudent."

The foolish virgins took insufficient oil to keep their lamps lit when the bridegroom delayed his arrival. The prudent virgins took enough oil. The foolish virgins had to go and buy additional oil to keep their lamps lit when the bridegroom's arrival was delayed. While they were away, "the bridegroom came, and those who were ready went in with him to the wedding feast; and the door was shut." The foolish virgins asked, "Lord, lord, open up for us" when they arrived. The bridegroom stated, "Truly I say to you, I do not know you." It will be too late for us when we breath our last breath and we have not entered a reconciled relationship with God through our faith in Jesus and accomplished the good works God has prepared for us to performs during our life. Jesus will tell us He does not know us when we stand before Him to examine our good works.

Jesus stated in Matthew 7:19-21:

"Do not store up for yourselves treasures on earth, where moth and rust destroy, and where thieves break in and steal. But store up for yourselves treasures in heaven, where neither moth nor rust destroys, and where thieves do not break in or steal; for where your treasure is, there will your heart be also."

We build up and store for ourself treasures in heaven when we obey Jesus' words in the Gospels and perform the good works God prepares for us to perform. We will receive the treasures associated with our good works we have stored in heaven when we enter the kingdom of heaven.

Jesus continued in Matthew 7:24:

"No one can serve two masters; for either he will hate the one and love the other, or he will be devoted to one and despise the other. You cannot serve God and wealth."

We must choose what motivates us as we make life choices and develop our character. Is it our love for and obedience to God, Jesus and the Holy Spirit, or is it our desire for wealth and the things of the world? The unrighteous who have rejected Jesus will be judged by what is written about them in the books that will be opened at the great white thrown judgment and thrown into the lake of fire. Those who claim they have but have not obeyed the words of Jesus in the Gospels and have only done their works to be noticed by others will be told by Jesus He does not know them, and they will be judged with the unrighteous.

The righteous who have good works that are destroyed by fire when they are examined by Jesus will suffer loss and receive less than a full reward, and some will be called least in the kingdom of heaven. However, they will be there. The righteous who have faithfully been obedient to the words of Jesus in the Gospels and accomplished the good works God has prepared for them to perform will receive a full reward, and they will be called great in the kingdom of heaven.

JUDGMENT OF THE UNRIGHTEOUS AND RIGHTEOUS

Judgment of the Unrighteous - the Great White Throne Judgment

The great white throne judgment will occur at the end of Jesus' 1,000-year kingdom. John described this judgment in Revelation 20:11-15. He stated:

> "Then I saw a great white throne and Him who sat upon it, from whose presence earth and heaven fled away, and no place was found for them. And I saw the dead, the great and the small, standing before the throne, and books were opened; and another book was opened, which is the book of life; and the dead were judged from the things which were written in the books, according to their deeds. And the sea gave up the dead which were in it, and death and Hades gave up the dead which were in them; and they were judged, every one of them according to their deeds. Then death and Hades were thrown into the lake of fire. This is the second death, the lake of fire. And if anyone's name was not found written in the book of life, he was thrown into the lake of fire."

Who will sit on the great white throne is not identified. Jesus indicated in John 5:22-23 that God "has given judgement to the Son, so that all will honor the Son." Therefore, Jesus will be the one who sits on the great white throne.

Everyone whose name is not written in the book of life will be judged according to what is written about them in the books that will be opened at the great white throne judgment. This will include the unrighteous who have rejected or not received Jesus as their Savior. Their judgment will relate to what is written about them in the books that will be opened. They will be judged and sentenced to eternal separation from God, Jesus and the Holy Spirit in the lake of fire. God gives the unrighteous freedom to shape their lives and develop their characters by their life choices. They will experience the eternal consequences of their choices when Jesus judges them.

There will be three groups who will claim they were followers of Jesus who will be judged with the unrighteous and sentenced to eternal separation from God, Jesus and the Holy Spirit in the lake of fire. The first group will include those who during their lives after entering a relationship with Jesus have performed no good works as required by God in John 15:1-6, have completed none of the actions Peter outlined in 2 Peter 1:4-11, and have performed works solely for personal recognition and gain Jesus warned not to do in Matthew 6:1-6. Jesus will declare He does not know these individuals, and they will be sentenced to the lake of fire with the unrighteous.

The second group will be those who, after receiving the knowledge of the truth of God's word in the Bible, continue in a life of willful sin. In Hebrews 10:26-31, the author stated:

> "For if we go on sinning willfully after receiving the knowledge of the truth, there no longer remains a sacrifice for sins, but a terrifying expectation of judgment and the fury of a fire which will consume the adversary.(Isaiah 26:11) Anyone who has set aside the Law of Moses dies without mercy on the testimony of two or three witnesses. How much severer punishment do you think he will deserve who has trampled underfoot the Son of God, and has regarded as unclean the blood of the covenant by which he was sanctified, and has insulted the Spirit of grace? For we know Him who said, 'Vengeance is mine, I will repay' (Deuteronomy 32:35) And again, 'The LORD will judge His people.' (Deuteronomy 32:36) It is a terrifying thing to fall into the hands of the living God."

The third group will be those who have accepted the redemption God offered them through Jesus and have internalized God's word in the Bible. However, they have allowed unforgiveness, bitterness, the concerns of the world, and their desire for wealth to take root and grow in their hearts. These eventually cause them to fall away from God and Jesus and reject the influence of the Holy Spirit in their lives. In Hebrews 6:4-6, the author stated when these occur:

> "For in the case of those who have once been enlightened and have tasted of the heavenly gift and have been made partakers of the Holy Spirit, and have tasted the good word of God and the power of the ages to come, and then have fallen away, it is impossible to renew them again to repentance, since they again crucify to themselves the Son of God and put Him to open shame."

Individuals in this group make a choice to reject God, Jesus and the Holy Spirit after receiving God's grace through Jesus and enlightenment from the Holy Spirit. The writer of Hebrews stated it will be "impossible to renew them again to repentance." They will be judged with the unrighteous and sentenced to the lake of fire.

The lake of fire will be where the unrighteous will experience the second death, which is eternal separation from God, Jesus and the Holy Spirit. This will be the eternal consequence of the deliberate choice they have made during their lives to reject God's provision for their redemption through His Son, Jesus. They will experience the second death because they have deliberately chosen to mock, dishonor and reject God.

Many do not understand why a loving God can and will condemn people to eternal separation from Him in the lake of fire. God brings us into the world for specific purposes and to fellowship and commune with Him. These purposes include accepting and receiving His love and grace for us through Jesus, loving and respecting Him in return, trusting Him and obeying His commandments and laws, and doing His will for their lives. These only have meaning when we have the freedom to choose whether to live our lives the way God desires. God will never force us to do anything we do not want to do, and He respects and honors the life choices we make. These are central to the human characteristics He creates within us. Therefore, He allows for the fact many will reject Him, His eternal values, and His purpose for their lives.

We start a slide away from God that will ultimately condemn us to eternal separation from Him, Jesus and the Holy Spirit when we deliberately choose to violate His commandments and laws, to mock, dishonor and reject Him, to do evil and worship other gods, etc. This is not God's choice for us; it is our choice that He honors. It is borne out by our consistently and deliberately choosing to live a life that rejects Him, His eternal values, and His Son, Jesus. Therefore, the eternal separation of the unrighteous from God in the lake of fire will be a continuation of the separation from Him they have consistently and deliberately chosen during their lives.

Dr. J. P. Morgan stated in Lee Stroble's book, *The Case for Faith* (2000):

> "Hell is not a place where people are consigned because they were pretty good blokes, but they just didn't believe the right stuff. They are consigned there, first and foremost, because they defy their maker and want to be at the center of the universe. Hell is not filled with people who have already repented, only God is not gentle enough or good enough to let them out. It's filled with people who, for all eternity, still want to be the center of the universe and who persist in their God-defying rebellion."

The position of the unrighteous will be sealed forever in the lake of fire after the great white throne judgment. It will never change. The messenger angel implied this in Daniel 12:2. Jesus indicated this in Matthew 25:41, 46. The angel indicated this to John in Revelation 14:11 and 20:10.

Judgment of the Righteous

The righteous will experience a judgment that is separate from the judgment of the unrighteous. Peter stated in 2 Peter 1:4-8, 10-11:

> "Now by these He has granted to us His precious and magnificent promises, so that by them you may become partakers of the divine nature, having escaped the corruption that is in the world by lust. Now for this very reason also, applying all diligence, in your faith supply moral excellence, and in your moral excellence, knowledge, and in your knowledge, self-control, and in your self-control, perseverance, and in your perseverance, godliness, and in your godliness, brotherly kindness, and in your brotherly kindness, love. For if these qualities are yours and are increasing, they render you neither useless nor unfruitful in the true knowledge of our Lord Jesus Christ. ... Therefore, brethren, be more diligent to make certain about His calling and choosing you; for as long as you practice these things, you will never stumble; for in this way the entrance into the eternal kingdom of our Lord and Savior Jesus Christ will be abundantly supplied to you."

Peter outlined the qualities we are to develop and display when we enter our relationship with God through our faith and trust in and obedience to Jesus and when we enter the "good works, which God prepared beforehand so that we would walk in them." (Ephesians 2:10) These qualities will render us "neither useless nor unfruitful in the true knowledge of our Lord Jesus Christ." God calls us to perform the good works He has specifically prepared for us to perform. With respect to our involvement in these good works, Paul stated in 2 Corinthians 5:10:

> "For we must all appear before the judgment seat of Christ, so that each one may be recompensed for his deeds in the body, according to what he has done, whether good or bad."

Jesus addressed the judgment the righteous will experience in the parable of the talents (Matthew 25:14-30). Jesus stated:

> "For it is just like a man about to go on a journey, who called his own slaves and entrusted his possessions to them. To one he gave five talents, to another two, and to another one, each according to his own ability; and he went on his journey."

A talent is a measure of weight. The Roman talent was 71 lb (32.3 kg). The value of 1 talent of gold today is around $1.3M and of 1 talent of silver is around $170K. The parable indicates the master expected his slaves to invest the talents he had entrusted to them. The slave who had received five talents earned five more talents. The slave who had received two talents earned two more talents. The slave who had received one talent buried his talent in the ground and earned nothing.

The master of the slaves after a long time came and settled accounts with them. The slaves who had received five and two talents showed him their gains of five and two talents. Their master said to them:

> "Well done, good and faithful slave. You were faithful with a few things, I will put you in charge of many things; enter into the joy of your master."

The slave who had received and buried the one talent appeared before his master with no gain. His master said to him:

> "You wicked, lazy slave ... you ought to have put my money in the bank and on my arrival I would have received my money back with interest. Therefore, take away the talent from him, and give it to the one who has the ten talents."

Then the master said:

> "For to everyone who has, more shall be given, and he will have an abundance, but from the one who does not have, even what he does have shall be taken away. Throw out the worthless slave into the outer darkness; in that place there will be weeping and gnashing of teeth."

The master's response in this parable is consistent with Jesus' statement in John 15:2 where He indicated those who are in a relationship with Him that do not bear fruit in the relationship will be removed from the relationship by God (John 15:1-2).

God apposes us when we are only motivated by acquiring wealth. He presents us with opportunities to acquire wealth when we have a proper attitude toward it. He requires us to use a portion of the wealth we acquire to support good works He calls us and others to perform in return. He blesses us by providing opportunities for us to acquire more when we are faithful to do this. He may take our wealth from us when we inappropriately and selfishly use it.

Jesus used the proper investment of wealth in His parable of the talents (Matthew 25:14-30) to describe what is required of us when we enter our relationship with God through Him. We are born with natural abilities and are given specific spiritual gifts by the Holy Spirit as God's servants. God requires us to develop and use our natural abilities and to discover, develop and use our unique spiritual gifts to perform the good works He has prepared for us to perform. We will receive our reward when we obediently and faithfully develop and use our natural abilities and spiritual gifts to perform these good works. We will suffer loss when we fail to do this and lose the reward Jesus desires to give us. What we have received or acquired may be taken from us. Jesus stated relative to the reward He desires to give us in His final message in Revelation 22:12:

> "Behold, I am coming quickly, and My reward is with Me, to render to every man according to what he has done."

Jesus' reference to His reward can refer to the full reward we hope to receive as indicated by John in 2 John 1:8-9 and to the recompense we expect to receive for our deeds indicated by Paul in 2 Corinthians 5:10.

Jesus identified a fourth group in His parable of the talents who claim to be His followers during their lives. Some individuals in the first group mentioned earlier may be included in this group that will be judged with the unrighteous at the great white throne judgement. This group, represented by the slave with one talent who buried his talent, will have professed Jesus is Lord and indicated they believed God raised Him from the dead. However, there will be no evidence of His presence and the transforming influence of the Holy Spirit in their lives. Jesus will declare He never knew these individuals, and they will be judged and sentenced to the lake of fire.

The righteous who stand before Jesus who have faithfully demonstrated their love for, faith and trust in, and obedience to Him will enter the kingdom of heaven and be invited to enter the joy of their Lord. Their good works will be examined and judged by Jesus. Paul addressed this in 1 Corinthians 3:9-15. He stated:

> "For we are God's fellow workers; you are God's building. According to the grace of God which was given to me, like a wise master builder I laid a foundation, and another is building on it. But each man must be careful how he builds on it. For no man can lay a foundation other than the one which is laid, which is Jesus Christ. Now if any man builds on the foundation with gold, silver, precious stones, wood, hay, straw, each man's work will become

evident; for the day will show it because it is to be revealed with fire, and the fire itself will test the quality of each man's work. If any man's work is burned up, he will suffer loss; but he himself will be saved, yet so as through fire."

Jesus is the foundation on which we build our life and develop our character. We build on His foundat1ion with care. The good works we do and our motives for doing them while building on Jesus' foundation will be revealed and tested with fire when we stand before Him. Good works represented by gold, silver and precious stones will be accepted by Jesus. Good works represented by wood, hay and straw will be rejected. We will receive a reward for those good works that are accepted, but we will suffer loss for those that are rejected. We will not lose our salvation because of those good works that are rejected. However, we may suffer loss with respect to our position in the kingdom of heaven. Our position will be fixed for eternity after our good works have been examined by Jesus; it will never change.

Summary

Questions are raised regarding those who have never had the opportunity to hear about God's saving grace through Jesus when His judgment is discussed. Paul responded to this in Romans 1:18-20 where he stated:

> "For the wrath of God is revealed from heaven against all ungodliness and unrighteousness of men who suppress the truth in unrighteousness, because that which is known about God is evident within them; for God made it evident to them. For since the creation of the world His invisible attributes, His eternal power and divine nature, have been clearly seen, being understood through what has been made, so that they are without excuse."

The existence of God has been made evident through His creation. He has placed a sen se of "His invisible attributes, His eternal power and divine nature" within us "since the creation of the world." Therefore, the unrighteous who have rejected God will be without excuse when they stand before Jesus at the great white throne judgment.

Several observations can be made from the preceding discussions:

- There is a difference between the kingdom of God and the kingdom of heaven. We enter the kingdom of God when we receive Jesus as our Savior and Lord of our life. The righteous will enter the kingdom of heaven after their good works and their motives for performing them have been examined and judged by Jesus. Not everyone who believe they have entered the kingdom of God will enter the kingdom of heaven.

- We are to grow in our knowledge of and internalize God's word in the Bible when we enter a relationship with Him through Jesus. We are expected to obey Jesus' commandments and words and to perform the good works God has prepared for us to perform.

- Our faith in God and Jesus develops and grows, and They reveal Themselves to and take up residence in us with the Holy Spirit as we grow in our knowledge of and internalize God's word in the Bible, and we yield ourself in obedience to Them.

- Our love for Jesus and obedience to Him must be the foundation on which we build our life and develop our character. These must motivate the good works we perform in His name. We then join the ranks of the righteous, God blesses and rewards us, and our names are written in the book of life.

- Our faith atrophies and dies when we fail to grow in our knowledge of and internalize God's word in the Bible, build our life and develop our character on the foundation of Jesus, and yield ourself in faith and obedience to Jesus. God may withdraw His Spirit from us when these occur, and we may join the ranks of the unrighteous.

- The righteous and unrighteous will be separated at the great white throne judgment. Everyone will be judged by the words Jesus spoke in the four Gospels. The unrighteous will then be judged by what is written about them in the books that will be opened at the great white thrown judgment and thrown into the lake of fire. Only the righteous whose names are written in the book of life will enter the kingdom of heaven.

- The good works of the righteous and their motives for doing them will be examined by Jesus. Some of their good works may be rejected, and they will suffer loss when this occurs. Other good works will be accepted, and they will receive a reward for them. This examination will determine the positions of the righteous in the kingdom of heaven for eternity.

- The righteous who have faithfully performed the "good works, which God prepared beforehand so that [they] would walk in them" will receive a reward when their good works are examined by Jesus.

- We do not know when Jesus will return or when we will breathe our last breath. We will spend eternity in the kingdom of heaven with God, Jesus, the Holy Spirit, the angels of God, and the righteous when we have had faith in, trusted and been obedient to Jesus during our life, and we have been fruitful in performing good works God has prepared for us to perform during our life. We will spend eternity in the lake of fire with Satan, his angels and the unrighteous when we have not sought and received God's redemption through Jesus. We will also be separated from God, Jesus and the Holy Spirit in the lake of fire when we have performed none of the good works God has prepared for us to perform in our relationship with Jesus during our life.

SHEOL, HADES, HELL, PARADISE AND HEAVEN

In Hebrews 9:27, the author stated:

> "And inasmuch as it is appointed for men to die once and after this comes judgement."

The Bible teaches our spirit and soul are separated from our physical body at the time of our death, and our physical body is placed in a grave in the ground. Sheol, Hades, hell, paradise and heaven refer to places where the Bible indicates our spirit and soul may go when we are judged by God after we die. Sheol is an Old Testament Hebrew word, and Hades is a New Testament Greek word that refer to the same place. Hell sometimes refers to the same place as Sheol and Hades in the Bible.

Jesus' parable of the rich man and Lazarus in Luke 16:16–31 presented a description of Hades/Sheol. They were a place that was divided into two regions. One region, referred to as Abraham's bosom, was a place of great comfort and rest. The righteous dead occupied this region. The other region, referred to as hell, was a place of great torment and suffering. The wicked dead occupied this region. A great chasm separated the two regions that prevented occupants of one region from crossing over to the other region.

Peter indicated in 1 Peter 3:18-20 Jesus went to Hades after He was "made alive in the spirit" after His crucifixion, but before the resurrection of His physical body where He made a "proclamation to the spirits now in prison" there. It is reasonable to presume these imprisoned spirits were in the region of Hades referred to as hell.

Jesus stated to the repentant criminal in Luke 23:43 while they hung on their crosses that he would be with Him that day in paradise. It is reasonable to presume Jesus went to Abraham's bosom in Hades where He made His proclamation to the spirits imprisoned in the region of Hades referred to as hell. Therefore, Jesus' reference to paradise may have referred to Abraham's bosom in Hades.

Matthew 27:52–53 implied the souls and spirits of the righteous in Abraham's bosom were released from Hades after Jesus' resurrection. They appeared to many in Jerusalem and then presumably were transported to heaven. Pauls' statement in Ephesians 4:8 implied this. Heaven at this time was and still is referred to as a spiritual realm.

Paul stated in 2 Corinthians 12:2-4 that he knew a man who 14 years earlier was caught up into the third heaven he referred to as paradise. This implied paradise is in heaven. This also implied Hades/Sheol only consisted of a single region where there is great torment and suffering, referred to as hell, after Jesus' resurrection.

Individuals when judged by God after they die will be received into heaven where there will be great comfort and rest when they have been redeemed by and reconciled to God through their faith and trust in and obedience to Jesus. They will be placed in hell when they have not sought and received God's redemption and reconciliation through Jesus where they will experience great torment and suffering.

THREE RESURRECTIONS

The Bible indicates there will be three resurrections where our spirits and souls will be reunited with physical bodies. They are:

- **The rapture** (Matthew 24:26-41, Mark 13:24-39 and Luke 17:22-37): The rapture will be a raising up of the living and a resurrection of the dead who have had faith in, trusted and were obedient to Jesus during their lives to meet Him in the air. Their names will be written in the book of life. The rapture will occur during the middle of the seven-year tribulation at the sounding of the 7th trumpet.

- **Resurrection of saints martyred during the great tribulation** (Revelation 20:4-6): This resurrection, referred to as the first resurrection in Revelation, will include those who remain faithful to God and Jesus and do not receive the mark of the beast during the great tribulation. Their names will be written in the book of life. This resurrection will occur after the return of Jesus at the end of the great tribulation and before He sets up His 1,000-year kingdom. Those in this resurrection will be priests of God and Jesus and will rule with Jesus during His 1,000-year kingdom.

- **Resurrection of the dead before the great white throne judgement at the end of Jesus' 1,000-year kingdom** (Revelation 20:11-15): This resurrection will include the dead who have not been redeemed by and reconciled to God through Jesus before the rapture and who have received the mark of the beast during the great tribulation. Their names will not be written in the book of life. This resurrection will also include all who die during Jesus' 1,000-year kingdom and who die at the end of His 1,000-year kingdom when the first earth and heaven pass away. Some will have been faithful and obedient to Jesus, and their names will be written in the book of life. Others will have rejected Jesus, and their names will not be written in the book of life. This last resurrection occurs after the first earth and heaven pass away at the end of Jesus' 1,000-year kingdom and before the great white throne judgement.

The names of those in the rapture, the first resurrection, and who are faithful to and obey Jesus during His 1,000-year kingdom will be written in the book of life. They will be immortal after their resurrections. Those in the resurrection before the great white throne judgement whose names are not written in the book of life will be placed in the lake of fire where they will be tormented and suffer forever.

OUR REWARD IN THE KINGDOM OF HEAVEN

Isaiah stated in Isaiah 40:10:

> "Behold, the LORD God will come with might,
> With His arm ruling for Him.
> Behold, His reward is with Him
> And His recompense before Him."

Jesus stated in Revelation 22:12:

> "Behold, I am coming quickly, and My reward is with Me, to render to every
> man according to what he has done."

Jesus will fulfill Isaiah's prophesy when He returns.

The Bible teaches we are to study and internalize God's word in the Bible. We will spiritually grow and mature through this study as our mind is renewed and our heart is transformed through the actions of the Holy Spirit in our life. As we spiritually grow and mature, we are to develop our natural abilities, discover and develop our spiritual gifts, and employ them in doing good works the Holy Spirit calls us to enter and perform.

John encouraged us in 2 John 1:8-9 to abide in the teachings of Jesus so that we will receive a full reward. Paul stated in 2 Corinthians 5:10 we will stand before the judgement seat of Jesus so that we can be recompensed for our deeds in the body. Paul indicated in 1 Corinthians 3:12-15 the quality of our works will be revealed and tested by fire when we stand before Jesus on the last day. Some works will be burned up while others will remain. We will suffer loss for our works that are burned up, but we will not lose our salvation through Jesus. Jesus, John and Paul indicated the righteous will receive a reward for the good works they have done when Jesus returns. However, they do not present information as to what this reward will be.

Jesus provided clues in His discourses in Matthew 24:42-51 and Matthew 25:14-36 regarding this reward. The faithful and sensible slave in Matthew 24:42-51 was put in charge of all his master's possessions. The slaves who were given two and five talents in Matthew 25:14-36 were told they will be put in charge of many things because of their faithfulness over a few things. These two discourses imply the reward the righteous will receive from Jesus will be related to positions of responsibility and leadership they will be given in the kingdom of heaven. These positions when awarded will be fixed for eternity.

Paul described three crowns in his letters the righteous will receive as a reward in the kingdom of heaven. They are:

The Crown of Righteousness: The crown of righteousness will be given to all those who have loved Jesus' appearing (2 Timothy 4:7-8).

The Crown of Life: The crown of life will be given to those who have persevered under trials (James 1:12, Revelation 2:10).

The Crown of Glory: The crown of glory will be given to elders (pastors) who have been faithful in shepherding the flocks (churches) that have been entrusted to their care (1 Peter 5:1-4).

The Imperishable Crown: The imperishable crown will be given to those who discipline their bodies to bring it into subjection to the righteousness of God. (1 Corinthians 9:25)

The Crown of Rejoicing: The crown of rejoicing will be given to those who rejoice at the coming of Jesus (1 Thessalonians 2:19).

THE NATURE OF OUR RESURRECTED BODIES

Paul gave us insight into the nature of the resurrection bodies the righteous will receive in 1 Corinthians 15:35-49. He stated:

> "But someone will say, 'How are the dead raised? And with what kind of body do they come?' You fool! That which you sow does not come to life unless it dies; and that which you sow, you do not sow the body which is to be, but a bare grain, perhaps of wheat or of something else. But God gives it a body just as He wished, and to each of the seeds a body of its own. All flesh is not the same flesh, but there is one flesh of men, and another flesh of beasts, and another flesh of birds, and another of fish. There are also heavenly bodies and earthly bodies, but the glory of the heavenly is one, and the glory of the earthly is another. There is one glory of the sun, and another glory of the moon, and another glory of the stars; for star differs from star in glory. So also is the resurrection of the dead. It is sown a perishable body, it is raised an imperishable body; it is sown in dishonor, it is raised in glory; it is sown in weakness, it is raised in power; it is sown a natural body, it is raised a spiritual body. If there is a natural body, there is also a spiritual body. So also it is written, 'The first man, Adam, became a living soul.' Genesis 2:7 The last Adam became a life-giving spirit. However, the spiritual is not first, but the natural; then the spiritual. The first man is from the earth, earthy; the second man is from heaven. As is the earthy, so also

are those who are earthy; and as is the heavenly, so also are those who are heavenly. Just as we have borne the image of the earthy, we will also bear the image of the heavenly."

The natural bodies of the righteous are perishable, weak and given to dishonor because of sin. Their resurrection bodies, however, will be bodies that will be raised imperishable in power and glory. The man from heaven is Jesus. The resurrection bodies of the righteous will be bodies that will be like Jesus' resurrection body. Paul affirmed this in Philippians 3:20-21:

"For our citizenship is in heaven, from which also we eagerly wait for a Savior, the Lord Jesus Christ; who will transform the body of our humble state into conformity with the body of His glory, by the exertion of the power that He has even to subject all things to Himself."

John reaffirmed this in 1 John 3:1-2:

"See how great a love the Father has bestowed on us, that we would be called children of God; and such we are. For this reason the world does not know us, because it did not know Him. Beloved, now we are children of God, and it has not appeared as yet what we will be. We know that when He appears, we will be like Him, because we will see Him just as He is."

The bodies of the righteous, like Jesus, will be placed in a grave when they die. Their bodies when resurrected will be like Jesus' resurrected body. They will:

- Consist of flesh and bones (Luke 24:39-40),
- Be similar in appearance to their natural bodies (Matthew 28:8-10, Luke 24:13-35, John 20:11-18),
- Be able to eat food (Luke 24:41-43, John 21:12-13),
- Be able to appear and disappear at will (Mark 16:12-14, Luke 24:31, 36-37, John 20:19-20, 26), and
- Be imperishable, eternal and immortal (1 Corinthians 15:53-54, 2 Corinthians 5:1).

Jesus stated in Matthew 22:30 and Luke 20:36 that we will be like angels with our resurrection bodies. The resurrection bodies of the righteous will not be corrupted by sin nor be subject to the constraints of known laws of physics and time even though they may resemble their natural bodies.

THE BOOK OF LIFE

Exodus 32:33 is the first reference to God's book in the Bible. The LORD said to Moses in response to the Israelites building and worshiping a golden calf after Moses had led them out of Egypt, "Whoever has sinned against Me, I will blot him out of My book." Other references to God's book in the Old Testament include:

- The Psalmist petitioned the LORD in Psalms 69:28 regarding those who were persecuting and afflicting him. He wrote, "May they be blotted out of the book of life and may they not be recorded with the righteous.

- The Psalmist wrote in Psalms 139:16, "Your eyes have seen my unformed substance; and in Your book were all written the days that were ordered for me, when as yet there was not one of them."

- The angel Gabriel told Daniel in Daniel 12:1:

  "Now at that time Michael, the great prince who stands guard over the sons of your people, will arise and there will be a time of distress such as never occurred since there was a nation until that time; and at that time your people, everyone who is found written in the book, will be rescued."

The names written in *My book* in Exodus 33:32, the *book of life* in Psalms 69:28, *Your book* in Psalms 139:16, and the *book* in Daniel 12:1 in the Old Testament referred to names written in *God's book*. The names written in the *book of life* mentioned in Philippians 4:3 and Revelation 3:5 and 21:27 in the New Testament can also refer to names written ins *God's book*.

God stated He will remove our name from His book when we have sinned against Him. The Bible teaches this will occur unless we repent of our sins and receive the redemption and reconciliation God extends to us through the blood of Jesus. We enter a reconciled relationship with God through Jesus when we approach Him, repent of our sins, and receive His gift of grace. We then begin a process through which God's book becomes for us the book of life. This process is discussed in Chapter 4. John was told in Revelation 20:15:

  "And if anyone's name was not found written in the book of life, he was thrown into the lake of fire."

Jesus stated in Revelations 3:5:

"He who overcomes will thus be clothed in white garments; and I will not erase his name from the book of life, and I will confess his name before My Father and before His angels."

Jesus' statement is a conditional statement. Our name will not be removed from the book of life when we have overcome temptation. The Bible implies this occurs when we overcome the trials and tribulations associated with our relationship with God through Jesus, and we have demonstrated our faith and trust in and our obedience to Jesus' words in this relationship. Jesus' statement also implies our name may be removed from the book of life when we have not overcome these trials and tribulations nor remained faithful and obedient to Jesus' words.

The Bible does not indicate during our life when God may remove our name from His book. The Bible also does not indicate when our name transitions from being written in God's book to being written in the book of life after we have entered a relationship with Him through Jesus.

Peter stated in 2 Peter 3:9:

"The Lord is not slow about His promise, as some count slowness, but is patient toward you, not wishing for any to perish but for all to come to repentance."

Paul stated in 1 Timothy 2:4 that God "desires all men to be saved and to come to the knowledge of the truth." God does not desire anyone's name to be removed from His book. Therefore, the Holy Spirit acts throughout our life to convict us of sin and draw us to repent and enter a reconciled relationship with God through Jesus. How we choose to respond to these acts of the Holy Spirit is up to us. Some choose to reject God, Jesus and the Holy Spirit. Some choose to enter a relationship with God through Jesus at an early age. Others make this choice later in their life. Some make this choice at the time of their death. God honors all these responses. However, He will remove our name from His book when our response has been to reject Him, Jesus and the Holy Spirit.

Psalms 139:16 indicates God has written our name in His book before we are born. Peter and Paul stated God desires "for all to come to repentance" and "to be saved and to come to the knowledge of the truth." The Bible teaches God through His grace provides the means through which we can be redeemed and reconciled to Him through our faith and trust in and obedience to Jesus. The Holy Spirit convicts us of sin and draws us to repent and enter a relationship with God through Jesus. We then begin a process through which our name will transition from being written in God's book to being written in the book of life. This occurs as we grow in our knowledge of and internalize God's word in the Bible, and we enter and perform the good works He prepares for us. Jesus' statement indicated

He will not remove our name from the book of life when we persevere and overcome the trials and tribulations we encounter because of our relationship with Him.

The Bible implies God will remove from His book the names of those who:

- Have sinned against Him (Exodus 33:32) and have not repented and received the redemption He extends to them through the blood of Jesus;

- Go on "sinning willfully after receiving the knowledge of the truth" (Hebrews 10:26-31);

- "After they have escaped the defilement of the world by the knowledge of the Lord and Savior Jesus Christ, they are again entangled in them and are overcome" by them (2 Peter 2:20-21);

- "Have once been enlightened and have tasted of the heavenly gift and have been made partakers of the Holy Spirit, and have tasted the good word of God and the power of the ages to come, and then have fallen away" from Him, Jesus and the Holy Spirit (Hebrews 6:4-6);

- Have only ministered to others in the name of Jesus to achieve personal gain and be noticed by others (Matthew 6:1-7, 25:31-46);

- Have done nothing to spiritually grow and mature in their relationship with Jesus after entering this relationship and have performed none of the good works God has prepared for them to perform (Matthew 25:14-30, Luke 19:12-27, and John 15:1-3); and

- Will worship the Antichrist during the great tribulation (Revelation 13:8, 17:8).

The Bible does not indicate when during the life of an individual his name may be removed from God's book. However, in Hebrews 9:27, the author indicated when this may occur:

> "And inasmuch as it is appointed for men to die once and after this comes judgment, so Christ also, having been offered once to bear the sins of many, will appear a second time for salvation without reference to sin, to those who eagerly await Him."

We will be judged by God after we die. Our position with Him will be fixed at this judgment for eternity. The names of those mentioned in the Bible verses listed in the preceding paragraph will have been removed from God's book when they stand before Jesus at the great white throne judgment. They will be thrown into the lake of fire because their names will not be written in the book of life.

God knows we will experience temptations and encounter challenges, adversities and persecution when we honor and obey Jesus' words. He knows we will not live a sinless life after we enter a reconciled relationship with Him through Jesus. He knows we will sometimes fail to obey Jesus' words and do some of the good works He has prepared for us. However, God through His grace extended to us through the atoning blood of Jesus will forgive us when these occur, and we seek His forgiveness. God is glorified by our perseverance demonstrated through performing the good works He has prepared for us (Matthew 5:16). Our names as a result will be written in the book of life.

The names of those who have not been removed from God's book will be written in the book of life. These individuals will stand before Jesus at a separate judgment on the last day (2 Corinthians 5:10). Some of their works may be rejected while others will be accepted when Jesus examines their life (1 Corinthians 3:9-15). They will receive their reward (Jeremiah 17:10, 1 John 1:8, Revelation 22:12) given to them by Jesus and enter the kingdom of heaven.

THE LAKE OF FIRE - THE SECOND DEATH

The lake of fire is referred to as the place of the second death in Revelation 20:14 and 21:18. The term second death refers to eternal separation from God, Jesus and the Holy Spirit. Jesus stated in Matthew 25:41 the unrighteous will be sent to "the eternal fire prepared for the devil and his angels." The lake of fire will be populated by:

- Satan (Revelation 20:10),
- The fallen angels (or demons) (2 Peter 2:4, Jude 6-7),
- The Antichrist and false prophet (Revelation 19:20),
- Death and Hades (Revelation 20:13), and
- Unrighteous whose names are not written in the book of life (Revelation 20:15).

Jesus indicated the lake of fire will be a place of:

- Unquenchable fire (Matthew 3:12),
- Unbearable thirst (Luke 16:24),
- Darkness (Matthew 25:30),
- Weeping and gnashing of teeth (Matthew 24:15, 25:30),
- Memory and remorse (Luke 16:19-31),

- Eternal fire (Matthew 25:41), and
- Eternal punishment (Matthew 25:46).

There is symbolism and reality in the Bible's description of the lake of fire. Fire symbolizes judgment and separation. The lake of fire will be a physical place. It will be a place of eternal punishment and separation from God, Jesus and the Holy Spirit. God will place an eternal barrier between those who will be with Him, Jesus and the Holy Spirit throughout eternity and those who will be eternally separated from Them.

Jesus referred to the lake of fire as a place of darkness. The darkness will be real darkness. It will also be a darkness associated with the absence of God. There will be no righteousness when God is absent; there will only be evil. There is no truth; there is only deception and despair. All that gives worth, value and meaning to life is stripped away when God is absent. This is the darkness that will exist in the lake of fire.

We often only consider God's attributes of love, mercy and grace; we ignore His attributes of holiness and justice. These attributes require God to judge the conscious and deliberate choices the unrighteous make during their lives to disobey His commandments and laws and to reject, revile and dishonor Him. God would diminish Himself if He did not act justly toward those who blatantly defied Him. Therefore, the lake of fire will be a place of God's eternal justice.

The unrighteous will suffer greatly in the lake of fire. It will be a place of great physical suffering. The unrighteous will have memory; they will know why they are there and what they are missing by being eternally separated from God. The emotional responses of shame, anguish, regret and remorse will torment them forever.

John was told in Revelation the unrighteous who worship the Antichrist and receive his mark (the mark of the beast) during the great tribulation will:

- Experience the undiluted divine wrath of God (Revelation 14:9-10),
- Have no rest both day and night (Revelation 14:11), and
- Be tormented both day and night forever (Revelation 14:11, 20:10).

CHAPTER 13
CREATION OF A NEW HEAVEN, EARTH AND JERUSALEM

DESTRUCTION OF THE FIRST HEAVEN AND FIRST EARTH

Revelation 20:11 indicates earth and heaven will flee from Him who sits on the great white throne. Revelation 21:1 states the first heaven and earth will pass away. There is no other mention in Revelation regarding the destruction of the earth and heaven. However, Peter presented an image of the destruction of the heavens and earth in 2 Peter 3:10:12:

> "But the day of the Lord will come like a thief, in which the heavens will pass away with a roar and the elements will be destroyed with intense heat, and the earth and its works will be burned up."

SIGNIFICANCE OF ZION

Jesus stated to His disciples in John 14:1-4:

> "Do not let your heart be troubled; believe in God, believe also in Me. In My Father's house are many dwelling places; if it were not so, I would have told you so; for I go to prepare a place for you. If I go and prepare a place for you, I will come again and receive you to Myself, that where I am, there you may be also. And you know the way where I am going."

Jesus indicated there are many dwelling places in His Father's house. The Psalms and Hebrews appear to present information on the location and description of this house. Psalms 9:11 states:

> "Sing praises to the LORD, who dwells in Zion,
> Declare among the peoples His deeds."

and Psalms 132:13-14 state:

"For the LORD has chosen Zion;
He has desired it for His habilitation.
'This is My resting place forever;
Here I will dwell, for I have desired it.'"

Psalms 48:1-3, 8, 12-14 present a description of Zion's beauty:

"Great is the LORD, and greatly to be praised,
In the city of our God, His holy mountain.
Beautiful in elevation, the joy of the whole earth,
Is Mount Zion in the far north,
The city of the great King. God, in her palaces,
Has made Himself known as a stronghold."

...

"As we have heard, so have we seen
In the city of the LORD of hosts, in the city of our God,
God will establish her forever. Selah."

...

"Walk about Zion and go around her;
Count her towers;
Consider her ramparts;
Go through her palaces,
That you may tell it to the next generation.
For such is God,
Our God forever and ever;
He will guide us until death."

Another description of Zion is found in Hebrews 12:22-24:

"But you have come to Mount Zion and to the city of the living God, the heavenly Jerusalem, and to myriads of angels, to the general assembly and church of the firstborn who are enrolled in heaven, and to God, the Judge of all, and to the spirits of the righteous made perfect, and to Jesus, the mediator of a new covenant, and to the sprinkled blood, which speaks better than the blood of Abel."

Readers of the Old Testament often believed *Zion* is a Hebrew word that came into use as a religious term long after Jerusalem became a city. *Zion* historically predated the Israelites and initially had no association with religious beliefs. The word *Zion* has an Arabic origin. The root Hebrew word for *Zion* means *dry place* or *parched ground*. Whereas the Arabic root word for *Zion* more appropriately means *hill crest* or *mountainous ridge*. The knoll or rounded hilltop of the ancient village of Jerusalem was called Zion before Jerusalem became a village.

Zion was first mentioned in 2 Samuel 5:7. It was located on the easternmost knoll of the two knolls that encompassed the ancient village of Jerusalem (Figure 8). Zion initially referred to the Jebusite fortress that was conquered by David. The area of and around the fortress became known as the City of David after being conquered by David.

Mount Zion initially referred to the location of the Jebusite fortress. The location of Mount Zion was moved to the top of the eastern Jerusalem knoll after the Temple of Solomon (the first Jewish temple) was erected there. This location is called the Temple Mount today. The final and current location of Mount Zion was moved to the more prominent western Jerusalem knoll. This is believed to be the location of the palace of king David. This location is west of the location of the City of David across the Tyropoeon Valley that separates the two knolls.

Zion has many meanings in ancient and modern Israel and in Old and New Testament history. It refers to the City of David, the ancient and modern City of Jerusalem, and the nation of Israel. With respect to Old and New Testament history, Zion is identified as the city of our God, the city of the LORD of hosts, the city of the living God, My holy mountain, etc. Zion along with Mount Zion represented the places throughout Old and New Testament history where God was believed to be present. Zion is the thread that ties together many of the narratives associated with Old Testament historic events. These events ultimately will lead to the future new Jerusalem, which God is building and will come down from heaven after heaven and earth pass away. "The Lord God the Almighty and the Lamb (Jesus)" will be its temple, and they will dwell there forever with the Holy Spirit, myriads of angels, and the righteous whose names are written in the Lamb's book of life. The new Jerusalem will be the house Jesus referred to in John 14:1-4 that His Father is building with many dwelling places for the righteous who will enter the kingdom of heaven.

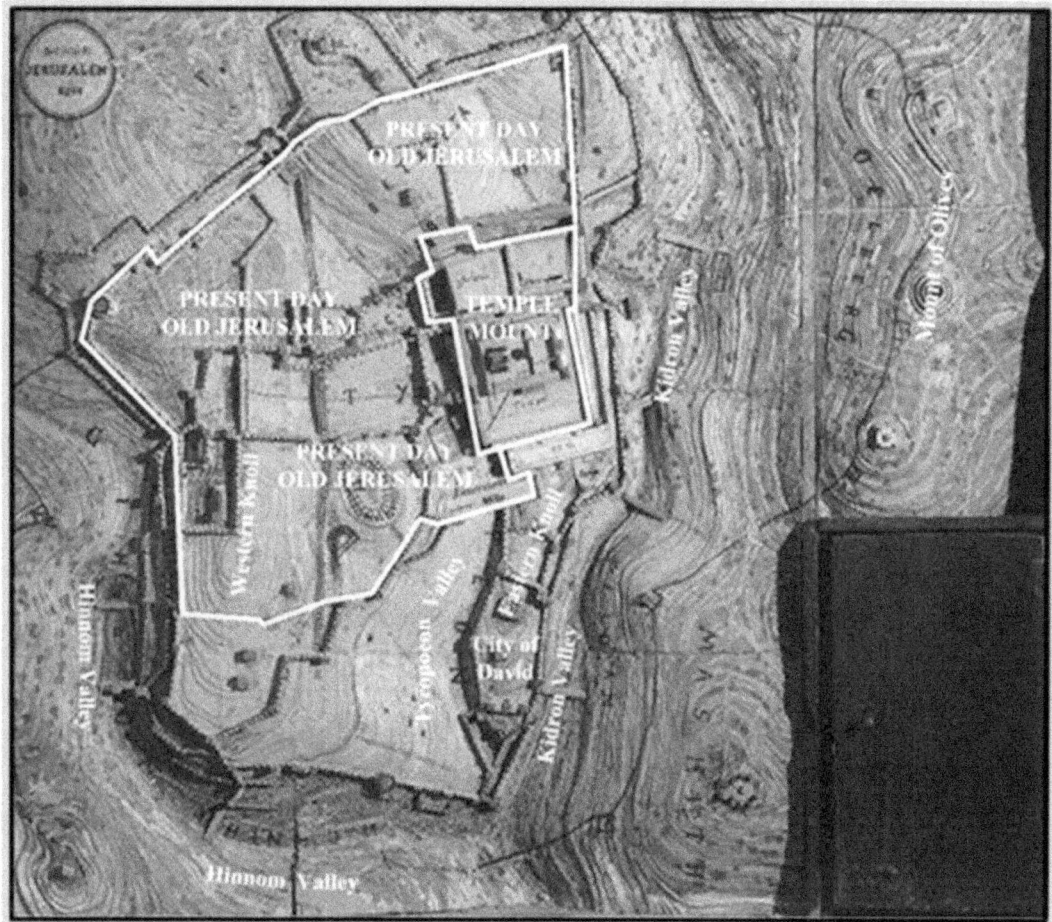

Thee Dimensional Model of Jerusalem: Conrad S. Schick (1822-1901) was a famous architect who lived in Jerusalem at the end of the 19th century. He created the three dimensional model as he envisioned Jerusalem during the Second Temple period shown in the above image. The size of this model was 99 by 85 cm, and its scale was 1:2500.

(Image photo contours sharpened and labeling and drawing of present day old Jerusalem boundaries added by D. D. Reynolds)

(Original Image sources: http://www.templemount.org/topo.html)

Figure 8

THE NEW EARTH, HEAVEN AND JERUSALEM

John was given a vision of the new heaven, earth and Jerusalem after his vision of the great white throne judgment in Revelation 21:1-3. The first heaven and earth had passed away. This is a confirmation of God's promised in Isaiah 65:17:

> "For behold, I create new heavens and a new earth;
> And the former things will not be remembered or come to mind."

His reference to new heavens refers to heavens that will exist beyond the new earth. These can refer to the creation of new or the recreation of existing solar systems and galaxies that will exist in the new heavens beyond the new earth. Regarding this promise, John stated in Revelation 21:3-7:

> "'Behold, the tabernacle of God is among men, and He will dwell among them, and they shall be His people, and God Himself will be among them, and He will wipe away every tear from their eyes; and there will no longer be any death; there will no longer be any mourning, or crying, or pain; the first things have passed away.' And He who sits on the throne said, 'Behold, I am making all things new.' And He said, 'Write, for these words are faithful and true.' Then He said to me, 'It is done. I am the Alpha and the Omega, the beginning and the end. I will give to the one who thirsts from the spring of the water of life without cost. He who overcomes will inherit these things, and I will be His God and he will be My son.'"

This verse and Isaiah 65:17 indicate God will create a new earth and heaven and a new solar system and galaxies that will exist in the heavens beyond the new earth.

Heaven and earth are currently separated by sin. There will be no sin on the new earth and in the new heaven God will create. Therefore, Revelation 21:3-7 indicates the new heaven will be on the new earth because God will be there. Jesus stated in Mathew 22:30 we will have bodies in heaven like angels. **Therefore, our bodies on the new earth will be immortal, and we will live there forever with God.**

John was also told the new heaven and earth will have no more:

- Hunger, thirst and heat from the sun (Revelation 7:16),
- Tears, death, mourning, crying and pain (Revelation 21:4),
- Sin (Revelation 21:27), and
- Curse (Revelation 22:3).

Our spirit and soul enter the current heaven when we die. This will be a transitional heaven. Our body there will be a spiritual body with a recognizable form and characteristics but with no mass. We will reside in this heaven from the time we die until we are resurrected at the rapture, at the first resurrection, or at the great white throne judgement.

Our spiritual body receives physical mass in the resurrection process when we are resurrected at the rapture, the first resurrection, or at the great white thrown judgement. We will have an immortal physical body when we enter the new heaven on the new earth.

Jesus gave us an understanding of the significance of the kingdom of heaven in Matthew 13:44-50 as it relates to our position in the new heaven on a new earth. He indicated the kingdom of heaven will be like:

- A treasure hidden in a field that, when found by a man, is hidden. He goes and sells everything he has so he can buy the field because of his great joy over finding it.

- A merchant who seeks fine pearls. When he finds one of great value, he sells everything he has so he can buy it.

- A dragnet that is cast into the sea to gather every kind of fish. It is dragged to the beach when it is filled where the good fish are separated from the bad. The good fish are placed in containers, and the bad are thrown away.

Jesus then stated in Mathew 13:49-50:

> "So it will be at the end of ages; the angels shall come forth, and take out the wicked from among the righteous, and they will throw them into the furnace of fire; in that place there will be weeping and gnashing of teeth."

John was given a vision associated with this separation in Revelation 14:14-20.

Jesus taught two important principles with respect to the new heaven and earth in the above verses in Matthew. First, the value of our ability to enter and live in the new heaven on the new earth is priceless; we would sell everything we own to purchase our entrance if we could. However, the Bible teaches it is impossible for us to enter or purchase the kingdom of heaven, relying on our own merit or worth. The Bible further teaches Jesus has paid the admission price for us. Second, the righteous and unrighteous will be separated at the end of the ages. The righteous, who have loved Jesus and obeyed the words He spoke, will reside in the new heaven, earth and Jerusalem. The unrighteous who have rejected Jesus will be thrown into the lake of fire.

John received a vision of the new Jerusalem in Revelation 21:10-25. The new Jerusalem in this vision appeared to descend from God from the existing heaven where it was created. It was suspended in midair above the new earth and showed the glory of God. John's vision indicated the new Jerusalem will:

- Be laid out in the shape of a cube (Revelation 21:16). Its length, width and height will each be 1,500 miles (2,414 kilometers). This is equal to the distance East-to-West from New York City to Denver, Colorado, and North-to-South from Canada to Florida in the United States.

- Have twelve gates (Revelation 21:12-13). There will be three gates each on the east, north, south and west sides of the city. An angel who will have one of the names of the twelve tribes of Israel written on him will be at each gate. Each gate will be made from a single pearl.

- Be separated into twelve levels (Revelation 21:14, 18-20). The city will be pure gold like clear glass, and the foundation stone of each level will be a different precious gem. The gems will be jasper, sapphire, chalcedony, emerald, sardonyx, sardius, chrysolite, beryl, topaz, chrysoprase, jacinth and amethyst. Each level will carry the name of one of the twelve apostles of Jesus. The walls of each level will be 216 feet (65.8 meters) high and made of jasper.

- Have streets made of pure gold (Revelation 21:21). The gold will be like transparent glass.

- Have no temple (Revelation 21:22). God and Jesus will be its temple.

- Have no need for the sun or moon (Revelation 21:23). The glory of God will illuminate the city, and its lamp will be Jesus.

- Have a river of the water of life flowing from the throne of God and Jesus (Revelation 22:1-2).

The water will be clear as crystal, and the tree of life will be present on both sides of the river. It will bear twelve kinds of fruit and yield its fruit every month, and its leaves will be for the healing of the nations.

Adam and Eve were driven from the Garden of Eden after they had sinned to prevent them from eating the fruit from the tree of life and live forever in a sinful state eternally separated from God (Genesis 3:22-23). This would have separated them and all men and women from God forever. The tree of life was then removed from the earth. It will, however, grow in the new Jerusalem, and its fruit will be available as food for the inhabitants of the city.

God initiated a system of offerings and feasts the Israelites were to offer and celebrate to temporarily atone for their sins and maintain fellowship with Him. These all pointed to the ultimate sacrifice Jesus was to make of Himself on a cross to atone for our sins. The offerings and two of the seven feasts initiated by God will be celebrated as a memorial to and in remembrance of what Jesus accomplished on the cross during the 1,000-year kingdom of Jesus. There will be no sin in the new earth, heaven and Jerusalem. Therefore, there will be no offerings and feasts to atone for sin in the new earth, heaven and Jerusalem.

The new Jerusalem will be the dwelling place of the heavenly hosts and saints of God. This will include God the Father and Jesus (Revelation 21:22, 22:1), the Holy Spirit (Revelation 22:17), and the myriads of angels who faithfully serve God (Hebrews 12:22-24). The angel in Revelation 21:9 referred to the new Jerusalem as the wife of the Lamb, implying the new Jerusalem will be the final dwelling place of the body of Christ, the Church. It will be the place Jesus' Father has prepared for men and women throughout the ages who trusted and had faith in His Son and who were obedient to Him. The angel told John in Revelation 21:27 only persons whose names are written in the Lamb's book of life will be allowed to enter the new Jerusalem.

John stated in Revelation 21:22-27:

> "I saw no temple in [the new Jerusalem], for the Lord God the Almighty and the Lamb are its temple. And the city has no need of the sun or of the moon to shine on it, for the glory of God has illumined it, and its lamp is the Lamb. The nations will walk by its light, and the kings of the earth will bring their glory into it. In the daytime (for there will be no night there) its gates will never be closed; and they will bring the glory and the honor of the nations into it; and nothing unclean, and no one who practices abomination and lying, shall ever come into it, but only those whose names are written in the Lamb's book of life."

The above vision affirms the Lord's intention to repopulate the new earth He indicated He will create in Isaiah 65:17.

The Lord then continued in Isaiah 65:18-23:

> "But be glad and rejoice forever in what I create;
> For behold, I create Jerusalem for rejoicing
> And her people for gladness.
> And there will no longer be heard in her
> The voice of weeping and the sound of crying.
> No longer will there be in it an infant who lives but a few days,

Or an old man who does not live out his days;
For the youth will die at the age of one hundred
And the one who does not reach the age of one hundred
Will be thought accursed.
They will build houses and inhabit them;
They will also plant vineyards and eat their fruit.
They will not build and another inhabit,
They will not plant and another eat;
For as the lifetime of a tree, so will be the days of My people,
And My chosen ones will wear out the work of their hands.
They will not labor in vain,
Or bear children for calamity;
For they are the offspring of those blessed by the LORD,
And their descendants with them."

The LORD concluded in Isaiah 66:22-24:

"'For just as the new heavens and the new earth
Which I make will endure before Me,' declares the LORD,
'so your offspring and your name will endure.
And it shall be from new moon to new moon
And from Sabbath to Sabbath,
All mankind will come to bow down before
Me,' says the LORD.
'Then they will go forth and look
On the corpses of the men
Who have transgressed against Me.
For their worm will not die
And their fire will not be quenched;
And they will be an abhorrence to all mankind.'"

The following observations can be made from the above scripture verses and preceding discussions:

- The righteous whose names are written in the book of life will live forever in the new Jerusalem. They will be immortal with bodies like angels (Mathew 22:30). Their positions on the earth will be determined by the results of their examination by Jesus and the reward they will receive from Him. This position will be fixed forever. They will neither marry nor conceive children.

- Individuals who repopulate the new earth will have a long lifespan. However, they will be mortal and eventually die. They will marry, conceive and bear children.

- The kings of the new earth will bring the glory and honor of the nations into the new Jerusalem, and nations will come to bow down before the LORD.

- The bodies of the unrighteous who have been condemned to the lake of fire will be observable and looked on by the inhabitants of the new earth as an example of those who have transgressed against God.

Finally, John stated in Revelation 22:1-5:

> "Then [the angel] showed me a river of the water of life, clear as crystal, coming from the Throne of God and of the Lamb, in the middle of its street. On either side of the river was the tree of life, bearing twelve kinds of fruit, yielding its fruit every month; and the leaves of the tree were for the healing of the nations. There will no longer be any curse; and the throne of God and of the Lamb will be in it, and His bondservants will serve Him; they will see His face, and His name will be on their foreheads. And there will no longer be any night; and they will not have need of the light of a lamp nor the light of the sun, because the Lord God will illumine them; and they will reign forever and ever."

The righteous, whose names are written in the Lamb's book of life, will see the face of Jesus in the new Jerusalem. His name will be written on their foreheads, and they will serve and reign with Him forever.

CHAPTER 14
GROWTH OF EVIL AND CULTURAL CONFLICTS AND CHANGES

GOD'S ACTIONS IN OUR LIFE AND THE WORLD

The Bible teaches God loves us and reaches out to us in His mercy to heal our broken relationship with Him caused by sin in a fallen world and in our life. It documents His desire to redeem and reconcile us to Himself by His grace extends to us through our faith in His Son, Jesus. The Bible indicates God and Jesus have sent the Holy Spirit into the world to convict us of sin, draw us into a reconciled relationship with Them, and reveal to us God's spiritual life principles and laws in the Bible that govern our life.

God requires us in our relationship with Him to study and internalize His word in the Bible as we grow and mature in this relationship. He requires us to live a life of faith and trust in and obedience to Jesus and to enter the good works He prepares for us to enter. These actions are designed by God to equip us to be used by the Holy Spirt to reach out to and share with others His desire to redeem and reconcile them to Himself as He has redeemed and reconciled us.

We must understand God is sovereign and in control of everything that occurs in His creation. He has established and executed His process for our individual redemption and reconciliation through our faith and trust in and obedience to Jesus to reestablish our broken relationship with Him caused by sin. He has achieved this through the birth, life, death and resurrection of Jesus. He has revealed to us in the Bible His plan to redeem His creation that has been corrupted by sin. He will accomplish this by destroying the existing heaven and earth that have been corrupted by sin at the end of this age and creating a new heaven and earth in which there will be no sin. He has revealed His process in the Bible for our judgment that will determine whether we will spend eternity with Him, Jesus and the Holy Spirt in the kingdom of heaven or whether we will be eternally separated from Them in the lake of fire.

The Bible describes the eternal conflict in the physical and spiritual realms between God and Satan. It appeared in the physical realm Satan had succeeded in this conflict to secure his position as the eternal god of this world when Jesus was crucified and died. He was dead, and His body had been laid in a tomb. However, Satan had been defeated and judged by

God in the spiritual realm when Jesus was resurrected from the dead and seated at His right hand in heaven. God had secured our individual redemption through Jesus' resurrection, and He continued His process to redeem His creation through the future destruction of the existing heaven and earth and the creation of a new heaven and earth.

God's conflict with Satan in the physical and spiritual realms after Jesus' resurrection did not end. It entered a new phase. Just as God has determined how He will engage Satan in this conflict, Satan has determined how he will resist God.

This and following chapters address anticipated future global conditions, events and Satan's involvement that will lead to the beginning of the tribulation. A major event leading to the tribulation will be the establishment of the global ten kingdom federation described by the profit Daniel in the Old Testament. Some speculate the establishment of a New World Order will precede the establishment of the ten kingdom federation. Elements of conspiracy theories that predict the establishment of a New World Order will be discussed in this and the following chapters. The resulting government will be a dictatorship that may transition into the ten kingdom federation. Much has been written concerning these conspiracy theories. Some of these writings are credible while others are questionable. The discussions that follow will not attempt to prove or disprove the credibility of these conspiracy theories nor will they go into details about them. However, they will be plausible discussions that address secret societies, global banking institutions and monetary systems, government agencies, and non-government organizations that will facilitate the potential establishment of a New World Order.

FACTORS THAT AFFECT THE GROWTH OF EVIL IN THE WORLD

The information for much of the discussions in this section was obtained from the book written by Richard Swenson titled, *Hurtling toward Oblivion* (1999).

Profusion and Exponential Growth

Swenson in his book, *Hurtling towards Oblivion* (1999), indicated we have become used to progress in our modern culture. Progress has resulted in the growth of everything at ever increasing rates of growth. He defined the process of *profusion* to describe this growth. *Profusion* is the process of creating and producing more of everything at continually increasing rates of growth. Profusion includes advances in all areas of medicine, science and technology, manufacturing, commerce, etc.; it includes advances and increases in everything. Swenson indicated the theoretical concepts and numerical values associated with profusion are sufficiently complex and vast that they can only be understood from a broad general perspective. However, this is enough to understand profusion's relation to events and their related growth in evil that will lead to the establishment of a New World Order, the tribulation and the return of Jesus.

   Profusion works through the processes of *differentiation* and *proliferation*. *Differentiation* implies moving from the simple to the more complex, from a single concept or product to many permutations of the concept or product. Once progress has differentiated a concept, design, materials, etc. associated with a product, *proliferation* then replicates the numbers of copies of the resulting products so more people can receive more. Progress is driven by advancements in science and technology and the desire for increased profits. It results in producing and receiving more of everything faster and cheaper.

   Profusion is based on two facts: the numbers of units of everything grow exponentially and each successive doubling period decreases. Exponential growth states there will be a doubling of what existed before over each successive doubling period. When what has previously existed is doubled over several iterations of growth, the overall growth will follow the formula:

$$\text{Units after n iterations of growth} = \text{Beginning Units} \times 2^n$$

where n is the number of doubling periods. The effects of exponential growth when successive doubling periods decrease can be illustrated by two examples.

Example 1: Assume 100,000 units of some element exist at the time of the birth of Jesus, which will be called year 0. This element can be people, units of food, units of mineral resources, number of weapons of war, etc. Let the number of units double every 150 years. The number of units will double 14 times (14 iterations of growth) from the birth of Jesus to the year 2100. The total number of units that will exist in the year 2100 will be 100,000 times 2 raised to the 14th power or around 1.64 billion units. Figure 17 shows the growth in the number of units from the birth of Jesus to the year 2100. This growth follows a curve that is specified by the function of 2 raised to the nth power (hence exponential growth).

Example 2: Assume changes in social customs, technology, or any other plausible reason cause the length of doubling period to decrease with each successive doubling iteration. Consider the following example to illustrate the effects of decreasing the lengths of each successive doubling period:

- 100,000 units exist at year 0.
- The first doubling period is 150 years.

- Each successive doubling period from the 2nd to the 15th doubling period decreases by 4 percent. That is, each successive doubling period is 96 percent of the preceding period.

- Each successive doubling period from the 16th to 23rd doubling period decreases by 15 percent. That is, each successive doubling period is 85 percent of the preceding period.

The results of this example are:

- Instead of 14 doubling periods from years 0 to 2100 there will be 23.

- The doubling period will decrease from 150 years for year 0 to year 150 to approximately 24 years for year 2083 to year 2107.

- The number of units that will exist in year 2107 will be around 839 billion instead of around 1.64 billion in the previous example.

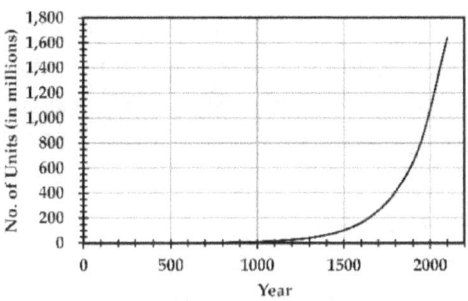

Figure 17

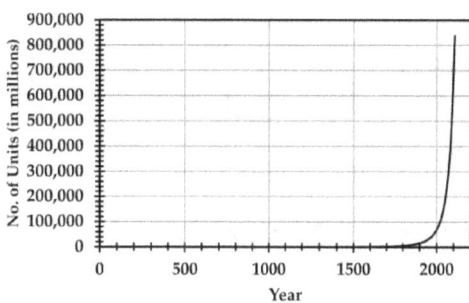

Figure 18

Figure 18 shows growth that occurs for this example in the number of units from the birth of Jesus to the year 2107. Some interesting observations can be made this figure. The curve is relatively flat, increasing slightly from year 0 through around 1865. The growth in the number of units rounds the *knee* of the growth curve through the next two doubling periods from years 1865 to around 1940. The growth for each successive doubling period is on the *steep slope* of the growth curve after 1940, which becomes steeper with each successive doubling period. This knee corresponds to an increase in profusion associated with advances in science and technology and the related increase in the demand for goods and services that occur from around 1800 to 2000. The steepening slope of the exponential growth curve beyond the knee of the curve is associated with the rapid increase in profusion projected to occur between 2000 and 2107. This growth will be fueled by increasing advances in science and technology and related increases in the demand for goods and services.

Swenson stated economic growth is the primary driving force in profusion. He indicated economics has become the dominant force in the modern world and dwarfs all other forces that affect profusion. He stated:

> "Because progress has proven so alluringly proficient, we have decided to build our entire economy around its twine engines of differentiation and proliferation. We have hitched our wagon to that star and progress has delivered on a grand scale, leaving us both gratified and awed. As a result, our way of life is predicated upon the growth that progress brings. Therefore, if we were to stop growing, both our economy and our way of life would collapse."

Swenson indicated progress driven by advances in science and technology and the desire for increased profits and economics are integrally and inseparably linked. Therefore, economics wins in the tug of war with all other forces that affect profusion. Nothing will be able to slow the growth of profusion because it fuels unhindered economic growth. It is interesting to note the economic Babylon (the world economic system) will be the final world institution that will be judged and destroyed by God during the great tribulation.

Profusion, Population Growth and Global Debt

Swenson did not address the effects of global population growth and debt on profusion. Population growth is essential for economic growth. It takes people to demand and buy the food, goods, services and products provided by profusion. A sustained growth in population is essential to support continued growth in profusion. Figure 19 indicates the global population will continue to grow. However, the United Nations predicts global population will peak at approximately 9.2 billion people around 2070. TED.com predicts the global population will peak at approximately 10 billion people around 2110.

Population growth, advances in science and technology, and economic growth are major driving forces that fuel profusion. Global population growth generates increased demand for the food, goods, services and products provided by profusion. Advances in science and technology facilitate differentiation and proliferation associated with the development of new products and advances in services associated with profusion. Economic growth motivates continued profusion. Ideally, profusion should result in increased global wealth to underwrite its costs.

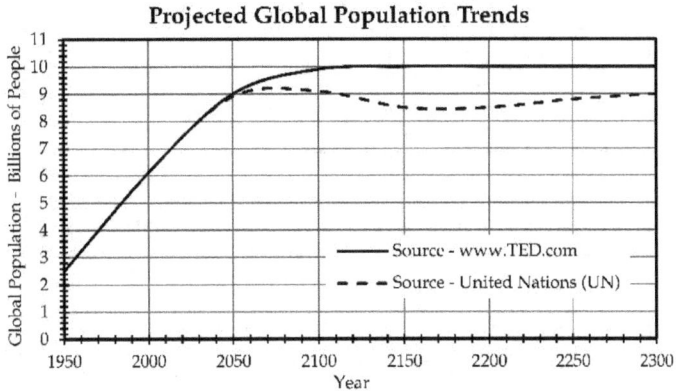

Figure 19

Debt is a major factor that affects profusion. Debt underwrites costs associated with profusion when it is unable to generate global wealth to underwrite these costs. Figure 20 shows exponential growth of global debt has significantly exceeded growth of global gross domestic product (GDP) since 1990. Global GDP represents global wealth available to underwrite increasing costs of profusion. Debt provides the financial resources to underwrite these costs when profusion is unable to do this. Debt must be repaid to the sources that supply it for healthy and stable global economics.

Figure 20 indicates global debt has grown to be more than 320 percent greater than global GDP. This growth in global debt is unsustainable because it is growing at a significantly grated rate than growth in global GDP. Global GDP growth represents the economic ability to repay global debt. The disparity between the growth in global debt and GDP left unaddressed will lead to a future global economic collapse.

Progress associated with profusion fueled by growth in population, science, technology and economics is presumed to provide a prosperous future. This progress requires continually increasing global resources, population growth and debt to sustain economic growth to underwrite the costs of profusion. A lack of continued population growth and growth in global debt will have major negative impacts on progress fueled by profusion. Figure 19 indicates population growth will begin to slow around 2050 and will cease between 2070 and 2110. Figure 20 indicates growth in global debt will continue to significantly exceed growth in global GDP. The combined effects of these two factors will have a major destabilizing effect on global economics that will lead to a future global economic collapse. Events leading to this collapse will initiate global conditions that will facilitate the establishment of a New World Order.

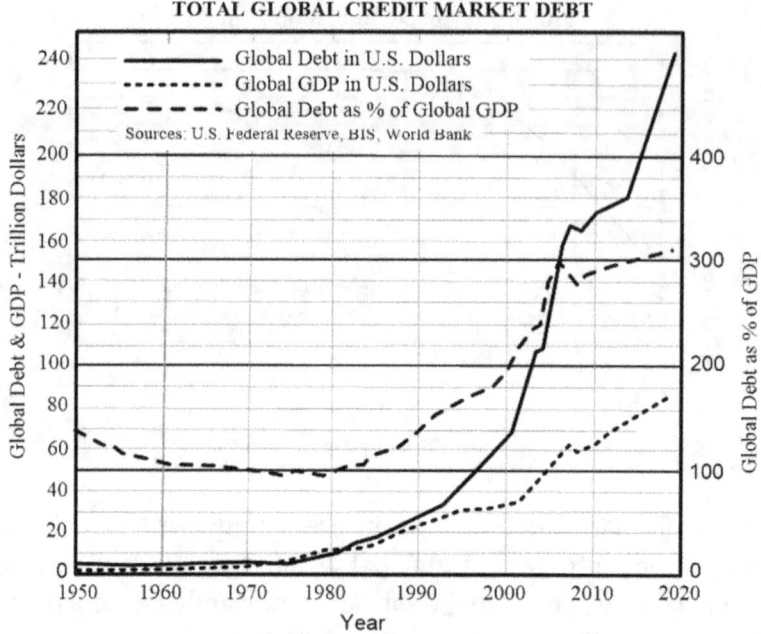

Figure 20

Profusion and Evil

Everything in God's original creation has become flawed because of sin. Nothing in all creation is perfect; all things are imperfect. Even those things that have been created explicitly for good have associated with them the potential for evil.

The presence of evil in the world and its potential existence in all good things have significant implication for profusion. Just as all things good and associated with good are increasing exponentially with time, so are evil and all things associated with evil. The growth in evil in the world can be seen in:

- Efforts to remove references to Jesus and God from schools, government buildings and public forums;

- The development and proliferation of weapons of mass destruction (WMDs);

- The spread of terrorism throughout the world;

- Increased efforts to redefine marriage and the structure of the family;

- The increase in sexual immorality and promiscuity and the corresponding increase in the number of babies born to unmarried women;

- The increase in the number of families with children without fathers;
- The easy access to pornography (even by children);
- The easy access to abortion;
- The increase in the distribution of illegal drugs and the related increase in drug addiction;
- Kids killing kids in schools and universities; and
- Workers killing co-workers in the workplace.

The growth in good associated with profusion and progress normally outweighs the related growth in evil. However, Swenson indicated evil has a unique lethal characteristic. The positives associated with good that exists in a situation may not be able to overcome the negatives associated with evil when these negatives are sufficiently dangerous and lethal. Evil can prevail when the benefits and advantages of good outweigh the dangers associated with evil once evil reaches a critical level of danger and lethality. Situations can arise in conflicts between good and evil in our individual lives and the world when the characteristic lethality of evil will allow it to dominate in a situation or event even though it is outweighed by good.

GROWTH OF EVIL AND GLOBAL TRANSFORMATIONS LEADING TO A NEW WORLD ORDER

General Global Conditions that will Facilitate the Growth of Evil

The growth of the global economic system and the related growth of evil in the world fueled by profusion will affect events that lead to the tribulation. Evil's characteristic of lethality will eventually overcome the good even though the growth of evil on a global scale will lag the corresponding growth of good associated with progress. The right set of conditions will facilitate evil to prevail on a global scale at some unknown time in the future.

The global economic system requires an ever-increasing availability and consumption of global resources and increasing global debt to sustain its growth. The global economic system will collapse when profusion has insufficient global resources and financial resources to sustain its growth and the global population ceases to increase. Life as we know it will radically change when this occurs. Few want to address the looming negative consequences associated with the continued growth of the global economic system and the corresponding growth of evil in the world. People want progress fueled by profusion to continue to give them the things they want. Eventually the right set of conditions associated with the lethality of evil and the over consumption of global resources will combine to result in the emergence of a New World Order, one-world government. This will facilitate the formation of the ten kingdom federation described by the prophet Daniel in the Old Testament. Jesus stated in Matthew 24:3-28 this will occur. Scenarios that may precede the formation of a ten kingdom federation are presented in Chapter 19.

The Bible presents some clues concerning when this may begin to occur. Gabriel in Daniel 12:4 indicated the end time will be characterized as a time of fast and efficient travel and a rapid increase in knowledge. These are occurring today. Paul stated in 2 Timothy 3:1-7:

> "But realize this, that in the last days difficult times will come. For men will be lovers of self, lovers of money, boastful, arrogant, revilers, disobedient to parents, ungrateful, unholy, unloving, irreconcilable, malicious gossips, without self-control, brutal, haters of good, treacherous, reckless, conceited, lovers of pleasure rather than lovers of God, holding to a form of godliness, although they have denied its power; avoid such men as these. For among them are those who enter into households and captivate weak women weighed down with sins, led on by various impulses, always learning and never able to come to the knowledge of the truth."

People today hold to a form of godliness but deny the power of God's word. They learn but do not come to a knowledge of the truth. They want a feel-good gospel and reject a disciplined life that leads to faith and trust in and obedience to Jesus.

Many today accept the philosophy of tolerance and reject the transcendent absolute truths of God. They accept the lie the Serpent extended to Eve in the Garden of Eden (Genesis 3:1-5). There were two parts to his lie:

- God would not hold her accountable for disobeying His command not to eat the fruit from the tree of the knowledge of good and evil.
- She would become like God, knowing good and evil, when she ate the fruit of the tree of the knowledge of good and evil.

Individuals who accept the Serpent's lie want to remove God from defining good and evil in their life, and they believe He will not hold them accountable for their defiance and disobedience. Peter stated in 2 Peter 3:3-4:

> "Know this first of all, that in the last days mockers will come with their mocking, following after their own lusts, and saying, 'Where is the promise of His coming? For ever since the fathers fell asleep, all continues just as it was from the beginning of creation.'"

There will be many in the last days who will deny the reality of the return Jesus and will believe everything is good and continue to live their lives as they always have. This is the prevailing belief of many today.

Many of the events associated with the tribulation discussed in preceding chapters center around the nation of Israel. The tribulation cannot begin until after Israel has become a nation again; this occurred in 1948. Therefore, all the conditions the Bible teaches must exist before the beginning of the tribulation now exist. The tribulation can begin at any time.

Transformations Leading to the Formation of a New World Order

Several regional and global transformations must occur before the future formation of a New World Order that will precede the ten kingdom federation described by the prophet Daniel. They include:

- People globally will turn away from a belief in and obedience to a transcendent God who is the creator and sustainer of the universe and all life, and governments will abandon their belief in and turn away from God.

- The government of the United States will develop ways to circumvent and ignore the U. S. Constitution in its governance of its citizens.

- The role of the United States as a global military superpower and police force will diminish.

- The control of global and regional military and police activities in which the U. S. military will participate will be transferred to the United Nations or another designated global authority.

- The role of the United States as the dominant global economy will diminish, and the U. S. dollar will cease to be the only world reserve currency used in international commerce and the international purchase of oil by nations of the world.

- A single global currency will be developed that will be managed by a single global bank.

- Cash transactions used in global, regional and individual commerce will be replaced with digital transactions that can be monitored and traced.

- Global governments will develop ways to indoctrinate their respective citizens with desired belief and value systems.

- Global governments will develop the ability to monitor and control all activities of their respective citizens.

- Global governments will develop the ability to track the movements and travels of their respective citizens.

The world will be ready for the formation of a New World Order after these transformations have occurred that will control the world population. The exact time frame over which these transformations will occur, and a New World Order will emerge is unknown. However, it is not a matter of if but when they will occur if biblical prophecy is true and to be believed.

CULTURAL CONFLICTS

Cultural conflicts in three major areas are shaping events that will lead to the formation of a New World Order that will precede the ten kingdom federation described in the prophet Daniel in the Old Testament. These three areas are:

- **Spiritual:** conflict between secular humanism and Christianity (and other religions)
- **Social-Political:** conflict between progressivism and conservatism
- **Economic:** conflict between socialism and capitalism

Conflict between Secular Humanism and Christianity

Two world views are contending for global prominence, particularly in western cultures. They are *secular humanism* and *Christianity*. The conflict between these world views will result in conditions that will eventually lead humanity on a global scale to turn away from God. A comparison of the characteristics of these world views will help better understand the nature of this conflict.

Secular Humanism

A summary of basic beliefs of secular humanists includes:

Origins: Secular humanists reject the existence of a transcendent God who exists outside of time and space as they are known and who is the Creator of the universe and all life. They believe the universe emerged from nothing, and everything in the universe has evolved through a sequence of random events. Mankind and the array of other life forms on earth have evolved from an accidental combination of chemicals that formed an initial single cell life form. This life form then randomly mutated over billions of years into the multiple life forms that exist on earth.

Identity: Secular humanists believe humans are only a collection of atoms and cells that have randomly mutated into an advanced animal life form. Humans have no greater value or significance than other animal life forms.

Purpose: The primary purpose in life for most secular humanists is to find some form of happiness through satisfying their basic emotional and physical needs and their motivational drives. It is difficult for them to find true purpose and meaning in life because they perceive life as an accident. Therefore, life for them is often viewed at one extreme as having little value or at the other extreme as being precious with humans having equal or less value than other animals.

Morality: Secular humanists reject the notion of any absolute transcendent moral values and laws. Moral and ethical values for them are derived from human and other natural sources. This usually translates into the development of relativistic values that are defined by group or cultural norms. These norms often change over time with changing perceptions of acceptable moral and ethical behavior.

Destiny: Secular humanist may strive to leave an earthly legacy. However, life for them ends after death. There is no afterlife.

Secular humanists and others with secular humanist beliefs and values want to fully control their lives. They want to be free to live as they choose and do what they want. Their life values often conflict with Christian values. Activists who represent secular humanist beliefs and values have and continue to work to remove the names and symbols of God and Jesus and the teaching of Christian principles and values from public schools and from government and public areas and forums. They have achieved significant success in accomplishing these objectives over the last 40-50 years. The elimination of the Christian world view on a global scale is essential to the future formation of a New World Order, one-world government.

Christianity

A summary of basic Christian beliefs includes:

Origins: Christians subscribe to the process of creationism. They believe the university and all life forms were created by a transcendent God who exists outside of time and space as they are known. They further believe the order, balances and complexities that exist throughout the universe and in all life forms were designed and created by this transcendent

God. Christians believe the creation narratives in Genesis are metaphors that describe the creation process. Some Christians believe God created the universe along with our solar system, earth and all life in six literal days, as described in the first two chapters of Genesis.

Identity: Christians believe humans are a unique and special creation, formed in the image of God. Adam was formed from the dust of the ground and Eve was formed from one of Adam's ribs. God then breathed into them the breath of life and they became living souls. They and all future humans were then to become caretakers of and exercise dominion over the earth. Adam and Eve disobeyed God, sin entered God's creation, and they and all humans after them became estranged from God. God in time sent His Son, Jesus, to be a Savior for all who would receive Him as their Savior, so their relationship with God could be restored.

Purpose: Christians know and love God and love one another. They reach out beyond themselves to serve God by bringing His message of redemption and salvation to a fallen world and by assisting others in addressing life struggles and in meeting their spiritual, emotional and physical needs. They believe this is the only way one can find true meaning and purpose in life.

Morality: Christians believe God alone establishes absolute transcendent moral laws that set boundaries for acceptable moral, ethical and interpersonal behavior. These laws are revealed in the Bible. They strive to live within these boundaries. However, they know they can approach God through Jesus with a repentant heart when they fail and sin (disobey God) and seek and receive His forgiveness.

Destiny: Christians believe humans are uniquely created with a spirit, soul and body. The spirit and soul separate from their physical body upon death, and the body eventually decays and returns to dust. The spirits and souls of those individuals who have appropriated the salvation God extends to them through Jesus will journey to a place Jesus referred to on the cross as paradise where they will be in the presence of God, Jesus and the Holy Spirit. The spirits and souls of those individuals who have rejected Jesus will journey to a place Jesus referred to as Hades where they will be separated from God. During events associated with the return of Jesus, both the dead and living who have accepted Jesus as their Lord and Savior will be resurrected and their spirits and souls will be united with an imperishable resurrection body in which there will be no sin. Those who are in Christ will be allowed to dwell with God, Jesus and the Holy Spirit at the final judgment for all eternity in the new heaven and earth He will create. Those who have rejected Jesus will be consigned to the lake of fire where they will be separated from God, Jesus and the Holy Spirit for all eternity.

The global influence of Christianity is diminishing because of growing world-wide opposition to Christian beliefs and values and because of changes that are occurring within major Christian denominations. Individuals in these denominations can be separated into two groups. One group can be classified as *orthodox* Christians. They:

- Christianity in the context of a restored active relationship with God through Jesus;
- Believe the Bible is the unchanging inspired word of God that is just as relevant today as it was when it was originally written;
- Accept as truth the creedal statements of the early Christian church; and
- Believe Jesus will return at the end of the tribulation to set up His 1,000-year kingdom on earth.

The other group can be classified as non-orthodox or *liberal* Christians. They:

- Believe many of the laws and related life principles and values presented in the Bible are culturally defined and must evolve and change as cultures advance and change;
- Believe many of the teachings, principles and values presented in the Bible are not relevant in today's world;
- Do not believe in a literal return of Jesus; and
- Want a form of godliness, but deny the power of God.

Orthodox Christian beliefs and values are being replaced by culturally defined relativistic beliefs and values. This transformation from orthodox to liberal Christian beliefs and values within Christian denominations continues to occur. It is nearly complete in many traditional Christian cultures of Europe and North America. In addition, Christians in many countries around the world are being persecuted and marginalized. Speech associated with some Christian values has been designated as hate speech in some countries, punishable under the laws of these countries. These trends, as they continue, decrease the influence of Christianity and increase the influence of secular humanism. This, as it continues, facilitates the emergence of a New World Order.

Conflict between Progressivism and Conservatism

Two social-political agendas are contending for global prominence. They are *progressivism* and *conservatism*. The nature of the conflict between these two agendas will define the global power structure that will facilitate the formation of a New World Order. A comparison of the characteristics of these agendas will help better understand the nature of this conflict.

Progressivism

A progressive is one who:

- Stands for change;
- Believes in moral and ethical relativism;
- Wants to move forward;
- Wants to be more enlightened; and
- Wants to socially evolve.

Progressives want to grow from the past into an enlightened and transformed future. They believe moral and ethical values, freedoms, economic systems and systems of law and governance must evolve to respond more effectively to changing global social, economic and cultural conditions. They want to forge a way to a future world liberated from archaic restraints of the past and to usher in moral freedom and humanistic and relativistic thought. Progressives in the United States view the Constitution as a flawed document that has served its purpose. It enabled the United States to be a leading force in the development of a better world. However, it has outlived its usefulness and must be discarded to make way for more enlightened and relativistic ways for governance. Their socialist agenda is designed to address social justice, global environmental change, and the redistribution of wealth on local, national and global levels. They want the government to control virtually everything, so all citizens and illegal aliens have access to education, healthcare, retirement benefits, vacations, housing and other unspecified creature comforts. They want to raise existing taxes and initiate new taxes to pay for these programs. This desired growth in the control of government will ultimately deny citizens their God given right to be free.

Progressive values and related socialist policies and programs prevail in the governments of most countries throughout the world. These policies and programs care for the lives and control the activities of their citizens from cradle to grave. The United States is the only major super power and economy where this is not the case. This must change for there to be a clear future path to the emergence of a New World Order.

Conservativism

A conservative is one who wants to maintain established:

- Moral and ethical values,
- Freedoms,

- Economic systems, and
- Systems of law and governance.

Conservatives want to maintain what they have and preserve the traditional structure of the family, control how they raise and educate their children, and continue to worship God in ways they have grown accustomed. Conservatives in the United States support the Constitution as the foundation of law and the Bill of Rights, which recognizes the God given rights of all U. S. citizens to be free. They support individual liberty, limited government, capitalism, the rule of law, faith, a color-blind society, national security, school choice, enterprise zones, tax cuts, welfare reform, faith-based initiatives, political speech, home owners' rights, and the war on terrorism. These stand as obstacles to the emergence of a New World Order.

Conflict between Socialism and Capitalism

Two economic systems are contending for global prominence. They are *socialism* and *capitalism*. The nature of the conflict between these two economic systems will influence the development of the global economic system that will facilitate the emergence of a New World Order. The difference between capitalism and socialism must be understood to fully understand events that will occur before the emergence of a New World Order.

Socialism

Socialism is an economic system where:

- The money and other physical and capital assets necessary to produce and market products, goods and services are owned by the government or the public.
- The society operates under the premise that what is good for one individual is good for all individuals.
- All businesses and companies are publicly owned and operated or owned and operated by the government.
- Everyone works to acquire wealth that is then redistributed to everyone. The government enacts laws and regulations that define how the wealth acquired by businesses, companies and individuals is to be redistributed to all individuals. This is to facilitate the distribution of wealth acquired by the very rich to those with little wealth.

- There are no competitive markets for products, goods and services. The government sets the salaries of the managers and workers within businesses and companies that create and provide products, goods and services, and it sets the price at which they can be sold or provided.

- The government provides many of the services (health, education, legal, etc.) to the people. Businesses, companies and people pay for these services through taxes that are often substantially higher than those that are imposed in a capitalist economic system.

A New World Order can only be established in an economic environment of a global socialist economic system.

Capitalism

Capitalism is an economic system where:

- The money and other physical and capital assets necessary to produce and market products, goods and services are privately owned.

- The economy operates through individuals who own and operate privately owned businesses and corporations and who make the decisions associated with the allocation of resources and assets necessary to produce products, goods and services. Most of the segments of the economy (manufacturing, technology development, health care, etc.) are privately owned.

- Businesses and corporations operate under the same or similar laws as individuals. They can sue and be sued, buy and sell property, and perform many of the same activities as individuals.

- All privately owned businesses and corporations have owners and managers. The owners and managers in small businesses and companies may be the same individuals. The owners may hire managers in larger corporations who may or may not have any ownership stake in the company.

- All businesses and corporation are motivated by making a profit. They exist to make money. Businesses and corporations with shareholders also seek to increase the price of the shareholders' stocks, thereby increasing their wealth.

- There are highly competitive markets for products, goods and services. Businesses and corporations establish the price associated with the products, goods and services they provide.

- It is the role of government to enact and enforce laws and regulations to level the playing field for small privately owned businesses and large privately owned corporations. The government also establishes laws that regulate how the profits achieved by businesses and corporations and the wealth received by individuals are to be taxed.

Capitalist based economies are major obstacles to the formation of a New World Order.

CULTURAL CHANGES

Cultural conflicts and cultural changes in the United States have facilitated and been facilitated by each other over five generations that include:

- Silent generation (1927-1945),
- Baby boomer generation (1946-1965),
- Generation X (1966-1980),
- Millennial generation (1981-1995), and
- Generation Z (1996-present).

Cultural changes that are addressed include:

- Attitudes toward Christianity, and
- Attitudes toward marriage, divorce and the family.

Changes in Attitudes towards Christianity

The United States identifies itself as a Christian nation. Major categories associated with Christian affiliations include Evangelical Protestants, non-Evangelical Protestant, liberal Protestant, Catholics and unaffiliated with any Christian group. The percent of the U.S. population among the generation groups that are unaffiliated with any Christian religion group is around (Source: Internet):

- Silent Generation – 9 percent
- Baby Boomers – 18 percent
- Generation X – 25 percent
- Millennial Generation – 28 percent
- Generation Z – 34 percent

The percent of the U.S. population that is unaffiliated with Christianity has increased from the Silent Generation to Generation Z.

Changes in Attitudes towards Marriage and Divorce

Generational marriage rate has steadily decline from the silent generation to generation Z. Marriage rates by generation are estimated to be:

- Silent Generation – 81 percent
- Baby Boomers – 61 percent
- Generation X – 53 percent
- Millennials – 44 percent
- Generation Z – 29 percent

These marriage statistics vary, depending on their source. Table 4 shows marriage, divorce and birth rates per 1,000 population in the United States between 1950 and 2020.

Table 4

Year	Marriages	Divorces	Divorces/Marriages	Births
Marriage, Divorce and Birth Rates per 1,000 Population in the United States				
1950	11.1	2.6	0.21	24.2
1960	8.5	2.2	0.26	22.7
1970	10.6	3.5	0.31	16.8
1980	10.6	5.2	0.49	15.0
1990	9.8	4.7	0.48	15.6
2000	8.2	4.0	0.49	14.2
2010	6.8	3.6	0.53	13.3
2015	6.9	3.1	0.45	12.3
2020	5.1	2.3	0.45	12.0

Attitudes toward marriage and divorce in the United States have changed, starting with the baby boomer generation. Baby boomers, referred to as the "me to" generation, pushed for more personal freedom, tolerance, openness, transparency, and equality between men and women in social and business environments. They also push against social and cultural behavioral boundaries established by previous generations. They placed more emphases in marriage on personal fulfillment than on fidelity and commitment. This contributed to the increase in the divorce rate per 1,000 population in the 1970's and 1980's that was facilitated by the adoption of no-fault divorce laws. However, the divorce rate has continued to decline from 1990 to 2020. The marriage rate has also declined from 1990 to 2020, resulting in a divorce/marriage ratio of 0.45 from 2015 to 2020. The birth rate has continuously declined from 1950 to 2020.

The baby boomer generation is credited with having the highest divorce rate among all the generations. Generation X was the first generation of children after the baby boomer generation who has come from divorced parents of baby boomers. The emotional trauma experienced by these children associated with the divorces of their parents has resulted in many of them getting divorced after being married. Therefore, the trauma of divorce on children continued into following generations. The increases in divorce in the 1970's and throughout the 1980's and 1990's have resulted in attitude shifts regarding marriage, divorce and co-habitation among the millennial generation and generation z. This will be addressed in the following sections.

Changes in the family

Cultural changes in the United States toward Christianity, marriage and divorce have resulted in corresponding cultural changes in the family. These changes in recent decades have centered around sexual orientation, gender identity, and changes in the makeup of the family. Maintaining the "traditional family" as created by God is essential for maintaining our freedoms in a free society.

God's Creation of the Family: Jesus reaffirmed in Mark 10:6-9 God's creation of the structure of the family:

> "But from the beginning of creation, God MADE THEM MALE AND FEMALE. FOR THIS REASON A MAN SHALL LEAVE HIS FATHER AND MOTHER, AND THE TWO SHALL BECOME ONE FLESH, so they are no longer two but one flesh. What therefore God has joined together, let no man separate."

Knowledge of God's creation of the family is essential to identify and understand how social and cultural changes are changing the family from what He created it to be. Jesus affirmed a family is established by the covenant relationship of marriage made before God between a man and woman as they become husband and wife. Its members include the husband, wife and biological children born to them. Their children today may also be adopted.

The family as God created it is:

- The foundational human institution of society (Genesis 2:20-25, Exodus 20:12); and
- Established by the covenant relationship of marriage (Genesis 2:20-25) that must be between one man and one woman.

Marriage as a union between a man and woman is:

- Ordained by God;
- A covenant before God between a man and a woman;
- Characterized by leaving the authority structures of one's parents to establish a new authority structure as husband and wife; and
- Characterized by Jesus' relationship with the church (Ephesians 5:22-33).

Marriage is also a commission from and blessing by God for husbands and wives to be fruitful and multiply (Genesis 1:27-28). Husbands and wives are given the responsibility to:

- Bring children into the world through the procreation process;
- Raise and teach their children; and
- Bring their children up in the discipline and instruction of the Lord so they may come to know Jesus (Ephesians 6:4).

Parents in marriage are responsible for and have been given authority from God to teach their children. Parents are responsible for their children's:

- General education (Galatians 4:1-2); and
- Spiritual and theological education (Deuteronomy 6:6-9, Proverbs 1:7)

Men and women historically have chosen to unit in the covenant of marriage to conceive, give birth to, and raise their children as a family. However, some men and women choose to remain single. Whatever their choice, God's love and grace through Jesus are extended to all men and women. He desires to use them, whether married or single, in ministry and service to others through their faith and trust in and are obedient to Jesus in a local Christian congregation.

God created the family to be a stable and safe environment where children are conceived, born into the world, and raised by their parents. The Bible presents the responsibilities of the husband and wife in their relationship with God and each other. It also presents the responsibilities of the husband and wife as parents in their relationship with their children and the responsibilities of children in their relationship with their parents. God blesses the family and commands it to be fruitful and multiply.

The Effects of Sin on the Family: The family often becomes an unstable and dangerous environment to raise children because of sin instead of being a stable and safe environment where children are raised by their parents. There are many examples of this in the Old Testament and examples of this in homes today.

The family has become the target of secular humanist who work to remove God, Jesus and the Holy Spirit from our society and culture and progressives with a socialist agenda to eliminate freedoms we enjoy in our society and culture. Secular humanists in 1962 successfully remove school-sponsored prayer from public schools through the U.S. supreme court's ruling of Engel v. Vitale as a violation of the 1st Amendment establishment clause. Progressives have taken over public schools and universities where children are educated. These have changed social and cultural attitudes toward marriage and the family as established by God. The LGBT community through actions associated with sexual orientation and gender identity have succeeded in redefining the family as established by God.

Changing Society and Cultural Attitudes toward the Family and Marriage

Attitudes toward marriage and the family among the millennial generation and generation Z are changing. Many in these generation believe marriage is unnecessary. Therefore, couples in these generation are choosing to co-habitat before considering marriage and to co-habitat without getting married. Many of these co-habitations result in breakups and divorces when co-habituating couples get married. Children are often involved in these breakups and divorces, and the resulting single parent is normally, but not always, the mother.

Effects of the LGBT Community

The LGBT community have been active in promoting changes in the family. Their activities have centered around sexual orientation and gender identity.

Sexual Orientation: Genesis 1:26-27 indicates God has created man as male and female to rule over the earth. He uniquely created man as male and female with physical and emotional characteristics and attributes necessary to conceive, give birth to and raise children to populate and subdue the earth. Therefore, God created the bodies of men and women and placed within them emotional, psychological and physical desires to accomplish these activities. He created men to be sexually attracted to women and women to be sexually attracted to men. However, the introduction of sin into God's creation has for some disrupted this attraction where men are attracted to men and women are attracted to women.

Moses was instructed by God to define homosexual attraction between men and women as sin when it results in sexual contact between two men or two women when He gave Moses the Law (Leviticus 18:22, 20:13). The Bible teaches God's nature and character are immutable; they do not change with time. Therefore, if God defined homosexual acts between men and women as sin when He gave Moses the Law, they are still defined by Him as sin today even though they are now culturally defined as acceptable behavior.

The U.S. supreme court in 2015 in the case of Obergefell v. Hodges redefined the makeup of the family. The supreme court ruled that marriage is also a legal union between same sex couples. This ruling has resulted in the split up of several mainline protestant denominations over the issues of performing same sex marriages in their churches and the ordination of homosexual ministers within their denominations. It has also resulted in the inclusion of homosexual relationships in public school sex education curricula down to primary grades and kindergarten.

Gender Identity: God in His creation has established gender to be determined by the physiological characteristics of our body at birth; they determine whether we are male or female. However, there is a disconnect within some individuals between the actual physiological characteristics of their gender and what they emotionally and psychologically desire for their gender to be. This can result in emotional and psychological trauma for them and in a desire to change their gender.

It is not uncommon for some children to experience some gender identity confusion as they progress through puberty. However, they normally successfully work through this confusion as they progress into adulthood when there is no intervention in their growth.

Gender identity is an agenda item within the LGBT community. They have worked to place information related to gender identity into sex education classes in public schools. This has the potential to increase gender identity confusion in young children.

Some individuals demand they be allowed to choose and declare their gender even though their choice differs from their biological gender. This has created problems where biological boys demand the right to use girl toilets and locker rooms and where biological girls demand the right to use boy toilets and locker rooms. Gender identity has created serious problems where biological men who declare themselves to be women want to compete against biological women in athletic events. Gender identity can have serious consequences where medical intervention is considered for use to change the gender of pubescent children.

Effects on the Makeup of the Family

The above issues associated with sexual orientation and gender identity have resulted in changes to the makeup of the family. A family is no longer only established by the marriage union of a man and women. It can now be established by a marriage union of two men or two women or of a man and/or women who claim to be a gender that is different from their biological gender. In addition, changes in the attitudes of the millennial generation and generation Z toward marriage and the family have resulted in an increase in co-habitation arrangements. Table 5 presents results of living arrangements between married and co-habitating couples between 1968 and 2018.

Table 5

Living Arrangements between Young Adults Ages 18 – 24
Living with a spouse: 1968 – 39.2 percent; 2018 – 7.3 percent
Living with a partner: 1968 – 0.1 percent; 2018 – 9.4 percent

Living Arrangements between Young Adults Ages 25 – 34
Living with a spouse: 1968 – 81.5 percent; 2018 – 40.3 percent
Living with a partner: 1968 – 0.2 percent; 2018 – 14.8 percent

Table 6

	Number of Children in Single Parent Households per 1,000 Population		
Year	Mother Only	Father Only	Total
1970	7.5	0.8	8.3
1975	10.2	1.0	11.2
1980	11.4	1.1	13.5
1985	13.1	1.6	14.7
1990	13.9	2.0	15.9

1995	16.5	2.5	19.0
2000	16.2	3.1	19.3
2005	17.2	3.5	20.7
2010	17.3	2.6	19.9
2015	17.0	2.8	19.8
2020	15.3	3.3	18.6

Breakups among co-habitating couples and divorces among married couples have resulted in an increase in the United States in single-parent families with children. Table 6 shows this trend from 1970 to 2020. Single-parent families with children have resulted from divorced married couples, separated co-habitating couples, deaths of a spouse or partner, desertions of fathers, unintended and planned pregnancies of unmarried women, and single-parent adoptions.

Effect of Single-Parent Families on Children

Children who live in single-parent families often face struggles that children who live in two-parent families do not face. These struggles include:

- **Less money for the family:** Single parents earn less money than two parents. This often results in food shortages, an inability to provide children with required necessities, no access to the internet, and a slip into poverty.

- **Lack of quality time, assistance and attention for children:** These occur because single parents often must work multiple jobs to financially survive. Therefore, they have less time to spend with and meet their children's needs.

- **Health and behavioral issues:** These occur because single parents do not have adequate time to meet the needs of their children. This often leads to feelings of insecurity and abandonment in their children. These feelings often lead to behavior issues that result in disobedient and aggressive behavior.

- **Future life issues:** Children from single-parent families often struggle with their desire and ability to obtain an education that is essential for them to secure employment as adults. Children from single-parent families often struggle with feelings of being socially and economically disadvantaged throughout their lives.

An objective of secular humanists, progressives and socialists in creating these struggles is to make children of single-parent families more receptive to receiving and being dependent on government assistance for survival.

Society and Cultural Impacts of Changes in the Family

The Bible teaches the family, as created by God, is the foundational human institution of society that is essential for maintaining a free society. Therefore, secular humanists, progressives and socialist work to remove God, Jesus and the Holy Spirit from our society and culture. One of the ways they work to facilitate this is to change the attitudes of children and young adults toward marriage and the family structure as God has created them. The minds of children in public schools and of students in universities are being conditioned to accept, and U.S. supreme court rulings are being used to accomplish this agenda. Changing the family from what God has created it to be is essential to condition and prepare people to accept the formation of a New World Order.

CHAPTER 15
GLOBALIZATION, NEW WORLD ORDER, AND SECRET SOCIETIES

GLOBALIZATION AND CALL FOR A NEW WORLD ORDER

Globalization is the process by which businesses, multinational corporations and other organizations develop international influence and operate on a global scale. It is essential for the future establishment of a New World Order, and:

- Requires the economic resources of capital, technology and information to sustain it and the flow of goods and services to people;
- Is driven by growth in the international flow of money, ideas and knowledge;
- Transcends national boarders; and
- Results in the sociocultural transformation of people.

Processes associated with globalization can be separated into three categories (Figure 21): economic, political and sociocultural. Global financial organizations, rapid global monetary and investment transactions, and businesses and multinational corporations support economic globalization. International political organizations, non-government organizations, and trade blocs support political globalization. The growth of the internet, development of dominant cultures, and spread of dominant religions support sociocultural globalization. All globalization is supported and affected by knowledge and information transfer, the migration of people, secret societies, the availability of people and natural resources, and the environment. The goal of globalization is to unify the people and governments of the world into a social, cultural, political and economic structure that will accept and support the emergence of a New World Order.

World leaders have proposed the establishment of a world government to address and manage challenges associated with globalization more effectively. They have proposed the establishment of a one-world government that is often referred to as a New World Order. Vice President Joe Biden in his address to the 2014 graduating class of the U.S. Air Force Academy stated the graduating cadets "will lead and shape a New World Order for the 21st century."

FACTORS THAT SUPPORT AND AFFECT GLOBALIZATION

Economic Globalization	Political Globalization	Sociocultural Globalization
Bank for International Settlements, IMF, World Bank	United Nations	Growth of the Internet
World Trade Organization	Power of multinational corporations	Emergence of English as the language of international relations
Rapid financial transactions	Trade blocs – EU, NAFTA, G8	Mass migration of people
Growth of multinational corporations	Non-government organizations	Growth of dominate cultures (American, Western)
Emergence of global markets	Professional organizations	
Global trade agreements	Economic sanctions	Spread of dominate religions (Christianity, Islam)
Global free trade regulations	Military intervention	

Figure 21

President George H. W. Bush stated in his 1991 State of the Union address:

> "What is at stake is more than one small country; it is a big idea: a New World Order, where diverse nations are drawn together in common cause to achieve the universal aspirations of mankind: peace and security, freedom, and the rule of law The world can, therefore, seize this opportunity to fulfill the long-held promise of a New World Order, where brutality will go unrewarded and aggression will meet collective resistance. We can find meaning and reward by serving some higher purpose than ourselves, a shining purpose, the illumination of a Thousand Points of Light. ... The winds of change are with us now."

This New World Order will usher in global "peace and security, freedom, and the rule of law" when it is established. It will also usher in an autocratic world government under the leadership of a single world ruler who will extend his authority over all the nations of the world. Former President Bush also stated at the U.N. General Assembly on March 21, 1991:

> "We have before us the opportunity to forge, for ourselves and for future generations, a New World Order. A world where the rule of law, not the law of the jungle, rules all nations. When we are successful – and we will be – we have a real chance at this New World Order. An order in which a credible United Nations can use its peacekeeping forces to fulfill the promise and vision of its founders."

French President Emmanuel Macron in his speech to the U.S. Congress on April 25, 2018, called on the United States to create "a new breed of multilateralism" to stop the spread of nationalism. To create a new breed of multilateralism is another way of saying expand globalization." He went on to state:

"We can build the 21st century world order, based on a new breed of multilateralism, based on a more effective, accountable and results-oriented multilateralism, a stronger multilateralism."

Dr. Henry Kissinger stated at the World Action Council on April 19, 1994:

"The New World Order cannot happen without U. S. participation, as we are the single most significant component. Yes, there will be a New World Order, and it will force the United States to change its perceptions."

He further stated in a 2008 CNBC interview after the election of President Obama:

"I think that his [Obama's] task will be to develop an overall strategy for America in this period, when really a New World Order can be created."

David Rockefeller stated in his memoirs:

"Some even believe we are a part of a secret cabal working against the best interests of the United States, characterizing my family and me as 'internationalists' and of conspiring with others around the world to build a more integrated global political and economic structure – one world, if you will. If that's the charge, I stand guilty and I am proud of it."

James Paul Warburg, son of Paul Warburg, the author of the 1913 Federal Reserve Act, in a senate Foreign Relations Committee hearing on February 17, 1950, stated:

"We shall have World Government, whether or not we like it. The only question is whether world government will be achieved by consent or conquest."

The Reverend Karol Wojtyla (Pope John Paul II) stated in 1990:

"By the end of this decade we will live under the first one-world government that has ever existed in the society of nations … a government with absolute authority to decide the basic issues of survival. One-world government is inevitable."

John Paul II on January 1, 2004 "stressed that to bring about peace, there needs to be a new respect for international law and the creation of a new international order based on the goals of the United Nations (CNN, January 2, 2004)."

Pope Benedict XVI in a 2005 Christmas speech stated:

> "Let the Child of Bethlehem take you by the hand! Do not fear, put your trust in Him! The life- giving power of His light is an incentive for building a new world order based on just, ethical and economic relationships."

Pope Francis on June 27, 2017, while speaking with Ecuador's Il Universo newspaper called for a one world government and political authority, indicating the creation of the one world government is necessary to combat major issues such as climate change. He stated the United Nations doesn't have enough power and must be granted full governmental control for the good of humanity.

Wikipedia defines the New World Order as referring "to the emergence of a totalitarian world government" that will encompass and replace the individual governments of sovereign nation-states around the world. For the discussions that follow, a New World Order refers to the emergence of an oligarchy style, one-world, dictatorial government.

The highly organized global network that is working to establish a New World Order is like a spider web that extends into:

- Secret societies and cults,
- Global banking and commerce,
- National governments and government agencies,
- Non-government organizations,
- Intelligence agencies and the military,
- Multinational corporations and global business structures,
- Education, religion and the judiciary,
- Medical and pharmaceutical research and heath care,
- Energy production and distribution, and
- Technology research and development.

The network is so locally and globally pervasive and organized that, as we live and work in its midst, it is difficult to see and recognize its impact on our lives. It is like the proverbial forest and trees. It is difficult to determine the extent of a forest when we are standing amid its trees.

We must be elevated on a high hill or mountain overlooking the forest to see the extent of the forest. It is the same with the New World Order network. We must elevate ourselves to identify its many components to see it and understand its impact on our lives. We will attempt to do this in this and following chapters where we will examine many of the factors and components associated with the New World Order network.

SATAN AND HIS DEMONIC HIERARCHY

Writers of the New Testament referred to Satan as the god of this world. He took Jesus to a very high mountain and showed Him the kingdoms of the world when he confronted Jesus in the wilderness with his three temptations (Matthew 4:8-9). He offered them to Jesus if He would bow down and worship him. Jesus did not dispute Satan's claim of dominion over the world even though He rebuked him and commanded him to leave. Therefore, it is reasonable to postulate:

- Satan, who is also referred to as Lucifer and is the god of this world, is behind the efforts to establish an anti-God New World Order; and
- The senior and top leadership of secret societies, cults, groups and organizations who support these efforts are disciples of Lucifer.

Satan offered his throne as god of this world to Jesus who rejected it. He will offer his throne to the Antichrist who will accept it during the tribulation.

Efforts to establish a New World Order play out in two realms. One is the physical realm where we live and work, and the other is the spiritual realm where Satan exists and works. Satan has established a hierarchy of demonic forces to assist him in his activities. Paul stated in Ephesians 6:12:

> "For our struggle is not against flesh and blood, but against the rulers, against the powers, against the world forces of this darkness, against the spiritual forces of wickedness in the heavenly places."

He divided Satan's hierarchy into rulers, powers, world forces of this darkness, and spiritual forces of wickedness. Knowledge of this hierarchy is essential to better understand how Satan works through the lives of individuals to carry out his agenda to establish a New World Order.

Rulers: Rulers are spiritual forces of Satan who exert influence and control over specific geographic areas and regions. These can be small areas, such as a village, town or small region within a large region. They can be larger regions, such as a large city or a region within a country. They can be a larger region, such as a country or continent. Rulers work to exclude God and Jesus from the geographic areas and regions over which they have control and to keep people who live there in bondage to Satan.

Powers: Powers influence and control people. Therefore, they are spiritual forces of Satan who exert influence on and work through:

- Individuals in local, regional and world executive, legislative and judicial governmental bodies,
- The leadership of businesses and corporations, public and private organizations, and religious groups and organizations,
- Schools, colleges and universities; and
- Cults.

They use this influence to accomplish Satan's objectives.

World forces of this darkness: World forces of this darkness are spiritual forces of Satan who work in the lives of individuals to oppose the influence of God through the Holy Spirit in their lives. They are lying spirits who blind "the minds of unbelievers, so they cannot see the light of the gospel of the glory of Christ, who is the image of God" (2 Corinthians 4:3-4).

Spiritual forces of wickedness: Spiritual forces of wickedness are spiritual forces of Satan who work to lure by deception individuals into activities that transgress the laws, statutes and ordinances of God. They are demonic spirits who create within us desires to satisfy "the lusts of the flesh and the lust of the eyes and the boastful pride of life" (1 John 2:16).

Satan and his demonic hierarchy can only accomplish activities in the physical realm by working through individuals who allow them to work through their lives. The following sections present secret societies, groups, organizations and networks through which Satan works to accomplish his agenda.

SECRET SOCIETIES

Information for this section was obtained from the article, "Mysteries" on the blog of Thomas C. Allen (http://tcallenco.weebly.com).

Brief History

Secret societies are essential to Satan's efforts to establish a New World Order that will precede the ten kingdom federation ruled by the Antichrist during the tribulation. Ancient secret societies consisted of individuals who believed there were few truly intelligent and mature minds in the world. They also believed they were the only ones to possess these intelligent and mature minds. Members of these secret societies regarded themselves to be the *illumined* ones who were exclusively chosen to be the guardians of the Mysteries of the ages. They were the first *Illuminists* who were trusted with the esoteric Mysteries they chose to believe in and who were then to teach the esoteric interpretations of these Mysteries to the masses. This gave them control over the masses. Many ancient secret societies traced their origins back to the Mysteries of Nimrod at the Tower of Babel (Genesis 11:1-9) and to the ancient mystery religions of Egypt.

The Mysteries that were at the heart of most ancient secret societies opposed the constraining spiritual influence of God and were used to free and enable men to become gods. The Mysteries normally centered worship on the death and later resurrection of a specific god or goddess and focused on fertility associated with regeneration, procreation and reproduction. Practitioners could obtain wealth, power and immortality by performing ritual magic, which was related to the secrets of the Mysteries. Religions associated with the Mysteries were used to exert control over the masses of ancient cultures. Practices of ancient secret societies ranged from extreme hedonism to extreme asceticism, based on the Mysteries they chose to believe in.

Ancient secret societies associated with the Mysteries include the Brotherhood of the Snake, Zoroastrianism, the cult of Mithra, and the Egyptian Mysteries of Isis and Osiris. After the death and resurrection of Jesus came the anti-Christian Gnostic sects and the anti-Islam Order of the Assassins. Following these came the secret societies of the Rosshaniya (based in Afghanistan), the Spanish Gnostic Alumbrado movement, and the Knights Templar.

The Templars were initially formed as a Christian society who supported and participated in the crusades and who were accountable only to the Pope. They later morphed into two separate non- Christian groups that were both eventually ordered to be disbanded and were ordered by the Pope to be exterminated as heretics. One group fell into an apostate and hedonistic lifestyle supported by the extreme wealth acquired by the Templars. The other group was based on a simple ascetic religious lifestyle closely related to Buddhism and the Mithras.

Many of these early secret societies were led by Illuminists who were disciples of Lucifer, and they had among their goals the:

- Absolute rule over the world,
- Elimination of private prosperity,
- Elimination of religions, and
- Elimination of nation-states.

These goals found their way into later anti-Christian secret societies that included the Luciferians, Rosicrucians and the Levellers and eventually into the Illuminati and Freemasonry. Many of these and other secret societies have as one of their rituals the death of the resurrection of Christ.

Basic Characteristics

There are four reasons why individuals may choose to join a secret society. The two major reasons are the desire to:

- Have access to secret knowledge and wisdom associated with the Mysteries and
- Be selected as one of the elect to join the society.

Two lesser reasons are the:

- Desire to be part of a fraternal organization that may be of advantage in business and politics and
- Belief that joining the society will place them in a position to contribute to society.

Most secret societies have two agendas. One is public and used to attract new initiates, and the other is secret known only available to members at the highest levels in the society who were Illuminists.

The following characteristics are typical of secret societies. They:

- Employ training through ascending tiers or degrees;
- Are organized into lodges or centers;
- Teach secret occult doctrines and have secret agendas;
- Require reciting horrible oaths and participating in occult initiation rituals;

- Require absolute loyalty and often require obedience to unknown masters; and
- Often threaten a death penalty for indiscretions and treason.

Most secret societies are anti-Christian and anti-God. Their secret doctrines include teachings related to occult magic and practices and Luciferian ideology. They require allegiance to and the worship of demonic beings or Lucifer at higher levels of membership. They also support his efforts to establish a New World Order. Lucifer may be called by a different name in some secret societies, such as God of Hades, God of the Underworld, the Great Architect of the Universe, or by the name of a demon, which when translated could refer to Lucifer. The demon may also be a high-ranking demon in Lucifer's hierarchy.

Most secret societies have a tiered (degree) system of training and related initiation rituals that initiates, called *adepts*, must successfully complete to advance in the society (Figure 22). The training at each tier (degree) teaches the adepts the myths and esoteric doctrines of the Mysteries of the society and requires them to participate in related occult initiation rituals that will commit and bind them to deeper levels of loyalty and mysticism associated with the society. The public agenda and related benefits of the society are emphasized at each tier (degree). Successfully completing and undergoing the related initiation ritual associated with a tier (degree) indicates increased loyalty to the society and allows the adepts to progress to the next tier (or degree). Adepts gain increased status within the society as they progress to higher tiers (degrees). The higher the tier (degree) successfully completed, the fewer the number of adepts at that tier (degree).

Motivation for belonging to a secrete society – Desire:
- To receive hidden Mysteries knowledge and wisdom;
- To be selected as one of the "elect" to join the society;
- For fraternal brotherhood and to do good for society.

Figure 22

An adept can only advance to the next tier (degree) by invitation from higher ranking members of the society at some tier (degree) and beyond after careful review and evaluation of his progress. Most adepts never progress beyond this tier (degree). The adepts that do not progress remain in the society to be used in support of its public face and agenda and in its political base. Adepts must reject Jesus and God, swear total allegiance to the society, accept and support Luciferian ideology, and worship and swear allegiance to Lucifer for them to progress to the highest tier (degree) in a secret society. Only adepts who progress to the highest tiers (degrees) in a secret society learn its true agenda.

Secret societies pursue either esoteric mystical knowledge and wisdom or some ultimate purpose with specified objectives. Both are normally pursued in secret. Secret societies can further be classified by type into societies of intellect and direction and societies of actions and conflicts. This results in a two-by-two combination matrix with four possible combinations by pursuit and type. Secret societies with different combination of pursuit and type often work in concert with each other to achieve the Luciferian goal of establishing a New World Order. Nearly all secret societies oppose submission to God and Jesus; however, not all secret societies support efforts to establish a New World Order. Figure 23 lists secret societies that are believed to support efforts to establish a New World Order.

Secret Groups and Societies that Support Efforts to Establish a New World Order

Illuminist Movements
Illuminati
Committee of 300

Secret Societies
Freemasonry (Blue and Craft Lodges, York Rite, Scottish Rite, Grand Lodges, and Grand Orients)
Round Table
Order of Skull & Bones, Scroll and Keys
Royal Order of the Garter
Priory de Sion
Rosicrucians
Knights of Malta
Thule Society

Figure 23

ILLUMINATI

The information for much of this section was obtained from the article, "A Primer on the Illuminati," written by William H. McIlhany and published the New American on June 12, 2004; the article, "Illuminist Organizationally," in the Blog of Thomas C. Allen (http://tcallenco.weebly.com); the article, "The 1782 Congress of Wilhelmsbad: The Illuminati Takeover," by E. A. Samuels, J.D., November 2006 (http://www.biblebelievers.org.au/wilhelms.htm) and an 18 part interview, titled "Svali 2nd Series - The Illuminati in America", by Svali as interviewed by HJ Springer,2000-2001 (http://www.bibliotecapleyades.net/sociopolitica/esp_sociopol_illuminati_svali01b.htm#menu2).

Brief History

The Illuminati trace their origin to ancient Babylon sometime around 3,900 B.C. They indicate their ideology and beliefs are founded on all ancient mystery religions and their related occult practices. The Illuminati as it is known today was created from the roots of the Knights Templar and Rosicrucians during the 17th century by financiers who financed the early monarchies of Europe. The idea of an Illuminati controlled global movement was made popular by Adam Weishaupt's movement during the latter part of the 18th century.

Adam Weishaupt, who was a Jesuit-trained professor of canon law at Ingolstadt University in Bavaria, Germany, established in the later part of the 18th century an organization structure to continue the worldwide assaults on Christianity and the monarch form of government present in Europe. Kölmer, a Danish Kabbalist Jew, initiated Weishaupt into the secret Mysteries of Osiris magic, the Kabbala, and the Spanish Gnostic Alumbrado movement. Weishaupt met a Jew named Mayer Amchel Rothschild during this time who would later finance his Illuminati movement.

Weishaupt is often credited with establishing the Illuminati. However, Svali in her interview with HJ Springer stated:

> "Weishaupt did not create the Illuminati; they chose him as a figurehead and told him what to write about. The financiers, dating back to the bankers during the times of the Templar Knights who financed the early kings in Europe, created the Illuminati. Weishaupt was their 'go fer' who did their bidding."

Weishaupt and his movement were used by the Illuminati to further expand their influence and efforts to eventually replace nation-states with a global government.

Weishaupt established the secret society named the Bavarian Order of the Illuminati on May 1, 1776. The public image of the Order was that of a charitable and philanthropic organization. This image attracted many German educators and protestant clergymen to the Order. The organizational structure of the Order was a pyramid structure like the one shown in Figure 22. Novices (adepts) were initiated into the Order believing it had a Christian and philanthropic orientation designed to create a better world. The adept's progress was closely monitored as he progressed through a tiered training program and related initiation rituals. Those adepts who displayed a willingness to abandon Christian and altruistic ideals were invited to progress to higher tiers of training where additional and more secretive information regarding the Order was revealed. Those adepts who did not display this willingness were kept at their current levels and were not told about the higher tiers in the Order. The higher tiers included training in Luciferian ideology and Satanism. The adepts entered the top tier of the Order below Weishaupt, who was its supreme leader, after they had progressed to a tier where they had proven their absolute loyalty to the Order and its secrets. They also had to take an oath to be loyal to and worship Lucifer and maintain the secrets of the Order. They then became Illuminists like Weishaupt.

They were introduced to the true agenda of the Order after this, which was the establishment of a deistic (Luciferian), global, dictatorial government that would abolish:

- Governments of all nation-states;
- All private property;
- All inheritance rights;
- Patriotism to nationalist causes;
- Social relationships within families, sexual prohibition laws and moral codes; and
- Religious disciplines based on faith in a living God, while promoting faith in nature, man and reason.

These goals were to be achieved by creating conditions and environments that would separate groups of people in ever increasing numbers into opposing groups along political, racial, social, economic, religious and other lines. The opposing groups would then be armed, after which an event would be fabricated and initiated to provoke them to fight each other, weakening themselves as they destroyed governments and religious institutions.

The **Hegal dialectic triad** was used to achieve specific social and policy outcomes that were initially judged to be unacceptable. The Hegel dialectic triad can be explained as follows:

Thesis: The thesis is an initial assertible proposition, desired outcome or a formulated event.

Antithesis: The thesis is opposed by an antithesis, which is an equally assertible proposition, desired outcome or a reaction to the formulated event.

Synthesis: The conflict between the thesis and antithesis is resolved on a higher level of truth by the synthesis, which is a third assertible proposition, desired outcome or a resolution to the formulated event.

As used by Weishaupt's Illuminati to achieve initially unacceptable desired outcomes, the Hegel dialectic triad can be stated:

Thesis: First formulate, create and initiate a crisis (event) designed to facilitate achieving a desired outcome that is initially judged to be unacceptable.

Antithesis: Then wait for a public outcry (reaction to the event), demanding something be done to resolve the crises.

Synthesis: Finally, offer a solution to resolve the crises (resolution to the event) that ensures achieving the desired unacceptable outcome.

Some postulate this technique has been used in some form or another to provoke many of the major revolutions, wars, and social unrest in targeted countries and regions of the world since the French revolution, which began in 1789.

In addition to using the Hegel dialectic triad to accomplish specific unacceptable objectives, Illuminist have used the following tactics developed by Weishaupt to achieve long term objectives:

- Gain control of education and church leadership;
- Express concern for humanity while making people indifferent to all other relationship;
- Gain control of book reviewers and booksellers and use them to promote Illuminist writers;
- Decry writers of notice who reject Illuminist plans;
- Promise emancipation to women, and use them to control men;
- Win support of the common people by pandering to their prejudices;

- Gain control of the military academies, publishers, literary societies, etc.;

- Secure control of the judiciary and the legal system to enact laws favorable to Illuminist ideology and win favorable rulings in courts;

- Assist and promote fellow Illuminists, giving them preference relative to all others of equal merit;

- Place people where they will do the most good for the advancement of Illuminist ideology;

- Surround people in authority who do not agree with Illuminist ideology with Illuminist; and

- Remain in the background and work through front organizations.

Threats, bribes, sex and blackmail were tactics commonly used with the above tactics.

Weishaupt was extremely successful in penetrating the economic, social, political and cultural elite in Bavaria and other areas in Germany with his Order. It is estimated that at least 2,000 members within Germany had joined the Order within a period of thirteen months after its establishment. These included lawyers, doctors, bankers, government officials, and clergymen who later rejected many of the basic tenants of Christianity. Many who joined the Order became Illuminists.

Weishaupt joined the Freemasonic lodge, Theodor zum guten Rat. Weishaupt's Illuminati with the help of Baron Adolf von Knigge was received into the Freemasonic lodges of Europe. Weishaupt and von Knigge on June 16, 1782, presented the "secrets which the Illuminati had to offer" to the representatives of three million members "of all the secret societies" of Europe. They met at the Congress of Wilhelmsbad near Hanau in Hessen. The Congress was held at the castle of Mayer Amschel Rothschild. The Congress "adopted organizational plans formulated by the Illuminati," resulting in a merger between the Illuminati and Freemasonry. "Illuminism was injected into Freemasonry by indoctrinating the Masonic leaders." Illuminists worked their way into the key leadership positions of Freemasonic lodges, extending the Illuminati ideology and agenda into Freemasonry in Europe and other parts of the world. This was particularly instrumental in the Illuminati's role through the Grand Orient Lodge in Paris in mobilizing Illuminist subversive revolutionaries to ferment the French revolution and unrest in Europe and other parts of the world.

An Illuminati currier in 1785 traveling from Frankfort to Paris on horseback was struck by lightning and killed. Incriminating papers about the Order and its role in the French revolution were discovered in his possession. These papers led to the discovery of other writings by Weishaupt, documenting the existence and agenda of the Illuminati in Bavaria.

Bavarian government officials based on this evidence outlawed the Order and closed many of the Freemasonic lodges in Bavaria that were known to be under Illuminist control. Weishaupt lost his position at Ingolstadt University and was forced to flee and live in exile in Gotha, located in Thurngia, Germany. He continued to write about and spread Illuminism even though he lived in exile. The Illuminati in the form established by Weishaupt was never reconstituted. However, Weishaupt's Illuminists migrated into Freemasonic lodges and other secret societies throughout Europe and other countries around the world.

Illuminati Today

Illuminists must be separated into two groups when discussing the Illuminati that exists today. The first group are Illuminists in the Illuminati. They are members of European monarchies and descendants of European royal families, "old money" European and United States financial and banking families, and families with unbroken generational occult bloodlines. All Illuminists have occult connections. This group of Illuminists very rarely recruits and marries outside the Illuminati, and they are very secretive regarding their involvement with the Illuminati. They comprise around one percent of the populations of major metropolitan regions around the world. They maintain and grow their membership through training and psychological mind-control programing of their children. These children are psychologically programmed, beginning at very young ages, to be loyal to and pursue Illuminati objectives as adults. This group of Illuminists is highly organized, intelligent, and possesses extraordinary wealth at its national and global leadership levels. It controls its members through a highly organized and controlling organizational structure. Figure 24 shows the United States Illuminati organization structure that was presented by Svali in her interview with HJ Springer.

The second group of Illuminists is comprised of individuals:

- Who join secret societies and progress through their tier (degree) training and occult ritual structure (Figure 22) to the highest tiers (degrees) in their secret societies.
- Who by invitation after significant screening are inducted into secret societies by virtue of their social/education status.

Figure 23 lists many of these secret societies. They are founded on Luciferian ideology, have strong occult connections, and require allegiance to and the worship of Lucifer. These individuals support and pursue the Illuminati agenda even though they become Illuminists through secret societies and may not be members of the Illuminati.

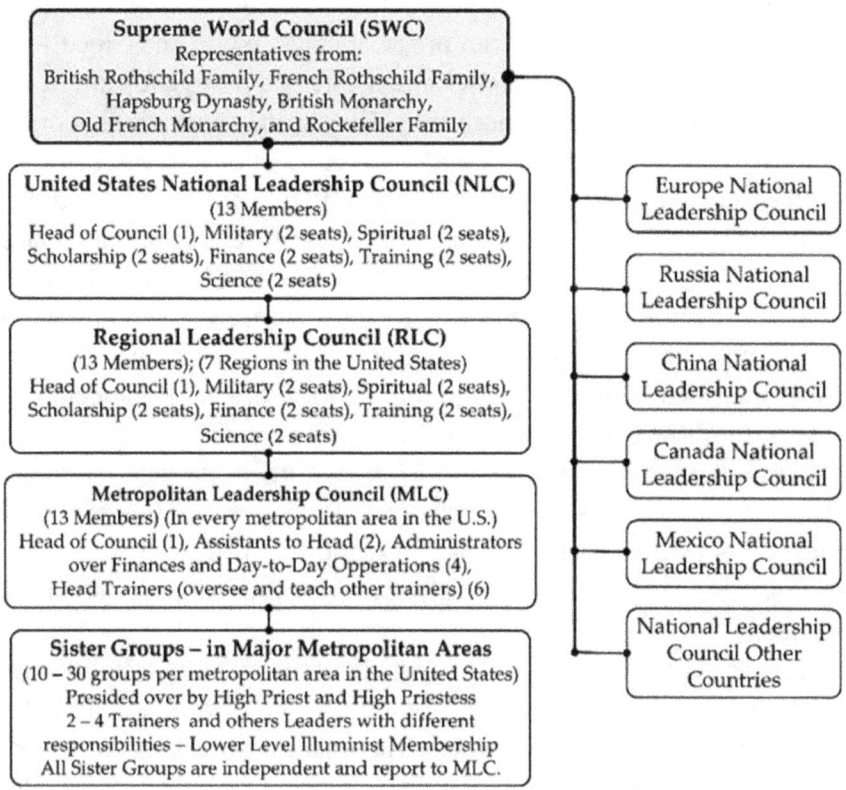

Figure 24

Illuminists in secret societies (sometimes under the fear of death) are required to swear an oath of allegiance to their respective secret societies. This oath often invalidates all prior oaths and commitments made by the Illuminists. It also takes precedence over future oaths and commitments they may make. Therefore, Illuminists' allegiance to their respective secret societies has priority over any oath of loyalty they swear when accepting any military, judicial or government position or office. Their allegiance to and support of the agendas of their respective secret societies take precedence over their obligations to and support of the position or office they are interring.

The above is true of Illuminists who are Illuminati members. Their training and psychological programming secure their allegiance to Illuminati objectives to establish a New World Order even though they may not have to swear an oath of allegiance.

Illuminism inside and outside the Illuminati is a highly organized and influential regional, national and global movement. Illuminists are socially upper middle and upper class. They are corporate and government insiders. They are the establishment and globalists. They are top leaders who direct and control secret societies. They are scholars and intellectuals in universities, think tanks and institutes. They are politicians, senior and executive government leaders, the executive leaders of government agencies and non-government organizations, and key executives in multinational corporations. They hold key positions in public education systems and are teachers in our schools and professors in our universities. They hold key positions in judicial systems and are judges in our courts. They are the national and global banking and financial elite. These Illuminists are loyal to and worship Lucifer, and they pursue the Illuminati global efforts to establish a New World Order. The Illuminism global movement is a heterogeneous movement. The major global factions are Illuminist groups in the European Union, the United States, Russia and China. Illuminist groups also exist in Canada, Mexico, and other countries around the world. There are significant organizational, cultural and societal differences between these factions. Illuminist factions inside and outside the Illuminati are often not unified in their pursuit of establishing a New World Order even though they all pursue this objective. There are according to Svali acrimony, back-biting and ladder-climbing within Illuminati groups in the United States. It is reasonable to postulate the same occurs within Illuminist groups in other countries and between global Illuminist factions.

Figure 25 created from information in the article "Illuminati Organizationally" in the blog by T. C. Allen shows a diagram of the operation structure of the Illuminati. It is a layered structure that can be represented by concentric rings that move outward from a central circle. The central circle represents the Illuminati Supreme World Council (SWC), which is the same as shown in Figure 24. The rings closer to the central circle represent organization elements that have greater influence and impacts in implementing the Illuminati plan to establish a New World Order. The rings that progressively move outward toward the edge of the rings represent those organizational elements that have progressively lesser influence and impacts.

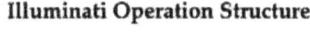

Illuminati Operation Structure

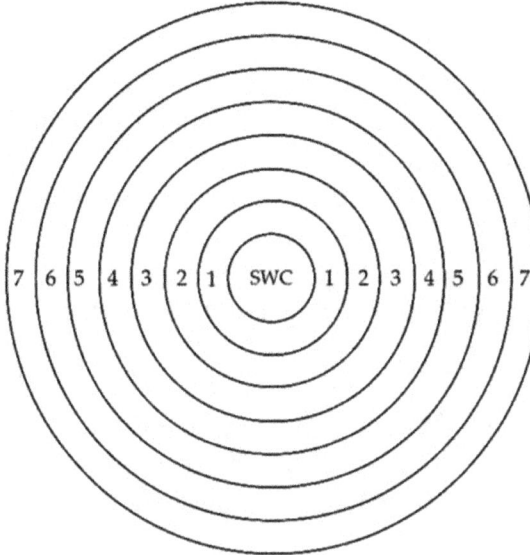

Supreme World Council (SWC)
Representatives from:
British Rothschild Family, French Rothschild Family,
Hapsburg Dynasty, British Monarchy,
Old French Monarchy, and Rockefeller Family

Layered Operation Leadership Structure

1. International Financiers/Bankers, Inner Circles of Freemasonry, Zionism, and New Age Movement

2. Establishment Elite

3. High Degree Members of Council of Foreign Relations, Bilderberg Group, Trilateral Commission, Freemasons, Theosophy Society, Major Philanthropic Foundations and Many Others

4. Leaders of the Governments of the United States, Europe, Australia, New Zealand, Canada, and Israel

5. Communist and leaders of the Governments of Russia and China

6. Leaders of Miscreant Governments, such as Libya and Iran and most Third World Governents of Importance

7. All sorts of expendable thugs, provocateurs, political leaders, dupes, fellow travelers, sympathizers, and low-degree members of Freemasonry and other Illuminostic and front organizations

Figure 25

The objectives and operation tactics of the Illuminati today are those presented by Weishaupt to advance the agenda of the Bavarian Order of the Illuminati. Illuminists use their positions and influence to further the Illuminati pursuit of its agenda. Using tactics presented by Weishaupt, they are involved in regional and global groups who continually oppose each other and are involved in ongoing conflicts. They are present in:

- The far right of conservatism and the far left of progressivism;
- Jewish and Muslim groups;
- Pro-western and communist groups;
- Christian and secular humanist groups;
- Liberal, fundamental, evangelical, Pentecostal and charismatic Protestant groups; and
- Other social, cultural and national groups who have opposing agendas.

Illuminists are present in all sides of conflicting groups to keep them from reconciling and resolving their conflicts. They frustrate, discourage and wear down opposing and conflicting groups by continually fanning the flames of conflict. This is done to prepare people to accept the emergence of a future New World Order.

Individuals may not be aware they are associated with or working for an Illuminist controlled institution, corporation, agency, organization, etc. The more open an Illuminist controlled group, organization, business, etc. and the less selectivity in hiring requirements, the more likely non- Illuminists will be unaware they are involved with an Illuminist controlled operation. Those Illuminist controlled groups, organizations, businesses, etc. that are more secretive regarding their operations and more selective in their recruiting and hiring will most often only hire known Illuminist.

Illuminati Supreme World Council (from Svali's interview with HJ Springer)

The Illuminati require their leadership to be descended from royal ancestry or unbroken generational occult bloodlines. They must be a member of a ruling European monarchy or a descendant of European royalty and of a family with extreme occult power.

Individuals who are members of the Illuminati Supreme World Council are:

- A descendant of the Hanover/Hapsburg dynasty who are one of the strongest lines for the occult.

- The head of the British Monarchy; (Svali said very little regarding possible occult ties of the British Monarchy. However, Fritz Springmeier has stated "the British Royal family have been leaders in Freemasonry Lots of testimony and circumstantial evidence leads one to believe that the Royal family has a secret occult side to them that is nasty.")

- A descendant of French royalty who are also in power in the occult;

- A member of the British Rothschild family who are powerful in the occult;

- A member of the French Rothschild family who are powerful in the occult; and

- A member of the Rockefeller family. (Svali said nothing regarding possible Rockefeller family occult ties. However, several Internet sources indicate they do have occult ties.)

Svali stated:

> "This council is already set up as a prototype of the one that will rule when the NWO comes into being. It meets on a regular basis to discuss finances, direction, policy, etc. and to problem-solve difficulties that come up. Once again, these leaders are heads in the financial world, old banking money."

She indicated there is extreme wealth associated with the leadership at the levels of the National Leadership Councils and the Supreme World Council. Svali mentioned the participation of the Rockefeller, Mellon, Carnegie and Rothschild families regarding the U. S. National Leadership Council. Figure 24 shows a diagram of the Illuminati global leadership structure as it relates to nations and related geographic regions around the world. She indicated there are Illuminati Sister Groups in every major metropolitan area in the United States and Europe. These groups comprise around one percent of the population in these areas.

Illuminati and the United Nations (from Svali's interview with HJ Springer)

The name "United Nations" was coined by President Franklin D. Roosevelt (Source - Wikipedia). The term was first used in the Declaration by the United Nations. This document was signed January 1, 1942, by representatives of 26 nations who pledged their governments' support in the fight against the Rome-Berlin-Tokyo Axis Powers during World War Two

The creation of the United Nations using the backdrop of World War Two was the culmination of a major effort by the Illuminati and government leaders from around the world. Many of these leaders may have been Illuminists. The concept of a United Nations was initially unpopular with the public and required a long-term major media campaign of "nation bashing" to gain public support. President Roosevelt, who Svali indicated along with his wife, Eleanor, were staunch Illuminists, worked hard to gain the acceptance of the U. S. public. The United Nations formally came into existence on October 24, 1945.

The Illuminati had two major reasons for supporting the establishment of the United Nations: the advancement of globalism and the neutralizing of nationalism. The United Nations according to Svali was to be "set up as a shadow, or forerunner, of the Supreme World Council that will represent every nation." She further indicated:

> "The UN has a stated goal of world peace and wants to incorporate under its fold military and peace-keeping functions. But in reality, giving this role to the UN weakens the individual military strength of nations, and encourages them to lean more and more on an external organization, making them less able to resist when the takeover occurs."

Illuminati Website

The Illuminati has historically operated in the background. However, it has now established an official website. The web address is www.illuminatiofficial.org.

FREEMASONRY

The information for much of this section was obtained from the article, "Freemasonry the Early Years," in the Blog of Thomas C. Allen (http://tcallenco.weebly.com).

The Public Face of Freemasonry

Freemasonry presents itself as a fraternal organization (a secret society) that draws its membership from many of the world religions. It requires its initiates to be of good moral character and to profess a belief in a "Supreme Being." It does not specify who this "Supreme Being" must be. It can be one of the many gods of Hinduism, Confucianism, Buddhism, or any other world religion. Freemasonry does not refer to itself as a religion. However, it positions itself as an organization as being above and able to bring together individuals from all world religions into a single brotherhood.

Freemasonry uses a tiered (degree) structure like the one described in Figure 22 for the training of adepts and for their related initiation rituals. It has an organizational structure based on Lodges. The first three degrees of Freemasonry are obtained in Blue Lodges, Craft Lodges, or Ancient Craft Lodges. Once an adept achieves his 3rd degree (Master Mason), he can apply to further advancement in Freemasonry through either the York Rite (Royal Arch Mason) or Scottish Rite (Lodge of Perfection) branch of Freemasonry. Most Freemasons do not progress beyond the 3rd degree. The 14th degree (Order of the Knights Templar) is the highest York Rite degree. The 33rd degree (Sovereign Grand Inspector General) is the highest Scottish Rite degree. Lodges are governed by national, state, regional or provincial lodges referred to as Grand Lodges or Grand Orients.

Freemasons claim their craft of masonry can be traced back to the Tower of Babel. The origin of their rituals and symbolism used in their lodges and initiation rituals are trace back to the Mysteries of Isis and Osiris in ancient Egypt. The present form of Freemasonry can be traced back to 1717 to the union of four London lodges to form the United Grand Lodge of British Freemasons (the Grand Lodge of London). The Grand Lodge of London dominated Freemasonry throughout the world by 1747. The United Grand Lodge of England was formed in 1813 by bringing together the Grand Lodge of London, the Grand Lodge of Ireland, and the Grand Lodge of Scotland.

The Secret Face of Freemasonry

Freemasonry claims publicly its beliefs and principles are compatible with those of Christianity. However, Freemasonry teaches Jesus is only one of many ways to be redeemed and achieve salvation. The Kentucky Monitor of Freemasonry states (pages 24-25):

> "All believed in a future life, to be attained by purification and trials; in a state or successive states of reward and punishment; and in a Mediator or Redeemer, by whom the Evil Principle was to be overcome and the Supreme Deity reconciled to His creatures. The belief was general that He was to be born of a virgin and suffer a painful death. The Hindus called him Krishna; the Chinese, Kioun-tse; the Persians, Sosiosch; the Chaldeans, Dhouvanai; the Egyptians, Horus; Plato, Love; the Scandinavians, Balder; the Christians, Jesus; Masons, Hiram [Abiff]."

Freemasonry teaches the Bible is only one of many sacred books of world religions and teaches Jesus is not:

- The ONLY mediator between God and man (1 Timothy 2:5),
- The ONLY redeemer and savior (John 14:6), and
- The ONLY name whereby men may be saved (Acts 4:12).

The name of Jesus is not allowed to be spoken in Freemasonic lodges, and Christians who enter Freemasonry must acknowledge Jesus is not the unique Son of God, is not God, and is not the only way to be redeemed and receive salvation.

The "Supreme Being" of Freemasonry is the Great Architect of the Universe who is the embodiment of all the gods of the many world religions, including the God of the Bible and Christianity. God in Deuteronomy 32:39 states:

> "See now that I, I am He, and there is no god besides Me; it is I who put to death and give life. I have wounded, and it is I who heal; and there is no one who can deliver from My hand."

He continues in Isaiah 46:9:

> "Remember the former things long past. For I am God, and there is no other; I am God, and there is no one like Me."

Finally, Deuteronomy 10:17 states:

> "For the LORD your God is the God of gods and the LORD of lords, the great, the mighty, and the awesome God who does not show partiality, nor take a bribe."

God referred to Himself during His conversation with Moses in Exodus 3:14 as "I AM WHO I AM." This reference of God to Himself as the four-letter word *YHWH* (pronounced Yahweh) implied He is the infinite God who is behind everything and to whom everyone in heaven and on earth is ultimately accountable. The "I AM WHO I AM" specifies that nothing and no one else defines who God is but God Himself. "The Great Architect of the Universe" is not the God of the Bible nor of Christianity. He is an imposter and a deceiver who seeks to draw unsuspecting Christians away from Jesus and to prevent others who do not know Jesus from being introduced to Him and receiving the true redemption and salvation that can only be received through Him.

Freemasonry, like all other secret societies founded on the ancient Mysteries, is anti-God and anti-Christian. It seeks at its core to remove from itself what it perceives is the constraining and restraining influences of God and Jesus. Freemasonry has replaced these constraining and restraining influences with its god, the Great Architect of the Universe, who is Lucifer.

Weishaupt's Illuminati along with its one-world, dictatorial government ideology was fully absorbed into Freemasonry at the Congress of Wilhelmsbad in 1782. This along with its ancient Mysteries and one-world government ideology radically transformed the secret face of Freemasonry. It is reasonable today to believe most, if not all, of the highest degree Freemasons and all the "inner circle" Grand Lodge leadership of Freemasonry are Illuminists. The Illuminist operational structure in Figure 25 implies this is the case. Svali stated, "I have never known a 32 degree or above who wasn't Illuminati, and the group helped create Freemasonry as a front for their activities."

The fact that the highest degree and the "inner circle" Freemasons are Illuminists does not imply all Freemasons are Illuminists. Most Freemasons as stated earlier do not progress beyond the 3rd degree (Master Mason). Many of these Freemasons are honorable individuals with high moral convictions and integrity who for some reason are not invited or choose not to progress to higher degrees. These individuals, as is the case with many secret societies, remain in Freemasonry. They bolster its public image and support its public agenda. However, they are not presented with the secret information that is presented to Freemasons who progress to higher degrees nor are they required to participate in the corresponding required initiations rituals.

CHAPTER 16
THE COMMITTEE OF 300

ORIGIN OF THE COMMITTEE OF 300

Dr. John Coleman's book titled, *"Conspirators' Hierarchy: The Story of the Committee of 300, 4th Edition,"* 1997-2006, presents one of the more comprehensive discussions on the activities and far-reaching influence of the Committee of 300. It was used as the source for most of the discussions in this section. The Committee of 300 is an outgrowth of the East India Company chartered in England by Queen Elizabeth I in 1600. Its headquarters was the London House in London, England. The Black Nobility banking families of Venice and Genoa, Italy, were included in the charter. In 1661, King Charles II granted the East Indian Company the right to add to its charter the ability to wage war and make peace with sovereign nations. This gave the East India Company the ability to gain full control over the opium poppy growing industry in India. The East India company reorganized in 1702 and became known as the United East India Company and later the British East India Company. The British East India Company by 1830 had control over all of India. According to Dr. Coleman:

> "The oldest families in England, Josiah Child, Thomas Papillion, Montague, Marlborough (Churchill), Russsell, and their cousins in the U. S. (especially the Warren Delano family) who grew immensely wealthy off the opium trade were now in a position to take virtual control of the world through a new entity that was known only to a select few as 'the Committee of 300'."

Dr. Coleman further indicated:

> "The Committee of 300 is the ultimate secret society made up of an untouchable ruling class, which includes the Queen of England, the Queen of the Netherlands, the Queen of Denmark, and the royal families of Europe. These aristocrats decided at the death of Queen Victoria, the matriarch of the Venetian Black Guelphs, that to gain world-wide control, it would be necessary for its aristocratic members to 'go into business with the non-aristocratic, but extremely powerful leaders of corporate business on a global scale. The Committee of 300 consists of certain individuals specialized in their own fields, including *Cultus Diabolicus*, mind altering drugs, and specialists in

murder by poison, intelligence, banking, controllers of all major commodities, pricing, demand and supply, transport and communication, and every facet of commercial activity. The Committee of 300 dictates what passes for United States foreign and domestic policies and has done so for more than 150 years."

Dr. Coleman indicated the Committee of 300 is comprised of:

- Members and descendants of European royal families;
- Members of the Illuminati;
- High ranking members of U. S. Freemasonry, the British Quator Coroati Lodge of Freemasonry, and the Italian P2 Masonic Lodge (especially those in the Vatican hierarchy);
- Members of the Circle of Initiates, Lucius Trust, the Order of the Elders of Zion, and the Nasi Princes;
- Members of the Order of Skull and Bones and Scroll and Keys;
- Members of the National and World Council of Churches and of the Jesuit Order (liberation theology);
- Members of the Bank of International Settlements, the International Monetary Fund, and the World Bank; and
- Members of the United Nations.

It is reasonable to speculate that members of the Committee of 300 are Illuminists who pursue the establishment of a New World Order.

ILLUMINATI AND COMMITTEE OF 300 ORGANIZATION STRUCTURE

The Illuminati traces its leadership back through two linages. One is through European royal ancestry and the other is through long occult bloodlines. Regarding the six seats on the Illuminati Supreme World Council:

- Three are associated with European royal ancestry: the head of the British monarchy, a descendant of the French royal family, and a descendant of the Hanover/Hapsburg dynasty; and
- Three are associated with occult bloodlines: the British Rothschild family, the French Rothschild family, and the Rockefeller family. These families are socially elite and elite world financial and banking families that control extraordinary wealth.

ILLUMINATI AND COMMITTEE OF 300
ORGANIZATIONAL STRUCTURE

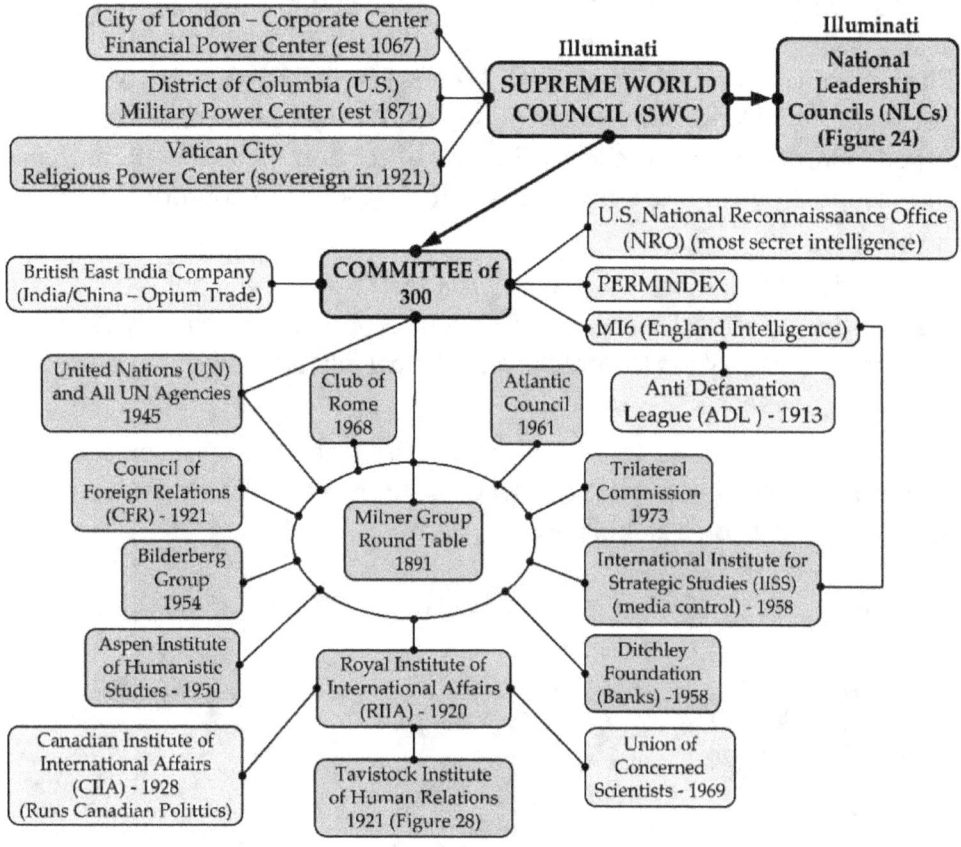

Figure 26

Figure 26 shows a diagram of the possible Illuminati and Committee of 300 organization structure. The network that proceeds from the Committee of 300 is derived from Dr. Coleman's book. The position of the Illuminati Supreme World Council in Figure 26 is drawn from information presented by Svali and T. C. Allen. The operations of the Illuminati Supreme World Council are shown extending in two directions. One is through the Illuminati National Leadership Councils shown in Figure 24. The Illuminati will use this council network to control nations and geographic regions after the New World Order has been established. The other is shown acting through the Committee of 300 network. The Illuminati organization structure show by T. C. Allen in Figure 25 imply the Illuminati Supreme World Council could work through the Committee of 300 network to facilitate accomplishing their political and operational agendas essential for establishing a New World Order.

The top of Figure 26 shows three unique city states that many believe will be integral to the establishment of a New World Order. These cities have unique laws that allow them to operate outside the laws of the governments of the countries where they are located.

- The City of London is the center of the English finance industry and is the global center for international banking operations. All major U.S. banks and banks from other countries have branches in the City of London that allow them to engage in international banking operations that are illegal in the countries where that are located.

- The District of Columbia is the seat of the U.S. Government but is not a part of any state in the U.S. The U.S. is undergoing a buildup of major military assists that can be used by a New World Order to project global military power and presence where and when needed.

- Vatican City is the global center for Catholicism. The Vatican has extensive financial assets and a global network that can be used by a New World Order to project its spiritual ideology on a global basis.

Figure 27 shows pictures of obelisks in the City of London, Washington D.C. and Vatican City.

 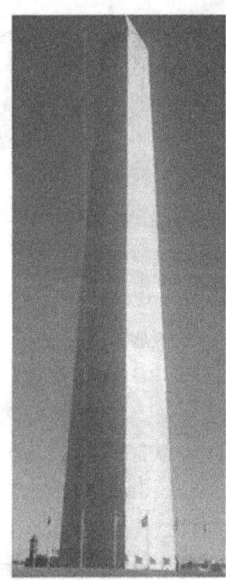 

City of London　　　**Washington D.C.**　　　**Vatican City**

Figure 27

Obelisk are carved rectangular stone pillars with a tapered top that forms a pyramid. They were erected to honor a god or an important individual or event. The obelisks in ancient Egypt represented the benben, which in ancient mythology was the primordial mound where the god Atum stood at the creation of the world. This mythology states he was the first god to exist on earth from the waters of Chaos, and he created the other gods and the universe.

The first obelisk appeared in ancient Egypt around 2575 B.C. and was a symbol of the sun god Ra. Atum and Ra were the same god in ancient and Egyptian mythology. The gods Osiris and Isis in Egyptian mythology were descended from Atum. Obelisks in ancient Egypt were placed in pairs at temple entrances to honor pharos who were believed to be gods on earth who acted as intermediaries between the gods and the people. Ra was believed to be present within the obelisks.

Obelisks signify accomplishment and success in illuminati symbolism. Therefore, it is not uncommon to find obelisks placed in prominent locations throughout the world to commemorate and honor the activities of illuminists. It is reasonable to speculate the Illuminate Supreme Council will have access to the global assets of the three city states represented in Figure 27 when a New World Order is established. (Clayton, M., *3 Corporations that Run the World: City of London, Washington DC, and Vatican City*; Waduge, S. D., *Three Corporations Run the World; City of London, Washington DC and Vatican City*; and CrossTheBorder. org, *The Empire of the City – The Unholy Trinity that Runs the World*)

COMMITTEE OF 300 NETWORK

Dr. Coleman stated the Committee of 300 accomplishes its agenda through a network of front groups, councils, commissions, and institutes. The Illuminati and Committee of 300 network operates through:

- Secret societies,
- International and national banking and commerce,
- Multinational corporations,
- Political and non-government organizations,
- Intelligence agencies and the military,
- Education and religious institutions and organizations,
- Entertainment and news media outlets, and
- Tavistock (Figure 28 show a diagram of the Tavistock network.).

Following are brief descriptions of organizations, many who have web sites on the Internet, who are part of the Committee of 300 network.

U. S. National Reconnaissance Office (NRO): The National Reconnaissance Office is a super-secret intelligence agency within the U. S. government. According to Dr. Coleman, Winston Churchill had a hand in setting it up during WW II. Until it was discovered by President Truman, only a handful of individuals outside of the Committee of 300 knew of its existence. Today the NRO supplies satellite intelligence to other U. S. intelligence agencies.

Military Intelligence Department Six (MI6): MI6 is a British intelligence agency that was set up under Queen Elizabeth I. It has grown to be one of the most renowned intelligence agencies in the world. MI6 is funded by and only accountable to the British monarchy.

PERMINDEX: According to Dr. Coleman, PERMINDEX is a MI6 front group used to conduct high level assassinations.

Anti-Defamation League (ADL): The Anti-Defamation League, headquartered in New York City, NY, is an international Jewish non-government organization that defines itself as a civil rights/human relations agency. It fights anti-Semitism and all forms of bigotry, defends democratic ideals, and protects civil rights for all through information, education, legislation and advocacy. It supports separation of church and state, opposes the teaching of creationism and intelligent design in public schools, and supports gun control and immigration reform. According to Dr. Coleman, "the ADL is a British intelligence operation founded in the United States by MI6," and was formally run by individuals from Tavistock.

Milner Group Round Table: Cecil Rhodes (established and funded the Rhodes Scholar program at Oxford) is credited with founding the Round Table secret society in 1891 to aid in the extension of British rule throughout the world and ultimately create a world government. After Rhodes' death in 1902, his quest was continued by Lord Alfred Milner, who established Round Table Groups in the United States and other countries throughout the world. The recruitment, training, monitoring and advancement of initiates in Round Table Groups were modeled after Adam Weishaupt's Bavarian Illuminati. The real objectives and goals of the Round Table Groups, which paralleled those of the Illuminati, were only revealed to those initiates who were judged to be well-proven and most loyal. The innermost members of the Round Table Groups have become international bankers, politicians, professors, and senior executives of major multinational corporations. The Round Table is often referred to as the Milner Group Round Table because of his efforts. Dr. Coleman indicated:

- The Round Table consists of a highly integrated and organized group of companies, banks, institutes, and educational institutions and units;

- The driving philosophy of the Round Table is to have Round Table groups in positions where they can formulate and carry out social policies through social institutions that can be used to manipulate the masses; and

- The Round Table plays an important role in forming U. S. foreign policy by supplying information to relevant government agencies through the office of the British ambassador in Washington D C.

Other groups established by or in the form of the Round Table include: Royal Institute of International Affairs (RIIA) - 1920, Council on Foreign Relations (CFR) - 1921, Aspen Institute of Humanistic Studies - 1950, Bilderberg Group - 1954, Ditchley Foundation - 1958, International Institute for Strategic Studies - 1958, Atlantic Council - 1961, Club of Rome - 1968, and Trilateral Commission - 1973. Many of these groups have both a public and secret face.

Royal Institute of International Affairs: The Royal Institute of International Affairs (RIIA), formed at the end of WW I and known as the Chatham House, is the operational arm of the Committee of 300. Publicly, it is portrayed as a nonprofit, non-governmental organization located at the Chatham House in London, England. Its mission is to analyze and promote the understanding of major international issues and current affairs. Secretly, it formulates, develops and controls the domestic and foreign policies of the governments of England, Canada, and the United States and develops strategies and initiates actions that are designed to advance the long-term agenda and objectives of the Committee of 300. Dr. Coleman indicated, "The Royal Institute of International Affairs was, and remains, totally interfaced with the British monarchy."

Council on Foreign Relations (CFR): The Council on Foreign Relations, located in New York City, publicly is an American nonprofit, nonpartisan and non-governmental organization and think tank that specializes in U. S. foreign policy and international affairs. It is the most influential foreign policy think tank in the United States. It develops and promotes foreign policies related to globalization, free trade, and the reduction of financial regulations on multinational corporations. It promotes the regional consolidation of countries into economic blocs. Examples are the development of the North American Free Trade Agreement (NAFTA) and the European Union (EU). Secretly, it works in conjunction with the Royal Institute of International Affairs and the Bilderberg Group to ensure that U. S. foreign policies agree with the long-term global agenda and objections of the Illuminati and Committee of 300 network. (Source - Wikipedia and Dr. Coleman's book)

Aspen Institute of Humanistic Studies: The Aspen Institute of Humanistic Studies (now referred to as the Aspen Institute), headquartered in Washington, D.C., has a public two-fold mission: foster values-based leadership that encourages individuals to reflect on the ideals and ideas that define a good society and provide a neutral and balanced venue for discussing and acting on critical issues. However, Dr. Coleman indicates the Aspen Institute is the front for and home of the Committee of 300 in the United States.

Bilderberg Group: The Bilderberg Group is a group that meets annually in secret with 120 to 140 attendees who are from the United States, Canada and Europe. Attendees annually include around 80 permanent members who are among the world's most powerful individuals plus others who are occasionally invited because of their expertise in areas of interest to the group. Members and attendees include heads of state, former heads of state, influential members of the U. S., Canadian and British governments, high ranking Pentagon and NATO officials, European royalty, and selected media individuals. The Council on Foreign Relations, the Trilateral Commission and the European Union are well represented, along with powerful central bankers from the U. S. Federal Reserve, the European Central Bank and the Bank of England. The Bilderberg Groups functions as a shadow government that influences the policies of the United States, Canadian and British governments. The group's steering committee determines whom to invite to participate in the group. Only those individuals who subscribe to an oligarchy style, *one*-world government controlled by a powerful elite are invited to participate. (Source - *The True Story of the Bilderberg Group* by Daniel Estulin)

Ditchley Foundation: The Ditchley Foundation, based at Ditchley House near Chipping Norton, Oxfordshire, England, publicly strives to promote international relations, especially Anglo-American relations, through a program of several annual conferences of international interest. Around forty participants are invited, drawn from senior levels of politics, business, the armed forces, media and academia. Dr. Coleman indicated the Ditchley Foundation also is a secret banker's club and a conduit for secret instructions from the Tavistock network. There are also an American Ditchley Foundation and a Canadian Ditchley Foundation.

Atlantic Council: The Atlantic Council, located in Washington, D.C., publicly "promotes constructive leadership and engagement in international affairs based on the central role of the Atlantic Community in meeting global challenges." Secretly, the Atlantic council is a spinoff of the Round Table.

International Institute for Strategic Studies (IISS): Publicly, the International Institute for Strategic Studies is a London-based British research institute and think tank in the area of international affairs. It describes itself as the world's leading authority on political-military conflict. However, according to Dr. Coleman:

"The Committee of 300 set up the International Institute for Strategic Studies (IISS) under the auspices of the Round Table. The IISS is the vehicle for MI6-Tavistock black propaganda and wet jobs (an intelligence cover name denoting an operation where 'bloodshed' is required), adverse nuclear publicity, and terrorism, which goes to the world's press for dissemination, as well as to governments and military establishments. The U. S. Department of Defense has become very much beholden to IISS. Membership in the IISS includes representatives of 87 major wire services and press associations, as well as 138 senior editors and columnist drawn from international newspapers and magazines."

Club of Rome: The Club of Rome, based in Winterthur, Canton in Zurich, Switzerland, publicly is a global think tank that addresses a variety of international political issues. It describes itself as "a group of world citizens, sharing a common concern for the future of humanity." Its members consist of current and former heads of state, UN bureaucrats, high-level politicians and government officials, diplomats, scientists, economists, and business leaders from around the world. Dr. Coleman referred to the Club of Rome as a secret executive branch and foreign policy arm of the Committee of 300. He further indicated the:

> "Club of Rome is a conspiratorial umbrella organization, a marriage between Anglo-American financiers and the old Black Nobility families of Europe, particularly the so-called 'nobility' of London, Venice and Genoa."

Along with other global activities, the Club of Rome has been behind:

- The development and implementation of global population control and reduction programs;
- The creation and support of many of the global environmental movements, efforts and programs;
- The destruction of the industrial and manufacturing base of the United States;
- The creation of the anti-nuclear power propaganda effort in the United States, and
- The creation of divisions and factionalism between the charismatic, fundamentalist and evangelical branches of Christian Protestantism in the United States, thereby reducing the influence of Christianity in the U. S.

Trilateral Commission: The Trilateral Commission, based in Washington, D.C., Paris and Tokyo, publicly, is a nonpartisan and non-governmental think tank established to foster closer cooperation among North America (U. S., Canada and Mexico), Western Europe (European Union), and Japan. Later the Japanese group was expanded to the Pacific Asian Group. Membership (members cannot hold public office) includes: North American Group (120), Western European Group (170), and Asian Pacific Group (117). Secretly, the Trilateral Commission is a partner of the Bilderberg Group in activities designed to facilitate achieving the long-term agenda and objectives of the Illuminati and Committee of 300 network.

Canadian Institute of International Affairs (CIIA): Publicly, the Canadian Institute of International Affairs was formed as a nonpartisan forum for the discussion, analysis and debate of Canada's role in international affairs. Its members include participants from government and non-government organizations, the private sector, academia, and the concerned public of Canada. Secretly, it performs the same functions designed to control Canadian foreign policy as the Council on Foreign Relations does in the United States.

Union of Concerned Scientists (UCS): The Union of Concerned Scientists, based in Cambridge, MA, is a MIT associated nonprofit advocacy organization instituted to "initiate a critical and continuing examination of governmental policy in areas where science and technology are of actual or potential significance" and to "devise means for turning research applications away from the present emphasis on military technology toward the solution of pressing environmental and social problems." Its members include scientists, engineers and private citizens. The UCS addresses environmental issues associated with global warming, deforestation, nuclear energy, renewable energy, and agriculture. Its positions are allegedly aligned with the agenda of the Illuminati and Committee of 300 network.

TAVISTOCK INSTITUTE OF HUMAN RELATIONS

Tavistock is deeply entrenched in governments and organizations connected with governments throughout the world. Elements of U. S. Tavistock institutions are embedded in all U. S. government agencies and control the development of U. S. domestic and foreign policies.

Tavistock, in conjunction with the Council of Rome and other Illuminati and Committee of 300 network groups, develops and initiates strategies for creating regional and global crises (wars, terrorism, social unrest, etc.). It disseminates in support of these strategies propaganda to influence public opinion to accept related government responses and actions that are initially unacceptable. This propaganda is also designed to manipulate regional and global populations in predetermined manners and directions that will ultimately result in their acceptance of a New World Order.

The Institute of Human Relations was created by the Royal Institute of International Affairs at Oxford University in 1921. It publicly portrays itself as a British charity concerned with group and organizational behavior and is currently headquartered in London, England. It is a unique institute that is self-funded and positioned between the worlds of academia and consultancy. It has expertise in disciplines associated with anthropology, economics, organizational behavior, political science, psychoanalysis, psychology, and sociology. Tavistock has secretly crafted and established a global distribution network for using scientifically developed methods for propaganda dissemination, behavior modification, brain washing, and mind control on whole generational and population segments. Major, but not all, components of this network are shown in Figure 28.

TAVISTOCK RESEARCH, PLANNING AND PROGRAM NETWORK

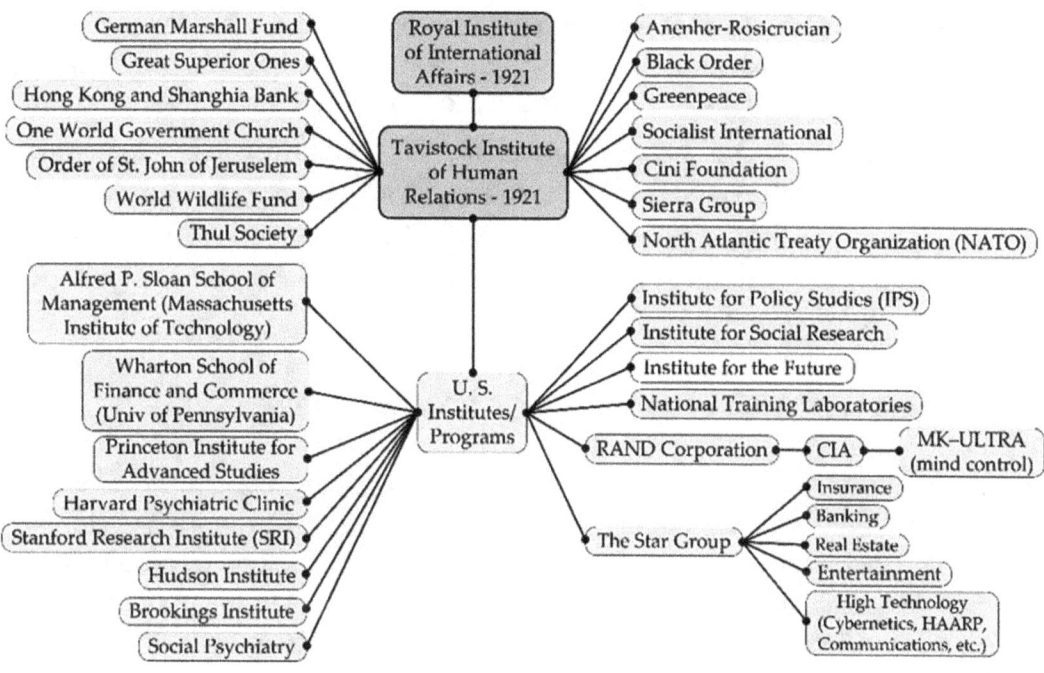

Figure 28

According to Dr. Coleman, the primary mission of Tavistock is to develop techniques that can be used to break down the psychological strength of individuals and render them incapable of opposing the dictators of the New World Order. Techniques designed to break down the family unit and family instilled principles associated with religion, honor, patriotism and sexual behavior are used by Tavistock scientists as weapons for population manipulation, control and behavior modification. Tavistock is involved in activities to achieve these objectives designed to:

- Take control of and destroy public education;

- Destroy the traditional family structure (husband, wife and children) associated with marriage and conceiving and raising children;

- Redefine traditional marriage (as a union between a husband and wife) to allow homosexual and other types of family unions;

- Remove and replace the role of Christianity and other world religion in defining moral and ethical values and behavior;

- Formulate, control and alter public opinion through the control and manipulation of media outlets;

- Manipulate and control the development of cultural and social customs and values in targeted population groups;

- Degrade the moral values of youth and adults through media, entertainment and music programing and encourage them to use drugs, participate in pornography and immoral and deviant sexual behaviors, and use abortions as a means of population control;

- Lead people into secret societies, Gnostic and other cults, occult practices, New Age groups and activities, and witchcraft and Satanism; and

- Discourage, depress and demoralize large segments of regional and world populations and lead them into the use of drugs and dependency on government agencies for their subsistence.

GLOBAL REACH OF THE COMMMITEE OF 300 NETWORK

The institutional and political assets available to the Illuminist organized movement through the Illuminati Supreme World Council and Committee of 300 network are globally far reaching. The Committee of 300 interacts with the United Nations to accomplish their global agenda both directly and through their networks of interconnected groups, institutes, commissions and councils shown in Figure 26. Tavistock works through its vast network shown in Figure 28 as the global propaganda, behavior modification, and mind control arm of the Illuminati and Committee of 300 network. Figure 29 shows many of the different types of organizations over which Illuminists associated with the Committee of 300 exert influence and exercises control. Groups, institutes, commissions and councils under the control of Illuminists associated with the Committee of 300 define and develop domestic, foreign and global policies that are promulgated through the United Nations, the governments of the United States and England, and other western and world governments. The presence of this influence is implied by the following statements:

- "Three hundred men, all of whom know one another, direct the economic destiny of Europe and choose their successors from among themselves." (Walter Rathenau - 1909. He was head of German General Electric, and he was Prime Minister of Germany until he was assassinated in 1922.)

- "Since I entered politics, I have chiefly had men's views confided to me privately. Some of the biggest men in the United States, in the fields of commerce and manufacture, are afraid of something. They know that there is a power somewhere so organized, so subtle, so watchful, so interlocked, so complete, so pervasive, that they had better not speak above their breath when they speak in condemnation of it." (Woodrow Wilson - former U. S. president - 1913).

- "Some conspiracy watchers believe that various branches of the '300' are the main players, but the Council on Foreign Relations (CFR), the Trilateral Commission, the Bilderberg Group, the Round Table, the Rhodes Foundation are only arms of this monstrous and well organized controlling body. The real leaders are found in the deep, secret societies of Freemasonry and offshoots like Skull and Bones, Scroll and Keys and the Thule Society and the Illuminati." (Dr. Coleman - *Conspirators' Hierarchy: The Story of the Committee of 300, 4th Edition*).

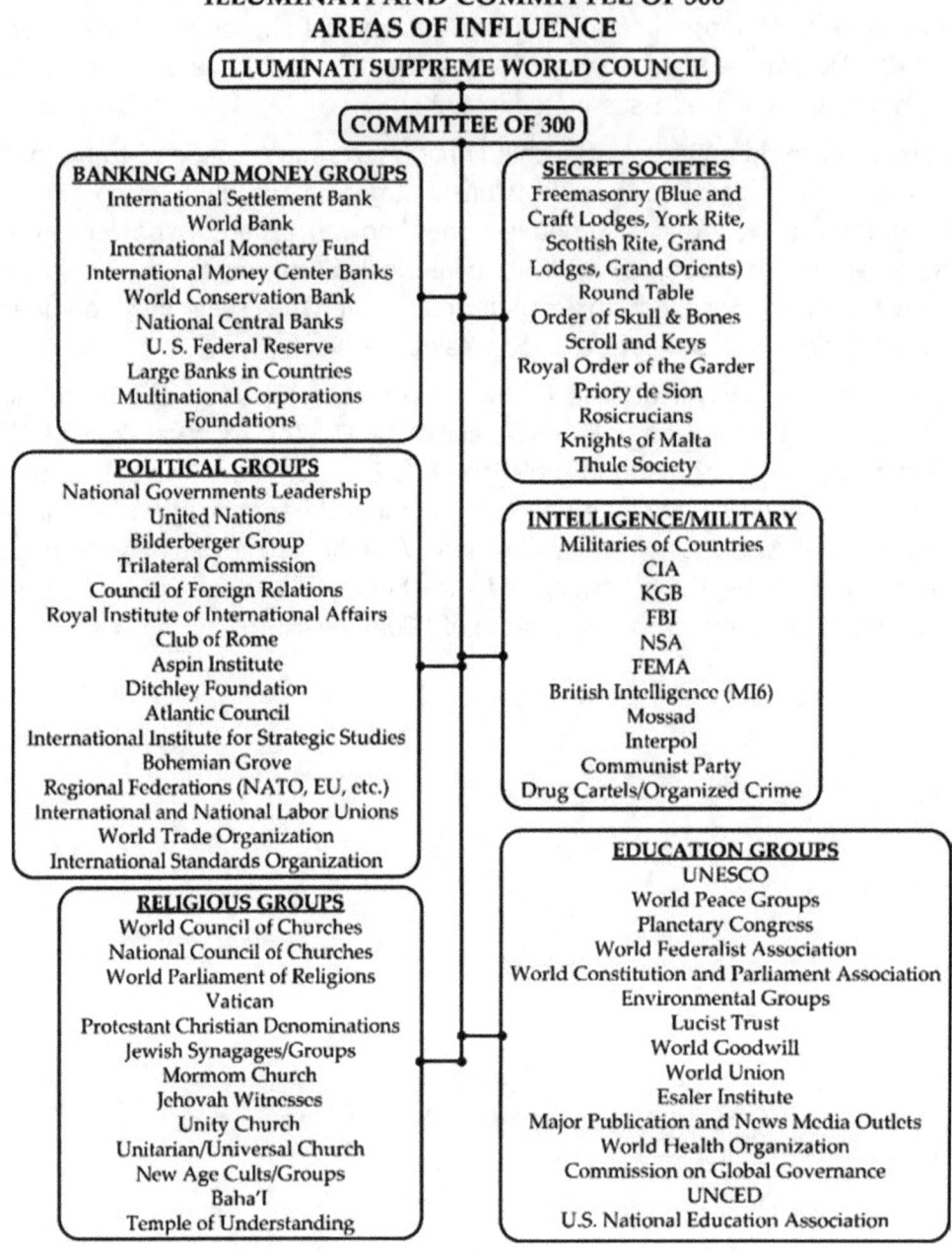

ILLUMINATI AND COMMITTEE OF 300 AREAS OF INFLUENCE

Source:

https://concisepolitics.com/2017/10/29/world-dictatorship-the-committee-of-300-led-by-british-swiss-rothschilds-crime-syndicate/comment-page-1/

Figure 29

GLOBAL AGENDA OF THE COMMITTEE OF 300 NETWORK

Following is the global agenda of the Illuminati and Committee of 300 network (also the New World Order) (*Conspirators' Hierarchy: The Story of the Committee of 300, 4th Edition*):

1. Establish a New World Order, which will be an oligarchy style dictatorship, with a unified church and monetary system under their direction. The One World Government began setting up its "church" in the 1920's/1930's.

2. Utterly destroy all national identity and national pride.

3. Destroy all religions, especially the Christian religion, and replace them with their own religion.

4. Establish the ability to control each and every person through means of mind control and technetronics.

5. Bring to an end all industrialization and the production of nuclear generated electric power in what the Committee calls "the post-industrial zero-growth society." Only service industries will remain. United States industries that remain will be exported to countries where abundant slave labor is available.

6. Encourage and eventually legalize the use of drugs and approve pornography as an art form.

7. Depopulate large cities according to the trial run carried out by the Pol Pot regime in Cambodia.

8. Suppress all scientific development except for those deemed beneficial by the Committee.

9. Cause by means of limited wars in advanced countries and starvation and disease pandemics in Third World countries the death of 3 billion people referred to as "useless eaters" by the year 2050. Under the terms of the Global 2000 Report, the population of the United States is to be reduced by 100 million by the year 2050.

10. Weaken the moral fiber of western nations by the degradation of the institution of marriage and by encouraging drug use, sex outside of marriage, the viewing of pornography, and severely immodest dress among women.

11. As jobs dwindle because of the Post Industrial Zero Growth policies, demoralize workers in the labor class who are no longer employable.

12. Keep people everywhere from deciding their own destinies by creating one crisis after another and then managing these crises. This will confuse and demoralize people, resulting in apathy because of too many failed choices in responding to the many crises.

13. Introduce new cults and continue to boost those cults already in existence. Use music as a means to attract and entrap people in these cults.

14. Continue to build up Christian fundamentalism begun by the British East India Company's servant, John Nielson Darby. Christian fundamentalism has been used to strengthen the Zionist state of Israel through identifying with Jews as "God's Chosen People" and to donate very substantial amounts of money in what is believed to be a religious cause in the furtherance of Christianity. Christian fundamentalism overlooks the fact that modern Israel has been established as a Zionist political state and not a Jewish religious state.

15. Encourage and support the spread of religious cults, such as the Moslem Brotherhood, Moslem fundamentalism, and the Sikhs, and carry out mind control experiments of the Jim Jones and "Son of Sam" types.

16. Export "religious liberation" ideas throughout the world to undermine all existing religions, especially Christianity.

17. Facilitate a total collapse of the world's economies and engender total political chaos.

18. Take control of all foreign and domestic policies of the United States.

19. Give the fullest support to supranational institutions, such as the United Nations (UN), the International Monetary Fund (IMF), the Bank of International Settlements (BIS), the World Court and, as far as possible, make local institutions of lesser effect by gradually phasing them out or bringing them under the mantle of the United Nations.

20. Penetrate and subvert all governments, and work from within them to destroy the sovereign integrity of nations represented by them.

21. Organize a world-wide terrorist apparatus and negotiate with lawful governments for their surrender whenever terrorist activities take place in their countries by allowing the U. S. to establish permanent military bases in those countries, which will be carried out under the banner of "bringing democracy."

22. Take control of education in the U. S. with the intent and purpose of utterly and destroying it.

CHAPTER 17
THE GLOBAL AND U. S. BANKING AND MONETARY SYSTEMS

GLOBAL BANKING AND MONETARY SYSTEM

Gaining control of the global banking and monetary system is a major objective in the establishment of a New World Order s. This is essential to the establishment of a global economy with a single world currency. Therefore, an understanding of the global banking and monetary system is important. Figure 30 shows a simplified organization diagram of the global banking system.

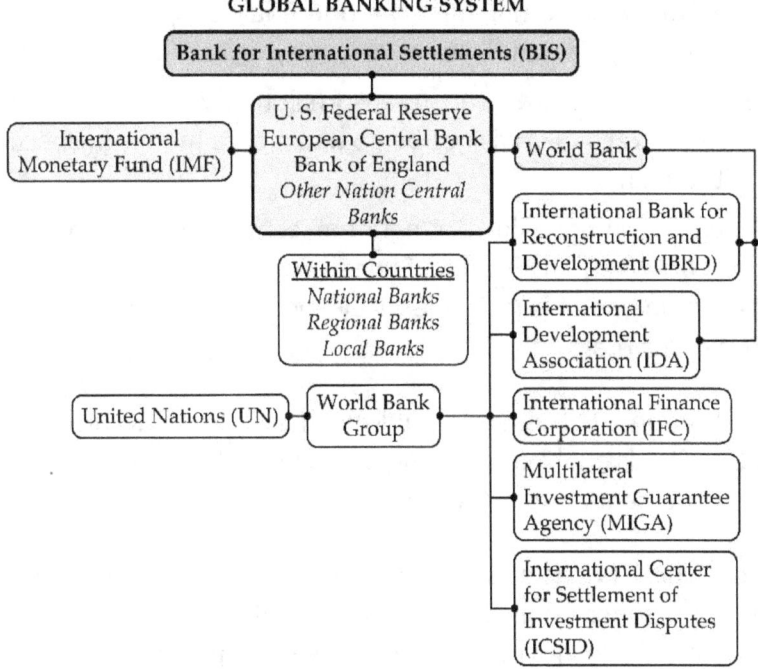

Figure 30

Bank for International Settlements (BIS)

The Bank for International Settlements that is headquartered in Basel, Switzerland was established in 1930 by a treaty between Belgium, England, France, Germany, Italy, Japan, United States and Switzerland. It was formed to facilitate reparation payments imposed on Germany by the Treaty of Versailles after World War One. It was originally owned by governments and private individuals but was reorganized after World War Two It is currently owned by sixty national central banks and operates in the private market as a counter party assets manager and lender for national central banks and international financial institutions. Revenue received from these activities is used to support other banking operations. The following national central banks own the controlling interest in the Bank for International Settlements: U. S. Federal Reserve, Bank of England, Bank of Italy, Bank of Canada, Swiss National Bank, De Nederlandsche Bank, Bundesbank, and Bank of France.

Activities of the Bank for International Settlements include:

- Regulate the valuation of equity and capital assets (capital adequacy) between national central banks to minimize the potential for speculative lending based on inadequate underlying capital and widely varying liability regulations.

- Set reserve control requirements to ensure liquidity and limit liability to the larger economy so central banks will not be able to create money in specific industries or regions without limit.

- Provide banking supervision to national central banks. There are significant differences between the United States, European Union, and United Nations regarding the degree of capital adequacy and reserve controls that global banking is required to maintain.

The Bank for International Settlements publishes its accounts in terms of SDRs (special drawing rights). One SDR is equivalent to 0.66 USD. One of the major objectives of the Bank for International Settlements is to establish:

> "A well-designed financial safety net, supported by strong prudential regulation and supervision, effective laws that are enforced, and sound accounting and disclosure regimes." (Source - Wikipedia)

Central and Reserve Banks

Central and reserve banks are an integral part of the global banking system. They are banks that control and manage the money supplies and currencies within their respective countries. A central or reserve bank is granted monopolistic control of a country's money supply by the government of the country in which it resides. It is often responsible for minting the nation's coins and currency, which serve as a nation's legal tender in commercial transactions. The central or reserve banks in most counties are privately owned and managed corporations that are subject to local, regional and national taxes and the laws that govern the operation of private corporations. They privately own deeded properties, their buildings, and other assets necessary to support their operations. Central or reserve banks are normally not accountable to or subject to government oversight since they are privately operated corporations. However, most central or reserve banks work in concert with executive branches of the governments in the countries where they reside to print money when it is requested.

Central and reserve banks manage a nation's money supply that:

- Sets the reserve requirements (required fraction of deposits that must be maintained as cash- on-hand) for commercial banks;
- Manages central and commercial bank lending interest rates;
- Acts as the lender of last resort for commercial banks during times of bank insolvency or times of financial crises;
- Injects money into the nation's money supply when needed; and
- Exercises supervisory powers to prevent commercial bank runs and commercial banks and other financial institutions from engaging in reckless or fraudulent behavior.

All global currencies are fiat currencies. A fiat currency is a currency a government has declared to be legal tender, but is not backed by a physical commodity, such as gold, silver or other precious metal. The value of fiat money is derived from the relationship between supply and demand of the money. The value increases when the demand is high, and the supply is low and decreases when the demand is low and the supply is high. In addition, the value is also highly influenced by faith in the government issuing it. Central and reserve banks essentially create money out of nothing when they create money by printing fiat currency because there is nothing of value to back the currency. As a result, printing large quantities of fiat currency often reduces its value.

International Monetary Fund

The International Monetary Fund (IMF), which is headquartered in Washington, D.C., was created in 1945 as an outgrow of the 1944 Brenton Woods Conference. The initial goal of the International Monetary Fund was to assist in the reconstruction of the global international payment system after World War Two. Initially, the two primary functions of the IMF were to:

- Oversee the fixed currency exchange rate agreements between countries established by the Brenton Woods Conferences, helping governments to manage these rates more effectively and to set priorities for economic growth; and
- Provide short-term capital loans to member countries when their capital outflow significantly exceeds their capital generation and inflow.

These functions were changed after currency exchange rates were permitted to float after former President Nixon removed the USD from the gold standard in 1971. The IMF became more actively involved in managing economic policies and development in countries with IMF loan agreements in addition to overseeing currency exchange rates between countries. The IMF currently has 188 member countries that are divided into two primary groups:

- Developed countries that contribute most of the IMF funds available for loans, and
- Emerging developing countries to whom most IMF loans are made.

The accounting unit used by the IMF is SDRs (special drawing rights). (Source - Wikipedia)

World Bank

The World Bank that is headquartered in Washington, D.C. was created in 1944 as an outgrow of the Brenton Woods Conference. It was initially established to provide reconstruction loans to European countries devastated by World War Two. The World Bank shifted its focus to non-European, Third-World governments for infrastructure loans, primarily for seaports, highway systems and power generating plants because of competition in Europe from the Marshall Plan and other funding sources for European reconstruction. It later approved Third-World government loans for social services and other sectors, as well as, for Third-World debt reduction. The World Bank expanded its loan programs after 1989 to include Third-World, non-governmental organizations and environmental groups. The World Bank currently has 188 IBRD member countries and 172 IDA member countries

(Figure 30). It operates under the guidance of the United Nations World Bank Group to remove poverty and increase employment in poor countries. The Word Bank receives monetary contributions from the stronger developed countries. (Source - Wikipedia)

Effects of Globalization

Globalization encompasses:

- Global financial markets and multinational corporations and financial institutions;
- National governments linked together through economic and military alliances, often led by the United States; and
- Establishment of global organizations, such as organizations within the United Nations, the International Monetary Fund, the World Bank, and the Bank for International Settlements.

Globalized monetary institutions, such as the International Monetary Fund, the World Bank and the Bank for International Settlements weaken the notion of nation-state sovereignty. The centralization of wealth and financial resources within these institutions gives them increased control over the internal affairs of countries who make use of these resources. This is particularly true of countries in emerging economic markets. Figure 30 shows the channels of power, control, indoctrination and distribution associated with increasing global wealth, resources and power.

The current global economic system is based on the U. S. dollar and euro and is supported by the United States, the European Union, and the International Monetary Fund. The reserve currencies are the U. S. dollar, euro and Japanese yen. However, there is an emerging movement to replace the current global economic and monetary systems with a new system based on a single global currency. Some indicate this new global currency will be a virtual digital currency modeled after bit coin. This is being recommended to bring greater stability to the global economy. It is also one of the major objectives of the Illuminati and Committee of 300 network in their effort to establish a New World Order. Control of the global banking and monetary systems is essential to their achieving this objective. Dr. Henry Kissinger stated in 1973, "Who controls the food supply controls the people; who controls the energy can control whole continents; who controls the money supply can control the world."

Dark Side of the Global Banking System

Collusions between banks, multinational corporations and governments have undermined the sovereignty of governments around the world, particularly in Third-World emerging economies. Desired assets and resources within a country are identified. Its government is then invited to receive major loans from the World Bank and/or the International Monetary Fund to develop these assets and resources. Money from these loans is often given to multinational corporations to carry out the development and necessary construction. Often little or no money from these loans is used to develop the country's infrastructure and economy or to address the needs of the people. As a result, the country is often unable to repay the loans and defaults on the payments. Elected leaders are then given the choice of submitting to the agenda of the lending institutions and the multinational corporations who received the money from the loans or face being replaced or the possibility of being assassinated. (Source: *Confessions of an Economic Hit Man* by John Perkins, 2004)

THE EIGHT TOP FINANCIALLY ELITE BANKING FAMILIES

There are eight major global banking families. These families are: Rothschild, Rockefeller, Lehman, Kuhn Loebes, Goldman Sachs, Warburg, Lazard, and Israel Moses Serifs. They indicate the control these families exert over the global economy that is internationally shrouded in secrecy cannot be overstated. Conspiracy theorist further claim these families have controlling interests in many of the eight central banks that control the Bank of International Settlements. Therefore, it is reasonable to believe they also control the activities of the Bank of International Settlements. However, it is difficult to find evidence to substantiate these claims because of the public secrecy surrounding these families. Regarding the influence and control these eight banking families and the increasing number of billionaires throughout the world exercise over the global banking and financial system, Louis Even in one of the appendices in his book, *In This Age of Plenty* (2012), stated:

> "The basic flaw of the present [global] financial system is that the banks create money as a debt, charging interest on the money that they create. The obligation for the debtor countries to repay the banks money that the banks did not create and money that does not exist eventually brings about unpayable debts. The Financiers know quite well that it is impossible for these countries to repay their debts, that the present financial system is defective at its base, and that it can only bring about crises and revolutions. But this is exactly what they want! As Clifford Hugh Douglas, the founder of

the Social Credit school, said: 'The Money Power does not, and never did, want to improve the money system - its consequences in war, sabotage and social friction are exactly what is desired. Why? It is because the Financiers believe that they are the only ones capable of governing mankind properly, and in order to be able to impose their will upon every individual and control the whole world, they invented the present debt-money system. They want to bring every nation in the world to such a state of crisis that these countries will think they have no alternative but to accept the miracle solution of the Financiers to save them from disaster: complete centralization, a single world currency, and a one-world government, in which all nations will be abolished, or forced to give up their sovereignty.'"

Conspiracy theorist indicate members of these families are members of the Illuminati and Committee of 300, are involved with the Illuminati upper hierarchy (Figures 23 and 24) and are committed to the establishment of a New World Order. David Rockefeller is quoted as saying, "We are on the verge of a global transformation. All we need is the right major crisis and the nations will accept the New World Order."

THE U. S. BANKING AND MONETARY SYSTEM

The U. S. Federal Reserve

The U. S. Federal Reserve, which is headquartered in Washington, D. C., is the reserve or central bank of the United States. It has twelve regional banks, the most influential being in New York City. The Federal Reserve was created in 1913 with the enactment of the Federal Reserve Act. The Act was enacted in response to a series of bank panics, the largest of which occurred in 1907. Three key functions of the Federal Reserve that were specified in the Act are:

- Achieve maximum employment within the United States;
- Establish economic stabilization by providing for greater financial stability within the U. S. banking system; and
- Monitor and moderate long-term bank interest rates.

The basic document that resulted in the Federal Reserve Act was drafted during a secret meeting held on Jekyll Island, Georgia, in 1910. The meeting was coordinated by then Senator Nelson Aldrich. Attending the meeting were Author Shelton, Aldrich's personal secretary; A.

Piatt Andrew, Assistant Secretary of the Treasury; Frank Vanderlin, president of the National City Bank of New York; Henry P. Davison, senior partner of J. P. Morgan Company; and Paul Warburg, a member of the banking house of Kuhn, Loeb.

Major banking interests were represented at the Jekyll Island meeting, and the meeting was shrouded in secrecy. As a result, conspiracy theorists claim the U. S. Federal Reserve system was established with predatory characteristics to work to the advantages of the banking industry and to provide a means for foreign banking interests to obtain a controlling interest of the system. As will be discussed later, there are predatory characteristics in U. S. banking system. However, evidence is difficult to obtain to support the conspiracy theorists' claims.

Figure 31 shows the organization structure of the U. S. Federal Reserve system. The system is independent within the U. S. government. Its four main components are:

- The Board of Governors,
- The Federal Open Market Committee (FOMC),
- Federal Advisory Council (FAC), and
- The twelve regional Federal Reserve banks.

The Board of Governors (BOG) is a federal agency comprised of seven members appointed by the President and confirmed by the U. S. Senate. It is responsible for the oversight of the twelve regional Federal Reserve banks.

The Federal Open Market Committee (FOMC) has twelve members. These include the seven BOG members plus five of the regional Federal Reserve bank presidents. The president of the New York City regional Federal Reserve bank is a permanent member. Presidents of four of the other Federal Reserve banks rotate onto the FOMC on an annual basis. The FOMC formulates and oversees U. S. monetary policy and controls the amount of Federal Reserve funds that are to be made available to commercial banks and thrifts through its regional Reserve Banks. This affects monetary and credit conditions associated with the U. S. money supply. Additionally, the FOMC directs Federal Reserve operations in foreign exchange markets.

U. S. FEDERAL RESERVE SYSTEM

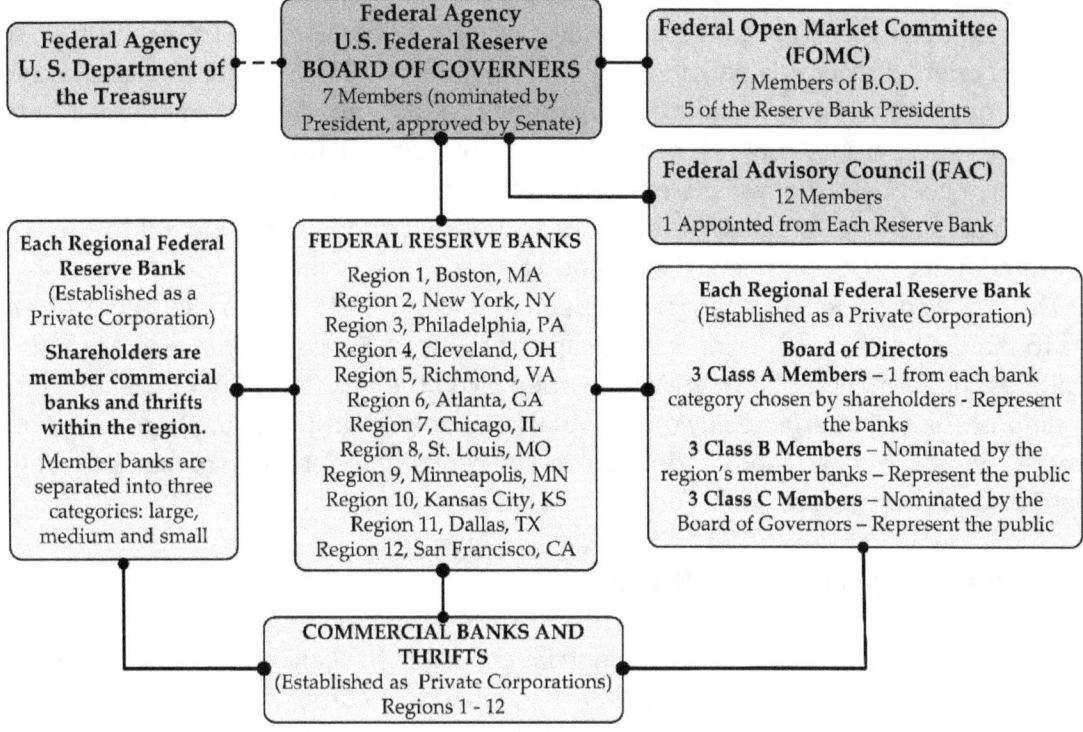

Figure 31

The Federal Advisory Council (FAC) is comprised of twelve representatives nominated by each of the twelve regional Federal Reserve banks. The FAC consults with and advises the BOG on matters that by law it can address.

Each of the twelve regional Federal Reserve banks are organized as a privately held corporation. The shareholders of the corporation are the member commercial banks and thrifts that are within the region. Unlike standard corporations where a shareholder's voting power is proportional to the number of shares owned, each member commercial bank or thrift has one vote regardless of size and number of shares owned.

Each regional Federal Reserve bank owns deeded properties, its buildings, and all other assets necessary to support its operations as a privately held corporation. It pays local taxes on its properties and is subject to laws that govern the operation of privately held corporations. Its employees are employees of a privately held corporation. They are not federal civil servants. A regional Federal Reserve bank is not accountable to nor subject to any government oversight since it is a privately held corporation. Unlike standard corporations in which corporate profits are distributed to its shareholders, profits accrued be regional

Federal Reserve banks are transferred to the U. S. Treasury. The U. S. Federal Reserve has monopolistic control over the U. S. money supply. It can create scarcity or oversupply of the money supply, depending on the money policies it institutes. The U. S. Treasury mints coins and prints currency on behalf of the Federal Reserve. The U. S. Treasury creates new money from nothing when it mints or prints money at the request of the Federal Reserve because the U. S. money supply is not commodity-backed. Additionally, it creates this new money on a debt basis that will be repaid to the Federal Reserve with interest. The printed money is sold to investors as U. S. Treasury securities or bonds or is loaned to the U. S. government or to U. S. commercial banks and thrifts.

The U. S. Federal Reserve can use monetary policies it institutes to exert control over and to manipulate the U. S. economy. It can direct the U. S. economy in a direction that facilitates the formation of a New World Order, given the right set of national and global conditions. This will be affected by the spiritual (secular humanist-Christian), social-political (progressive-conservative) and economic (socialist-capitalist) orientation of members of the Board of Governors and regional Federal Reserve bank presidents.

U. S. Commercial and Retail Banks

A major characteristic of the U. S. commercial and retail banking system is its corporate diversity represented by the large number of independent corporately owned banks that offer commercial and retail banking services. This contrasts with other countries where these services are offered by only a few independent corporately owned banks. Figure 32 shows a trend in the decrease in the number of U. S. banks that began around 1985. This represents a disturbing consolidation of commercial and retail banking services, if this trend continues that will be provided by a small number of large major banks. The four largest U.S. banks are J P Morgan Chase, Bank of America, Wells Fargo and Citibank.

A major function of banks is making business, corporate, equity, personal, mortgage, etc. loans. The aggregate number and sizes of these loans can have a significant impact on the U. S. money supply and the value of the U. S. dollar. The method associated with making these loans is referred to as *fractional reserve banking*. This is a banking system in which only a fraction of bank deposits is backed by actual cash-on-hand and are available for withdrawal by bank customers. This banking system is used to expand the economy by freeing up capital that can be loaned out to other parties. Economic expansion with this system is achieved through increasing debt. Fractional banking allows commercial and retail banks to create new capital for economic expansion from nothing.

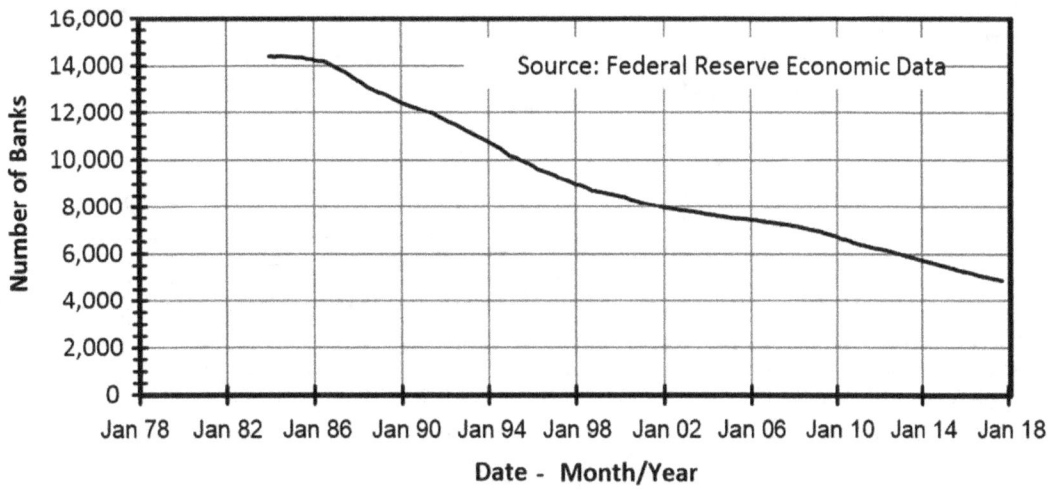

Figure 32

Fraction banking works as follows. Assume a bank receives an initial deposit of $100 and must keep a reserve of cash-on-hand of 20 percent of its deposits. Therefore, the bank keeps a reserve of $20 and lends $80 to a third party. The third party spends the $80, and the spent $80 is deposited by a fourth party into the original bank making the $80 loan or into another bank. Regarding this deposit, the bank keeps a reserve of $16 and lends out $64. Figure 33 shows the results of 10 iterations of this process. At the end of ten iterations, $357.05 has been lent out and $89.26 has been kept in reserve. Following this process to the point where no money is left to lend, a maximum of $400 will have been lent out, a maximum of $100 will have been kept in reserve, and the maxim deposits will be $500. An addition of $400 in deposits was created out of nothing in this example from the original $100 deposit. The possible total deposit from an initial deposit can be obtained by dividing the initial deposit by the reserve ratio. The reserve requirement of 20 percent relative to the above example results in a reserve ratio of 0.2. Therefore, the maximum total deposits are 100/0.2 or $500 (Figure 34).

Deposit Number	Amont Deposited	Amount Lent Out	Amount In Reserve
1	$100.00	$80.00	$20.00
2	$80.00	$64.00	$16.00
3	$64.00	$51.20	$12.80
4	$51.20	$40.96	$10.24
5	$40.96	$32.77	$8.19
6	$32.77	$26.21	$6.55
7	$26.21	$20.97	$5.24
8	$20.97	$16.78	$4.19
9	$16.78	$13.42	$3.36
10	$13.42	$10.74	$2.68
Total	$446.31	$357.05	$89.26

Initial Deposit	$	100.00
Reserve Ratio		0.2
Total in Reserve	$	100.00
Total Deposits	$	500.00
Total Lent Out	$	400.00

Initial Deposit	$	1,000,000.00
Reserve Ratio		0.05
Total in Reserve	$	1,000,000.00
Total Deposits	$	20,000,000.00
Total Lent Out	$	19,000,000.00

Figure 33   **Figure 34**   **Figure 35**

The required reserve for banks usually varies from 3-5 percent. Assume an initial deposit of $1,000,000 and a required reserve of 5 percent. The maximum deposits will be (1,000,000/0.05) or $20,000,000 (Figure 35). Therefore, a total of $19,000,000 in additional deposits or capital would be created out of thin air, injecting $19,000,000 into the money supply.

Predatory Aspects of the U. S. Banking System

U. S. commercial and retail banks are privately held corporations that, in addition to providing the financial services they provide, exist to increase the wealth of their shareholders. Figure 36 shows the increase in bank assets of U. S. commercial and retail banks. A comparison of Figures 35 and 31 indicates the increases in bank assets are being consolidated into a decreasing number of banks and bank shareholders. The increase in bank assets, which has translated into increased wealth for bank shareholders, has been achieved at the expense of increases in corporate and consumer debt. The U. S. Federal Reserve and commercial and retail banks exercise control over interest rates associated with lending money. They can control or manipulate economic and business cycles in the following manner:

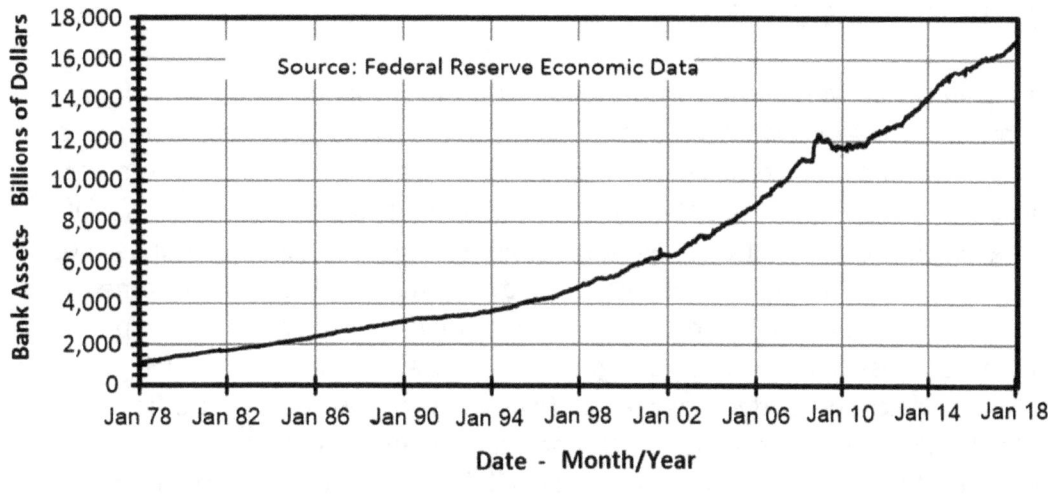

Figure 36

- **Phase 1:** The Federal Reserve places large sums of money into circulation at low interest rates. Banks increase the money supply in circulation by making low interest loans using fractional reserve banking. This creates an economic boom that creates new jobs. Consumer spending increases, resulting in economic growth. This results in an increase in consumer spending and related loan activity for larger homes, cars, travel, etc., and in business and corporate loan activity to increase infrastructure and manufacturing capabilities to meet increased demands for their products and services. The net result of this phase is increased consumer, business, corporate and other related debt and a decrease in the value of the currency.

- **Phase 2.** The Federal Reserve increases its interest rate, causing banks to increase their interest rates. As a result, loan activity decreases, and banks increase their requirements for approving loan applications. More money is needed to repay loans as interest rates rise, and less money is in circulation to buy products and services. More money is needed to pay for products and services because of the decrease in the value of the currency associated with Phase 1. Company profits decrease, jobs are lost, and some businesses and companies go out of business. Some individuals, businesses and companies can no longer repay their loans and default on their payments. Banks then acquire the real wealth, which are the lands, properties and other related assets that were used as collateral for the loans banks made with money they created out of thin air. This cycle has been used repeatedly during the past and has given the financial elite who are major investors in many of the commercial and retail banks the ability to acquire the real wealth in the world.

NEGATIVE IMPACT OF DEBT

Increases in U. S. government, corporate and consumer spending and growth of the U. S. economy are facilitated by the creation of debt. The U. S. government must borrow because it spends more than it receives in tax revenues. Businesses and corporations must borrow because there is always a lag between the requirement to pay expenses associated with creating, producing and marketing goods and services and the receipt of funds in payment for these goods and services. Consumers borrow because they lack the income to initially pay for major goods (homes, cars, etc.) and travel, medical, education, etc. expenses. They must pay for these loans over time. Figure 37 shows a summary of the U.S. government, corporate and consumer debt, as well as the total for these debts. The figure does not include the debt associated with state and local governments and the projected debt associated with U.S. government unfunded liabilities associate with entitlements.\

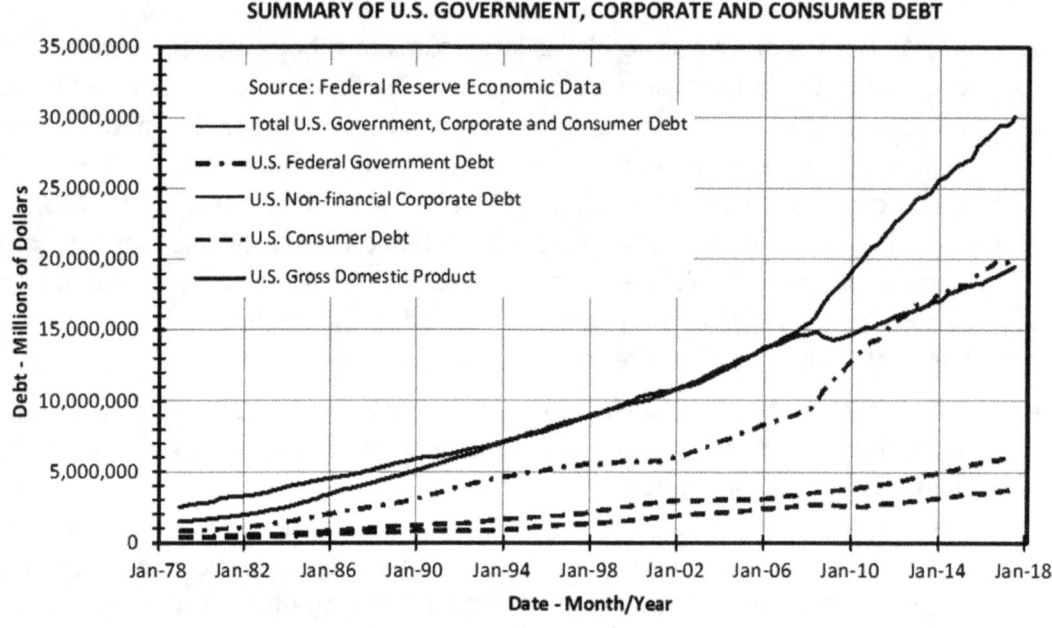

Figure 37

The corresponding increase in U.S. gross domestic product (GDP) is also shown in Figure 37. The GDP represents the total dollar value of all goods and services produced in a country over a specified time, normally a year. It is used as an indicator to gauge the size and health of a country's economy.

Two areas of concern arise from Figure 37. The first is the size of the U.S. federal government debt as it relates to U.S. GDP. Investors like to use the U. S. government debt-to-GDP ratio as a measure of economic health. This ratio compares a country's sovereign debt to its total economic output for the year, which is measured by GDP. Figure 38 shows the U. S. government debt-to-GDP ratio. It gives investors a rough gauge as to the United States' ability to pay off its debt. Investors start to worry when the debt-to-GDP ratio exceeds around 77 percent for an extended time. They will eventually demand higher interest rates for government securities because of the higher risk for default. The U. S. Government debt-to-GDP ratio has been above 77 percent since 2009. This can eventually result in a U. S. debt crisis because investors will eventually demand higher interest rates for U. S. Treasuries. (Source: World Bank, Finding the Tipping Point).

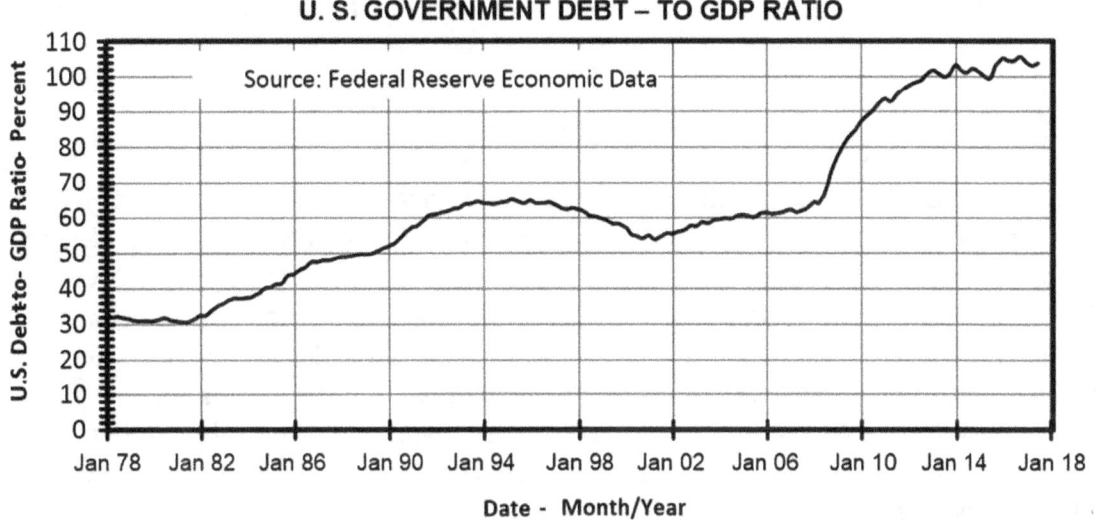

Figure 38

The relation of combined U.S. government, corporate and consumer debt to the U.S. gross domestic product is of concern. Figure 39 indicates the U.S. combined debt-to-GDP ratio increased from around 60 percent to 100 percent between 1979 and 1994. The ratio remained relatively constant at 100 percent between 1994 and 2007. The ratio has increased to 155 percent between 2007 and the beginning of 2018.

U. S. COMBINED DEBT – TO GDP RATIO

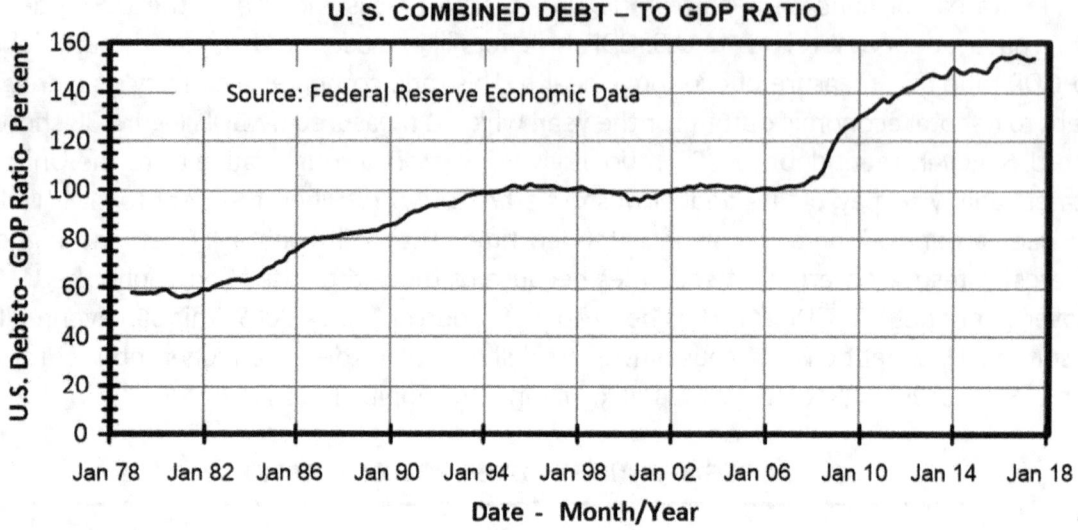

Source: Federal Reserve Economic Data

Date - Month/Year

Figure 39

It is not possible for the United States to create enough wealth represented by its gross domestic product to sustain the debt in Figures 36 and 38. The combine U.S. government, corporate and consumer debt was around $30 trillion in 2018. The unfunded U.S. government liabilities, which include social security, Medicare parts A, B and D, federal debt held by the public, and federal employee and veteran pension plans, is $115 trillion (www.usdebtclock.org). The total for the above debt plus unfunded liabilities is $145 trillion. This is over 7.2 times the U.S. gross domestic product, and this debt does not include state and local government and private pension unfunded liabilities. It is impossible to indefinitely sustain this debt with a U. S. gross domestic product of around $27 trillion per year (Figure 37).

CHAPTER 18
ESTABLISHMENT OF A
NEW WORLD ORDER

STRUCTURE OF THE NEW WORLD ORDER

The New World Order announced by former President George H. W. Bush in his 1991 State of the Union address includes the organizations identified in Figures 22 - 26. They are pursuing the Illuminati and Committee of 300 global agenda. The path to the establishment of a New World Order that will be an oligarchy style global dictatorship is one filled with deception and manipulation. Recruitment into the New World Order leadership and related training occur through Illuminati controlled secret societies. Many of these secret societies are listed in Figure 23 and 28. Many have a pyramid training structure like the one shown in Figure 22. Adepts' progress is closely monitored as they progress through secret training programs and participate in related secret occult initiation rituals. Only those adepts who show a clear willingness to reject God and Jesus and to swear allegiance to and worship Lucifer (Satan) are elevated to top leadership positions in the secret societies. They then receive full knowledge of their roles in the New World Order agenda (same as the Illuminati and Committee of 300 global agenda) and become agents and key leaders in the New World Order. They are trained to enter their respective professions and spheres of influence to carry out the New World Order global agenda. Those adepts closer to the base of the pyramid only have access to information associated with their lower positions in the secret societies. They do not receive information related to the New World Order global agenda.

The objectives of the New World Order are an extension of Weishaupt's Illuminati objectives They are the establishment of a New World Order that will:

- Be a global dictatorship;
- Have a single global economy;
- Have a single global money system;
- Have a global military; and
- Have a single global Religion.

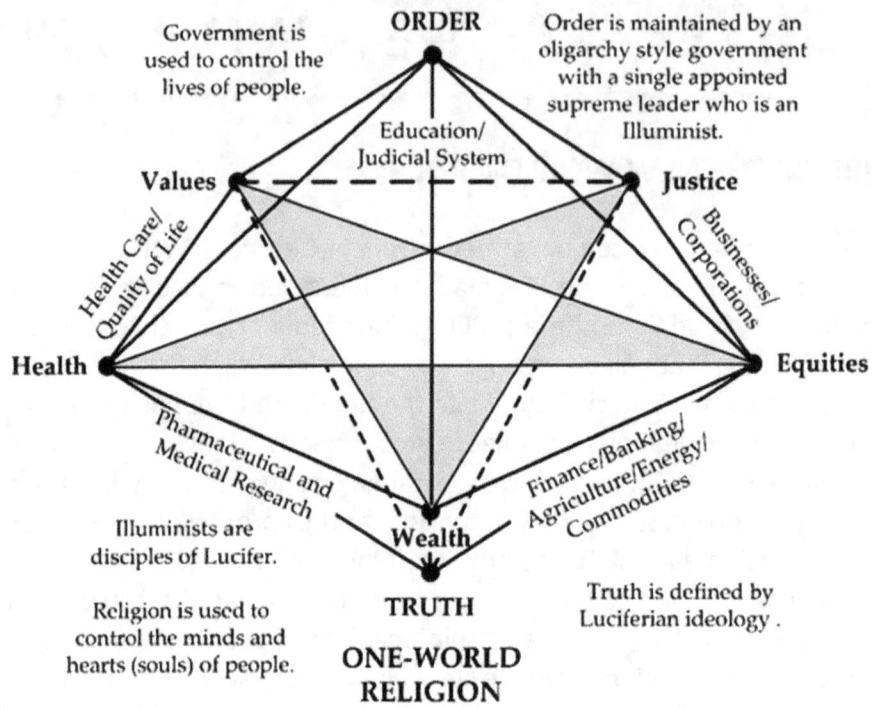

NEW WORLD ORDER
ORGANIZATION STRUCTURE

ONE-WORLD GOVERNMENT

ORDER

Government is used to control the lives of people.

Order is maintained by an oligarchy style government with a single appointed supreme leader who is an Illuminist.

Education/Judicial System

Values

Justice

Health Care/Quality of Life

Businesses/Corporations

Health

Equities

Pharmaceutical and Medical Research

Finance/Banking/Agriculture/Energy/Commodities

Illuminists are disciples of Lucifer.

Wealth

Religion is used to control the minds and hearts (souls) of people.

TRUTH

Truth is defined by Luciferian ideology.

ONE-WORLD RELIGION

Figure 40

These objectives will be achieved with absolute control under the leadership of an Illuminist global dictator who is a disciple of Lucifer. These objectives are compatible with the establishment of the ten kingdom federation foretold in Daniel that will be ruled by the Antichrist during the tribulation. The organization structure of the New World Order can be represented by a decahedron shown in Figure 40. Order is at the top of the decahedron, and Truth is at the bottom. Order will be enforced by an oligarchy style Illuminati controlled dictatorial government. Truth will be defined by Luciferian ideology and Satanism. The surfaces of the five sides of the decahedron form double pyramids shown in Figure 41. The top pyramid represents the management and control structure associated with the activities specified for each side of the decahedron. The bottom pyramid represents the occult religious leadership and training structure associated with Illuminati controlled secret societies. Key senior executives and executive managers in the management and control structure are Illuminists who are disciples of Lucifer in secret societies that support the New World Order.

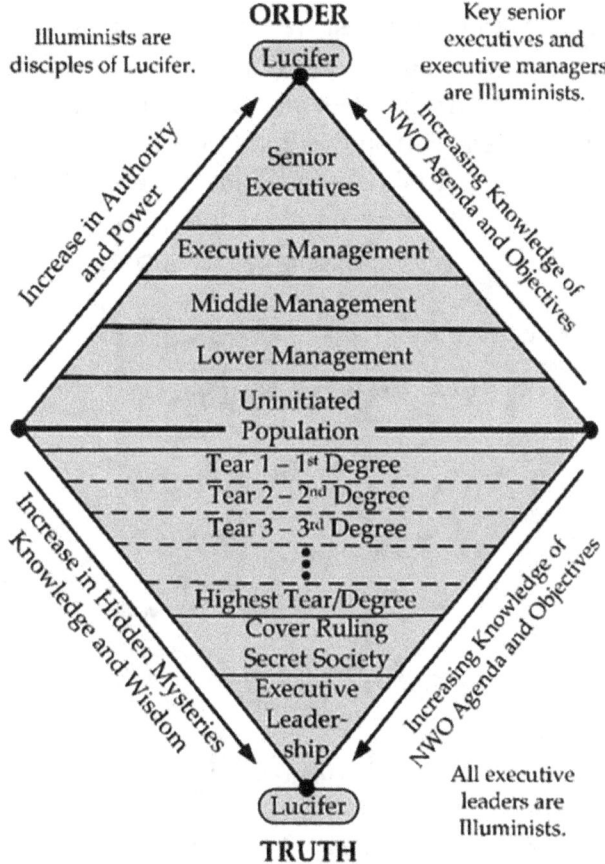

NEW WORLD ORDER ORGANIZATION STRUCTURE

Figure 41

A five-point pentagram is at the midpoint between the top and bottom of the decahedron in Figure 40. The points on the pentagram represent Wealth, Equities, Justice, Values and Health. Wealth (of Illuminist global bankers and financial elite) enables, supports and controls the other four points on the pentagram. The side between the points of Justice and Values opposite the point of Wealth represent the New World Order's control of global education essential for public indoctrination, manipulation and control and of the global judicial system essential for the manipulation and control of the world's courts. Both are necessary for the New World Order to achieve its global agenda. The side between the points of Equities and Justice represents the New World Order's control of the global corporate and business structure. The side between the points of Health and Values represents the New World Order's control over global quality of life and health care. The side between the points of Wealth and Equities represents how the New World Order global bankers and financial elite will increase their wealth and control global banking, commerce, agriculture, and energy generation and distribution. The side between the points of Wealth and Health represents the New World Order global banker's and financial elite's control of pharmaceutical and medical research and distribution. The two front sides of the triangle formed by the points of Health, Wealth and Equities represent the total control the New World Order global bankers and financial elite will have over the research and wealth generation necessary to control a global economy and society.

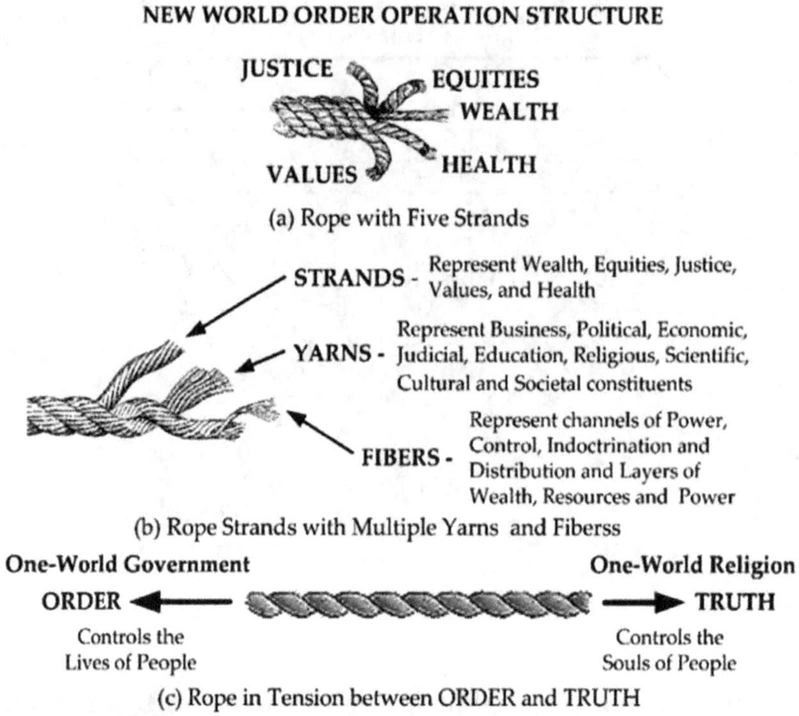

NEW WORLD ORDER OPERATION STRUCTURE

JUSTICE   EQUITIES
           WEALTH

VALUES   HEALTH

(a) Rope with Five Strands

STRANDS - Represent Wealth, Equities, Justice, Values, and Health

YARNS - Represent Business, Political, Economic, Judicial, Education, Religious, Scientific, Cultural and Societal constituents

FIBERS - Represent channels of Power, Control, Indoctrination and Distribution and Layers of Wealth, Resources and Power

(b) Rope Strands with Multiple Yarns and Fiberss

One-World Government   One-World Religion
ORDER ◄——— ▨▨▨▨▨▨▨▨▨▨▨ ———► TRUTH
Controls the   Controls the
Lives of People   Souls of People

(c) Rope in Tension between ORDER and TRUTH

Figure 42

The multiple components of the Illuminati and Committee of 300 networks are integrally interwoven into regional, national and global societal, cultural and government organizations, agencies and groups. Referring to the New World Order organization structure in Figures 40 and 41, its highly integrated and sophisticated operation structure can be visualized as a rope with five intertwined *strands*. The *strands* represent Wealth,

Equities, Justice, Values and Health as shown in Figure 42(a). The multiple intertwined *yarns* that make up the *strands* represent business, political, economic, judicial, education, religious, scientific, cultural and societal constituents that direct and control integrated activities within and between the five *strands* in Figure 42(b). *Fibers* that make up the *yarns* of the *strands* in Figure 42(b) represent channels of power, control, indoctrination and distribution associated with the labeled vertical segments of the pyramid in Figure 43. Moving from the bottom to the top of the pyramid, *fibers* also represent channels of progressively increasing wealth, resources and power associated with the horizontal layers of the pyramid. Illuminists represented by *fibers* in the *yarns* facilitate coordinated and integrated activities represented by *yarns* within the *strands* and by *yarns* that operate between the *strands*.

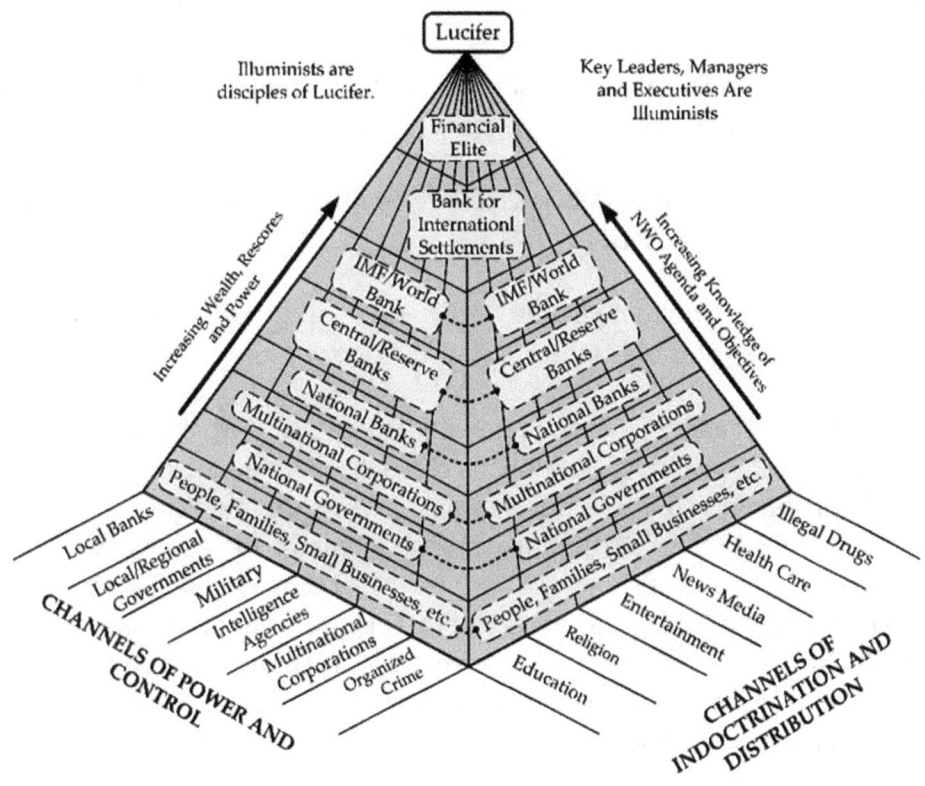

Figure 43

The rope comprised of the five *strands* with their multiple *yarns* and *fibers* can be visualized as being held in tension by *Order* and *Truth* [Figure 42(c)]. *Order* is maintained by the New World Order, oligarchy style, global, dictatorial government that controls the lives of people.

Truth is defined by Luciferian ideology and Satanism through a global religion that controls the minds and hearts (souls) of people. Lucifer's influence and control are present throughout all operational elements represented by the rope's *strands*, *yarns* and *fibers*. These are achieved through Illuminists among the global social, financial and banking elite who are descended from European royalty and families with generational unbroken occult bloodlines.

OBSTACLES TO THE ESTABLISHMENT OF A NEW WORLD ORDER

Three major obstacles oppose the establishment of a global New World Order. They are:

- The presence of Christianity in the world that functions through the Christian Church;
- The nature and character of the people of the United States and of the U. S. Government; and
- The strong and vibrant capitalistic economic system of the United States that dominates the global economic system.

A New World Order can only be established after these obstacles have been neutralized or removed. Jesus told Peter in Matthew 16:18:

> "And I also say to you that you are Peter, and upon this rock I will build My church; and the gates of Hades shall not over power it."

The presence of the Christian Church, even with its faults and weaknesses, was essential to the development of Western civilization. Its character defined the character of Western cultures, and Christianity led in the development of science, medicine and education in Europe and the United States. Satan through the Illuminist movement will not be able to establish a New World Order that will assume total dominion over the world until the Christian Church and Christians are neutralized. This can only occur after the Christian Church and Christians have been removed from the world at the rapture.

The greatness, stability and global dominance of the United States are sustained by the country's commitment to and support of:

- Its Jewish-Christian heritage and the resulting belief in a transcendent God who is the creator of the universe and who has given us a transcendent set of absolute spiritual and moral laws that govern our lives and define our nation's character.
- The traditional family unit that is defined as a husband and wife who are married and who conceive, give birth to and raise their children.

- The traditional family unit that provides a safe, stable and nurturing environment where children can grow in maturity to adulthood and where moral and ethical values associated with religion, honor, patriotism and sexual behavior are instilled in children.

- A democratic constitutional republic government whose primary functions are to support and facilitate the development of a highly educated citizenry, to provide a stable environment where its citizens can develop a strong and vibrant society and economy, and to protect its citizens from foreign threats and intervention.

- The establishment and maintenance of a dedicated, strong, well trained, and technologically superior military.

- The development and maintenance of a strong industrial base.

- The development and maintenance of a strong and stable middle class.

NEUTRALIZING THE PRESENCE OF THE CHRISTIAN CHURCH AND CHRISTIANITY

Neutralizing Christianity

Evangelical Protestant denominations in the United States and the Catholic Church throughout the world are major obstacle to the Illuminati's and Committee of 300 network's efforts to establish a New World Order.

(Source: Blog of Thomas C. Allen, "Gaining Control;" http://tcallenco.weebly.com)

The Illuminati and Committee of 300 network have worked throughout the last half of the 20th century and into the 21st century to neutralize the global influence of Christianity. They have infiltrated and gained a high level of influence over and control of Protestant denominations and segments of the Catholic Church (see Figure 29). Examples of this effort include:

- The liberation theology movement, sometime referred to as Christianized Marxism, was initiated in the Catholic Church. It focused on improving the plight of the poor in Third World countries.

- The social gospel movement was initiated in mainline Protestant denominations. It focused on using social reform and socialism to reduce economic and other inequities related to the poor.

- Liberal Protestant denominations have abandoned orthodox Christian beliefs and accepted the notion that Jesus is only one of many ways to approach God.

Beliefs supported by information in the Bible are being supplemented with or replaced by beliefs based on feelings, personal experiences and sociocultural norms. These strip Jesus of His divine nature and infuses modernism and liberalism into Christian theology. Mainline Protestant denominations are abandoning their historic opposition to homosexuality, transsexuality, the redefining of marriage to include homosexual unions, divorce, abortion and euthanasia. The defining of sin as a violation of God's laws is being abandoned (see God's laws in Chapter 2). The belief that God's salvation is available to everyone irrespective of their beliefs, life choices and lifestyles is becoming common.

During the presidency of Franklin D. Roosevelt, Freemasons gained a majority on the U. S. Supreme Court that continued through the Nixon presidency. Freemasons controlled the Supreme Court from 1941 to 1971. As a result, the Supreme Court adopted the Freemasonic view of law, which is "law is largely in the interpretation and not in the text." Consequently, Chief Justice Evan Hughes stated, "the Constitution means what the Supreme Court says it means." The Supreme Court removed nearly all vestiges of God and Christianity from public schools during this period, transforming them into institutions influenced by secular humanism, Gnosticism, Pantheism, and other forms of religion, except Christianity.

The Evolution of a New World Order Religion

The New World Order seeks to replace the belief systems of Christianity and other monotheistic world religions with its own one-world religion.

Efforts to establish a one-world religion were presented in previous discussions related to the ancient Mysteries, early secret societies, the Illuminati, Freemasonry, and the Committee of 300. Activities of these groups and those of the Tavistock network have resulted in the abandoning of traditional historic Christian beliefs in liberal Protestantism and Catholic modernism. Elements of Pantheism and Gnosticism have found their ways into the belief systems of secret societies and cults, and they and elements of Eastern religions facilitated the emergence of the New Age moment during the 1970's and 1980's. Figure 25 indicates inner circle members of the New Age movement, Zionism and Freemasonry hold high level leadership positions in the Illuminati/Illuminist movement.

Pantheism

(Source: Blog of Thomas C. Allen, "Illuminism Religiously;" http://tcallenco.weebly.com)

Pantheist believe God and the Universe are one. God is the sum of all that exists, and the Universe is a great inclusive unity that absorbs God. Therefore, the Universe is God. God is the forces and laws of nature, the life- or God-force that flows through all living things (trees, plants, animals, humans, etc.). The God-force flows through all living things, including humans. Therefore, it reduces all mankind to a global oneness, a collective consciousness, in which all men and women lose their individual identities, worth and value. Men and women will never die because mankind is united with and a part of God. This leads to the belief in reincarnation in religions that derive part of their belief system from Pantheism.

There is no personal, transcendent God in Pantheism, and truth is only revealed through nature and natural events. Truth is not revealed through divine revelation from God. Since men and women will never die, they have no need of a personal savior since they will never have to fear standing in judgment before God.

Gnosticism

(Source: Theopedia, "Gnosticism;" http://www.theopedia.com/Gnosticism)

Gnostics believe all that is spirit is good and all that is made up of physical matter in the material universe, including the human body, is evil, and there is great tension between spirit and physical matter. They believe the material universe was created by a lesser god who was evil, while God who is Spirit and wholly transcendent is far removed from the material universe. He is too perfect and pure to interact with the evil material universe. The evil lesser god is sometimes called a *demiurge*. Humans are believed to be stray sparks of the same spiritual essence of God that are trapped in physical bodies. Humans sin because they are ignorant of their true spiritual nature and their potential unity with God.

Salvation for Gnostics is the ability for their spirit/soul to escape from their physical bodies and be reunited with God. God initiates the process for salvation because He wants to draw back to Himself the stray sparks of His Spirit. Therefore, God sends emanations of Himself to secretly teach some of the sparks of His Spirit the true nature of their existence and how they can return to Him. They can begin their journey back to God once they receive this secret knowledge. Therefore, salvation for Gnostics is achieved through receiving and acting on the secret knowledge that enlightens them regarding the true nature of their existence and teaches them how they can return to God.

Most Gnostics consider themselves to be Christians even though Christianity considers Gnosticism to be a heretical belief system. They perceive Jesus to be a spiritual messenger from God. However, they reject the notions of God becoming man in the physical body of Jesus (the incarnation), dying, and then being resurrected. The perfect purity of God could not have cohabitant in the evil body of Jesus. They believe that whatever spiritual presence interred Jesus at His baptism left Him before He died on the cross.

New Age Movement

(Source: Got Questions.org, "What is the New Age movement?"; http://www.gotquestions. org/ new-age-movement.html)

The New Age movement became popular in the 1970's and 1980's. The movement is attractive to those individuals who have become disillusioned with organized religion and who desire spiritual reality but do not want to give up materialism, deal with moral problems, and come under any type of religious authority and accountability.

The New Age movement draws many of its beliefs from elements of Pantheism, Gnosticism and Eastern religions. New Agers accept the Pantheist's concept of the all-inclusive unifying nature of God and the Universe. They believe in the related Pantheist's collective oneness and consciousness of God and mankind. This consciousness is often referred to as a *cosmic consciousness*. They must train their minds to ignore existing reality and to tap into this cosmic consciousness to create their own unique reality.

New Agers, like the Gnostics, believe mankind's fall into sin was a result of ignorance. They must become enlightened and attuned to the universal cosmic consciousness of God and mankind to address this fallenness. They achieve this through contacts with spirits and *Ascended Masters* in the spiritual realm (the Gnostic's emanations of God) through channeling with spiritual mediums. They become like God and can create their own reality once they achieve this enlightenment.

There are no absolute truths for New Agers because for them there is no distinction between good and evil. Truth and reality are what they determine them to be. They create their own reality by what they choose to believe is truth. Many New Agers believe in reincarnation. Some believe that, like the Pantheists, they will never die. Others believe that, like the Hindus, they will be absorbed into the universal cosmic consciousness when they finally die, while others believe that, like the Buddhist, they will cease to exist when they finally die. Both Hindus and Buddhists believe in reincarnation.

New Agers believe there is a New Age coming when there will be a oneness of world human consciousness. This will then lead to the establishment of a New World Order.

Summary

Pantheism, Gnosticism and the New Age movement reject the exclusive Christian belief in and requirement of redemption and salvation by means of God's grace through faith in Jesus. They rely on individual efforts to:

- Escape God's judgment by believing they will never die,

- Work out their respective means of being reunited with God or being absorbed into a universal cosmic consciousness when they die, or

- Cease to exist when they die.

Evil is present in the world and has and continues to cause untold individual and global human suffering. However, the presence of the Christian Church, sustained by the Holy Spirit, has been and continues to be a restraining presence in the world. Its presence prevents evil along with Satan from assuming absolute dominion over the world. Satan through secret societies, false religions, cults, the Illuminati, and Committee of 300 network continues to work to marginalize the influence of Christianity and neutralize the activities of the Christian Church in the lives of men and women and in local, regional and global affairs.

There will be a time, which is currently unknown, when global conditions will facilitate the establishment of a New World Order. The ten kingdom federation foretold by Daniel will be established when this occurs, and the tribulation will begin. The Christian Church along with all Christians both living and dead, who have lived throughout history, will be removed from the world at the rapture after the Antichrist commits the abomination of desolation in the temple in Jerusalem. The Antichrist through Satan will be given absolute dominion over the world after this occurs, and evil will prevail.

CHANGING THE PERCEPTION OF THE PEOPLE OF THE UNITED STATES AND THE U. S. GOVERNMENT

The capitalist economic and sociocultural structure of the United States and the constitutional republic form of the U. S. government are major obstacles to the Illuminati's and Committee of 300 network's efforts to establish a New World Order.

Dr. Henry Kissinger has stated,

> "A New World Order cannot happen without U. S. participation, as we are the single most significant component. Yes, there will be a New World Order, and it will force the United States to change its perceptions."

The Illuminati, Committee of 300 and the Tavistock networks have been engaged in activities designed to change the perceptions of the United States. These activities are at the heart of the spiritual (secular humanism/Christianity), social-political (progressivism/conservatism), and economic (socialism/capitalism) cultural conflicts discussed in Chapter 14. There are three cultural components (spiritual, social-political and economic) with two elements in each component. Therefore, there are six possible cultural group combinations, and it is reasonable to assume all six combinations exist within the population of the United States. Secular humanist/progressive/socialist groups are at the far left of these combination, and Christian/ conservative/capitalist groups are at the far right of this combination.

Organizations and institutes within the Tavistock network have developed and have used and are using generational behavioral programming directed at young children, youth and young adults who will become the future generations of the U. S. Their objective has been and is to manipulate the movement of individuals in all cultural group combinations to the far left combination. This is essential to changing the perception of the population of the United States, so it will accept the establishment of a future New World Order.

Three Pillars of the U. S. Sociocultural Structure

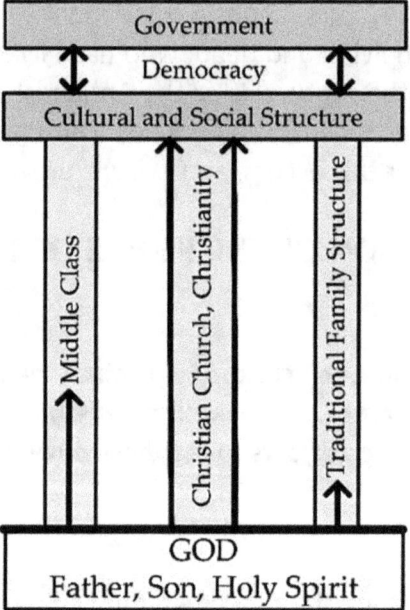

Figure 44

The United States is a nation that has been founded on and developed with a strong Christian heritage. God establishes through the Christian church the moral and ethical values that define the cultural and social structure of a nation when He is the underlying foundation of the nation (Figure 44). He defines and establishes the structure and character of the family, provides how a strong and stable middle class can develop, and provides for the establishment of a government that is responsive to and supported by the people.

The presence of the Christian church and Christianity, a strong and stable middle class, and the traditional family structure have been three pillars that have historically defined, supported and sustained the cultural and social structure of the United States. They also played a major role in defining, developing and maintaining the structure and character of the U. S. government. The result has been the establishment of a democratic constitutional republic form of government that is accountable and responsive to the people. These pillars must be neutralized or removed to change the perception of the people and government of the United States. Also, a means must be created within the U. S. government that, given the right conditions, can be used to change the character of the government. The neutralization of Christianity and the Christian church was discussed in the previous section. The disappearance of the middle class, the decline of the traditional family structure, and how the character of the U. S. government can be changed will be discussed in this section.

U. S. Capitalist Economic Structure and Disappearance of the Middle Class

The U. S. capitalist economic structure has been supported and sustained in part by the presence of a large, stable middle class. The middle class has been historically sustained by:

- A strong and healthy nationwide industrial and manufacturing base that has supported a large workforce and provided apprentice training for those just entering the workforce; and

- Income parody between lower, middle and upper income wage earners.

Figure 45

The industrial and manufacturing base of the United States has experienced a substantial loss of manufacturing jobs even though it is one of the strongest in the world. Figure 45 indicates the number of manufacturing jobs in the United States has declined from a peak of around 19.5 million in 1978 to around 12 million in 2014. Manufacturing employment, as a percentage of the total U. S. workforce, has declined from 28 percent in 1950 to 11 percent in 2010. The decrease in manufacturing employment has resulted from many labor-intensive manufacturing operations moving out of the United States and the automation of many manufacturing operations that remain in the United States. The significant loss of manufacturing jobs has resulted in a bifurcation of the U. S. workforce. At the bottom end are workers who for various reasons accept low-skill, low-paying employment with no or little chance for advancement. At the middle to top end are semi-skilled and skilled workers with educational and professional training who can secure well-paying employment with reasonable opportunities for advancement.

Figure 46 shows the annual income disparity that has developed and continues to increase between the bottom 90 percent income population (Group A) and the top 10 and 1 percent income populations (Groups B and C). Figure 47, which is an expanded representation of Figure 46 that shows the threshold curve for Group B, indicates the average annual income for individuals in Group A must increase by at least 400 percent to reach the threshold income level of Group B.

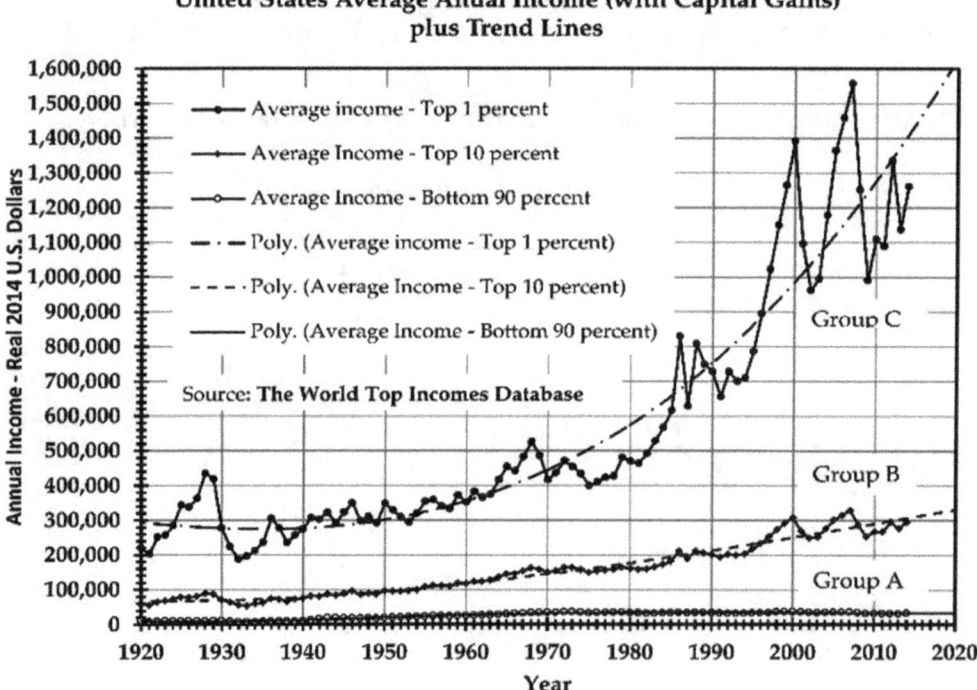

Figure 46

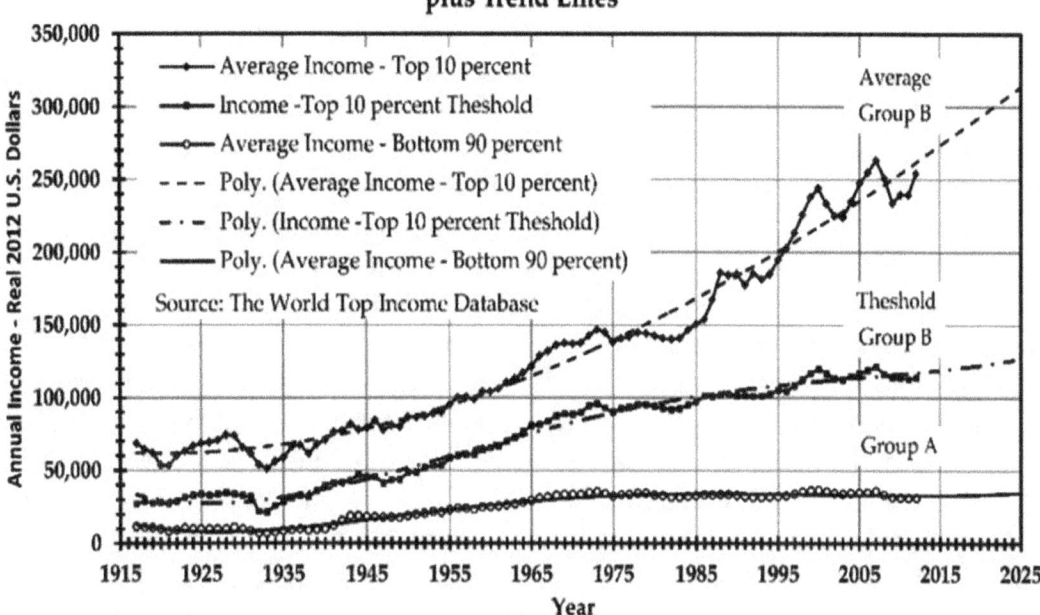

Figure 47

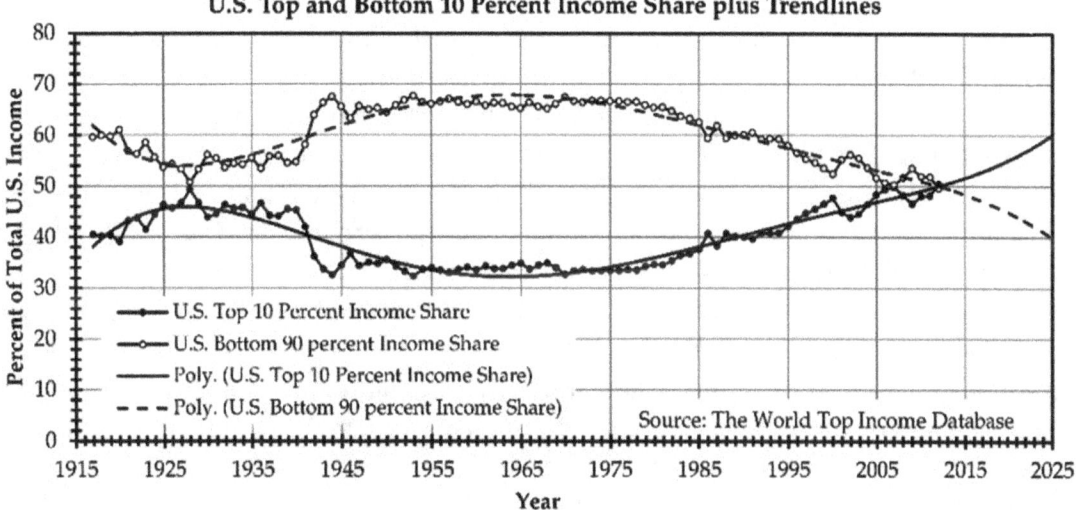

Figure 48

Figure 48 indicates a paradigm shift is occurring in the distribution of wealth in the United States. Group B accounted for around 33 percent of the total U. S. income from around 1950 to 1980, while Group A accounted for around 77 percent. The income distribution between Groups A and B will become equal at 50 percent around 2018. Group B will account for around 55 percent of the total U. S. income by 2025 if the trend lines reasonably forecast the future, while Group A will account for only 45 percent. This trend implies the eventual bifurcation of the U. S. population into two economic classes. Referring to Figures 45 and 46, there will be the wealthy and very wealthy (Groups B and C) and those who are financially struggling to survive (Group A). This will result in the possible disappearance of the middle class as it exists today.

The U. S. income distribution paradigm shift and possible disappearance of the middle class can have significant economic consequence. Many single parent households in Group A currently must receive government subsistence help to cover monthly expenses. Both spouses in two-parent households in Group A often must work to cover monthly expenses.

The number of single and two parent households in Group A who have insufficient incomes to cover their monthly expenses associated with housing, food, health care, and other basic needs will continue to increase if their average annual incomes do not significantly increase. This has resulted in the increase in homelessness in major urban areas that will eventually lead to social dislocation and unrest that will require government intervention. This intervention will eventually result in the establishment of government socialist policies that will lead to the redistribute of wealth between the wealthy and poor. This will be necessary to facilitate the establishment of a New World Order. Another consequence of the paradigm shift in U. S. income distribution will be the continued growth of debt in the United States. Individuals in Groups A, B and C must spend money for the purchase of expensive items, such as homes, automobiles, education, vacations, etc., to support continued economic growth. Those in Group C will have enough cash reserves to pay for many of these items. However, those in Groups A and B will have to borrow through bank loans to pay for these items, increasing their personal debt. Figure 37 indicates that, even though there was a slight dip in consumer debt after 2007, consumer debt has continued to increase. Consumer debt, along with corporate and U. S. Government debt are re-inflating the debt bubbles. These bubbles will burst at some time in the future, creating another economic collapse in the United States. The population segment that will be most severely impacted will be Group A. This will further increase their dependence on U. S. government support for their subsistence and survival.

Increased illegal immigration from Mexico and Central America is another factor that is and will continue to have a negatively impact on those in Group A. The large influx of illegal immigrants is placing a severe strain on private and government social service networks and public education. These immigrants are also competing for low-paying, low-skill jobs.

U. S. Sociocultural Structure and Decline of the Traditional Family Structure

The U. S. cultural and social structure has been supported and sustained by the predominant presence of the traditional family structure. This structure has historically consisted of a husband and wife, united together in marriage, who have joined together to conceive, give birth to, and raise their children. This structure is based on the biblical definition of marriage and thousands of years of Jewish and Christian history.

The traditional family structure provides a safe, stable and nurturing environment where:

- Children can grow in maturity to adults;
- Children can develop healthy self-esteem and learn how to persevere and effectively deal with life's successes, disappointments and challenges;
- Moral and ethical values associated with religion, honor, patriotism and sexual behavior can be instilled in children; and
- Boys and girls can learn through instruction and observation how to properly interact in a moral and healthy manner with members of the opposite sex and begin the process of learning and developing parenting skills they will need when they become parents.

Men and women emotionally, intellectually and physically respond differently to life experiences and challenges. Often it requires both male and female perspectives to effectively respond to them. It takes the presence of a father and mother for children to effectively learn and understand these differences as they grow into adults.

The perception and future course of a nation rest with the proper nurturing and education of its young children and youth. These functions are traditionally performed by the family, religious institutions and schools in the United States. Transforming the character and functions of these institutions will change the perception and future course of a nation.

The traditional family structure is in decline as it has historically existed in the United States. Statistics that document this decline include (source - Internet):

- 50 to 60 percent of heterosexual couples cohabitate before getting married with 67 percent of these marriages ending in divorce;
- The divorce rate increased from 28 percent in 1960 to 42 percent in 2012;
- The percent of births to unmarried women increased from 7.7 percent in 1965 to 40.7 percent in 2012, not including the number of pregnancies terminated by abortion;
- The percent of single parent households increased from 9 percent in 1960 to 26 percent in 2011; and
- The number of children who live in single parent households in 2012 was 24,75,0020.

Children who are born into and live in these home environments are denied the balanced male and female nurturing and learning environment provided by a father and mother in a traditional family structure.

Marriage has been redefined to include same sex marriage. The Supreme Court in a 2014 ruling (Obergefell vs Hodges) struck down all state laws and state constitutional amendments banning same sex marriage. States now allow homosexual couples to adopt children.

Religious institutions and Christian churches have become less effective in instilling God-based and Christian life principles and moral values in the lives of generations of youth and young adults. Similarly, the Supreme Court has removed nearly all vestiges of God and Christianity from public schools. Many public school districts are hostile toward the teaching of God-based and Christian life principles and moral values. Instead they offer instruction and teach courses related to alternate lifestyles, which include homosexual, transsexual and trans gender lifestyles, the requirement of tolerance regarding these lifestyles, sexual experimentation, and alternative family structures.

Generations of youth and young adults have succumbed to sociocultural behavioral modification programing in the absence of being exposed to a God-based and Christian value system and world view. This programming, which is hostile toward God and Christianity, in various forms has been incorporated into music, media and entertainment, public education, colleges and universities, and other related venues and activities. It often makes youth and young adults hostile toward God and Christians and encourages them to:

- Resist authority and avoid relationships that require accountability;
- Become sexually active and engaged in pornography;
- Accept abortion as a means of birth control;
- Become addicted to drugs and participate in drug related activities;
- Become involved in cults and occult activities; and
- Become intolerant of sociocultural and religious values and views they disagree with.

U. S. Political Structure and Continuation of Government of the U. S. Government

(Sources: "FEMA Executive Orders;" http://www.theforbiddenknowledge.com/hardtruth/fema_ executive_orders.htm)

Discussions in Chapters 14 and 15 indicate there are individuals within the U. S. government (congress, office of the president and federal agencies who support the United States' participation in efforts to establish a New World Order. These individuals normally identify with secular humanist, progressives, socialists and closely allied groups. They want to transform:

- The U. S. Government from a constitutional republic of the people, by the people and for the people to one that believes it knows what is best for and wants to control the people; and

- The United States from a nation that believes in and is a nation under God to a nation that denies the existence of and turns away from God.

This has created tension with those individuals in the U. S. government who normally identify with the far right (Christian/conservative/capitalist) and with groups closely allied with this group. The far-left cultural group normally identifies with the democratic party, while the far right cultural group normally identifies with the republican party. The cultural, social and political agendas of these two groups are irreconcilable. This has significantly impeded the abilities of democrats and republicans in state legislatures and the U. S. congress to compromise and reach agreement on issues of local and national importance. This has sometimes been true relative to disagreements between the executive and congressional branches of the U. S. government. Is it possible that individuals within the Illuminati, committee of 300 and Tavistock networks have gained influence over and control of the extreme elements of the far left and far right cultural groups and are creating and manipulating the tension that exists between them?

Presidents have in the past have used and currently use their authority to issue Executive Orders (EO) to reorganize and create agencies within the executive branch of the U. S. government that have been authorized by enabling legislation enacted by the congressional branch of the U. S. government. An area of importance associated with presidential executive orders has been and is the requirement for the branches of the U. S. government to effectively continue to function in the aftermath of a major global or national event or series of events that would have a devastating impact on the United States. To address this requirement, presidents have issued Executive Orders that would have or will allow the U. S. government to:

- Take over all modes of transportation and control of highways and seaports (EO 10990);

- Seize and control the communication media (EO 10995);

- Take over all electrical power, gas, petroleum, fuels and minerals (EO 10997);

- Seize all means of transportation, including personal cars, trucks and vehicles of any kind and total control over all highways, seaports, and waterways (EO 10998);

- Take over all food resources and farms (EO 10999);

- Mobilize civilians into work brigades under government supervision (EO 11000);

- Take over all health, education and welfare functions (EO 11001);

- Designate the Postmaster General to operate a national registration of all persons (EO 11002);

- Take over all airports and aircraft, including commercial aircraft (EO 11003);

- Allows the Housing and Finance Authority to relocate communities, build new housing with public funds, designate areas to be abandoned, and establish new locations for populations (EO 11004);

- Take over railroads, inland waterways and public storage facilities (EO 11005);

- Assigns emergency preparedness function to federal departments and agencies, consolidating 21 operative Executive Orders issued over a fifteen-year period (EO 11049);

- Gives the Office of Emergency Planning authorization to put all Executive Orders into effect in times of increased international tensions and economic or financial crisis (EO 11051);

- Grants authority to the Department of Justice to enforce the plans set out in Executive Orders, to institute industrial support, to establish judicial and legislative liaison, to control all aliens, to operate penal and correctional institutions, and to advise and assist the President (11310); and

- Allows the Federal Emergency Preparedness Agency to develop plans to establish control over the mechanisms of production and distribution, of energy sources, wages, salaries, credit and the flow of money in U. S. financial institutions in any undefined national emergency. It also provides that when a state of emergency is declared by the President, Congress cannot review the action for six months (EO 11921).

Many of these Executive Orders were written to address specific events that are long past. Some have been rewritten and incorporated into more recent comprehensive Executive Orders. Others may have been withdrawn or still may be active.

President Carter with the issuance of Executive Order 12148 created the Federal Emergency Management Agency (FEMA). All the activities associated with the Federal Emergency Preparedness Agency, along with many previous Executive Orders, were rolled into FEMA. The authority of FEMA was further consolidated and enhanced by the inclusion of actions authorized by the following legislative acts:

- **Act of August 29, 1916:** The act authorizes the Secretary of the Army, in time of war, to take possession of any transportation system for transporting troops, material, or any other purpose related to the emergency;

- **National Security Act of 1947:** The act permits the strategic relocation of industries, services, government, and other essential economic activities and allows the related rationing of manpower, resources, and production facilities;

- **Defense Production Act of 1950:** The act gives the President sweeping powers over all aspects of the economy; and

- **International Emergency Economic Powers Act of 1977:** The act allows the President to seize the property of foreign countries and nationals.

The primary function of FEMA was to assure the survivability and continuation of the U.S. government in the event of a nuclear attack during the Cold War. FEMA was also tasked with coordinating the U. S. government's response to domestic disasters, such as earthquakes, floods and hurricanes. However, most of its annual budgets and assets have been directed to functions associated with the continuation of government.

FEMA's primary function continued to be the assurance of the continuation of the U. S. government after the end of the Cold War. However, in addition to responding to a possible nuclear attack against the United States, this function has been expanded to respond to:

- Acts of international and national terrorism against the United States;

- Major global and national economic and financial crises, pandemics, widespread demonstrations and related social unrest, and crippling mega disasters; and

- Any other major global or national event or series of events that, in the judgment of the president, pose a serious threat to the United States and the continuation of the U. S. government.

Presidential Executive Order 12656 and the Patriot Act of 2001 were designed to increase the effectiveness of the U. S. government in addressing threats to the United States by global and national terrorism. The Executive Order established the National Security Council (NSC) as the principal body to address issues related to emergency government powers and authorizes the U. S. government to increase domestic intelligence and surveillance of U. S. citizens. In the case of a declared national emergency by the president, it also authorizes the restriction of freedom of movement within the United States, the isolation of large groups of U. S. citizens, and the National Guard to be federalized and used to seal all U. S. borders and take control of U. S. air space and all ports of entry.

The Patriot Act was enacted to respond to the terrorist attack against the United States on September 11, 2001. With respect to individuals and groups suspected of engaging in terrorist activities against the United States, the act suspends their Constitutional and Bill of Rights safeguards against unlawful search and seizure, electronic and other forms of surveillance, and arrest. The act authorized increased electronic and other forms of surveillance without appropriate court approval of individuals and groups suspected of terrorist activities against the United States. The U. S. government has the technology to monitor all phone, email and texting communications and all financial, banking, monetary and credit card transactions, using the capabilities of the National Security Agency (NSA) and other federal agencies. The U. S. government can monitor and track the movement and travel of people, using satellite surveillance, RIFD chips and GPS tracking.

Using the authority granted by relevant Presidential Executives Orders declaring a national or global emergency, with the stroke of the president's pen the U. S. government can assume control over:

- All movement within the United States and where people can live;
- All modes of public and private transportation;
- Financial, banking and monetary activities and salaries and wages;
- Commodity and food production, water availability and their distribution;
- Manufacturing and distribution of manufactured goods;
- Energy production and distribution (includes electricity, oil and gasoline);
- News, media and entertainment outlets;
- Medical and health services; and
- All Educational activities.

The above actions of the executive branch of the U.S. government have been authorized by presidential executive orders. These executive orders have been issued in accordance with enabling legislation enacted by the congressional branch of the U. S. government. They cannot be implemented in an unlawful manner that circumvents the U. S. Constitution and Bill of Rights. However, the public protection afforded by the U. S. Constitution and Bill of Rights can cease to exist in the aftermath of a major global or national event or series of events where branches of the U. S. government are rendered incapable of or unwilling to perform their constitutional functions.

Summary

This and the previous section address religious, economic, cultural and societal changes occurring in the United States that, given the development of the right set of global or national conditions, can result in a change in the perception of people in the United States and lead them to accept the establishment of a New World Order. The U. S. government could circumvent the U. S. Constitution and Bill of Rights and assist in the establishment of this New World Order, given the development of the right set of conditions.

Two questions should be asked at this point. Are the changes that have been discussed and continue to occur the result of the normal evolution in the development and growth of a global culture and society, or are they being programed and conditions being manipulated to facilitate their occurrence? There are no clear and provable answers to these questions.

Illuminists use terrorism and other related tactics to create circumstances and events that cause prolong regional and global unrest and fear, and they use the Hegel dialectric triad to create regional and global crises to accomplish what would otherwise be unachievable objectives. It is worthwhile to restate David Rockefeller's statement in which he said, "We are on the verge of a global transformation. All we need is the right major crisis and the nations will accept a New World Order."

UNITED NATIONS AGENDA 21

(Source: United Nations Sustainable Development - Agenda 21; United Nations Conference on Environment & Development; Rio de Janeiro, Brazil; June 3 - 14, 1992)

Agenda 21 is a little publicized United Nations program that was adopted by more than 178 governments, including the United States, at the United Nations Conference on Environment and Development held in Rio de Janeiro, Brazil, June 3 - 14, 1992. It is presented as a comprehensive plan of action to be globally, nationally and locally undertaken in all areas where humans impact the environment by relevant organizations of the United Nations, national governments, regional and local governments, and major non-government groups. This program appears to be a plan that, under the umbrella of environmentally sustainable land development and use, establishes a strategy to control global population demographics. This can then be used to control consumption of agricultural and non-agricultural global and regional resources. Agenda 21 also appears to be a response to information developed by the Club of Rome and published in the book titled, *Beyond the Limits, Confronting Global Collapse Envisioning a Sustainable Future*, which was published in 1992.

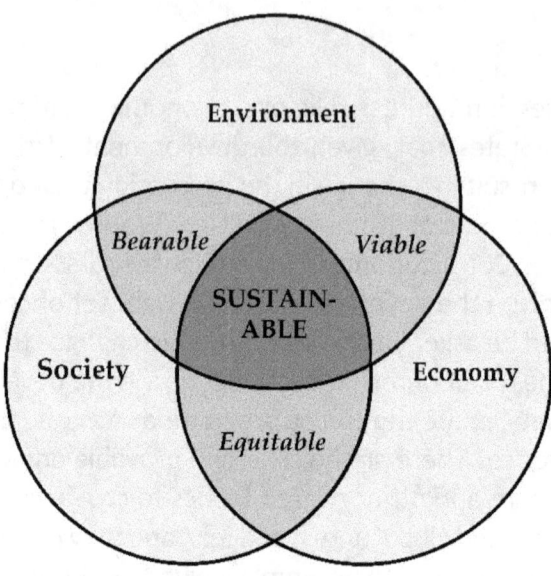

Figure 49

Agenda 21 presents a complex decision, management and financial matrix relative to environmentally sustainable land development and use that considers environmental, economic and societal factors, as shown in Figure 49. These address human impacts on air, water and land environments. Agenda 21 focuses on developing counties. However, it also applies to developed countries. Agenda 21 will result in a major socialistic redistribution of global wealth from developed to developing countries when and if fully implemented. Existing and proposed land development and use will be examined and evaluated based on the possible existence of toxic wastes and their anticipated effects on human health, species and area biodiversity. Agenda 21provides for major national and regional relocations of large population groups when determined necessary. Agenda 21 is not a proposed treaty. Therefore, it did not require congressional approval for the United States to sign on to it. Agenda 21 can bypass the approval process of national governments and be implemented on regional and local levels. As a result, conspiracy theorist believe Agenda 21 can be implemented in ways that circumvent the national sovereignties of those countries that have signed on to it. They also believe the adoption of Agenda 21 is another step toward the eventual formation of a New World Order. The facts that desired outcomes of Agenda 21 are compatible with information developed and published by the Club of Rome and agenda items of the Illuminati and Committee of 300 tend to support these beliefs.

CHAPTER 19
TEN KINGDOM FEDERATION, ANTICHRIST GLOBAL DICTATORSHIP, AND A SUMMARY

SCENARIOS FOR A TEN KINGDOM FEDERATION

John indicates in Revelation 13:5 the Antichrist will be given authority to rule the people and nations of earth for forty-two months (1,260 days) during the great tribulation (Figure 9). Daniel 7:7-8 and other related Bible verses indicate ten kings will assist the Antichrist in his rule of earth. They will accomplish this through a ten kingdom federation. Chapter 7 indicates these kings will come from a revived Roman Empire that may come from or be the European Union. How the ten kingdoms of these kings and their ten kingdom federation will be formed are unknown.

Two plausible scenarios are presented that describe how a ten kingdom federation may be formed. The ten kings in this federation in both scenarios are presumed to come from the European Union.

Scenario 1: The ten kingdoms that form the ten kingdom federation will be ruled by kings who come from their kingdoms. These kingdoms may be countries that are members of the European Union. A ten kingdom federation is established from these kingdoms when their kings pledge their support and allegiance to the Antichrist. Their federation will then become the Antichrist's global dictatorship.

Scenario 2: Nations on earth will be separated into ten regional territories. The nations in each regional territory may have similar cultural identities and economic interests. The Antichrist with the assistance of the ten kings who will rule a kingdom in the ten kingdom federation will facilitate this separation. A ten kingdom federation is established from these kingdoms when their kings pledge their support and allegiance to the Antichrist. The federation then becomes the Antichrist's global dictatorship.

The emergence of a New World Order will precede the establishment of the ten kingdom federation formed by one of the above scenarios. A global environment that may facilitate these scenarios is presented in the following sections of this chapter.

ALBERT PIKE AND THREE WORLD WARS

Albert Pike was a 33rd degree Freemason of the Scottish Rite. He was Sovereign Grand Commander of the Supreme Council of the 33rd degree and Supreme Pontiff of Universal Freemasonry. He remains a significant figure in Freemasonry.

Albert Pike is alleged to have written a letter, dated August 15, 1871, to Giuseppe Mazzini, who was an Italian revolutionary. Pike described in this letter three world wars that would bring about a one-world global government. Some state there is no evidence this letter was written. It is presented because it provides a framework in which a New World Order can come into existence before the start of the tribulation.

The first two world wars, as described by Pike, have occurred. A Third World War has yet to occur. However, conditions that could provoke a Third World War currently exist and continue to evolve in the Middle East.

Pike stated in his letter:

"The First World War must be brought about in order to permit the Illuminati to overthrow the power of the Czars in Russia and of making that country a fortress of atheistic Communism. The divergences caused by the 'agentur' (agents) of the Illuminati between the British and Germanic Empires will be used to foment this war. At the end of the war, Communism will be built and used in order to destroy the other governments and in order to weaken the religions. The Second World War must be fomented by taking advantage of the differences between the Fascists and the political Zionists. This war must be brought about so that Nazism is destroyed and that the political Zionism be strong enough to institute a sovereign state of Israel in Palestine. During the Second World War, International Communism must become strong enough in order to balance Christendom, which would be then restrained and held in check until the time when we would need it for the final social cataclysm. The Third World War must be fomented by taking advantage of the differences caused by the 'agentur' of the Illuminati between the political Zionists and the leaders of the Islamic World. The war must be conducted in such a way that Islam (the Muslim Arabic World) and political Zionism (the State of Israel) mutually destroy each other. Meanwhile the other nations, once more divided on this issue will be constrained to fight to the point of complete physical, moral, spiritual and economical exhaustion."

"We shall unleash the Nihilists and the atheists, and we shall provoke a formidable social cataclysm which in all its horror will show clearly to the nations the effect of absolute atheism, origin of savagery and of the most bloody turmoil. Then everywhere, the citizens, obliged to defend themselves against the world minority of revolutionaries, will exterminate those destroyers of civilization, and the multitude, disillusioned with Christianity, whose deistic spirits will from that moment be without compass or direction, anxious for an ideal, but without knowing where to render its adoration, will receive the true light through the universal manifestation of the pure doctrine of Lucifer, brought finally out in the public view."

"This manifestation will result from the general reactionary movement which will follow the destruction of Christianity and atheism, both conquered and exterminated at the same time." (Source: Albert Pike in a letter to Giuseppe Mazzini, excerpt from *Pawns in The Game* by William Carr 1978).

Svali, regarding a Third World War predicted by Albert Pike, in her interview with HJ Springer stated:

"The [current] conflict in the Middle East is only to the advantage of the Illuminists. They hate Israel, and hope one day to see it destroyed, and are biding their time. One of the olive branches offered by the UN when it takes over is that they will prevent war in the middle east, and this will be greeted with joy by many. At the same time, the Illuminati covertly supply guns and funds to both sides to keep the conflict fueled. They are very duplicitous people. They used to funnel guns through the USSR to Palestine, for example, in the name of promoting *friendliness* between the USSR and this state and other Arab nations. Then, the US Illuminists would help funnel guns to Israel, for the same reason."

She then stated the following, regarding how the Illuminati believes a New World Order may be ushered in:

- "There will be continued conflict in the Middle East, with a severe threat of nuclear war being the culmination of these hostilities."
- "An economic collapse [will occur] that will devastate the economies of the U. S. and Europe, much like the great depression."
- "One reason that our economy continues limping along is the artificial supports that the Federal Reserve had given it, manipulating interest rates, etc."
- "But one day, this won't work (or this leverage will be withdrawn on purpose), and the next great depression will hit."

- "The government will call in its bonds and loans, and credit card debts will be called in."

- "There will be massive bankruptcies nationwide."

- "Europe will stabilize first, and Germany, France and England (surprise) will have the strongest economies and will institute through the UN an international currency."

- "Japan will also pull out, although their economy will be weakened."

- "Peacekeeping forces will be sent out by the UN and local bases [will be established] to prevent riots."

- "The leaders will reveal themselves, and people will be asked to make a pledge of loyalty during a time of chaos and financial devastation."

- "The Antichrist will require the inhabitants of the earth to receive his mark during the great tribulation in order to carry out acts of commerce."

Daniel stated at the end of Daniel 9:27, regarding events that may precede the start of the tribulation, "Even to the end there will be war, desolations are determined." How a future Third World War may be provoked and how its outcomes may facilitate the Antichrist's rise to power are unknown. The following discussion presents a plausible sequence of events that may lead to the Antichrist and a ten kingdom federation gaining control of earth after a future Third World War.

A Third World War before the start of the tribulation may result from:

- God will draw Russia and its allies to invade Israel as described in Ezekiel 38 and 39 and presented at the end of Chapter 7.

- The invasion of Israel may result in an immediate response by the United States to support and defend Israel. This response will result in a clash between United States and Russian military forces that may initiate a nuclear exchange between the two countries. This may result in a nuclear exchange between the United States and China if Russia and China are allies with a mutual defense agreement.

Ezekiel indicated God will defend Israel in this invasion by Russia and its allies, and He will destroy their invading armies. However, the United States government and military may not know this, resulting in their immediate response to Russia's invasion of Israel.

Results of Russia's and its ally's invasion of Israel, the United States' response to this invasion, and God's destruction of the invading military forces of Russia and its allies may be:

- The armies of the Muslim allies of Russia will be destroyed by God. This will destroy their abilities to have any future influence on global events.

- The infrastructures of the United States, Russia and China will be severely damaged by their nuclear exchanges, and their military capabilities will be significantly diminished. This will significantly limit their abilities to respond to future global events.

- The global fallout from the nuclear exchanges between the United States, Russia and China may have devastating effects on Third World countries that do not have infrastructures capable to address the fallout.

- Countries in the Europe Union, because they may not have engaged in the nuclear exchanges, may experience minimal destruction to their infrastructures, and they may be able to address the effects of the global nuclear fallout in their countries. Therefore, their infrastructures and military capabilities may remain intact.

These global conditions may reduce the effort required by the Antichrist and the ten kings who support him to form their ten kingdom federation necessary for the Antichrist to establish his global dictatorship.

The military capabilities of the Muslim countries who invade Israel will be destroyed by God. The military capacities of the United States, Russia and China may be significantly diminished by the nuclear exchange associated with the start of a world war. However, the military capabilities of countries in the European Union that may be part of a future revived Roman Empire referred to in Daniel 7 and discussed in Chapter 7 may remain intact. Therefore, the Antichrist, ten kings, and their federation may be able to engage in the Antichrist's military conquest to establish his global dictatorship with reduced resistance. This conquest and its consequences are addressed in the first four seal judgements in Revelation 6:1-8 and discussed in Chapter 8.

The catastrophic reduction in the population of earth may also reduce the effort required by the Antichrist, ten kings and their federation to gain control of earth and establish the Antichrist's global dictatorship before the start of the great tribulation. One-fourth of earth's population will die because of the military conquest of the Antichrist and ten kings (Revelation 6:7-8). One-third of the remaining population on earth will die because of the sixth trumpet judgement (Revelation 9:13-19).

Over one half of earth's population will be dead by the start of the great tribulation because of:

- A Third World War before the start of the tribulation;

- The military conquest of the Antichrist and ten kings to gain control of earth to establish the Antichrist's global dictatorship (Revelation 6:8); and

- The results of the sixth trumpet judgements (Revelation 9:17-19.

Global population from 2065 to 2100 is projected to peak at 9 to 10 billion people (Figure 19). One-half of this population will range from 4.5 to 5 billion people. This reduction in earth's population will have catastrophic local, regional and global effects. Government and public and social services that enable governments to function will be catastrophically reduced. This may also result in a global economic and societal collapse. The unimaginable desolation, devastation and destruction responsible for this population loss will also contribute to the ability of the Antichrist and ten kings to gain control of earth before the start of the great tribulation. God will then allow them to maintain this control during the forty-two months (1,260 days) of the great tribulation.

Pike may have been correct in his statement that the one-world government, New World Order he envisioned "will receive the true light through the universal manifestation of the pure doctrine of Lucifer." The Antichrist's terrifying global dictatorship that will rule earth during the great tribulation will occur with the assistance of Satan. His government will not be like the government depicted in Figure 44. That government is one that is undergirded by God, who defines the cultural and social structure of the people. The cultural and social structure of the people then defines the nature and character of the government. The nature and character of the Antichrist's terrifying global dictatorship will be defined by Satan, the Antichrist and the false prophet (Figure 50). The Antichrist's global dictatorship will then define the cultural and social structure of the people of earth.

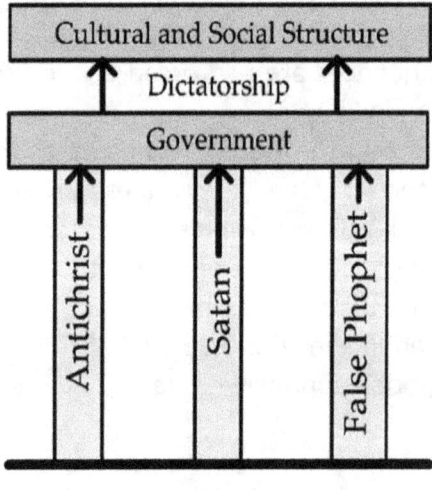

Figure 50

SUMMERY OF EVENTS LEADING TO GOD'S JUDGEMENT OF PEOPLE ON EARTH AND OUR REDEMPTION THROUGH JESUS

Events are summarized below that will lead to:

- The establishment of a New World Order;
- The formation of a ten kingdom federation and the Antichrist's global dictatorship;
- God's resulting judgement of the unrighteous on earth;
- Our redemption through and resurrection by Jesus; and
- Our living on a new earth with God, Jesus and the Holy Spirit.

The sequence of these events may differ from what is listed. They include:

- God will redeem and receive into His presence people on earth who have faith in, trust and are obedience to Jesus' words in the Gospels. He accomplishes this through the blood Jesus shed on a cross. (Chapter 4)
- God will support and nurture people on earth who have received Jesus as their Savior and Lord of their lives through the presence of the Holy Spirit in their lives. (Chapter 5)
- Profusions will continue to facilitate the growth of good and evil on earth. The conflicts between secular humanism and Christianity, progressivism and conservatism, and socialism and capitalism will continue. The growth in evil will reach the point when it will dominate. Secular humanism, progressivism and socialism will become dominant cultural forces on earth. (Chapter 14)
- The global influence of Christianity will continue to decline even though the gospel of Jesus is being proclaimed throughout the earth. (Chapter 18)
- The family formed by a covenant of marriage ordained by God between a husband (male) and wife (female) who come together to conceive, give birth to, and raise children will continue to decline in the United States and other western countries. (Chapter 18)
- The global economic and military influence of the United State will continue to decline. (Chapters 14 and 18)
- The decline in the global influence of Christianity, in the family as a covenant relationship between a man and woman as husband and wife, and in the global economic and military influence of the United States will facilitate the formation of a New World Order. (Chapters 14 – 18)

- The New World Order will facilitate the emergence of a revived Roman Empire that may be or come from the European Union. The ten kings and the Antichrist will come from this empire. (Chapters 7 and 19)

- The Antichrist and ten kings will establish a ten kingdom federation that will become the Antichrist's terrifying global dictatorship. (Chapters 7 and 19)

- Israel will be invaded by Russia and its allies before the start of the tribulation. This invasion may provoke World War Three. Albert Pike indicated this war will cause the nations of earth "to fight to the point of complete physical, moral, spiritual and economic exhaustion." (Chapters 7 and 19)

- The Antichrist will enter a covenant with Israel that will guarantee its existence for seven years at the conclusion of this war and after the formation of the ten kingdom federation and his dictatorship. The tribulation and great tribulation will follow the approval of this covenant. The Antichrist will terminate this covenant during the middle of the tribulation. (Chapters 7 and 10)

- Earth will experience a time of great distress, desolation and destruction during the end time that is prophesied by the angel Gabriel in Daniel, Jesus in the Gospels, and John in Revelation. This will be the time of the tribulation, great tribulation, and return of Jesus. (Chapters 7 – 10)

- It will take the Antichrist 1,297 days (around three and one-half years) after the start of the tribulation to consolidate his control of and be given authority by God to rule the people and nations of earth. The saints will then be given into his hands at the start of the great tribulation, and he will enter a war with and overcome them during the great tribulation. One-half or more of the population of earth will be dead before the start of the great tribulation. (Chapters 7 and 10).

- Saints who have died before the start of the middle of the tribulation and who will be alive during the middle of the tribulation will be raptured from the earth during the middle of the tribulation. (Chapters 5 and 9)

- All restraints on the Antichrist will be removed by God at the start of the great tribulation. He will be given authority to rule over the people and nations of earth during the great tribulation. Gentiles will invade Israel and occupy Jerusalem for forty-two months (1,260 days) during the great tribulation. (Chapter 7 - 10)

- The marriage of Jesus (the Lamb) and His bride (the Church) will occur in heaven at the end of the great tribulation. Jesus will return to earth with the hosts of heaven and defeat the armies of the Antichrist and kings of earth at the battle of Armageddon. Satan, the Antichrist and the false prophet will be placed alive in the lake of fire after this battle. (Chapter 10)

- Jesus will establish His 1,000-year kingdom after the battle of Armageddon. The existing heaven and earth will pass away at the end of His kingdom. God through Jesus will execute the great white throne judgement. Saints whose names are written in the Lamb's book of life will be received into the presence of God, Jesus and the Holy Spirit. Those whose names are not written in the Lamb's book of life will be placed in the lake of fire. (Chapters 11 and 12)

- God will create a new heaven, earth and Jerusalem where there will be no sin, death, pain, suffering and tears after the great whit throne judgement. The new heaven will be located on the new earth because God will be present there with Jesus and the Holy Spirit. Saints who were resurrected at the rapture during the middle of the tribulation, at the first resurrection at the end of the great tribulation, and at the resurrection before the great white throne judgement will have immortal physical bodies without sin. They will live forever on the new earth with God, Jesus and the Holy Spirit. (Chapter 13).

THE SPEAR OF DESTINY AND THE ANTICHRIST

Brad Meltzer in one of his Decoded series episodes on the History channel hosted a program on the Spear of Destiny. The Spear of Destiny is reported to be the spear that was thrust into Jesus' side at His crucifixion. Mythology claims the person who possesses this spear will be able to control the destiny of the world. Both the Vatican and a museum in Vienna, Austria, claim to have possession of the Spear of Destiny. However, some experts believe neither spear is the actual spear that was thrust into Jesus' side. Some also speculate the Spear of Destiny may be in a sunken German U-boat off the east coast of the United States.

Meltzer interviewed Chris Blake, a retired bodyguard, at the end of this episode of Decoded. Blake indicated one of his former clients claimed to have stolen the Spear of Destiny from Adolf Hitler near the end of World War Two. His client then stated he belonged to a group known as Sons of the Fallen who are disciples of Lucifer. He indicated this group is working to facilitate the rebuilding of the Temple in Jerusalem.

One who has been selected from within their group will take the spear they claim to be the Spear of Destiny into the Holy of Holies in the rebuilt Temple and use it to shed his own blood in the temple after it has been rebuilt. He will then claim he is the messiah. Will this be the abomination of desolation committed by the Antichrist foretold by the angel Gabriel in Daniel and by Jesus? The Sons of the Fallen believe they will then rule over the earth. Will they, who may be led by the Antichrist, be the ones into whose hands control of earth will be given at the start of the great tribulation, as foretold in Revelation?

CHAPTER 20
JESUS - OUR HOPE FOR THE FUTURE

SOME CLOSING THOUGHTS

Past efforts to establish and maintain regional and global empires have failed. These empires collapsed even though they were successfully established and initially thrived. Therefore, the establishment of a future New World Order and global dictatorial government by the Antichrist can be perceived as being impossible. Past failed efforts to establish regional and global empires focused on the use of military force to establish and maintain them. Current efforts to establish a New World Order focus on indoctrination, deception, manipulation and creation of major regional, national and global crises. These crises are designed to create dependency on government(s) for resolution and thereby neutralize resistance to the formation of a dictatorial, one-world government. The formation of this government will be perceived as being essential for survival and can be viewed as fulfilling Bible prophesy related to the seven-year tribulation. This will facilitate the formation of the Antichrist's future global dictatorship.

Evil and the persecution and murdering of Christians will continue to increase up to the beginning of and into the seven-year tribulation. These will continue to increase until Christians are removed from the earth at the rapture during the middle of the tribulation. Evil will prevail throughout the earth after the rapture and into the great tribulation. Those who will accept Jesus as their Savior and Lord after the rapture during the great tribulation will be martyred in unimaginable numbers.

THE SECURITY OF GOD AND SUPREMACY OF JESUS

We are secure in our relationship with God through our faith and trust in and obedience to Jesus. Nothing can separate us from God and Jesus in this relationship. Jesus stated in John 10:27-30:

> "My sheep hear My voice, and I know them, and they follow Me; and I give eternal life to them, and they will never perish; and no one will snatch them out of My hand. My Father, who has given them to Me, is greater than all; and no one is able to snatch them out of the Father's hand. I and the Father are one."

Paul described the relationship we have with God through Jesus in Romans 8:15-17:

> "For you have not received a spirit of slavery leading to fear again, but you have received a spirit of adoption as sons by which we cry out, 'Abba! Father!' The Spirit Himself testifies with our spirit that we are children of God, and if children, heirs also, heirs of God and fellow heirs with Christ, if indeed we suffer with Him so we may also be glorified with Him."

We become adopted children of God through our relationship with Jesus and joint heirs with Jesus of God with all the privileges of being an heir of God.

Paul implied our relationship with Jesus will result in difficult life challenges and suffering. Jesus affirmed in Matthew 28:19, "All authority has been given to Me in heaven and on earth." He has authority in our relationship with Him to equip us through the presence of the Holy Spirit in our life with the means to preserve through and triumph over difficult life challenges and suffering in our life.

THE PROMISES OF JESUS IN REVELATION 2 AND 3

God's righteousness and justice will ultimately prevail in the conflict between good and evil. He instructed us to have faith and trust Him in difficult and troubled times. David stated in Psalm 37:38-40:

> "But transgressors will be altogether destroyed; the posterity of the wicked will be cut off. But the salvation of the righteous is from the LORD; He is their strength in time of trouble. And the LORD helps them and delivers them; He delivers them from the wicked, and saves them, because they take refuge in Him."

Jesus delivered messages to seven churches in Asia in Chapters 2 and 3 of Revelation. These were actual churches during John's day. Some Bible scholars today indicate these churches represented churches with different cultural, sociological and theological characteristics that have existed down through the ages and that exist today. Others indicate they represented different church ages from the days of the apostles to the present day.

Jesus' promises at the end of each message can be interpreted to be specific to the people of each church or church age. He prefaced each promise with the statement, "He who has an ear, let him hear what the Spirit says to the churches." The promises were made to those who would remain faithful and obedient to Him in each church or church age. We can argue that all seven promises apply equally to all who have been and will remain faithful and obedient to Jesus throughout the ages.

Jesus prefaced each promise with the phrase, "to him who overcomes." He will grant what He has promised to those who persevere through difficult times, hardships and trials that result from their faith and trust in and obedience to Him. Jesus promised those who overcomes:

Promise 1:

"To him who overcomes, I will grant to eat of the tree of life, which is in the paradise of God." (Revelation 2:7)

Adam and Eve were driven from the garden of Eden when they disobeyed God and sinned, so they would not be able to eat the fruit of the tree of life and be eternally separated from God (Genesis 3:22-24). The tree of life then disappeared from the earth. The tree of life will be present in the new Jerusalem, and all whose names are written in the book of life will be allowed to eat its fruit. Access to the tree of life was the first thing that was denied Adam and Eve after they had sinned; it is the first thing Jesus promised to return to the righteous in his eternal kingdom.

Promise 2:

"He who overcomes will not be hurt by the second death." (Revelation 2:11)

All whose names are written in the book of life will not experience the second death that is eternal separation from God.

Promise 3:

"To him who overcomes, and to him I will give some of the hidden manna, and I will give him a white stone, and a new name written on the stone which no one knows but he who receives it." (Revelation 2:17)

The manna that was given to the Israelites during their forty-year journey in the wilderness was enough to satisfy the needs of their physical hunger (Exodus 16:3-18). The hidden manna can refer to the sufficiency of God's grace that is extended to the righteous through Jesus to satisfy their spiritual hunger (John 6:47-51). A white stone during John's day was used to vote for the acquittal of an accused person. This statement indicates the righteous will be acquitted before God and given new names in His eternal kingdom.

Promise 4:

> "And he who overcomes, and he who keeps My deeds until the end, to him I will give authority over the nations; and he shall rule them with a rod of iron, as the vessels of the potter are broken to pieces, as I also have received authority from my Father; and I will give him the morning star." (Revelation 2:26-28)

This is the only one of Jesus' seven promises with a condition in addition to remaining faithful and obedient to Him. This condition is a possible reference to Jesus' statement in His parable of the talents (Matthew 25:14- 30). He indicated those who are faithful to perform the good works God prepares for them during their lives will be given the authority to exercise leadership in His eternal kingdom. Lucifer was called the star of the morning in Isaiah 14:12 before he sinned and rebelled against God. This was a reference to the special position he had in God's kingdom before he was cast out of heaven. To be given the morning star can imply those who meet the special condition of this promise will be given special positions in God's eternal kingdom.

Promise 5:

> "He who overcomes will be thus clothed in white garments; and I will not erase his name from the book of life, and I will confess his name before My Father and before His angels." (Revelation 3:5)

The righteous will be given bodies without sin and that will not be corrupted by sin. Their names will never be removed once they have been written in the book of life.

Promise 6:

> "He who overcomes, I will make him a pillar in the temple of My God, and he will not go out from it anymore; and I will write upon him the name of My God, and the name of the city of My God, the new Jerusalem, which comes down out of heaven from My God, and My new name." (Revelation 3:12)

Jesus promised in John 14:2-3 He was going to prepare a place for us. This place is in the kingdom of heaven, and more specifically, in the city of God, the new Jerusalem. The righteous will be allowed to enter the temple of God and His very presence. The names of God, the new Jerusalem, and the new name of Jesus will be written on the righteous.

Promise 7:

> "Behold, I stand at the door and knock; if anyone hears My voice and opens the door, I will come in to him, and will dine with him, and he with Me." (Revelation 3:20)

Jesus has extended this promise to everyone down through the ages. It is an invitation that requires a response. We must open the door of our heart and invite Him into our life. We can keep the door shut, or we can open it and invite Jesus in. The choice is ours, and He will honor the choice we make. Jesus promised to enter, commune and fellowship with us when we open the door to our heart and invite Him in. He will allow those who open the doors of their hearts to Him to sit with Him on His throne throughout eternity.

JESUS IS OUR HOPE FOR THE FUTURE

God will at a time of His choosing direct His judgments against men and women and the earth, and He will bring this present age to an end. He will destroy the existing heaven and earth and create a new heaven and earth where there will be. We must acknowledge the reality this can occur at any time in the future. Therefore, we must be prepared by accepting the redemption and reconciliation God extends to us by means of His grace through our faith in and obedience Jesus

Proverbs and Ecclesiastes in the Old Testament give us answers to these questions. Solomon and other writers present sound and practical wisdom in Proverbs regarding life's challenges. Solomon stated in Proverbs 3:1-12:

> "My son do not forget my teaching,
> But let your heart keep my commandments;
> For length of days and years of life,
> And peace they will add to you.
> Do not let kindness and truth leave you;
> Bind them around your neck,
> Write them on the tablet of your heart.
> So you will find favor and good repute
> In the sight of God and man.
> Trust in the LORD with all your heart,
> And do not lean on your own understanding.
> In all your ways acknowledge Him,
> And He will make your paths straight.

Do not be wise in your own eyes;
Fear the LORD and turn away from evil.
It will be healing to your body
And refreshment to your bones.
Honor the LORD from your wealth,
And from the first of all your produce;
So your barns will be filled with plenty,
And your vats will overflow with new wine.
My son, do not reject the discipline of the LORD,
Or loathe His reproof,
For whom the LORD loves He reproves,
Even as a father, the son in whom he delights."

When we incorporate the wisdom Solomon and others give to us in Proverbs, we will:

- Find peace in our soul,
- Experience a long life,
- Find favor with God and man,
- Receive health and refreshment for our body,
- Be prosperous, and
- Accept discipline from the LORD with a right attitude.

Solomon encouraged us to turn away from evil, fear God, develop a personal relationship with and be in fellowship with Him, and trust and lean on Him. God will guide and make the paths of our life straight when we do these.

Solomon addressed many important life issues and the futility of things in life that we often incorrectly believe are important in Ecclesiastes. He encouraged us to enjoy life to the fullest and recognize it as God's gift to us. He admonished us to avoid the futility of pursuing things in life that do not have eternal value and direct us away from God. Solomon indicated God has given us life to enjoy while He expects us to live it in obedience to Him. Solomon concluded in Ecclesiastes 12:13-14:

> "The conclusion, when all has been heard, is fear God and keep His commandments, because this applies to every person. For God will bring every act to judgment, everything which is hidden, whether it is good or evil."

We must enter a redeemed and reconciled relationship with God through faith in and obedience to Jesus to enjoy meaning and purpose in our life. We can find true meaning, purpose and joy only when we enter this relationship and allow the Holy Spirit to transform us into the person God has created us to be. Paul stated in Galatians 2:20:

> "I have been crucified with Christ; and it is no longer I who live, but Christ lives in me; and the life which I now live in the flesh I live by faith in the Son of God, who loved me, and delivered Himself up for me."

We have been redeemed by God's grace through our faith in and obedience to Jesus. God freely extends His gift of redemption to us because of His love, mercy and grace. He promises to place His Spirit in us through Jesus and the Holy Spirit and walk with us as we encounter life's challenges, disappointments and joys. He will prepare our way and equip us to persevere. Jesus is our hope for the future.

EPILOGUE

WHAT JESUS SAID

I asked the Holy Spirit in 1982 to help me better understand God's word in the Bible as it relates to our relationship with Him through Jesus when I agreed to His request to write my initial *REDEEMED BY GOD* book. His assistance over a span of 39 years has given me an understanding of God's word in the Bible necessary to write my series of four *REDEEMED BY GOD* books. I will use words Jesus spoke in the Gospels of Matthew and John to summarize my understanding of the basis for our relationship with God and the redemption He extends to us through our faith and trust in and obedience to Jesus.

I begin with Jesus' statement in John 3:16-17:

> "For God so loved the world, that He gave His only begotten Son, that whoever believes in Him shall not perish, but have eternal life. For God did not send the Son into the world to judge the world, but that the world might be saved through Him."

Jesus indicated God, His Father, made the conscious decision to redeem the world through Him, and this redemption results in eternal life for those who are redeemed. Jesus, as the Son of God, is our Lord who God sent into the world to be our Savior. Jesus stated in John 4:34:

> "My food is to do the will of Him who sent Me and to accomplish His work."

Jesus affirmed His agreement with His Father's decisions to redeem the world through Him even though He knew this decision would ultimately result in His sacrificial death on a cross. Jesus stated in John 8:10:

> "I am the Light of the world; he who follows Me will not walk in the darkness, but will have the Light of life."

Jesus came into the world to show us how to live in a manner pleasing to God and that will result in our receiving eternal life.

Paul indicated in Ephesians 2:8 we are saved by God's grace through faith. He indicated God's grace is offered to us as a gift, and he referred to this gift as being free in Romans 5:15-17. God offers us His grace with no cost to us because we can do nothing independent of His love to obtain it.

Jesus stated in Matthew 5:17-18:

> "Do not think that I came to abolish the Law or the Prophets; I did not come to abolish but to fulfill. For truly I say to you, until heaven and earth pass away, not the smallest letter or stroke shall pass from the Law until all is accomplished."

Jesus confirmed He came to fulfill the Law and the Profits, not to do away with them. Therefore, the Ten Commandments and their extension in the moral law remain to define and convict us of sin.

Jesus stated in John 12:47-50:

> "If anyone hears My sayings and does not keep them, I do not judge him; for I did not come to judge the world, but to save the world. He who rejects Me and does not receive My sayings, has one who judges him; the word I spoke is what will judge him at the last day. For I did not speak on My own initiative, but the Father Himself who sent Me has given Me a commandment as to what to say and what to speak. I know that His commandment is eternal life; therefore the things I speak, I speak just as the Father has told Me."

Jesus reaffirmed He did not come to judge the world, but to save it. He indicated God, His Father, instructed Him to speak the words He spoke, and it is these words that will judge us at the last day. Jesus' words are recorded in the four Gospels of the New Testament. Therefore, we will do well to read, study and internalize them.

Jesus stated in John 10:27-30:

> "My sheep hear My voice, and I know them, and they follow Me; and I give eternal life to them, and they will never perish; and no one will snatch them out of My hand. My Father, who has given them to Me, is greater than all; and no one is able to snatch them out of the Father's hand. I and the Father are One."

Jesus affirmed we know Him and hear his voice when we enter a relationship with Him. He reaffirmed He gives us eternal life, and He stated no one will be able to separate us from our relationship with Him because God, His Father, sustains this relationship.

Jesus stated in John 14:15, 21, 23:

> "If you love Me, you will keep my commandments. ... He who has my commandments and keeps them is the one who loves Me, and he who loves Me will be loved by My Father; and I will love him and will disclose Myself to him. ... If anyone loves Me, he will keep My word, and My Father will love him, and We will come to him and make Our abode with him."

Jesus indicated we demonstrate our love for Him by keeping His commandments and the word He spoke. He stated He will reveal Himself to us, and He and His Father will love and take up residence in us when we do this.

Jesus stated in Matthew 10:37-39:

> "He who loves father or mother more than Me is not worthy of Me, and he who loves son or daughter more than Me is not worthy of Me. And he who does not take his cross and follow after Me is not worthy of Me. He who has found his life will lose it, and he who has lost his life for My sake will find it."

Jesus indicated our love for Him must be greater than our love for anyone or anything that may become an object of our love. Our love for Him must motivate us to obey His words in the Gospels. We risk losing our eternal life when anyone or anything other than Jesus becomes the primary object of our love. We will receive eternal life when we lose our life because of our faith and trust in and obedience to Jesus.

Jesus stated in John 14:1-3, 6-7:

> "Do not let your heart be troubled; believe in God, believe also in Me. In My Father's house are many dwelling places; if it were not so, I would have told you; for I go to prepare a place for you. If I go and prepare a place for you, I will come again and receive you to Myself, that where I am, there you may be also. ... I am the way, and the truth, and the life; no one comes to the Father but through Me. If you had known Me, you would have known My Father also; from now on you know Him and have seen Him."

These are words Jesus spoke to His disciples. He stated He is going to prepare a place for us in God, His Father's, house in heaven, and He will return to receive us to Himself so we can be where He is. Jesus stated we can come to God, His Father, only through Him, and we come to know God as our Father when we know Him.

Jesus stated in John 15:1-6:

"I am the true vine, and My Father is the vinedresser. Every branch in Me that does not bear fruit, He takes away; and every branch that bears fruit, He prunes it so that it may bear more fruit. You are already clean because of the word which I have spoken to you. Abide in Me, and I in you. As the branch cannot bear fruit of itself unless it abides in the vine, so neither can you unless you abide in Me. I am the vine, you are the branches, he who abides in Me and I in him he bears much fruit, for apart from Me you can do nothing. If anyone does not abide in Me, he is thrown away as a branch and dries up; and they gather them, and cast them into the fire and they are burned."

These are words Jesus spoke to His disciples. He stated He is the true vine, and God, His Father, is the vinedresser who will remove branches from the vine that do not bear fruit. Jesus' statement indicated we are to bear fruit in our relationship with Him, and God, His Father, will remove us from this relationship when we do not bear fruit in it. Knowing God will remove us from our relationship with Jesus when we do not bear fruit in this relationship is distressing and a shock. However, God can do as He wills. Jesus indicated we can bear fruit only when we abide in Him, and He abides in us. He emphasized we can do nothing independent of our relationship with Him. Jesus continued in John 15:7:

"If you abide in Me, and My words abide in you, ask whatever you wish, and it will be done for you."

Jesus indicated we can request anything from Him in prayer when we abide in Him, and His words abide in us. He assures us our requests will be granted. Our requests must be compatible with God's nature and character.

Paul stated in Romans 10:8-10 we enter a relationship with Jesus when we profess with our mouth He is Lord and believe in our heart God raised Him from the dead. The Bible teaches we are to grow and mature in this relationship after we enter it. Peter instructed us in 1 Peter 2:1-3 to long for the pure milk of the word so we can grow in respect to salvation. Paul instructed us in Philippians 2:12-13 to work out our salvation with fear and trembling so God can will and work His good pleasure through us. He also instructed us in 1 Corinthians 3:10-15 to build our life on the foundation of Jesus. These actions prepare and equip us to do good works referred to by Paul in Ephesians 2:10 that God prepares for us to perform.

Paul indicated in Romans 12:4-8, 1 Corinthians 12:3-11, 28, and Ephesians 4:11-13 the Holy Spirit gives us supernatural spiritual gifts that uniquely enable and equip us to perform our good works. Our good works are the fruit on Jesus' vine that God prunes so we can bear more fruit. Jesus instructed us in Matthew 5:16 to let our light shine before men so they can see our good works. Our good works are performed to glorify God, and they are proof of the presence of Jesus and the Holy Spirit in our life.

James indicated we demonstrate our faith by our works in James 2:14-24. He indicated faith that does not result in works is useless; it is dead. Our faith must motivate us to do the good works God has prepared for us to perform as it grows and matures.

Jesus stated in Matthew 7:13-14:

> "Enter through the narrow gate; for the gate is wide and the way is broad that leads to destruction, and there are many who enter through it. For the gate is small and the way is narrow that leads to life, and there are few who find it."

Jesus' parable of the Sower in Matthew 13:1-9, 18-22 helps us understand His statement. Jesus indicated in this parable that sharing His words with others is like a sower who spreads seeds over the ground. Some seeds fall beside a road and are immediately eaten by birds. Some seeds fall on rocky places where there is little soil. They initially grow, and then they dry up when the sun shines on them because they do not have deep roots. Some seeds fall among thorns, and the thorns grow and chock them when they grow. Some seeds fall on good soil, and they grow and produce fruit. Jesus identified those represented by the Sower's seeds in Mathew 13:18-22:

- **Seeds that fall beside a road** represented individuals who hear Jesus' words and do not understand them. Therefore, Satan deceives and snatches them from Jesus.
- **Seeds that fall on rocky places where there is little soil** represented individuals who eagerly receive Jesus' words with joy, but they fail to learn what His words mean. They fall away from Jesus when afflictions or persecutions arise. This occurs because Jesus' words do not form the foundation of their lives.
- **Seeds that fall among thorns** represented individuals who receive and understand Jesus' words, but the worries of life and the deceitfulness of wealth overshadow and obscure His words. As a result, they do not produce fruit in their relationship with Jesus. Therefore, God removes them from the relationship.
- **Seeds that fall on good soil represented** individuals who receive, understand, and build their lives on the foundation of Jesus' words. As a result, they produce fruit in their relationship with Jesus. Therefore, they are among the few who Jesus indicated find life.

There are individuals who enter a relationship with Jesus who do not grow and mature in this relationship and perform good works God has prepared for them to do in this relationship. Therefore, they do not bear fruit in this relationship. This normally occurs because they are not motivated to grow and mature in their relationship with Jesus and perform good works God has prepared for them to do in the relationship. They may also do nothing after receiving God's gift of grace through Jesus because they believe this gift is free, and therefore, they do nothing after receiving it.

There is no acceptable reason for our light not to shine before men as proof of our bearing fruit through our good works in our relationship with Jesus. Therefore, individuals who do not bear fruit in this relationship will be removed from the relationship by God. This will occur when their failure to bear fruit through their good works has not been addressed and corrected before they stand in judgement before God after they die (Hebrews 9:27-28).

I want to return to God's love for us demonstrated by sending His Son, Jesus, into the world so we can receive eternal life after we die. Jesus' sacrificial death on a cross enables God to redeem and reconcile us to Himself by means of His gift of grace.

God gives us the freedom to choose to either accept or reject His gift of grace and receive His redemption, and He gives us to the end of our life to make this choice. Ignoring or avoiding this choice has the result of our rejecting God's gift of grace and redemption. The Bible teaches we will be judged by God when we stand before Him after we die, and we will be separated from God, Jesus and the Holy Spirit forever when we have not received His gift of grace and redemption. We will initially be in Hades after we die and then in the lake of fire after the great white throne judgement. The Bible also teaches we enter a redeemed and reconciled relationship with God through Jesus after we receive His gift of grace and His redemption, and we will be with God, Jesus and the Holy Spirit in the kingdom of heaven forever after we die.

Some individuals do not believe or recognize there are requirements when they enter a reconciled relationship with God through Jesus because Paul referred to God's gift of grace as being free. Christian denominations also teach the salvation we receive through Jesus is free. This creates a false perception we do not need to do anything before and after we receive our salvation. However, previous paragraphs indicate, and the Bible teaches there are requirements when we enter a reconciled relationship with God after we have been redeemed by His grace through Jesus.

The Bible teaches God and Jesus bless and reward us when we do what is required of us after we are redeemed by God and have entered a reconciled relationship with Him through our faith and trust in and obedience to Jesus. These blessings and rewards begin while we are alive and continue after we die. The Bible also teaches we will experience God's judgement when we stand before Him after we die, and we have done none of these requirements while we were alive.

CLOSING COMMENTS

Moses gave us the Law that established the moral code God expects us to live by. The Law defined sin that separates us from God when it is present in our life. The Law convicts us of sins in our life. It cannot redeem us from these sins and reconcile us to God. Therefore,

God extended His love and grace to us by sending us a Savior, Jesus, to redeem us from the consequences of our sins and reconcile us to Himself. Jesus stated in Matthew 5:17-19 that nothing shall be removed from the Law until heaven and earth pass away. This will not occur until the great white throne judgement.

Joshua stated in Joshua 1:8:

> "This book of the law shall not depart from your mouth, but you shall meditate on it day and night, so that you may be careful to do according to all that is written in it; for then you will make your way prosperous, and then you will have success."

It is impossible for us to live a life without sin. Therefore, God sent Jesus into the world to be a sacrifice for and to save us from the consequences of our sins. God forgives and redeems us from our sins through Jesus when we repent of our sins and seek and receive His forgiveness and redemption through our faith in Jesus.

God gives us freedom to choose to or not to seek His forgiveness, redemption and reconciliation through Jesus. We are separated from Him, Jesus and the Holy Spirit forever when we die, and we did not repent of our sins and seek God's forgiveness and receive His redemption and reconciliation through Jesus while we were alive. We will be sent to Hades (hell) after we die and then to the lake of fire after the great white throne judgement. We are redeemed by God and reconciled to Him when we repent of our sins and receive Jesus as our Savior and Lord of our life. We then enter a bilateral relationship with Him, Jesus and the Holy Spirit in the kingdom of God on earth.

God, Jesus, the Holy Spirit and we have obligations in this bilateral relationship. God and Jesus will honor their covenants and promises that are presented in the Bible. We are to spiritually grow and mature as we grow in our faith and trust in and obedience to Jesus. This is a lifelong process. The Holy Spirit facilitates our ability to spiritually grow and mature in our relationship with God through Jesus though our faithful and disciplined study of the Bible. He then equips us to perform good works in Jesus' name that God prepares for us to perform. We secure our entrance into the kingdom of heaven after we die by performing our good works in service and ministry to others for God's glory because we love Jesus and obey His words (1 Timothy 4:14-16, 2 Peter 1:5-11). God then acts through the Holy Spirit in our relationship with Him through Jesus to make our "way prosperous" and enable us to "have success" during our life.

REFERENCES

1. Bevere, J., *Driven by Eternity: Make Your Life Count Today and Forever*, Messenger International, Inc., 2016

2. Brickel, B. and Jantz, S., *Guide to the End of the World*, Harvest House Publishers, 1999.

3. Carr, W. G., *Pawn in the Game*, St. George Books, 1970.

4. Coleman, J., *Conspirators' Hierarchy: The Story of the Committee of 300, 4th Edition*, World International Review, Inc., 2007.

5. Coleman, J., *The Tavistock Institute of Human Relations: Shaping the Moral, Spiritual, Cultural, and Political*, Global Review Publishers, 2006.

6. Evens, L., *In This Age of Plenty*, CreateSpace Independent Publication Platform, November 11, 2012.,

7. Grant, R. D. and Wells Miller, A., *Recovering Connections*, Harper San Francisco, 1993.

8. Heeren, Fred, *Show Me God*, Day Star Publications, 1997.

9. LaHaye, T. and Jenkins, J. B., *Are We Living in the End Times?*, Tyndale House Publishers, 1999.

10. Meadows, D. H., Meadows, D. L., Randers, J., *Beyond the Limits, Confronting Global Collapse Envisioning a Sustainable Future*, Chelsea Green Publishing Company, 1992.

11. Miller, J. K., *The Secret Life of the Soul*, Broadman & Holman Publishers, 1997.

12. Perkins, J., *Confessions of an Economic Hit Man*, Berrett-Koehler Publishers, Inc., November 9, 2004.

13. Reynolds, Douglas D., *Redeemed by God - Our Relationship with God through His Son, Jesus Christ*, Trafford Publishing, 2006.

14. Rhodes, R., *Angels Among Us*, Harvest House Publishers, 1994.

15. Stoner, Peter W., *Science Speaks: An Evaluation of Certain Christian Evidences*, Chicago: Moody, 1963.

16. Swenson, R. A., *Hurtling toward Oblivion*, Navpress, 1999.

17. Tenney, M.C, (ed.), *Pictorial Bible Dictionary*, The Southwestern Company, 1971.

18. Webb, Chris, *The Fire of the Word - Meeting God on Holy Ground*, IVP Books, 2011.

19. Wilmington, H. L., *Willmington's Guide to the Bible*, Tyndale House Publishers, 1981.

20. *Nelson's Illustrated Bible Dictionary*, Thomas Nelson Publishers, 1986.

Internet References

21. Allen, T. C., "Gaining Control," blog; blog: http://tcallenco.weebly.com.

22. Allen, T. C., "Illuminist Organizationally," blog: http://tcallenco.weebly.com.

23. Allen, T. C., "Illuminism Religiously," blog: http://tcallenco.weebly.com.

24. Allen, T. C., "Mysteries," blog: http://tcallenco.weebly.com.

25. Allen, T. C., "Freemasonry the Early Years," blog: http://tcallenco.weebly.com.

26. Century- One Bookstore, "Fascinating Facts about the Discovery at Qumen," http://www. centuryone.com/25dssfacts.html.

27. Clayton, M., "3 Corporations that Run the World: City of London, Washington DC and Vatican City," THE INVESTIGATIVE, https://www.theinvestigative.com/3-corporations-that-run-the- world-city-of-london-washington-dc-and-vatican-city/, August 9, 2018.

28. Custance, A. C., "The Virgin Birth," Volume IV; http://custance.org.

29. Got Questions.org, "What is the New Age movement?"; http://www.gotquestions.org/new- age-movement.html

30. Manning, Scott, "Process of copying the Old Testament by Jewish Scribes." March 17, 2007; http://www.scottmanning.com/archives/scribeswritingoldtestament.php.

31. McIllhany, W. H., "A Primer on the Illuminati," New American, Internet, June 12, 2004.

32. Svali as interviewed by HJ Springer, "Svali 2nd Series - The Illuminati in America," December 18, 2000 - July 12, 2001; http://www.bibliotecapleyades.net/sociopolitica/esp_sociopol_illuminati_svali01b.htm#menu2.

33. Samuels, E. A., "The 1782 Congress of Wilhelmsbad: The Illuminati Takeover," November 2006; http://www.biblebelievers.org.au/wilhelms.htm.

34. Springmeier, F., "Predators in Power: a Look at the British Royal Family, Jimmy Saville & Child Abuse," MERCY TRIUMPHS Web Site; http://mercytriumphs.org/mercytriumphs/2014/02/15/predators-in-power-a-look-at-the-british-royal-family-jimmy- saville-child-abuse-by-fritz-springmeier/.

35. Theopedia, "Gnosticism;" http://www.theopedia.com/Gnosticism.

36. The Empire of the City - The Unholy Trinity that Rules the World, CrossTheBorder.org, https:// nicklasarthur.wordpress.com/2013/08/08/the-empire-of-the-city/.

37. Waduge, S. D., "Three Corporations urn the World: City of London, Washington DC and Vatican City," htp://www.sinhalanet.net/three-corporations-run-the-world-city-of-london- washington-dc-and-vatican-city, May 31, 2014.

38. Walker, D. B., "First Century Manuscript? Clarification statement about the discovery of several New Testament papyri," http://www.dts.edu/read/wallace-new-testament-manscript-first- century/

39. Wikipedia, "Bank for International Settlements (BIS)."

40. Wikipedia, "Central Bank."

41. Wikipedia, "International Monetary Fund."

42. Wikipedia, "World Bank."

43. Wikipedia, "Federal Reserve System."

44. Wikipedia, "Commercial Bank."

45. Wikipedia, "Retail Bank."

46. "FEMA Executive Orders;"
    http://www.theforbiddenknowledge.com/hardtruth/fema_ executive_orders.htm.

47. *United Nations Sustainable Development - Agenda 21*; United Nations Conference on Environment & Development; Rio de Janeiro, Brazil; June 3 - 14, 1992.

APPENDIX A
PROPHESIES CONCERING JESUS

PROPHESIES CONCERNING EVENTS IN THE LIFE OF JESUS

	Events in Jesus' Life	Old Testament Prophesies	Fulfilled in the New Testament
1.	Born of a woman	Genesis 3:15	Galatians 4:4 Matthew 1:20
2.	Born of a virgin	Isaiah 7:14	Matthew 1:18, 24, 25 Luke 1:26-35
3.	Son of God	Psalm 2:7 1 Chronicles 17:11-14 2 Samuel 7:12-16	Matthew 3:17 Matthew 16:16 John 1:34, 49
4.	Seed of Abraham	Genesis 22:18 Genesis 12:2-3	Matthew 1:1 Galatians 3:16
5.	Son of Isaac	Genesis 21:12	Luke 3:23, 34 Matthew 1:2
6.	Son of Jacob	Numbers 24:17	Luke 3:23, 34 Matthew 1:2 Luke 1:33
7.	Tribe of Judah	Genesis 49:10	Luke 3:23, 33 Matthew 1:2 Hebrews 7:14
8.	Family line of Jesse	Isaiah 11:1, 10	Luke 3:23, 32 Matthew 1:6

9.	House of David	Jeremiah 23:5 2 Samuel 7:12-16	Luke 3:23, 31 Matthew 1:1
10.	Born in Bethlehem	Micah 5:2	Matthew 2:1 Luke 2:4-7
11.	Presented with gifts	Psalm 72:10 Isaiah 60:6	Matthew 2:1, 11
12.	Herod Kills Children	Jeremiah 31:15	Matthew 2:16
13.	Jesus' pre-existence	Micah 5:2 Isaiah 9:6, 7 Isaiah 41:4; 44:6; 48:12 Psalm 102:25	Colossians 1:17 John 1:1-2; 8:58 John 17:5.24 Revelation 1:17, 2:8 Revelation 22:13
14.	He shall be called Lord	Psalm 110:1 Jeremiah 23:6	Luke 2:11 Luke 20:41-44
15.	He shall be Emmanuel	Isaiah 7:14	Matthew 1:23 Luke 7:16
16.	He shall be a prophet	Deuteronomy 18:18	Matthew 21:11 Luke 7:16 John 4:19, 6:14, 7:40
17.	He shall be a priest	Psalm 110:4	Hebrews 3:1, 5:5-6
18.	He shall be a judge	Isaiah 33:22	John 5:30 2 Timothy 4:1
19.	He shall be a king	Psalms 2:6	Matthew 21:5, 27:37 John 18:33-38
20.	He shall be anointed by the Holy Spirit	Isaiah 11:2 Isaiah 42:1, 61:1-2	Matthew 3:16-17 Mark 1:10 Luke 4:15-21, 43 John 1:32
21.	He shall have a zeal for God	Psalm 69:9	John 2:15-17

22.	He shall be preceded by a messenger	Isaiah 40:3 Malachi 3:1	Matthew 3:1-2 John 1:23 Luke 1:17
23.	Jesus' ministry was to begin in Galilee.	Isaiah 9:1	Matthew 4:12-13, 17
24.	Jesus was to have a ministry of miracles	Isaiah 35:5-6	Matthew 9:32-35 Matthew 11:4-6 Mark 7:33-35 John 5:5-9, 9:6-11 John 11:43-47
25.	Jesus was to teach in parables	Psalm 78:2	Matthew 13:34
26.	Jesus was to enter the temple	Malachi 3:1	Matthew 21:12
27.	Jesus was to enter Jerusalem on a donkey	Zechariah 9:9	Luke 19:35-37 Matthew 21:6-11
28.	Jesus was to be a "stone of stumbling" to the Jews	Psalm 118:22 Isaiah 8:14, 28:16	1 Peter 2:7 Romans 9:32-33
29.	Jesus was to be a light to the Gentiles	Isaiah 60:3 Isaiah 49:6	Acts 13:47-48 Acts 28:28
30.	Jesus' resurrection	Psalm 16:10, 30:3 Psalm 41:10 Hosea 6:2	Acts 2:31 Luke 24:46 Mark 16:6 Matthew 28:6
31.	Jesus' ascension	Psalm 68:18	Acts 1:9
32.	Jesus to sit at the right hand of God	Psalm 110:1	Hebrews 1:3 Mark 16:19 Acts 2:34-35
33.	Jesus to be betrayed by a friend	Psalms 41:9, 55:12-14	Matthew 10:4 Matthew 26:49-50 John 13:21

34.	Jesus sold for 30 pieces of silver	Zechariah 11:12	Matthew 26:15, 27:3
35.	Money to be thrown in God's house	Zechariah 11:13	Matthew 27:5
36.	Silver to be used to buy Potter's Field	Zechariah 11:13	Matthew 27:7
37.	Jesus to be forsaken by disciples	Zechariah 13:7	Mark 14:27, 14:50 Matthew 26:31
38.	Jesus to be accused by by false witnesses	Psalm 35:11	Matthew 26:59-61
39.	Jesus to be dumb before accusers	Isaiah 53:7	Matthew 27:12-19
40.	Jesus to be wounded and bruised	Isaiah 53:5 Zechariah 13:6	Matthew 27:26
41.	Jesus to be smitten and spit upon	Isaiah 50:6 Micah 5:1	Matthew 26:27 Luke 22:63
42.	Jesus to be mocked	Psalm 22:7-8	Matthew 27:31
43.	Jesus to fall under His cross	Psalm 109:24-25	John 19:17 Luke 23:26 Matthew 27:31-32
44.	Jesus' hands and feet to be pierced	Psalms 22:16 Zechariah 12:10	Luke 23:33 John 20:25
45.	Jesus to be crucified with thieves	Isaiah 53:12	Matthew 27:38 Mark 15:27-28
46.	Jesus made intercession for His persecutors	Isaiah 53;12	Luke 23:34
47.	Jesus was rejected by His own people	Isaiah 53:3 Psalm 69:8, 118:22	John 1:11, 7:5, 48 Matthew 21:42-43
48.	Jesus was hated without a cause	Psalm 69:4 Isaiah 49:7	John 15:25

49.	Friends stood far off when He was crucified	Psalm 38:11	Luke 23:49 Mark 15:40 Matthew 27:55-56
50.	People shook their heads at Jesus when He was crucified	Psalm 22:7, 109:25	Matthew 27:39
51.	Jesus was stared upon when He was crucified	Psalm 22:17	Luke 23:35
52.	Jesus' garments were parted and lots were cast for them when He was crucified	Psalm 22:18	John 19:23-34
53.	Jesus was to suffer thirst when He was crucified	Psalm 22:15, 69:21	John 19:28
54.	Gall and vinegar were to be offered to Jesus when He was crucified	Psalm 69:21	Matthew 27:34 John 19:28-29
55.	Jesus was to feel forsaken by God when He was crucified	Psalm 21:1	Matthew 27:46
56.	Jesus was to commit Himself to God when He was crucified	Psalm 31:5	Luke 23:46
57.	None of Jesus' bones were to be broken when He was crucified	Psalm 34:20	John 19:23
58.	Jesus' heart was to be broken when He was crucified	Psalm 22:14	John 19:34
59.	Jesus' side was to be pierced	Zechariah 12;10	John 19:34
60.	Darkness was to come over the land when Jesus was crucified	Amos 8:9	Matthew 27:45
61.	Jesus was to be buried in a rich man's tomb	Isaiah 53:9	Matthew 27:57-60

PROPHESIES CONCERNING THE SECOND COMING OF JESUS [1]

	Bible Verse	Prophesy
1.	Psalm 50:3-6	Jesus will return to execute judgment and to gather His people, Israel, to Himself. Refers to the return of Jesus at the end of the Tribulation.
2.	Isaiah 9:6-7	Jesus will return to rule during His millennial kingdom.
3.	Isaiah 66:18	Jesus will return to gather the nations of the world to Himself. Refers to Jesus setting up His millennial kingdom.
4.	Daniel 7:7-8	Ten-kingdom federation will be formed with the Antichrist as its head.
5.	Daniel 7:13-14	Jesus will be given dominion to set up His kingdom on earth during the middle of the tribulation.
6.	Daniel 7:26-27	The Antichrist will be judged and dominion o of the earth will be given to the followers of Jesus.
7.	Daniel 8:23-25	The Antichrist's power will be derived from Satan. The Antichrist will make war against Jesus, who will defeat him.
8.	Daniel 9:24-27	Tribulation will be seven years. The Antichrist will commit abomination of desolation and break 7-year covenant with Israel during the middle of the tribulation.
9.	Daniel 11:31, 12:11	The Antichrist commits abomination of desolation.
10.	Ezekiel 38-39	Israel will be invaded by the king of the north (Russia) and the king of the south (Egypt).

11.	Zechariah 12:10	Israel will recognize Jesus as her Messiah and will acknowledge with deep contrition that He was the One whom their forefathers had nailed to a cross when He returns to set up His millennial kingdom.
12.	Zechariah 14:1-9	Jesus will return with the armies of heaven to battle the Antichrist and the armies of the kings of the ten-kingdom federation at the battle of Armageddon. He will return by way of the Mount of Olives.
13.	Matthew 24:15-18 Mark 13:5-13 Luke 21:8-9	Prophesies by Jesus concerning the first half of the Tribulation.
14.	Matthew 24:15-18 Mark 13:14-16	Prophesies by Jesus concerning the abomination of desolation during the middle of the Tribulation.
15.	Matthew 24:19-25 Mark 13:17-23 Luke 17:22-37	Prophesies by Jesus concerning the great Tribulation (last three and one-half years of the Tribulation).
16.	Matthew 24:26-41 Mark 13:24-29 Luke 17:22-37	Prophesies by Jesus concerning the rapture.
17.	Acts 1:9-11	Jesus will return in the same way that He ascended to heaven. He ascended from the Mount of Olives to the east of Jerusalem and He will return by way of the Mount of Olives.
18.	1 Corinthians 15:51-52	Jesus will return to gather Christians to Himself at the rapture at the sound of the last trumpet.
19.	1 Thessalonians 1:10	Jesus will rescue us from the wrath of God duringthe great tribulation.
20.	1 Thessalonians 4:13-17	The dead in Christ will rise first, after whichthose who are alive will be caught up with Jesus at the rapture.

21. 1 Thessalonians 5:9-10   Jesus will rescue Christians from the wrath of God during the great tribulation by gathering them to Himself at the rapture.

22. 2 Thessalonians 2:1-4   Jesus will return to gather Christians to Himself at the rapture after the abomination of desolation by the Antichrist.

---

[1]   Does not include prophesies in the Revelation of John